Art in Motion
Animation Aesthetics

Art in Motion
Animation Aesthetics

Maureen Furniss

School of Film and Television
Chapman University, California

John Libbey
JL
LONDON · PARIS · ROME · SYDNEY

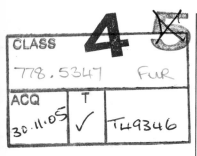
Cover image from Jules Engel's Meadow (1995). *Courtesy of the artist.*

The publisher and author have undertaken all efforts to acquire permission to reproduce the illustrations used in this book. If any infringement occurs it is unintentional.

National Library Cataloguing in Publication Data:

Furniss, Maureen

    Art in motion: animation aesthetics.

    Includes index.

    ISBN 1 86462 038 2 (hbk.).
    ISBN 1 86462 039 0.

    1. Animation (Cinematography). 2. Motion pictures – Aesthetics.
    3. Animated films. I. Title.

    778.5347

Published by

John Libbey & Company Pty Ltd,
Level 10, 15–17 Young Street, Sydney NSW 2000 Australia.
Telephone: +61 (0)2 9251 4099
Facsimile: +61 (0)2 9251 4428
E-mail: jlsydney@mpx.com.au

John Libbey & Company Ltd, 13 Smiths Yard, Summerley Street,
  London SW18 4HR England;
John Libbey Eurotext Ltd, 127 Avenue de la République,
  92120 Montrouge, France.

Printed in Malaysia by Vivar Printing Sdn. Bhd.

Contents

† 'Colour plate' abbreviated as 'CP' throughout.

CP 1	*Furies*	Sara Petty
CP 2	*The Man Who Planted Trees*	Frédéric Back/CBC
CP 3	*The Mighty River*	Frédéric Back/CBC
CP 4	*The Cow*	Alexander Petrov
CP 5	*The Monk and the Fish*	Michael Dudok de Wit
CP 6	*Kakania*	Karen Aqua
CP 7	Paint on glass technique	Clive Walley
CP 8	'Divertimenti'	Clive Walley
CP 9	*Ride to the Abyss*	Georges Schwizgebel
CP 10	*Sophie's Place*	Larry Jordan
CP 11	*A Colour Box*	Len Lye
CP 12	*Algorithms*	Bärbel Neubauer
CP 13	*Moonlight*	Bärbel Neubauer
CP 14	*The Boy Alchemist*	Larry Jordan
CP 15	Sample primary, secondary and tertiary colours	
CP 16	*World*	Jordan Belson
CP 17	*Fireflies I*	Trnka Studio
CP 18	*Gerald McBoing Boing*	Robert 'Bobe' Cannon/UPA
CP 19	*Gerald McBoing Boing*	Robert 'Bobe' Cannon/UPA
CP 20	*When the Stars Came Dreaming*	Jean Poulot/Will Vinton Studios, Inc.
CP 21	*Meet the Raisins*	Will Vinton Studios, Inc.
CP 22	'The Gumby Show'	Art Clokey
CP 23	*The Hand*	Jirí Trnka
CP 24	*Toy Story*	John Lasseter/Walt Disney Pictures
CP 25	*Gas Planet*	Eric Darnell and Michael Collery/PDI
CP 26	*Sleepy Guy*	Raman Hui/PDI
CP 27	*The Cat and the Two Sparrows*	Fantôme Animation
CP 28	'Insektors'	Fantôme Animation
CP 29	'ReBoot'	Mainframe Entertainment
CP 30	'Insektors'	Fantôme Animation
CP 31	'ReBoot'	Mainframe Entertainment
CP 32	*Hippoposterous*	Modern Cartoons, a concept in development
CP 33	*Meadow*	Jules Engel

Introduction

*I*t was about ten years before the publication of this book – back in 1987 – that I completed my Master's Thesis, 'The Current State of American Independent Animation and a Prediction for its Future', at San Diego State University. I then embarked on the study of animation at the University of Southern California, despairing at what was then a great lack of information in the field. I am glad to say that the situation is finally changing, so that today's reader is fortunate to find many, if not yet abundant, sources of information on animation history, theory and aesthetics.

What this book represents is the synthesis of all the information I have found throughout those ten years, by attending festivals and digging through archives, and by conducting interviews and receiving donations from generous colleagues. Its structure is developed around a course outline that I initiated at the University of California, Santa Cruz (my first university teaching job, thanks to Margaret Morse) and continued to use at Chapman University, where I am now employed.

In *Art in Motion: Animation Aesthetics*, I have done my best to cover a broad range of subjects. Admittedly, the focus is somewhat oriented toward American work, reflecting both the domination of the country in the realm of animation and my own area of expertise. However, I have made an effort to balance my discussion with examples of animation produced throughout the world. To ensure accuracy, I have cross-checked information with many experts in the field. I apologise in advance if any mistakes have slipped through and welcome writers to expand upon and clarify my work.

In writing this book and many other aspects of my work I owe thanks to Janet Benn, Karl Cohen, Scott Curtis, David Ehrlich, Jules Engel, Elfriede Fischinger, Robert Haller, Jo Jürgens, George Griffin, Jere Guldin, Tom Klein, J.B. Kaufman, Mark

Langer, Ron Magliozzi, Donald McWilliams, William Moritz, Linda Simensky, and Cecile Starr. I especially appreciate the help in proofreading and corrections given to me by Henry Selick and Art Clokey, and am grateful for the time and energy of many, many other people along the way, including Brian Barker, who created the index.

My appreciation goes to my publisher, John Libbey, for being so supportive of my work and the field of animation studies, and also to Karen Enkelaar, who did a wonderful job designing, desktopping and editing *Art in Motion: Animation Aesthetics*. This is my first book and I entered into the publication process without knowing what to expect, but having heard a few horror stories from my colleagues. However, I have nothing but good things to say about my experience. Karen was very enthusiastic and helpful to me throughout; she and John made the whole publication process a pleasure.

A great deal of thanks also go to Bob Bassett, Dean of the Chapman University School of Film and Television, and others at the University for supporting my research so generously.

Finally, I must of course thank my parents – my mother in particular – who in more ways than one have helped to make space for me and my work.

Maureen Furniss

Part 1
FUNDAMENTALS

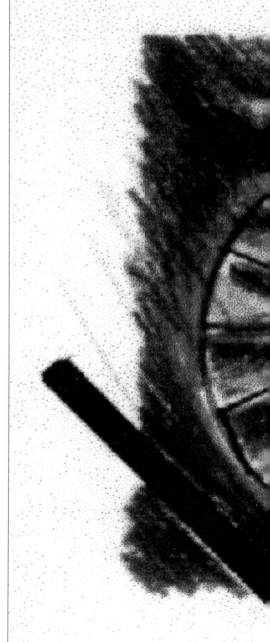

1

Introduction to animation studies

*A*lthough Cinema Studies has developed greatly since its general introduction into university programs during the early 1960s, Animation Studies has largely remained on the sidelines – while many colleges and universities have animation production courses, the study of the form's aesthetics, history and theory generally has been relegated to the status of an elective 'special course' offered only on an occasional basis or not taught at all.[1] In some cases, when animation is discussed, it is subsumed under another subject matter, such as avant-garde film. The discussions of James Whitney, Jordan Belson, Stan Brakhage or Pat O'Neill, all of whom used frame-by-frame animation techniques at some point, probably are found primarily in that context.

The denigrated status of Animation Studies in the university is largely due to the belief held in many countries that animation is not a 'real' art form because it is too popular, too commercialised, or too closely associated with 'fandom' or youth audiences to be taken seriously by scholars. This impression is faulty because there is a wide range of animation that is not commercially – or child – oriented and, in any case, these areas also merit study.

Fortunately, some indicators have suggested that the situation of Animation Studies is beginning to improve. A significant factor has been the influence of post-modernism on Media Studies, which has helped to legitimise the study of popular forms of entertainment. Also, people are realising that there is an immediate need to document previously marginalised areas, including animation history, which is slipping away quickly: many artists from the early days have died without proper documentation of their contributions; films and cels, many of the early ones on nitrate, are disintegrating; and documentation material, once believed to be of little value by studios, has been discarded or housed unavailable to historians (and often without any organisation) in studio warehouses.

For many years, the documentation of animation history largely was carried out by a relatively small and cloistered group of individuals – mostly hard core fans, collectors, and historically minded practitioners. However, some organised efforts to preserve animation history did exist. The organisation that has been perhaps most active in fostering and preserving the art of animation is l'Association Internationale du Film d'Animation, generally known as ASIFA (the International Association of Animated Film), which was founded in 1960 and continues to operate an international chapter as well as local groups in countries throughout the world. But, during the late 1980s, there were other signs that the area of Animation Studies was beginning to grow in strength.

The late 1980s saw increasing concern with the preservation of animation as an art, among both industry professionals and scholars. Walter Lantz was among the first to speak up for the future of animation. With his financial assistance, the American Film Institute hosted two conferences, in 1987 and 1988, and published two anthologies of critical writing on animation.[3]

At about the same time, Harvey Deneroff founded the Society for Animation Studies (SAS), which has held annual conferences since 1989 in order to present the research of its members. Although SAS members and others began to produce a stream of animation research in the 1980s, for some years it remained difficult to place essays on animation in the majority of media journals, which are geared toward live-action motion pictures. As a result, a lot of animation research languished undeveloped and without proper distribution. To address this problem, *Animation Journal*, the first peer-reviewed publication devoted to animation studies, was founded in 1991; the journal publishes animation history, theory and criticism related to studio and independent animation created throughout the world.[4]

Another sign of growth in the field was the establishment of Women in Animation (WIA) by former *Animation Magazine* publisher Rita Street in late 1993. This non-profit, professional organisation is dedicated to preserving and fostering both the contributions of women in the field and the art of animation. The organisation of a historical committee was among the first of WIA's activities and an oral history program has begun to document the work of women in the field, which for years has been undervalued.[2] The above list includes only a few milestones in the growth of animation studies, which is more thoroughly documented elsewhere.

DEFINING ANIMATION

One of the concerns that has resurfaced periodically in animation scholarship relates to definition. It seems that, before one attempts to understand the aesthetics of 'animation', it is essential to define its parameters: just what is meant by the term?

A number of people have offered definitions of animation. One attempt appears in a 1989 essay by Edward S. Small and Eugene Levinson, which is entitled 'Toward a Theory of Animation'.[5] In fact, the article is less a development of theory than an attempt to define what animation means. The conclusion? The authors claim 'we have adopted as definition for animation "the technique of single-frame cinematography" '.[6] A lot of energy was spent to reach this point, but little has been achieved; such a simplistic definition provides the reader with only the most basic characteristic of the practice.

Charles Solomon had arrived at an expanded version of Small and Levinson's definition a year earlier in his essay, 'Animation: Notes on a Definition'.[7] In it he discusses a variety of techniques that he says can be called 'animation'. He finds that 'two factors link these diverse media and their variations, and serve as the basis for a workable definition of animation: (1) the imagery is recorded frame-by-frame and (2) the illusion of motion is created, rather than recorded'.[8] Ultimately, he finds that 'filmmaking has grown so complicated and sophisticated in recent years that simple definitions of techniques may no longer be possible. It may be unreasonable to expect a single word to summarise such diverse methods of creating images on film'.[9]

One of the most famous definitions of animation has come from Norman McLaren, the influential founder of the animation department at the National Film Board of Canada. He once stated:

> Animation is not the art of drawings that move but the art of movements that are drawn; What happens between each frame is much more important than what exists on each frame; Animation is therefore the art of manipulating the invisible interstices that lie between the frames.[10]

In this case, McLaren is not defining the practice of animation, but rather its essence, which he suggests is the result of movement created by an artist's rendering of successive images in a somewhat intuitive manner. Although McLaren wrote of 'drawings' in his original definition, he later indicated that he used that word 'for a simple and rhetorical effect; static objects, puppets and human beings can all be animated without *drawings* ...'.[11]

Each of these individuals has a different interpretation of the term 'animation'. McLaren discusses an inherent aesthetic element (movement – an issue that will expanded on later in this book), while the other authors attempt to illustrate the borders of the practice, to display the qualifications that allow an object to be discussed as animation. Despite these and other attempts, arriving at a precise definition is extremely difficult, if not impossible. It is probably safe to say that most people think of animation in a more general way, by identifying a variety of techniques such as cel animation, clay animation, puppets and so forth.

One way to think about animation is in relation to live-action media. The use of inanimate objects and certain frame-by-frame filming techniques suggest 'animation', whereas the appearance of live objects and continuous filming suggest 'live action'. However, there is an immense area in which the two tendencies of overlap, especially when an individual is writing on the subject of aesthetics. Rather than conceiving of the two modes of production as existing in separate spheres, it is more accurate for the analyst to think of them as being on a continuum representing all possible image types under the broad category of 'motion picture production' (Fig. 1.1).

In constructing this continuum, it is probably best to use more neutral terms than 'animation' and 'live action' to constitute the ends of the spectrum. Although the terms 'mimesis' and 'abstraction' are not ideal, they are useful in suggesting opposing tendencies under which live-action and animated imagery can be juxtaposed. The term 'mimesis' represents the desire to reproduce natural reality (more like live-action work) while the term 'abstraction' describes the use of pure form – a suggestion of a concept rather than an attempt to explicate it in real life terms (more like animation).

There is no one film that represents the ideal example of 'mimesis' or 'abstraction' – everything is relative. A work that combines live action with animation, such as *The Three Caballeros* (directed by Norman Ferguson, 1943), would appear somewhere in the middle of this continuum, while a documentary like *Sleep* (directed by Andy Warhol, 1963), a real-time account of a person sleeping, would be far to the side of mimesis. A live-action film employing a substantial amount of special effects, such as *Jurassic Park* (directed by Stephen Spielberg, 1993), would appear somewhere between *Sleep* and *The Three Caballeros*. On the other hand, a film like *Hen Hop* (directed by Norman McLaren, 1942), which contains line drawings of hens whose bodies constantly metamorphose and break into parts, would appear on the other side of the spectrum, relatively close to the abstract pole because the film is completely animated and its images are very stylised. Even further toward abstraction would be *Kriese* (Circles; directed by Oskar Fischinger, 1933), which is composed of circular images that are animated to the film's score. However, the Disney animated feature *Snow White and the Seven Dwarfs* (directed by David Hand, 1937) has a relatively naturalistic look and employs some characters based on human models, so it would appear on the abstraction side but closer to the mid-point of *The Three Caballeros*. While it may seem strange to describe *Snow White* as an example of an 'abstract' work, its characters and landscapes can be described as caricatures, or abstractions of reality, to some extent.

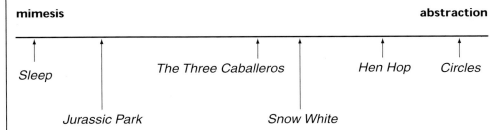

Fig. 1.1 *A live action – animation continuum*

Actually, the placements suggested by this description are somewhat arbitrary. There is no exact spot where any one film should appear and it is completely reasonable that various people might argue for different placements than the ones described here. The point is that the relationship between animation and live action, represented by mimesis and abstraction, is a relative one. They are both tendencies within motion picture production, rather than completely separate practices.

One advantage of this kind of system is that it facilitates discussion of someone like Frank Tashlin, whose work overlaps the realms of both live action and animation. It has been said that his animated works for Warner Bros., Columbia and Disney during the 1930s and 1940s are strongly influenced by live-action conventions, while the live-action features he directed after his career in animation tend to be very 'cartoony' in nature. One can easily see the crossover in examining one of his characters, Rita Marlow (played by Jayne Mansfield), in *Will Success Spoil Rock Hunter* (1957). With her big hair, large bosom, small waist and exaggerated mannerisms, she is clearly a descendant of the cartoon female 'bombshell' one finds in such films as Tex Avery's *Red Hot Riding Hood* (1943), produced at Metro-Goldwyn-Mayer (MGM), with animation by Preston Blair.

The difference between a continuum and a definition is that a continuum works with similarities to position items in relation to one another, while a definition seeks difference, to separate items in some way. Using a continuum, one can discuss a broad range of materials without qualifying the extent to which each example belongs to a precisely defined category called 'animation'. This book employs the continuum approach, drawing examples from across a broad spectrum, incorporating motion pictures that are easily described as animated (e.g. Disney or Warner Bros. cartoons) along with others that are not as commonly discussed under that heading (e.g. some of the work of Stan Brakhage or the animated special effects used to enhance live-action features). Rather than limit its examples according to some defining criteria, this book expands outward from a basic conception of what animation means, under the premise that it is discussing motion pictures on a broader level.

CONDUCTING ANIMATION RESEARCH

The goal of this book is not only to overview basic concepts of animation aesthetics, but also to encourage subsequent research by its readers. As this chapter already has pointed out, the need for Animation Studies research is great. Because it is anticipated that this book will be used in introductory courses on animation aesthetics, a bit of information on basic research techniques will be presented here.[12]

This book strongly advocates a contextual approach to the study of aesthetics. It contends that, to fully understand the aesthetics of a single art work or a group of works, it is necessary to know something about the production context – the historical, economic, social, technological, industrial and other influences upon any work at the time of its making. Consider how the content of animation might be affected due to different political backgrounds; for example, between Germany during World War II and the United States in the 1970s. Consider the way in which the depiction of racial groups might be affected by differences in social attitudes between animation produced in the United States during the 1910s and the 1980s. Consider the way in which the techniques used in an animated work might be affected by the economic situations of an independent, self-funded animator working today and a director at a large Hollywood studio. These examples employ contrasts that make the influence of production context quite obvious. However, a true analysis of production context takes into account many, many influences upon a given work, some clear and obvious, and others more subtle and elusive.

Understanding production context helps to situate a work as a product of its time, and provides more objectivity in discussing sensitive subjects such as racial representation or sexism that can be viewed as offensive; or dated approaches, such as computer effects that do not match the standards set today. By understanding the many forces that shaped the making of a production, we are able to think about a work within its context and avoid judgements based only on contemporary standards of what is socially correct, technically proficient, beautiful, and so on. This knowledge allows the researcher to consider the production and reception of a work within its time period and also provides perspective on the ways in which things have changed since that time.

In considering production context, it is advisable to extend an analysis to at least the ten years before a production was made, the period during which a context was becoming established. For example, in discussing work of World War II, one should keep in mind the devastating effects of the Depression during the 1930s, for although economic hardships became less evident, they had lasting repercussions on the attitudes and working practices of people during the 1940s.

The methodology described above is one that is primarily historical in nature. Researching history can be difficult because it requires access to information that can be hard to locate. Often, records from the distant past are incomplete, sometimes reflecting the priorities of the individual(s) who preserved them. Reading books on the subject is the most common way that individuals find out about historical information; however, information printed in books typically represents one individual's perspective of the subject at hand, at the time of the book's publication. Accordingly, researchers should always look at the year in which a publication was released. Sometimes an old book is useful for assessing attitudes held at a certain point in history, but one should be careful about quoting outdated information as if it were true at the present time – people change their opinions, companies go out of business, new technologies are developed, and so on.

In the realm of Animation Studies, the beginning researcher must be very careful to scrutinise the content of any so-called history of animation. One finds that a disproportionate amount of books on animation history have been written by what can be described as a knowledgeable animation fan, often with another fan or other casual reader in mind. One of the clearest signs of what might be called a 'fan-oriented publication' is a lack of documentary material in the way of endnotes, bibliographies and filmographies. Very often these kinds of books contain a substantial amount of anecdotal material, perhaps written by an individual who worked in the industry and is recalling what occurred, or by an author who compiles a number of amusing stories about the 'golden days' of years gone by. Another probable indicator of a fan-oriented book is a large number of photos or illustrations. In some cases, what might be called 'coffee table books' on animation, filled with glossy colour pictures and relatively little writing, serve as showcases of a studio's productions and are more of a promotional product than an historical account with any level of objectivity.

Today, there is a new source for highly anecdotal, fan-oriented writing: the Internet. However, despite the uneven quality of information available on it, the Internet actually is not a bad place to conduct preliminary research, especially for the beginning writer. News groups (such as rec.arts.animation) can be used to find information on anything from today's most popular productions to obscure animation from the past. Individual Web sites (home pages) related to animation are largely created by fans and marketing organisations and can provide interesting information and occasional interviews with industry professionals. Probably the best Internet site related to animation is the Animation World Network (www.awn.com). It contains a wide range of useful research material. Of course, the reliability of information taken from the Internet varies widely; discretion must be used in assessing the credibility of any site before it is used for research purposes.

This is true of all kinds of fan writing, whether it appears in books, magazines, or elsewhere. While it often makes interesting reading and can contain a high degree of accurate information, the animation researcher must be able to recognise the signs of casual documentation and use these sources with caution, if at all, when compiling the body of his or her scholarly research. One of the main reasons to avoid them for research purposes is their lack of precision in documenting historical occurrences. It is dangerous to quote these sources as 'fact' in a paper because the content might reflect more of a good story or marketing pitch than an unbiased account of what really occurred.

Fortunately, in recent years, a number of reliable books have come into wide circulation. For example, Giannalberto Bendazzi's book *Cartoons: One Hundred Years of Cinema Animation*[13] or Donald Crafton's *Before Mickey: The Animated Film 1898–1928*,[14] offer much more objective perspectives on animation history. As Animation Studies continues to establish itself as a recognised field of scholarship, it is imperative for research to continue in the direction of these authors' research, employing more rigorous approaches to historical documentation.

More advanced researchers who wish to go beyond the limited number of scholarly books on animation history should make an effort to visit one of the many libraries and archives across the world that house information pertaining to animation history. Almost every major library maintains clipping files that contain an assortment of newspaper articles, magazine stories, event notices, and other odds and ends related to the file's subject. Clipping files provide a good place to start, to gather a range of information that might not be available elsewhere. Some archives contain special collections materials, such as production records, oral histories (interviews), and artwork, as well as films and videos that can be viewed on the premises. Generally, clipping files can be viewed without an appointment, but more specialised collections often require a letter of application and a reservation. Many of these materials cannot be duplicated and so must be viewed on site. However, some materials (such as American patents and other information in the public domain) are available to anyone who wishes to have a copy. The Library of Congress and other government offices can provide more information on particular materials. If it is impossible to go to an archive in person, sometimes a reference librarian can assist a researcher with limited requests for information, often charging an hourly fee. Some archives have extensive guides to their collections on-line through the Internet, so that researchers can do preliminary research without travelling to the site.

In very special cases, researchers may be given access to collections housed on studio lots. However, studios often are reluctant to reveal sensitive information, such as budgets and inter-office memos, because they do not want the public to have access to it. One of the most accessible studio archives is run by the Walt Disney Company; however, researchers need to give proof of academic credentials and in any case may be given access only to the most basic level of information, primarily consisting of clipping files and press books. Some production companies and individuals in the field have donated their files to university or other media archives. For example, Walter Lantz gave many of his studio holdings to the Arts Special Collections Library at the University of California, Los Angeles. Warner Bros. files are available at the University of Southern California's Cinema-Television Library.

An alternative to visiting an archive is to create one's own data, perhaps by writing to or interviewing individuals who worked on a given production. Often, the best interview subjects are the 'sidelines' people whose contributions are generally overlooked; for example, camera operators, colour key artists, producers, and exhibitors. However, interviewing is not always the easy way to get information. Sometimes interview subjects are unable or reluctant to divulge actual details of a matter, either because they have forgotten what occurred or they do not want to put themselves in a compromising light. The contents of 'oral history', the term for a growing movement in interview-based historical documentation, can be as subjective as the anecdotal fan publications discussed previously – the researcher must use caution when incorporating any kind of interview response into historical research. This is where the researcher's own knowledge of history and production context comes into play – to interject balance into the recollections of the interview subject. Also, it can help to interview a number of people on overlapping topics, to see where accounts of an event come into conflict.

Another method for creating first-hand information is through focus groups. For example, the responses of a group of individuals can be obtained by giving them questionnaires, perhaps after they have watched a certain animated production. Some people use special interest groups on the Internet for similar purposes; it is common to see requests posted for information that will be used in research papers. The findings of an informal survey conducted by a beginning researcher who has yet to acquire skills in regard to sampling, question formatting, and other important matters obviously will not be authoritative. Nonetheless, questionnaires and other sampling methods can provide interesting perspectives that go beyond the basic information written in books.

Another option that is likely to be employed in courses on Animation Aesthetics is what is called 'textual analysis'. This method involves the interpretation of some aspect of an animated work without consideration of any factors outside the 'text' (another name for the actual animated production, which is 'read' in some manner). For example, one might consider the way in which character design gives meaning to a work, or perhaps the use of colour and music in a production. In some cases, theoretical models will be applied to further the analysis. This occurs frequently when individuals discuss aspects of symbolism in a work. Some of the most common approaches include the use of psychological theory derived from Freudian or Jungian models, sometimes with a more specialised focus, such as a Feminist reading. Theoretical research is often relatively a-historical, meaning that it does not take into account many, if any, factors pertaining to production context. Theoretical analyses can be useful for understanding more about thought processes and the ways in which a society expresses itself. However, this book encourages analysis that blends historical and theoretical analysis, as opposed to historical research that avoids theoretical implications or theoretical work that ignores the influence of historical circumstances.

Thanks to the burgeoning home entertainment market, today we have access to many more animated productions from around the world than ever before. Students should be encouraged to expand their viewing and researching interests beyond the mainstays of most writing on the subject of animation: Disney, Warner Bros. and other major American studios. However, the proliferation of home entertainment media not only expands the potential topics of focus, but also the aesthetic issues that must be considered when conducting an analysis.

In viewing animated works on home entertainment formats, certain issues affecting the aesthetics of the work should be kept in mind. For example, when viewing work that was originally produced on film and projected in a theatre, the ideal circumstance is to view it in the same manner. Unfortunately, the researcher today commonly has access only to a copy of the production on a videocassette or a laserdisc, which he or she plays on a small monitor. In this format, it becomes difficult to make definitive statements about the quality of colour, resolution, sound, and other factors in a given production. Videotape, particularly, lacks the fine grain of most film stocks and images on television monitors are not able to achieve the same degree of resolution that one finds in theatres. An added problem can arise in respect to the quality of the print used to make the video or laserdisc duplicate. Unfortunately, a significant number of copies have been made from very worn prints, which can result in poor image and sound quality.

Another consideration is that any one production can exist in many different versions.[15] Censorship, changing attitudes toward a subject, or a host of other factors can cause re-editing of sounds, images and actions, with the result that the production viewed as a home entertainment product looks very different than it did in its original form. When doing an in-depth analysis of a work, the researcher should document the version of the animation that he or she studied, whether it was taped from a broadcast, purchased from a shop, viewed in a theatre, and so on. Distributor information is vital to help other researchers discern which version of a production was used in the writing of a paper.

Home entertainment formats also engender a host of other potential problems. For example, the image that appears on a home video may be very differently framed than the original work because the duplicated version does not conform to the aspect ratio (screen dimensions) of the original work. The Academy ratio of 1.33:1 can be captured fairly well on a videocassette, but to get the entire image of a wide screen (e.g. a 1.85:1 or 2.35:1) aspect ratio, letterboxing must be used. Letterboxed images include a black strip at the top and bottom of the screen, to make the total image relatively wider, and represent a viable way to maintain proper framing. However, it is often believed that consumers do not like letterboxing because it cuts down on the total image size seen on a monitor or screen (letterboxed images do not fill the screen from top to bottom). As a result, film productions shown in theatres today sometimes are made with a 'TV safe area', the central portion of the frame, in mind. If no action appears at the edge of a wide screen production, nothing vital will be lost when it is transferred to video. *Beavis and Butt-Head Do America* (Mike Judge, 1996) provides an example of a feature that was made with the transfer to video in mind.[16]

Although it may be illegal to make duplicates of copyrighted work, it is sometimes the case that a researcher will find him or herself in the position of viewing a copy made from a copy of a copy of something passed on by a friend of a friend of a friend. This situation brings up the common problem of generational quality loss, which occurs when someone makes a copy of a copy. As copies move further away from the original source footage, images and sounds suffer from increasingly greater degrees of distortion. But even original tapes are not free from the possibility of image and sound distortion. As tapes age, metallic particles chip off and cause damage as well. Stopping a tape midway through its run and storing it that way for a period of time also tends to damage the portion of exposed tape, causing visual and audio problems.

Again, when discussing the potential problems of viewing theatrical work on video, one must consider the difference between seeing a production on a theatre screen, with a large image and a powerful sound system, and viewing it on a television monitor at home. Our perception is affected by the way in which light shines through film to project an image on a theatre screen and by the presence of other viewers, who add ambiance in the way of laughter and so forth. For these reasons, it is quite likely that the television viewing experience will lack the overall impact of the theatrical screening. This is not to suggest that made-for-television animation necessarily lacks the power or quality of theatrical work, but rather that animation made specifically for screening in a theatre will appear quite different when it is viewed from a video copy.

The aesthetics of made-for-television animation fare somewhat better when it comes to videocassettes, since the original transmission and the reviewing are in much the same context. However, differences can occur in terms of commercial breaks, which are a component of most made-for-television work produced in the United States, at least – home videos do not include commercials, thus changing the flow of the narrative and the viewing experience as a whole. As in all research, the key factor is the researcher's understanding of the production context; in this case, the intended exhibition venue for which an animated work was created. However, exhibition is just one aspect of production context that must be taken into consideration in order to have a full understanding of aesthetic issues. The twelve chapters of this book present many more of them, covering a wide spectrum of subjects and animated works.

Notes

1. For a list of colleges and universities that offer animation courses, see Gunnar Strøm, comp., *ASIFA List of Animation Schools* 2 (Volda, Norway: Møre and Romsdal College, 1993).
2. Jayne Pilling (ed.), *A Reader in Animation Studies* (London: John Libbey, 1997), xii–xvi.
3. Charles Solomon (ed.), *The Art of the Animated Image: An Anthology* (Los Angeles: American Film Institute, 1987); John Canemaker (ed.), *Storytelling in Animation: The Art of the Animated Image* (Los Angeles: American Film Institute, 1988).
4. Prior to my founding of *Animation Journal*, a number of non-refereed publications published writing on animation that was, to various degrees, scholarly in nature. One of the most notable in this category is *Animatrix*, published by graduate students in the Animation Workshop at the University of California, Los Angeles. Other journals have run special issues on the subject of animation; see *The Velvet Light Trap* 24 (Fall 1989) or *Film History* 5, 2 (June 1993). For information about *Animation Journal*, contact Maureen Furniss, Film Studies, Chapman University, 333 N. Glassell Street, Orange, CA 92866 USA.
5. E.S. Small and E. Levinson, 'Toward a Theory of Animation', *Velvet Light Trap* (1989): 73.
6. Id.
7. Charles Solomon, 'Toward a Definition of Animation', *The Art of Animation* (Los Angeles: AFI, 1988), 9–12, 10.
8. Ibid., 10.
9. Id.
10. Georges Sifianos has published a letter McLaren wrote to him in 1986, which clarifies his meaning. The date McLaren originally made this statement is unknown, but it is likely he came up with this definition during the 1950s. It appears in André Martin, *Les cinéastes d'animation face au movement* (Poitiers: Imprimerie Daynac, n.d.) and *Cinema 57* 4 (1957), and is reprinted in several more recent publications. Georges Sifianos, 'The Definition of Animation: A Letter from Norman McLaren', *Animation Journal* 3, 2 (Spring 1995): 62–66.
11. Ibid., 63.
12. For an introduction to historical research and possible models, consult the chapter 'History, Historiography, and Film History: An Advanced Introduction', in David Bordwell and Kristin Thompson, *Film History: An Introduction* (New York: McGraw-Hill, 1994), xxxi–xlii; and Robert Allen and Douglas Gomery, *Film History: Theory and Practice* (New York: Knopf, 1985).
13. G. Bendazzi, *Cartoons: One Hundred Years of Cinema Animation* (London: John Libbey, 1994).
14. Donald Crafton (1982), *Before Mickey: The Animated Film 1898–1928* (Cambridge, MA: MIT, 1987). For another excellent model for animation scholarship, see Donald Crafton, *Emile Cohl, Caricature, and Film* (Princeton: Princeton UP, 1990).
15. Eric Walter addresses the issue of multiple versions in his article, 'Whatever Happened to the Fleischer Popeye Cartoons, Anyway?' *Animato!* 25 (Spring 1993): 30–33.
16. Janet Benn, interview with the author (Jan. 1997).

2

Foundations of studio practices

DOMINANT TRAITS OF THE ANIMATION INDUSTRY

*I*n every type of cultural production, there are dominant forms of expression that tend to define it within the minds of people in the general public, if not specialists in the field. Within the realm of animation, one can identify at least four such traits: animation is (1) American and (2) created with cel artwork (3) made by famous men (4) at the Disney studio.

An interesting question to ask is, how did these characteristics become dominant? Surely their success cannot be attributed solely to inherent quality; rather, a complex combination of factors determined their domination within the realm of animation. This chapter will discuss each of the four traits, to illustrate what can be described as the foundation of contemporary animation practices.

Development of the American film industry

Long before 1895, the year in which a motion picture was screened publicly for the first time, models for both live-action and animated films had been established by optical toys and various forms of projected images involving sequential movements. Among these 'cinematic precursors' are the painted and photographed glass slides of magic lantern shows, which date back to the mid-seventeenth century, as well as several other kinds of entertainment that had been popular since the early- to mid-1800s; for example, the two-state animated images of the thaumatrope, the cyclical multi-step animation produced for a phenakistiscope wheel, and the cyclical multi-step animation produced for the linear strips of paper used in a zoetrope. Equally interesting in terms of cinematic models are the motion studies conducted by Englishman Eadweard Muybridge and Jean Etienne Marey, which allowed scientists as well as artists to understand better the dynamics of human and animal movement.

Eventually, the technology was developed that allowed the recording of sequential images on a flexible film base. The French brothers Auguste and Louis Lumière, using their versatile Cinématographe projector/camera/printer, were the first to project films publically in 1895, but it did not take long for others to join them, resulting in the growth of what would shortly become a major industry. During the first twenty years of film history (1895–1915), film production sprang up in Russia, Italy, Germany, Japan and a number of other countries. Although the United States was the largest consumer of motion pictures during these early years, it did not dominate in terms of production. Rather, France was the world's leading producer of films.

Silent film historian Eileen Bowser writes:

> ... the production of films in America in 1907 was still a handcrafted amusement industry, trying in vain to keep up with the rapidly expanding market. There were only about 1,200 films of one reel or less, mostly less, released in the entire United States in that year, and only about 400 of them were made in America. Most of the others were French, with the largest number coming from Pathé Frères.[1]

In December 1907, the domination of Pathé Frères was solidified when it was granted a license to use legally certain patents in the United States. Since the 1890s, Thomas Edison, whose company owned many essential processes and technologies, had been waging a patents war upon American companies that infringed on his rights.[2] Edison did not register his patents overseas, so he was unable to sue filmmakers outside the United States. When he decided to grant rights to Pathé Frères, he aided the French production company by limiting its competition from other foreign filmmakers. The only other foreign company licensed by Edison was that of Georges Méliès; the license was granted to his American office, which was run by his brother, Gaston.[3] Silent film historian Charles Musser describes Méliès as 'undoubtedly the world's leading filmmaker during the first years of the new century ...'.[4]

In 1908, Edison established the Motion Picture Patents Company (MPPC) as an alliance among most of the major American film production companies, along with Pathé Frères and Méliès. One of the factors that helped the MPPC to control the American film market was its agreement with Eastman Kodak, the leading manu-facturer of film stock in the United States, to sell only to MPPC members. Despite the organisation's power, independent production managed to grow. Within three to five years' time the MPPC lost much of its power; firstly because of the growth of the independent market, and secondly because the government began to question its legality. Nonetheless, the MPPC did assist the American film industry in stand-ardising equipment and processes that had been developing in many different directions during the first ten years of film history; as unified members of an organisation, companies could agree on which direction they would take as a unit. Also, by narrowing the competition, the MPPC helped to establish a strong and unified national industry, in contrast to the unorganised group of autonomous producers that had worked against one another during the earliest years of film production in the United States.

Although the power of the MPPC was waning by 1914, other changes helped the United States to secure its place as the world leader of film production. In *Exporting Entertainment*, Kristin Thompson explains that, after the start of World War I in 1914, a series of restrictions passed in England (which had been the world's most powerful nation and the American distribution point for the European film market), causing the United States to change its distribution system.[5] Rather than go through London, the American film industry began direct distribution to foreign markets. Thompson points out that 'the long-range success of the USA resulted not simply from a rise in manufacturing and exports, but also from the build-up of the facilities for supporting export: shipping and financial organizations'.[6]

In 1916, the United States government established a Division of Films within its Committee on Public Information (known as the Creel Committee, after its chairperson, George Creel), aiding the American filmmakers' ability to take over the world market. Thompson explains that the Division of Films worked with the commercial film industry to promote educational and theatrical films across the world.[7] New markets such as South America and Australia were exploited to make up for temporarily diminished sales to war-torn European nations. When the countries of Europe began to regain their economic stability, Americans were able to glut this market with a back-log of films made during wartime. This domination of screen time further entrenched the American film industry as a world leader.

In fact, the only national film industry in Europe to emerge from World War I in a relatively strong position was Germany's. To circumvent the sale of German films, the Creel committee made a 'patriotic' decree that no American films would be rented to a theatre that showed productions from Germany.[8] This restriction helped to assure American dominance within the world market, since most theatres were willing to forgo German films in order to have American productions, which had gained popularity with international audiences during the wartime period.

As the world power in filmmaking and distribution, the technical, formal and thematic content of American productions has significantly impacted the creation of conventional standards across the world. Although individual countries have developed their own styles of filmmaking throughout history (e.g. Italian Neo-Realism and the French New Wave), American live-action cinema has remained commercially dominant on an international level, continuing to set aesthetic norms for viewers. In terms of animation, the situation has been similar. American – that is, 'Hollywood' – animated productions have continued to be very popular with foreign audiences; the Disney studio, for one, makes its feature films in a host of languages, anticipating widespread international release.

But, like live-action industries, indigenous and sometimes rather specialised animation practices have flourished in many countries. During the 1920s and 1930s, experimental artists in France, such as Marcel Duchamp (in *Anémic cinéma*, Anemic Cinema, 1927) and Fernand Léger (in *Ballet mécanique*, Mechanical Ballet, 1924), were using animation techniques in conjunction with their work in other fine arts. In the United Kingdom, during the 1930s the General Post Office supported the production of a number of films created by experimental animators Len Lye and Norman McLaren (who became one of the world's most influential animators and who, in 1943, organised the animation department at the National Film Board of Canada). England also was home to the Bauhaus-influenced Hungarian animator

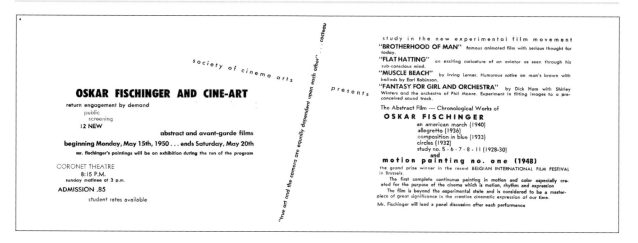

society of cinema arts

presents

"true art and the camera are equally dependent upon each other" . . . cocteau

OSKAR FISCHINGER AND CINE-ART

return engagement by demand
public
screening
12 NEW
abstract and avant-garde films

beginning Monday, May 15th, 1950 . . . ends Saturday, May 20th

mr. fischinger's paintings will be on exhibition during the run of the program

CORONET THEATRE
8:15 P.M.
sunday matinee at 3 p.m.

ADMISSION .85

student rates available

study in the new experimental film movement

"BROTHERHOOD OF MAN" famous animated film with serious thought for today.
"FLAT HATTING" an exciting caricature of an aviator as seen through his sub-conscious mind.
"MUSCLE BEACH" by Irving Lerner. Humorous satire on man's brawn with ballads by Earl Robinson.
"FANTASY FOR GIRL AND ORCHESTRA" by Dick Ham with Shirley Winters and the orchestra of Phil Moore. Experiment in fitting images to a pre-conceived sound track.

The Abstract Film — Chronological Works of
OSKAR FISCHINGER
an american march (1940)
allegretto (1936)
composition in blue (1933)
circles (1932)
study no. 5 - 6 - 7 - 8 - 11 (1928-30)
and
motion painting no. one (1948)
the grand prize winner in the recent BELGIAN INTERNATIONAL FILM FESTIVAL in Brussels.
The first complete continuous painting in motion and color especially created for the purpose of the cinema which is motion, rhythm and expression
The film is beyond the experimental state and is considered to be a masterpiece of great significance in the creative cinematic expression of our time.
Mr. Fischinger will lead a panel discussion after each performance

Fig. 2.1 *Oskar Fischinger film program at the Coronet Theatre, May 1950 Courtesy Elfriede Fischinger*

John Halas who in 1940 founded a studio with British animator Joy Batchelor (later, the two married); the Halas and Batchelor studio produced numerous important films, including *Animal Farm* (1954).

Eastern European countries have had strong traditions of animation production as well. For example, the Zagreb School of Animation earned an international reputation during the 1950s, employing a modern, experimental style of animation. Among the important animators working in Germany was the abstract painter Oskar Fischinger, who came to the United States in 1936. Subsequently, he influenced the formation what has been called the West Coast School of American abstract animation, which includes such artists as Harry Smith, Jordan Belson, James Whitney, and John Whitney. More recently, the popularity of Japanese *anime* has greatly impacted the American animation market. This list of world animation practices is hopelessly incomplete; Giannalberto Bendazzi's history of animation, *Cartoons: One Hundred Years of Cinema Animation*, is the best place to read about the many, many places outside of 'Hollywood' in which animation has been produced.[9]

Despite the breadth of animation practices worldwide, many people continue to regard American cel animation – particularly that of the Disney studio associated with the 'nine old men' animators (or, more generally, 'Disney-style') – as the epitome of animation art. The remaining sections of this chapter will discuss further these foundational aspects of studio animation.

Innovations in animation techniques

By the mid-1910s, animation production in the United States already was dominated by the techniques of cel and paper, which developed into the conventional narrative storytelling tradition associated with studios such as Disney and Warner Bros. However, when the film industry was in its infancy, other techniques such as the use of objects, clay and puppets, also appeared with some frequency in various types of productions. The eventual domination of cel animation arose from a variety of circumstances, including the technique's compatability with other industrial systems.

A brief survey of some filmmakers and productions of the time shows the variety of techniques that were employed during the early years. One of the earliest object animation was done by Arthur Melbourne of Great Britain. His 1899 film, *Matches: An Appeal*, uses animation techniques in asking citizens to give matches to troops fighting in the Boer War.

During the next ten years or so, object animations appeared with frequency. In his book, *Before Mickey: The Animated Film 1898–1928*, Donald Crafton discusses the work of pioneering French filmmaker Georges Méliès.[10] The filmmaker used stop motion – that is, stopping the camera, then adding or removing an object and starting the camera again – a practice that Crafton considers to be a technical predecessor of frame-by-frame animation. For example, in *Voyage dans la lune* (Trip to the Moon, 1902), aggressive Moon inhabitants (called selenites) burst into flames and 'disappear' after explorers from Earth hit them with umbrellas.

By 1907, the Spaniard Segundo de Chomón, who worked for French and Italian production companies under the name of Chomont, had created his popular *El hotel eléctrico* (The Electric Hotel, perhaps 1905, but not released until at least 1907).[11] This film and many others, including American J. Stuart Blackton's *Haunted Hotel* (1907), played on the novelty of 'spooky' or 'haunted' surroundings, wherein objects seem to move of their own accord or due to the forces of some evil spirit.

Blackton worked with clay animation in the 1910 film *Chew Chew Land*. In his book, *Clay Animation*, Michael Frierson discusses this film and several other uses of clay in films made prior to 1910.[12] Cut-outs and animated puppets also appeared in various films made around that time. For example, puppets were animated in the 1907 film, *The Teddy Bears*, directed by the American Edwin Porter, who is perhaps best known for his direction of the live-action short, *The Great Train Robbery*, in 1903. American Willis O'Brien, who became famous for his special effects animation in the features *The Lost World* (directed by Harry Hoyt, 1925) and *King Kong* (directed by Merian C. Cooper, 1933), was creating object animation in the mid-1910s in short works such as his *The Dinosaur and the Missing Link* (1915). The Russian-born filmmaker Ladislas Starewicz also had a long career animating objects, including extremely realistic-looking insect models in his *Mest' Kinomatograficheskogo Operatora* (The Cameraman's Revenge, 1912) and other films. As this brief overview has suggested, the early years of film history saw the application of various techniques in animation produced throughout the world. However, there were historical and industrial factors that helped determine that cels – and not clay or puppets, for instance – would become the dominant technique of commerical animation production.

As this chapter already has explained, many changes in the film industry occurred during the 1910s. In the United States, while the MPPC solidified the power of studios, the mode of live-action film production in America moved from an individual and small-group process toward an assembly-lined method employing large numbers of people in narrowly defined job classifications.

Donald Crafton has discussed the animation industry's movement toward a similar assembly-line process during the early 1910s. He explains that this re-organisation developed from a set of principles known generally as Taylorism, named for a pioneer in management theory, Frederick W. Taylor.[13] Taylor's system of scientific management and assembly-line methods advocates the use of machines and standardised, mechanised processes to assure uniform, predictable output. The division of labour is a key element in this system; management is clearly separated from the general labourers, whose work can be regulated systematically. The notion of individual craftsmanship is anathema to Taylorist principles, so there is no need for the general labourers to be 'unique' or particularly qualified for creating any given product.

Taylorism was most influential during the period 1910–1915, particularly after the publication of Taylor's book, *Principles of Scientific Management*, in 1911.[14] It had a great impact not only on the motion picture business, but across American industry on a wide scale. This impact not only influenced the way in which animation was created during the early years of film production, but had lasting repercussions on the organisation of the American animation industry.

A significant reason why paper-based and then cel animation came to dominate the American industry during the early years of film history is that these techniques lend themselves to a central component of Taylorism, an assembly-line method of production. Whereas clay or puppet animation is most labour intensive during the shooting stage, when objects must be manipulated in front of the camera by a small crew of people, paper and cel animation tend to be most labour intensive during the production stage, when a large number of people can work on drawing and colouring the thousands of images that will be filmed. The distribution of labour that can be achieved with drawn animation allows key creative individuals to do initial design work on a project, while less-skilled (and lower-paid) workers complete the more repetitive tasks, allowing the key creators to move on to another project. Because animation is such a labour-intensive process, the industry could not have flourished in a competitive environment without finding a means of cutting costs and speeding-up production. An assembly-line method of production proved to be an effective solution.

During the 1910s, there were various production methods in use, including 'retracing' and the 'slash system'. Retracing, which requires each element of a piece of art to be drawn over and over again, is perhaps the most basic method used to create animation. This system necessarily limits the amount of detail allowable in any given shot, since it is time-consuming to redraw relatively inconsequential elements. In addition, with more elements there is an increased possibility of poorly aligned images and other drawing errors. Consequently, one will find that environmental details on early animation made through retracing tend to be kept to a minimum.

Significant changes to this system were introduced by Canadian Raoul Barré, a painter who moved to New York in 1903 and began making animated advertising and entertainment films. Barré generally is credited with making two major contributions to animation production: the 'slash system' (also called 'slash and tear') and the 'perf and peg' alignment system. Using the slash system, an individual was freed from tedious retracing: the artist drew one background and laid it over another sheet containing the moving elements, cutting out a space so that images on the underlying sheet of paper could be seen. Retracing was still required to draw any figures that moved, but at least backgrounds could be reused and so could become more elaborate. One drawback of the slash system is the fact that the cut marks on the paper sometimes can be seen in the finished film.

Barré's other invention has proved to have a more long-lasting impact on animation production. In fact, it is still in use today. His standardised perf and peg system involves the use of punched holes at the bottom (or top) of animation paper (or cels) and a similarly designed peg-bar that holds sheets for drawing or shooting, all of which allows for precise registration of images. Today, the most commonly used peg-bars are made for the Oxberry and Acme animation stands, although exact designs vary throughout the world.[15]

The invention that has had the largest impact on the animation industry is the clear, flexible sheet of drawing material generally known as a cel (also spelled 'cell', especially during the early years of film history). Foreground moving images are drawn onto cels, which can be layered and placed over a background drawing or painting. This system was invented and patented by animator Earl Hurd in 1914. It was not entirely new, since a similar idea using cels as background overlays (as opposed to foreground overlays, as in Hurd's method) previously had been invented by another leader of the early animation industry, Joseph Randolph Bray.

In retrospect, it seems obvious that cels are better for moving parts, as Hurd supposed, since the clear sheets allow an animator to redraw only the moving portion of a figure (e.g. just the eyes, if they are all that move); however, it should be remembered that the cels of the 1910s were very different from the cels of today. For one thing, they were relatively expensive in comparison with plain paper, so a budget-minded studio probably would want to use them sparingly. In addition, the cels at that time were thicker – it was recommended that no more than three layers of them be used, as opposed to the five layers or so that can be used today. These early cels had a yellowish cast, which often made images look dark when photographed. For all these reasons, it might not have occurred to Bray to use cels for rendering the moving figures. Using them only for background art probably seemed quite effective.

Still, when Hurd patented his process, Bray immediately hired him and made him a partner in the Bray-Hurd Patent Company. Bray himself was an inventor and patented a number of labour-saving devices, all of which aided him in the development of an efficiently-run animation studio. Giannalberto Bendazzi describes Bray as having 'laid the foundations for American animation' through his no-nonsense approach to production, 'rationalising labor, cutting out unnecessary effort and speeding production line'.[16] Joining forces with Hurd was an extremely wise business move on his part, since the cel system of animation eventually became the dominant mode of production among American animation studios. It fit well into the Taylorist notion of an efficient assembly-line process.[17]

Fig. 2.2 *Paramount Studios' New York animation unit, circa 1921. Bill Tytla, aged 17, sits in the second row, far left*
Courtesy Adrienne Tytla and John Canemaker

At first, the development of the cel system was hampered by the fact that any studio wishing to use it had to pay royalties to the Bray-Hurd Patent Company, increasing the expense of an already expensive system. Still, as production time became an increasingly significant consideration, more and more studios began using cels. It was not until 1932, when the patent came into the public domain, that cel animation really became the industry norm.

To make the system more affordable during its early years, studios saved money by reusing cels. This could be done by cycling motions (repeating a set of movements, as in a walk cycle) in one or more films, or by washing the cels and reusing them for future productions. Martha Goldman Sigall, who painted cels for the Warner Bros. animation unit (at the time, Leon Schlesinger Productions) from the late 1930s until the early 1940s, says the studio washed cels six times before they were no longer painted.[18] The practice of cel washing is one that horrifies many people today, especially since the recent vogue for cel collecting has made animation artifacts of all kinds in great demand.

Another factor that has contributed to the demise of early cel art is the fact that, from the introduction of the process in the 1910s until the 1950s, animation cels – like 35 mm film stocks – for the most part were made with a nitrate base that was quite flammable and deteriorated relatively easily.[19] Sigall says that, at Warner Bros., she and other painters used easels (not the light boxes used by the animators) that were lit by small lamps with flexible hook necks, and that cels would catch on fire if the lamp got too close to them.[20]

Mass-production and creative control

During the early years of animation production, as in the case of live-action production, films tended to be created by a rather small crew. A good example of this mode of operation is Winsor McCay, who worked with an assistant (who traced backgrounds) to create such films as *Little Nemo* (1911), *Gertie the Dinosaur* (1914) and *The Sinking of the Lusitania* (1918).

However, as the film industry grew, production became much more complex, making it increasingly difficult for directors and other artists to retain creative control over their work. By the mid-1910s, standardisation of distribution and exhibition practices, as well as the expanding markets associated with World War I, required faster and more reliable production schedules. In addition, film formats were becoming standardised at longer lengths and with more complex narratives, both of which required the combined efforts of a team of writers, artists, directors and other personnel. Although many early animators had started their careers as newspaper cartoonists and so were used to working alone on their projects, a small-scale method was no longer viable when it came to the animation industry of the mid-1910s and 1920s.[21] Larger production crews and a division of labour became the key to running the American film industry as an efficient, money-making enterprise.

Nonetheless, it is common for people today to identify animated short films (and other motion pictures) produced at studios by the names of their directors (the reader probably is already aware that, in fact, this book abides by the convention of identifying a film by its director and year of production). Personalities such as Chuck Jones, Friz Freleng, Tex Avery, Shamus Culhane, Disney's 'Nine Old Men' (the original group animators who are closely identified with the studio's classical era) and a select few others have attracted a lot of attention, becoming the subjects of a great deal of admiration and writing. Some might say that these directors have reached the status of *auteur*, a term that French *cineastes* used to describe a live-action film director who was thought to be particularly gifted and to have controlled the production process, producing a distinctive body of films while working within the industry.

This concept of the distinctive artist/controller of a work is a common one throughout the arts. In his book *Art Worlds*, Howard Becker describes what he calls an 'intensely individualistic theory of art and how it is made' that sometimes is used to assess the reputation of an artist and his or her work. He says this theory includes the following features:

> (1) Specially gifted people (2) create works of exceptional beauty and depth which (3) express profound human emotions and cultural values. (4) The work's special qualities testify to its maker's special gifts, and the already known gifts of the maker testify to the special qualities of the work ...[22]

American critic Andrew Sarris elaborated on similar criteria of the auteur theory found in '*la politique des auteurs*', as it was called in *Cahiers du cinéma*, where it was first published in April 1957. In 1962, Sarris wrote about several premises that can be considered as measures of value in any filmmaker's work: technical competence, the distinguishable personality of the director, and the interior meaning or 'soul' of the production(s).[23] He envisioned these criteria as three concentric circles, with 'the outer circle as technique; the middle circle, personal style; and the inner circle, interior meaning. The corresponding roles of the director may be designated as those of a technician, a stylist, and an auteur', as he or she passes through them.[24]

The notion of a film 'author', or auteur, can be useful in considering the aesthetics of animation, just as the concept of genre (classifications based on content and style) are useful for organising critical discourse. However, the idea of the 'director as artistic controller' is not without its problems, whether one thinks of animated or live-action media. The most common argument against this approach points out that studio pictures are produced by the efforts of many people (producers, writers, camera operators, and so on), and not the director alone. To say that an animated short is the product of 'Chuck Jones', or whoever the director is, ignores the input of all the other workers. Of course, as the director takes on other roles – also becoming the producer, the writer, and so on (especially likely on small, independent productions) – his or her authorial control becomes more arguable.

It also can be argued that the auteurist approach is problematic because, throughout the history of the studio system, there has existed a relatively strong undercurrent that has worked against the control of individuals and toward more automated,

VARIETY   87

CARTOONS STEP FORWARD
PEN AND INKERS SPEED PRODUCTION

NEW developments to speed production and raise entertainment values made cartoons the leader in the shorts field during past 12 months. Increasing costs of turning out the one and two-reelers taxed leading pen-and-inker studios to limit of their ingenuity in finding methods to defeat higher budgets and at the same time assure a profit with no lessening of entertainment. New cameras, use of oil paints for backgrounds instead of water colors, new lighting methods, a reflection process to cut number of drawn frames of film, are among leading developments in technique contributed to the industry by top cartoon plants.

Walt Disney centered technical improvements at his plant around camera developments, and maintains a standing staff of engineers whose exclusive duty is camera research. To facilitate future camera developments, Disney has given department eight times more room at the new Burbank studio than under present setup at the Hyperion lot. Department has put in majority of its time on building of a new multiplane camera, now nearly completed and which will be used on 'Pinocchio,' second of Disney's animated features.

SIX LEVEL CAMERA

NEW camera will have six levels, instead of five as in older models, and the field range has been increased to twice its former capacity. Enlarged focusing depth, new lighting capable of 20,000 watts per camera plane, against 2,000 on present camera, are some of the outstanding developments by the Disney crew. While working hard on the new multiplane camera, department was also busy improving standard Disney cameras having only one level, all of which were regular motion picture cameras adapted to cartoon work. Redesigning of machines, such as placing the magazine on top side of the crane and other switches in placements have all resulted in cameras now being ideal for animated pictures photography, where all scenes are shot vertically.

Another innovation put into effect at the Disney plant is gradual change from nitro cellulose film to acetate film, latter's slow-burning qualities being a decided safety factor over highly combustible nitro cellulose. This change has also resulted in a paint formula switch to conform to new film. Progress also has been made during the year in the paint department, laboratory

having been given enlarged quarters and improved equipment. Paints are now more uniform in color, shade, texture and brilliance, with particular improvement noted in those used for water effects and as shadows.

IMPROVEMENT IN CARTOONS

ALL in all, the 12 to 18 Mickey Mouses, Donald Ducks and Silly Symphonies Disney will turn out for RKO release during the 1939-40 season will show a decided improvement over previous product, as will the feature-length cartoons, headed by 'Pinocchio,' since various departments have learned new and better technique for bringing full-length animated features in color to the screen.

Metro's cartoon department, recently enlarged by a third unit headed by William Hanna and Joe Barbera, to supplement those of Hugh Harman and Rudolf Ising, is forging rapidly ahead in way of improvements to speed production of the 18 one-reelers promised for the new season. Cartoon department is headed by Fred C. Quimby.

MIRRORS CUT COSTS

MOST important improvement undertaken at Metro is use of a reflection process to minimize the amount of drawn frames of film, in which mirrors serve same purpose as many drawings. Savings in production time and labor will be considerable over a period of time. New process, currently tagged 'Reflection,' comes from the reflection of one master drawn frame of film, reflected on many rippled mirrors, as the frame is being photographed. Thus many frames are photographed from one frame and its reflections on the mirrors.

Use of an 'on-the-beat' method of musical scoring has also resulted in considerable improvement in cartoons' music at Metro. Each member of the scoring orchestra, wearing earphones, co-ordinates the beats of the action and musical notes, resulting in an easier-achieved and more nearly flawless musical score. Constant efforts of the cartoon department to tighten each step in turning out the animated works simplifies each succeeding job and keeps it continually a step ahead of the next production need.

18 METRO CARTOONS

SIX cartoons each will be contributed by the three production units at Metro. The Ising unit will deliver two built around his

bear character, with likelihood there will be a whole series of Bear Family cartoons in addition to others. Harman's six will be led by 'The Blue Danube' with Strauss' music as the background; 'Peace On Earth,' anti-war pen-and-inker, and 'Gray's Elegy,' based on Thomas Gray's 'Elegy In a Country Churchyard.' Tilted for series of six to be produced by the Barbera-Hanna unit have not been selected as yet.

SCHLESINGER SKEDS 42

LEON SCHLESINGER'S Looney Tunes and Merrie Melodies, distributed by Warners, are undergoing many new treatments for the 1939-40 season. Scheduling 42—of which 26 are Melodies in Technicolor and 16 Looney Tunes with Porky Pig in black and white.

Schlesinger is well underway on his 10th year as a Warners cartoon producer. Plant's new method of using oil paints for backgrounds is understood to have resulted in an excellent three-dimensional effect, as well as achieving unusually beautiful scenic values. To obtain utmost in oil backgrounds, James Swinnerton, cartoonist and desert landscape artist, has been signed to handle paints on 'The Mighty Hunters,' which will mark screen debut of cartoonist's Canyon Kiddies.

MORE WB BURLESQUES

SCHLESINGER also will continue his successful satires and caricatures on newsreels and travelogs, after first introducing the burlesque with 'Pingo Pongo' in 1938. Latest of this group, released this season, are 'Detouring America' and 'The Land of the Midnight Fun.' Patriotic subjects are also slated as follow-ups on 'Old Glory,' a pen-and-inker starring Porky Pig, portraying various highlights in American history.

Down in Miami, (tax-exmpt) Florida, where Max Fleischer set up his cartoon studio to escape New York taxes, producer is prepping a feature-length cartoon 'Gulliver's Travels,' plus 12 Popeye shorts; 12 Stone Age cartoons, and six color classics for Paramount's release during 1939-40. Fleischer employs approximately 300 artists, plus about 400 art students undergoing cartoon training, in his modern air-conditioned studio, erected on the edge of the Everglades just outside of Miami a year ago.

Production is largely concentrated at present on rushing 'Gulliver's Travels' for a Christmas release by Paramount.

Fig. 2.4 Variety *article, 1942, describing a more efficient production process*

mechanised and (therefore) less expensive production. Reports of wonderful new inventions and break-through processes that save time and money by elimininating the work of the artists are relatively easy to find within the pages of a trade journal such as *Daily Variety*. For example, a 1942 article, 'Cartoons Step Forward: Pen and Inkers Speed Production', foregrounds some of the latest cost-cutting measures.[25] It lists various 'new developments' of the previous year, including 'new cameras, use of oil paints for backgrounds instead of water colors, new lighting methods, [and] a reflection process to cut number of drawn frames of film'. An article from 1957 entitled 'New Process Offers Automation Animation' mentions a new device called the Artiscope, invented by a Los Angeles man named Norman Maurer, which promised to 'reduce the cost of animated subjects to one-fifth the present cost' by eliminating the animator. Apparently a variation on rotoscoping, the process was described as functioning 'electronically, with up to 90 percent of all artist hand labor scrapped ...'.[26] Whether or not these new processes were embraced within the system is less significant than the general point that the reduction of artwork was of concern within the industry, a point that complicates our understanding of the director as a freely creative auteur.

Exhibition requirements related to technology and scheduling have also affected the way in which animation is made and the freedom of a director's expression. During the early years of film production, one method of standardising production was through fixed reel lengths. Today, too, there are general parameters set for the running times of feature-length films, allowing them to fit into a regular exhibition schedule; overly long films limit an exhibitor's ticket sales and, therefore, bring in less profit. Made-for-television animation in the United States must fit into blocks of time that include commercial breaks, so narratives must be structured accordingly. All these factors affect the way in which stories are told; to some extent, the creative vision of every artist working within the industry must be fit into pre-designated models.

More examples could be given, but in the end the point would be the same. For the artists involved, the dilemma often has been one of keeping creative expression alive within the parameters of a profit-making enterprise. Clearly, there are many restrictions that influence the way in which a director operates. At the very least, the issue of authorship must be evaluated on a case-by-case basis.

Marketing through innovation and differentiation

The final section of this chapter focuses on the fourth corner in the 'foundation' of animation, the dominance of the Disney studio. Because this company will be discussed within a later chapter, the information presented here is relatively limited in its scope. The main purpose of this section is to point out how commericial success came about by careful use of two opposing tendencies; one toward 'formula' and one toward 'novelty' – or, in the words of Mark Langer, how 'imitation of the successful product of one company was counterbalanced by the need to distinguish the product of one company from that of another firm'.[27] This strategy helped to propel Disney into its dominance of the animation industry.

During the earliest years of film history, like today, filmmakers sometimes tried to guarantee their profits by remaking the stories of successful films using similar plots.[28] Another common borrowing practice was the duplication of very similar character types. For example, the highly successful Krazy Kat (Hearst/Barré, et al.) appeared in 1916 and spawned many imitators. One of them, Felix the Cat, became the most famous cat figure in animation. Sharing many of Charlie Chaplin's attributes, Felix was one of the most recognisable figures worldwide during the 1920s. A further spin-off was a character named Julius, who was the animated sidekick of a live-action girl in Disney's 'Alice Comedies' of the 1920s. Russell Merritt and J.B. Kaufman contend that Disney's distributor, Margaret Winkler, who also distribued the 'Felix the Cat' series, suggested that the Julius character be developed; they say 'it seems quite likely that she saw it as a form of leverage to help keep the recalcitrant Pat Sullivan in check'.[29] The 'Alice Comedies' series (1924–1927) was itself part of a trend for live-action/animation combination films, following the success of others, such as the 'Out of the Inkwell' series (1919–1926) featuring Ko-Ko the Clown, produced by Max Fleischer.

It might seem that these kinds of manoeuvres would result in a group of films that were very much alike. To avoid that situation, studios tried to differentiate their products in some manner, to make their fairly similar films unique in some way. Langer notes that innovations in animation technology was one means by which distinctions were made. He says that, within the American animation industry, these innovations were 'motivated chiefly by competition between the two major animation companies – Fleischer Studios, Inc. and Walt Disney Productions'.[30]

The Fleischers and Disney, along with Pat Sullivan (producer of the 'Felix the Cat' series), were important forces within the American animation industry during the mid-1920s. However, the extent to which they embraced innovative technology helped to determine each company's continued success. For example, the popularity

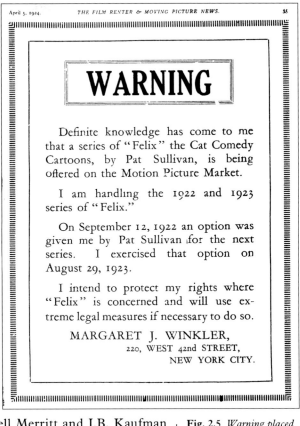

Fig. 2.5 *Warning placed in a trade publication* The Film Renter & Moving Picture News *(5 April 1924), by distributor Margaret J. Winkler*

of Felix as an animated character was fading in the late 1920s, and all but ceased after Sullivan refused to adopt sound technology in 1928. The distributor of the 'Felix' series dropped Sullivan's contract that year. With the ensuing stock market crash and Sullivan's own medical problems, Felix's better years were then behind him.

Unlike Sullivan, both Fleischer and Disney were among the first American producers to create animated pictures with sound. Evidence of the Fleischer Studios interest in sound is clear in their series of 'Sound Car-Tunes', launched in 1924. Films in the series invited viewers to sing along and 'follow the bouncing ball' through the lyrics of popular songs. Some of these films were synchronised to the early De Forest Phonofilm system, although orchestral scores were available as well. Disney also embraced sound with relish. In fact, it can be argued that the fame of Mickey Mouse was due in part to the character's association with the new sound technology. He appeared in one of the first animated shorts made with synchronised sound recorded on the film itself, *Steamboat Willie* (1928).[31]

But sound was not the only, nor even the first, innovation used by Fleischer and Disney as a marketing ploy. Mark Langer shows that technological differentiation became a 'central feature' of the competition between the two studios.[32] He demonstrates how Fleischer and Disney met each other almost invention for invention, in an attempt 'to find some advantage over its competitor, even though rational long-term economic interests argue against this approach'.[33] Langer lists a 'chronology of technical innovations' that occurred between the 1920s and the early 1940s, demonstrating 'a competitive pattern of innovation and product differentiation'.[34] Some examples of their competitive achievements include:

- the Fleischers' use of rotoscoping in a live-action/animation series, 'Out of the Inkwell', starring Ko-Ko the Clown (beginning 1919);

- Disney's live-action/animation series, 'Alice Comedies' (beginning 1923);

- the Fleischers' 'Song Car-Tunes' (beginning 1924);

- Disney's first sound-on-film production, *Steamboat Willie* (1928);

- the Fleischers' first use of sound-on-film processes with the De Forest Phonofilm system (1924–1925) and *Noah's Ark* (1929);

- Disney's three-year exclusive contract with Technicolor (beginning in 1932);

- the Fleischers' use of other colour systems and introduction of the Stereoptical Process (1934), which enhanced dimensionality in the films;

- the Fleischers' move to longer (two-reel) 'special' formats when it was able to use Technicolor (1936);

- Disney's introduction of the multiplane camera in *The Old Mill* (1937), which enhanced dimensionality in the films;

- Disney's feature-length film, *Snow White and the Seven Dwarfs* (1937); and

- the Fleischers' feature-length film, *Gulliver's Travels* (1939).

By the early 1940s, both companies were verging on disaster because, financially, they had extended themselves completely. Disney was able to ride the wave, while the Fleischer studio slid into insolvency.[35] In subsequent years, the Disney studio secured its position as a dominant force in the American and world markets through other strategic manoeuvres, combined with a commitment to aesthetic integrity.

Today, The Walt Disney Company's reputation as the leader of Classical-era animation continues to assure the success of its animated productions.

As a result of the Disney studio's rise to power, the dominance of its favoured production technique, cel animation, has been further reinforced. Recent years also have seen more interest in techniques other than cel animation and increased productivity at other studios, so Disney's power within the animation industry is not as absolute as it was ten or twenty years ago. These changes have come in part because of the rise of independent production throughout the world and increasingly stronger industrial animation production in countries other than the United States. In addition, peoples' perceptions have been altered due to the greater availability of animated products in terms of exhibition, thanks in large measure to international festivals and home entertainment formats such as videos and laserdiscs. The following chapter will examine some alternatives to mainstream studio production.

Notes

1. Eileen Bowser, *The Transformation of the Cinema 1907–1915* (Berkeley: UCP, 1990), 22.

2. Other patents holders, such as Thomas Armat and Woodville Latham were bringing suits against infringers as well. For more information, see Charles Musser, *The Emergence of Cinema: The American Screen to 1907* (Berkeley: University of California, 1990), 236–40.

3. Georges Méliès distribution in the United States was fraught with problems stemming from business dealings with his brother and American business representative, Gaston. Apparently, his brother double-crossed him by setting up his own company and failing to send profits back to France. For more on this situation, see Bowser, op. cit., 30. A letter from Méliès to William Selig suggests that, in 1909, Méliès had little idea of what his brother was doing. He wrote: '... I am anxious enough to know what happened about this story of Geo. Méliès Co. at Chicago. I certainly never had all the particulars concerning this trial of my brother which has been purely disastrous for me, and I should be very pleased to hear them from you, if you know them.' Georges Méliès, letter to William Selig (26 Aug. 1909), Folder 466, Correspondence, Margaret Herrick Library.

4. Musser, op. cit., 364.

5. Kristin Thompson, *Exporting Entertainment: America in the World Film Market* (London: BFI, 1985).

6. Ibid., 62.

7. Ibid., 93.

8. Ibid., 96.

9. Giannalberto Bendazzi, *Cartoons: One Hundred Years of Cinema Animation* (Bloomington: Indiana University Press, 1994).

10. Donald Crafton, *Before Mickey: The Animated Film, 1898–1928* (Cambridge, MA: MIT, 1987).

11. Although the exact year of the film's production and the process by which it is made is still open to question, Louise Beaudet speculated that it was created in 1905 using both animation techniques and 'invisible threads' to manipulate items on the set. She explains that, although Chomón had only a crank camera that exposed eight frames per rotation, it is likely that he used a partial crank, exposing more than one frame at a time, but still achieving an acceptable animation effect. Louise Beaudet, *In Search of Segundo de Chomón* (Annecy: Annecy Animation Festival, 1985), n.p.

    Donald Crafton writes, '*El Hotel eléctrico*, although attributed to 1905, was not released in Paris until after Blackton's *Haunted Hotel*, and not in the United States until December 1908. These late dates make it seem possible that Blackton had influenced Chomón'. Donald Crafton, op. cit., 24.

12. Michael Frierson, *Clay Animation* (New York: Twayne, 1994).

13.   Donald Crafton, op. cit., 162–168.

14.   Frederick W. Taylor, *The Principles of Scientific Management* (New York: Harper Brothers, 1911).

15.   In the earliest years of animation history, animation was photographed as live-action images were, with a camera positioned horisontally. Eventually, a vertical animation stand was developed, including two lights placed at 45-degree angles and a glass plate to hold down the artwork, and a pan bar was added to allow for moving backgrounds. In his research on animation technology, Mark Wolf indicates that, by 1926, a number of items had become standard accessories, including 'an automatic focusing device, an automatic actuating mechanism for advancing the film a frame at a time, and an automatic dissolving shutter for fades and effects, as well as attachments for doing rotoscoping'. The Oxberry animation stand, now one of the industry standards, was first marketed in 1946. Mark Wolf '*Crusader Rabbit* and the Adaptation of Animation to Television', unpublished paper written at the University of Southern California, ca. 1992.

16.   Bendazzi, op. cit., 20. In 'Institutional Power and the Fleischer Studios: The Standard Production Reference', Mark Langer discusses Bray's use of Taylorism and efficient studio methods. Producer Max Fleischer was one of Bray's foremost employees. The article focuses mainly on a production 'bible' known as the Standard Production Reference that was utilised beginning in 1942. In later years, the same bible was used by another studio, Perpetual Motion Pictures. Mark Langer, 'Institutional Power and the Fleischer Studios: The Standard Production Reference', *Cinema Journal* 30, 2 (Winter 1991): 3–22.

17.   For more on the advantages of cel animation in relation to the new studio system, see Langer, 'Institutional Power and the Fleischer Studios', op. cit., 5–6. In another article, Langer notes that a strict division of labour was not truly enforced at most studios, 'especially before the mid-1930s ... [descriptions of] rigid division of studios into ranks of work specialisation, like the management theories of Frederick W. Taylor, upon which they were based, exists more purely on paper than in actual practice. Informal lines of communication among job ranks, mobility up, down, and laterally in job classifications, and the generally relaxed atmosphere that can exist within family businesses acted as modifying factors in small institutions like animation studios. While hardly a unique example, Fleischer Studio people often held a number of positions, sometimes simultaneously on an *ad hoc* basis ... Rather than being highly disciplined dictatorships, most animation studios were managed as benevolent, patriarchal oligarchies, where employees at most levels were encouraged to contribute whatever was needed'. Langer's reference to 'patriarchal' might be understood as implying that such flexibility related to male employees in all but a few instances, but he has clarified that the flexibility occurred with women as well as men. He cites the example of Edith Vernick, who is mentioned in Chapter 12. Langer, 'Working at the Fleischer Studio: An Annotated Interview with Myron Waldman', *Velvet Light Trap* 24 (Fall 1989): 3–19, 14. Mark Langer, correspondence with the author, 15 May 1996.

18.   Martha Goldman Sigall, interview with Tom Sito, Los Angeles (12 March 1997).

19.   A *Daily Variety* article of 1942 indicates that Disney already was making the switch to safety film stocks, and that the change created repercussions in other aspects of the animation process. The article explains, 'Another innovation put into effect at the Disney plant is gradual change from nitro cellulose film to acetate film, latter's slow-burning qualities being a decided safety factor over highly combustible nitro cellulose. This change has also resulted in a paint formula switch to conform to new film.' Anonymous, 'Cartoons Step Forward: Pen and Inkers Speed Production', *Daily Variety* (8 March or May 1942), 87.

20.   Sigall, interview with Tom Sito, op. cit.

21.   Langer draws a similar conclusion: 'Due to their inability either to produce animated films in large quantities or to control the costs of producing such films, early practitioners like Cohl and McCay were eliminated from animation by 1921. The next generation of filmmakers would be those who controlled costs and regularised mass production.' Langer, 'Institutional Power and the Fleischer Studios: The Standard Production Reference', *Cinema Journal* 30, 2 (Winter 1991): 5.

22.   Howard Becker, *Art Worlds* (Berkeley: University of California Press, 1982), 352–53.

23. Andrew Sarris, 'Notes on the Auteur Theory in 1962', *Film Culture* (Winter 1962–63), reprinted in Gerald Mast and Marshall Cohen, *Film Theory and Criticism: Introductory Readings* (Oxford: Oxford UP, 1985), 527–540, 537–538.
24. Ibid., 538–539.
25. Anonymous, 'Cartoons Step Forward: Pen and Inkers Speed Production', *Daily Variety* (8 March or May 1942), 87.
26. The articles explains: 'A combo live action-animation technique, live action is converted into animation action on cells, to get the smoothness and realism of live action in drawings.' The 'veepee' of the company that manufactured the Artiscope equipment was Moe Howard, one of the stars of 'The Three Stooges'. The *Variety* article noted that a demonstration film 'lacks the refinement which can be added to the process, it is claimed'. Anonymous, 'New Process Offers Automation Animation', *Variety* (8 April 1957).
27. Mark Langer, 'The Disney–Fleischer Dilemma: Product Differentiation and Technological Innovation', *Screen* 33, 4 (Winter 1992): 343–60, 351.
28. Others took an even easier route in early cinema history, by just duplicating the actual films, hoping not to get caught. For example, the films of Georges Méliès were so popular that they were 'commonly pirated, and Méliès had to open a sales office in the United States in 1903 to protect his interests'. Kristin Thompson and David Bordwell, *Film History: An Introduction* (New York: McGraw-Hill, 1993), 16.
29. Russell Merritt and J.B. Kaufman, *Walt in Wonderland: The Silent Films of Walt Disney* (Baltimore, MD: Johns Hopkins, 1993), 63.
30. Langer, 'The Disney–Fleischer Dilemma', op. cit., 351.
31. For more information on Disney's use of sound in early 'Mickey Mouse' films, see J.B. Kaufman, 'The Transcontinental Making of *The Barn Dance*', *Animation Journal* 5, 2 (Spring 1997): 36–44. Kaufman points out that, although it is often said that *Steamboat Willie* is the first sound-on-film cartoon, it really is not. He writes, 'the DeForest process was also sound-on-film. *Steamboat Willie* is one of those famous film "firsts" that really wasn't. Like most such cases, it became so popular that everyone thought it was first.' J.B. Kaufman, correspondence to the author (5 August 1997).
32. Langer, 'The Disney–Fleischer Dilemma', op. cit., 352.
33. Langer likens this approach to the 'Prisoner's Dilemma', a non-zero-sum, unco-operative model developed out of games theory. For more on this theoretical model, see Langer, 'The Disney–Fleischer Dilemma', op. cit., 351.
34. The following list is drawn largely from Langer's article, 'The Disney–Fleischer Dilemma', op. cit.
35. Langer, 'The Disney–Fleischer Dilemma', op. cit., 353–4.

3

Alternatives in animation production

MODES OF ANIMATION PRODUCTION

*C*hapter 1 demonstrated how live-action and animation can be discussed as a continuum within the general category of 'motion picture production techniques'. This chapter demonstrates that 'industrial animation' (also known as commercial animation) and 'independent animation' also form a kind of continuum, under the general heading of 'modes of animation production'. It shows that industrially and independently produced animation are not completely separate modes of production, but are in fact interrelated in complex ways.

Film scholar David James discusses the nature of marginalised forms in relation to dominant modes of production, finding that any alternative practice 'speaks not only of what it is, it speaks of what it is not; it speaks of its other'.[1] That is, any mode that exists as an alternative – as avant-garde or experimental – does so only in contrast to the dominant, conventional form. Therefore, the two cannot be seen as separate entities; they can be characterised only in relation to each other. James explains that some influential historians, such as P. Adams Sitney, erroneously have viewed the independent and commercial modes of production as two separate entities. He contends that such readings result from an 'inability to accommodate the diversity of the alternative cinemas and their ongoing negotiations with Hollywood'.[2]

Although James's observations focus primarily on live-action films, they are relevant to a discussion of animation. It is impossible to understand independent animation as a cultural product without acknowledging its relationship to hegemonic forms, such as animated or live-action Hollywood films. Other industrial products, such as made-for-television animation and animated advertising, also have relevance to the independent 'fine art' animator and his or her work. To realise this, one need only consider that most of the celebrated practitioners of independent animation at some point have worked on a large studio production or created advertising.[3]

A more complex variation on the continuum model used previously in this book can be used to demonstrate the characteristics of commercial and independent production. The two columns in the following table represent extremes to which few cultural products could adhere completely; but, by evaluating a particular text in terms of the various paradigms, it is possible to see a given work as generally being related to one mode of production or the other.[4]

TABLE I — TENDENCIES OF INDUSTRIAL AND INDEPENDENT FORMS

Traditional/industrial/ hegemonic forms tend to:	Experimental/independent/ subversive forms tend to:
have big budgets	have small budgets
be made by groups	be made by individuals
utilise traditional techniques	utilise techniques other than traditional ones and alter media
be intended for mainstream audiences	be limited to personal or small-scale exhibitions
be dominated by marketing concerns	be dominated by aesthetic concerns
be narrative	be non-narrative
be mimetic	be abstract
be linear	be non-linear
reflect Western, traditional societal norms	reflect alternative lifestyles
support dominant beliefs	challenge dominant beliefs
be made by artists from dominant social groups and reflect their concerns	be made by artists from marginalised social groups and reflect their concerns

The model depicted in Table 1 alleviates the need to make exacting distinctions between independent animation and commercial production. Virtually every independent animator – even one who works exclusively in a 'one person, one film' mode of production – has some degree of commercial affiliation. If nothing else, an artist generally depends on the commercial world for equipment and materials. If an animated work is going to be publicly exhibited, he or she will be influenced by systems of distribution and exhibition.

This model helps to overcome some discriminatory beliefs that have been held by animation scholars. For example, take the case of what collectively might be called 'Saturday Morning Cartoons'; until the late 1980s, it was not uncommon to see animation historians such as Charles Solomon and Leonard Maltin deny the association of most television series with so-called 'real' animation because it had lower budgets and aesthetic standards that were quite different from theatrical features.[5] The model shown in this chapter is non-judgemental because it allows us to discuss made-for-television series, or any other type of animation, for what it is: one sort of animation among many.

The model provided here also addresses an assumption held by some newcomers to the field that most artists who begin working in a relatively independent mode are trying to expand into a more industrial model (i.e. the desire is to achieve widespread 'commercial success'). This assumption is sometimes based on stories of how first-time directors working with limited means, such as the live-action filmmakers Jim Jarmusch and Spike Lee, have 'graduated' to higher budgets and more complex productions after gaining initial acceptance. It is important to understand that a sizeable number of individuals do not see independent production as a step toward greater fame and more complex production methods; rather, they operate within the independent realm in order to achieve goals not generally associated with the commercial sector. These concerns are suggested in the right-hand column of the model.

This figure suggests that independent artists are not as concerned with exhibition, which is in some respects misleading. Perhaps it is more accurate to say that these artists tend not to cater to expectations about what the commercial marketplace finds useful and, therefore, their work generally finds limited exhibition opportunities. However, in recent years, there has been a growing number of venues for the exhibition and distribution of motion pictures made by independent animators. One of the primary ways in which this kind of work is shown today is in the context of animation festivals, which occur in many places throughout the world. Major competitions take place every two years in: Annecy, France; Hiroshima, Japan; Ottawa, Canada; Zagreb, Croatia; and many other places throughout the world. These festivals tend to focus on independently produced animated shorts, but often have categories for commercial features, advertising, made-for-television series, and other kinds of productions.

After the festival circuit has been completed, some independent animators find distribution possibilities in touring festival packages of animation and the home

Fig. 3.1 *Some delegates from the Annecy Festival 1960: André Martin, Claire Parker, Alexandre Alexeîeff, Paul Grimault, Ivan Ivanov Vano, Ernest Pintoff, Grant Munro, Henri Gruel, Pierre Barbin, Dimitri Babitchenko, John Hubley*

From Le quotidien *1, Centre International du Cinéma d'Animation (30 May 1995): 11*

entertainment mediums of video cassettes and laserdiscs. Today, the Internet also provides substantial opportunities for the exhibition of independent work; for example, the World Wide Web site 'Absolut Panushka', produced by American animator Christine Panushka for Absolut Vodka, contains information about many experimental artists as well as clips of their works (its address is http://www.absolut vodka.com). The dissemination of animation through such media as laserdiscs, video cassettes and the Internet provides many professional advantages for independent artists, even beyond possible royalties. Works that students and scholars can view easily tend to remain in the public awareness because they are incorporated into teaching programs and books. The availability of materials greatly affects the writing of history and possibly the prestige obtained by any given artist. Historical merit and prestige can, in turn, affect one's ability to sell work, get commissioned for projects, and be supported by grants.

The model depicted in Table 1 also suggests that independent artists tend to employ production techniques that differ from mainstream commercial processes. The remainder of this chapter will focus on some of the techniques that offer an alternative to industrial cel animation practices. It focuses on two-dimensional animation ('2D' – created using media that have height and width, but no depth). Three-dimensional animation ('3D' – created using media that have all three dimensions, such as clay and puppets) is discussed in Chapter 8.

TWO-DIMENSIONAL ANIMATION AS AN EXTENSION OF OTHER ARTS

Many independent animators have worked as fine artists in various media, often using the time-based medium of animation as a way to expand their explorations of movement and temporality in still paintings and drawings.[6] During the 1920s, a number of animated films were created by artists who had gained renown within the realm of the avant-garde: examples include Marcel Duchamp's *Anémic cinéma* (Anemic Cinema, 1927), Fernand Léger's *Ballet mécanique* (Mechanical Ballet, 1924), Walter Ruttmann's 'Opus' series (ca. early 1920s), Hans Richter's *Rhythmus 21* (1921) and Viking Eggeling's *Diagonal Symphonie* (1924). Throughout the twentieth century, many other examples of 'fine art' animation have been produced with various 2D techniques.

This chapter overviews some of these techniques and their aesthetics. To begin, there is a discussion of the wide range of animation made with drawing and painting, but not employing cels in the dominant studio style. Other techniques discussed here are cameraless animation, as well as animation made with drawings and paintings on paper, silhouettes, under-lit sand, collages, strata-cut clay and wax, or a pinboard. In each of these categories, certain practitioners have gained prominence by developing the technique and exploring its unique aesthetic potential. The following discussion focuses on these exemplary uses, and does not attempt to fully explicate the history of the use of each technique.

Drawing and painting

From the beginning of animation history, one of the most common alternatives to drawing and painting on clear cels has been drawing or painting on various other surfaces: most notably on paper, but also on frosted (or opaque, as opposed to clear) cels and other materials.

In the early years of animation history, drawing and inking on paper was an alternative used by industrial studios in large measure because the cost of the cels or the license to use the patented technique was too high; however, drawing and painting as techniques of animation always have appealed to independent animators for aesthetic reasons. As suggested previously, the temporal element of animation has been attractive to artists who wish to explore elements of time or movement. A great many animators who began as artists working in the realms of still drawing or painting have become interested in animation because it offers an opportunity to set their images in motion.

Drawn animation can be created with the use of regular pencils, coloured pencils, pens, pastels, Conté crayons, Aquarelles or any other materials available to still artists. These items can be used in combination with various bases, including paper and frosted cels, each with different results. The advantage of using frosted cels is that it is possible to draw on their surface using any of the above materials, while only acetate-adhering inks and paints can be used on clear cels. The main problem with frosted cels is that, because you cannot see through them very well, they cannot be used in multiple layers. However, an opaque cel can be varnished, so that its surface turns clear, in which case multiple levels and backgrounds can be used.

Paper presents its own challenges. Sheets of paper are generally too dense to be used in multiple layers, unless they are under lit (allowing the lines on lower sheets of paper to show through). Even if they are under lit, sheets of paper are opaque and textured (both in terms of the surface, with may range from smooth to rough, and the fibers that show through when paper is under lit). It is often the case that animated productions created with images composed on paper are rendered so that all images appear on one sheet (moving images, still images, backgrounds, etc.). For that reason, everything must be entirely redrawn for every new frame. In the early days of animation history, artists such as Winsor McCay worked in that manner.

The possibilities of drawn or painted animation are virtually endless. In *Sisyphus* (1974), Hungarian Marcell Jankovics employs bold black lines and deceptively simple character design on a white background. British animator Joanna Quinn uses kinetic, sketchy caricatures in her film *Britannia* (1994). British artist Candy Guard uses cleaner lines and cartoony style in films such as *Wishful Thinking* (1988) and *What about Me?* (1990). In *Preludes in Magical Time* (originally entitled *Picture Window*, 1987), American Sara Petty lets the texture of the paper show through her abstract forms rendered with Prismacolor pencils and a bit of charcoal. In *Furies* (1977) (see CP 1), Petty achieves a soft texture by using pastels and newsprint, which has a very smooth surface. In some of his work, American David Ehrlich creates hazy, dreamlike images with soft lines by using a combination of Prismacolor pencils and tracing paper, sometimes layered and lit from below; examples include *Vermont Etude* (1977), *Vermont Etude, No. 2* (1979) and *A Child's Dream* (1990). American Paul Glabicki's hard-edged figures in *Object Conversation* (1985) seem more like computer-generated renderings than the hand-drawn illustrations that they are. The relatively hard, 'contrasty' look of photocopied images is employed in *Deadsy* (1989), a collaboration

**Figs 3.2 (a) & (b)
(top left & right)**
Britannia *by Joanna
Quinn (1994)*
Courtesy the artist

between British animator David Anderson and writer Russell Hoban on the subject of the arms race between nations of the world. Each of these artists' techniques creates a certain ambiance in his or her work, affecting the way in which the viewer experiences it.

In *L'homme qui plantait des arbres* (The Man Who Planted Trees, 1987) (see CP 2), which won an Academy Award as well as thirty other international awards, German artist Frédéric Back used coloured pencils with turpentine on frosted cels. This process causes his sketchy lines to blur together, so that they almost appear to be painted.[7] Back used a similar style in his next film, *Le fleuve aux grandes eaux* (The Mighty River, 1993) (see CP 3). He describes his drawing style as 'very realistic, especially in [these two] films, because I want to create dreamlike images that are

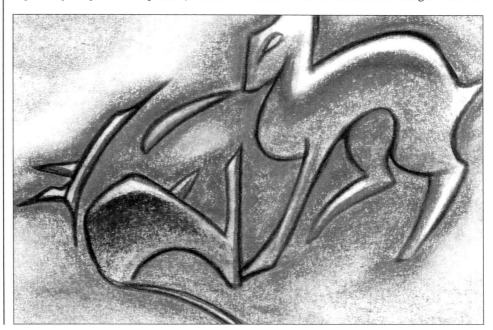

Fig. 3.3 Furies *by
Sara Petty (1977)*
Courtesy the artist

close to reality'.[8] It took Back more than five years to complete *The Man Who Planted Trees*, a 30-minute film, because he tends to create most of his drawings himself. He explains that he used that type of production process in *The Mighty River*:

> About 80 per cent of the drawings I did myself. I had one assistant who did the in-betweens in some places, but most of the work I had to do myself. There are so many different scenes in the film, so I had to do the animation, the calculations for the camera work, the backgrounds and the colouring.

> As in my previous films, I used colour pencils on frosted cels. When the drawing is finished, I sometimes varnish off the frosting around the drawing to get the transparency of a normal cel. When I did all the animation in one drawing, I only used one level of cels. But when I had landscapes, water and ships, I had to use three or four levels, sometimes even five or six. So I had to have good transparency.[9]

Back complains that he has trouble with the type of frosted acetate that is currently being manufactured, because it is made primarily for the use of engineers and architects. He says it is:

> ... too smooth and does not keep the colour of the pencils as did the older material, which was more granulated, but also more fragile. One can still get acetate similar to the old stuff, but I had great difficulties when making *Le fleuve aux grandes eaux* with this less interesting acetate – the colours do not come out so well and the lines are not as strong.[10]

In most cases, animators who choose to draw their images, whether on acetate cels or paper, must create many different drawings. However, it is sometimes the case that an artist will use a 'modified base' technique,

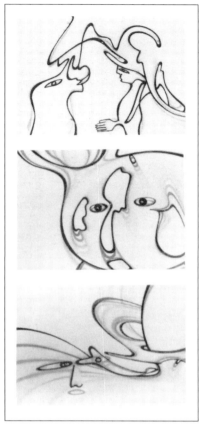

Fig. 3.4 (above)
Vermont Etude, No. 2
*(1979) by David Ehrlich,
and* **Fig. 3.5 (left)**
A Child's Dream *(1990)*
Courtesy the artist

in which a single base-image is created and recorded as it is constantly modified. Although many drawing tools (such as pencils and pens) remain relatively fixed on a drawing surface, pastel chalks and charcoals are soft enough that they can be erased

or smudged for use in a modified-base technique. One artist who is known for his use of a modified-base technique is Polish animator Piotr Dumala, who paints and etches images into a plaster base and photographs each modification frame by frame.[11] This method was used to create his film *Franz Kafka* (1992), which was used as the basis for a ten-second commercial for MTV in 1995.

Norman McLaren applied the modified-base technique in *La poulette grise* (The Grey Hen, 1947). In his film notes, he explains: 'The visuals were shot in 16 mm by a continuous chain of abutting 40-frame camera mixes or dissolves, with the camera trained on a single colour-pastel drawing, which was modified between each mix.'[12] The modified-base technique works well with painted images, particularly if the animator uses oils, which are relatively malleable. Oil paints remain wet for long periods of time, allowing the artist to modify his or her work with relative ease; animators who have used oil paints often work on glass or another hard surface, to facilitate the movement of the paint.

Two very different effects of using oil paints were achieved by the German-born Oskar Fischinger in *Motion Painting No. 1* (1947), which is mostly composed of oil paint on Plexiglas, and Russian animator Alexander Petrov in *Korova* (The Cow, 1989) (see CP 4), which is made with black paint on glass. Fischinger's film uses well-defined, brightly coloured geometric images and was painted as an experimental work, in order to reveal the process by which a painting develops. On the other hand, Petrov's work is a narrative film using representational figures and soft, dreamlike imagery in neutral tones. Through a combination of top lighting and underlighting he has created a luminous quality that compliments the film's story, a boy's fond recollections of his family's cow.

Using paint on glass, Welsh painter Clive Walley has made a series of six animated films collectively entitled 'Divertimenti 1991–1994'.[13] In these films, Walley combines his still and motion picture work through a type of motion painting, achieving

Fig. 3.8 La poulette grise *(1947) by Norman McLaren Courtesy NFB*

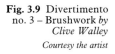

a multiplane effect by shooting through several sheets of glass placed some distance from each other. His films are derived 'from the paintings by virtue of a special but simple, multi-plane rig, which conceptually extends the techniques of painting directly to the cinema/TV screen'.[14] His *Divertimento no. 3 – Brushwork* (see also CPs 7 and 8), which opens and closes with views of an artist's easel, has been described as a 'contemplative, strangely dimensioned world which opens up to a painter when the work is in progress'.[15] As the action progresses, in what appears to be a zoom out through planes of space located within a painting, various images appear before the viewers: we track through a door, see a vase compose itself, watch a woman appear on a chair. Walley explains that, in the films, he was exploring:

> ... the axis of depth in a painting which archives its history ... And more than that, I was interested in imaging the process of painting rather than the results, because in much analysis of modern painting process is a key idea. The problem is that people who are not painters have no feeling for what 'process' might contribute to the meaning of a painting, so *Brushwork* was an attempt to use the extra dimension of time in a moving image to emphasise it.[16]

Each of Walley's 'Divertimenti' are different in character, ranging from total abstraction to relative representation, and sometimes hinting at character – for example, in *Divertimento no. 5 – Slapstick*, globs of paint run through various containers and channels, seeming to overcome hurdles and blockages.

Because it has body, or plasticity, paint offers the possibility of actual surface texture and a certain amount of dimensionality (oils can be applied thickly, as can acrylic paints). One example can be found in Walley's *Divertimento no. 2 – Love Song*, which includes both smooth and dimensional surfaces. Similarly, the texture of paints can be seen to varying degrees in the films of Swiss animator Georges Schwizgebel; for example, in *La course à l'abîme* (The Ride to the Abyss, 1992) (see CP 9) and *L'année du daim* (The Year of the Deer, 1995). Paints such as watercolours, tempera and India

Fig. 3.10 L'année du daim *(1995) by Georges Schwizgebel*
Courtesy the artist

inks lack body and do not offer the same malleability and texture as oils; however, a bit of oil can be mixed with these water-based paints to prevent them from drying so quickly.

However, some artists prefer the more translucent quality of water-based paints. An excellent example can be found in *Le moine et le poisson* (The Monk and the Fish, 1995) (see CP 5), an Academy Award-nominated film by Dutch animator Michael Dudok de Wit. The animator used a brush and India ink to render the lines of his cel figures and felt that watercolours on paper provided an aesthetically pleasing background for these images, though both choices increased the time and work involved in the production. He explains:

> I did hundreds of watercolor [backgrounds] and only selected sixty. This is something you cannot touch up ... I chose watercolor because the ink line of the characters is liquid and watercolor is liquid and I wanted the two to be harmonious ... you can really tell it has been done by hand.[17]

American Caroline Leaf used a combination of paints in her ten-minute film, *The Street* (1974), which took a year and a half to complete. She explains that she:

> ... did a lot of experimenting and ended up using waterbase tempera colours on milk glass with some oil added, to keep the paint from drying. It was like finger painting ... I wanted something that would be waterbased, so that it would be easy to wipe up with a cloth.[18]

While some animators prefer the unique qualities that oil-based paints offer, others – such as American Faith Hubley – prefer to use watercolours. In *Women of the World* (1975) and most of the other films by Hubley, watercolours are used to create muted tones and soft edges that complement her themes of compassion for all things and non-violent living. Watercolours, like drawings, require that complete separate images be created for each frame.

With so many media to use, perhaps the most important aesthetic consideration is how a given technique will help to create meaning in a work. In order to create a desired effect, it may be necessary to employ not one, but many different animation techniques. In *Slike is Sjecanja* (Pictures from Memory, 1989), Zagreb animator Nedeljko Drajic used various types of painting, along with different drawing styles, to depict memories of what occurred in his life between 1940 and 1960. The artist's multi-media approach seems well suited to the portrayal of different types of memories, from the child-like caricatures of youth to the splattered abstractions of war and the 'perfect' icons of American culture that invaded his country as well.

Drawing and painting on paper or frosted cels are techniques that have tended to remain in the realm of independent animation. In a purely technical sense, they are not well suited to a commercial studio mode of production because they do not lend themselves to an assembly-line method to the degree that clear-cel animation does. This is particularly true of the modified-base technique, in which most of the work occurs under the camera and not in pre-production.

Caroline Leaf explains why her method of making films is not well suited to commercial production. She says that 'the way I work, under the camera, I don't think I can work as a team'; she adds that her techniques are not commercially viable because, without explicit storyboards, a client 'couldn't see beforehand what I was going to do'.[19] When John Canemaker asked Leaf: 'If it were possible to direct other people in your technique, would you be interested in doing a feature?', she responded: 'No, I wouldn't. I can't imagine directing other people, and also I have a lot of fun when my fingers are doing it and I discover for myself little things. That's what keeps me going.'[20] Leaf's comments reflect some of the motivations for the creation of independent animation, as well as the difficulties of incorporating alternate techniques into the commercial studio system.

'Cameraless' animation

It is not necessary to record images with a camera in order to create animation. Cameraless animation, also called direct-on-film animation, is made by working directly on the surface of clear, white or black film-leader, or on pieces of exposed and developed film containing other images. Some artists choose to work in a relatively conventional way, treating each frame of film as a separate image, while others think of the entire strip of film as a 'canvas' and so create images up and down the acetate without consideration of where each frame lies. In any case, a variety of visual effects can be achieved. Linear images created along the length of the film move fluidly in a vertical motion when projected. Horizontal images seem to float in space. Random images pop on and off the screen in a split-second's time.

This technique, which represents a variation on the drawn and painted animation discussed previously, might seem to be a very simple way to create animation, but actually it can be one of the most challenging. There are three primary reasons for possible difficulty: the relatively small size of the drawing; the near impossibility of maintaining the registration of images (as a result, the images of cameraless animation tend to be fairly shaky); and the necessity for the artist to work on the project with little or no assistance from a crew (because of the size of the working area and due to the fact that every image created becomes a permanent fixture in the flow of the animation, the artist him or herself usually takes total control of the project).

However, there are ways to minimise the difficulties inherent in cameraless animation. For example, to combat the problem of image size, artists often work on larger film stocks – although any size of film is relatively small in comparison to most other drawing surfaces. When she made *Two Sisters* (1990), Caroline Leaf used 70 mm colour film stock. It took Leaf a year and a half to scratch the drawings necessary to create thirteen minutes of film. She explains that she worked on two pieces of film:

Fig. 3.11 (above)
Two Sisters *(1990)*
by Caroline Leaf
Courtesy NFB

> ... so that frame 1, 3, 5, 7 would be on one strip, then frame 2, 4, 6, 8 on the other one. I had a little metal plate with two pegs the same size as the sprocket holes in the film that I laid on a light-table. I laid my first strip down and did the first drawing, put the second strip on top of that so I could see through, and did the next frame.'[21]

To achieve colour in the film, she removed various amounts of emulsion. She explains that 'if I scratch a strip of colour film and scratch just a little bit, the red emulsion comes off and you get the green, and if I scratch more I get to the yellow and when I scratch all the way down, it is white. As for the blue, I used blue film'.[22]

Fig. 3.12 (below)
Caroline Leaf scratching
film for Two Sisters
Courtesy the artist

Most artists who create cameraless animation tend to capitalise on rather than fight against the technique's kinetic qualities. In fact, animators working in cameraless animation tend to be artists who are interested in exploring qualities of movement in a general sense. Such was the nature of the Scotsman Norman McLaren, who was a master of virtually every animation technique, including cameraless animation. Works such as *Fiddle Dee Dee* (1947) and *Begone Dull Care* (1949), both created during McLaren's long employment with the National Film Board of Canada, exemplify the kineticism that is characteristic of the form. These films were made by first recording a soundtrack and then cutting lengths of film to match various parts of the music. The strips of film were then painted with inks and dyes that were given texture by various means.

However, in contrast to these exuberantly kinetic films, McLaren also created cameraless animation with imagery that

is greatly controlled in its movement: *Lines Vertical* (1960), *Lines Horizontal* (1962) and *Mosaic* (1965). McLaren made these films as a personal challenge, to see if he could create direct-on-film animation that had the smoothness of movement generally found in more conventionally created animation. He made *Lines Vertical* by etching on 35 mm black leader. The lines were made by knives sharpened to various thicknesses and run along a straight-edge draftsman's rule that was six feet in length (which was the length of the film strips being used).[23] After the film was completed, its music score was composed by Maurice Blackburn. It should be noted that McLaren worked with an assistant in creating his cameraless animations and other projects. In many cases it was Evelyn Lambart, an artist whom McLaren felt closely shared his aesthetic sensibilities.

Fig. 3.13 (above)
Norman McLaren
working on Begone
Dull Care
Courtesy NFB

Fig. 3.14 (right)
Begone Dull Care
(1949) by Norman
McLaren
Courtesy NFB

Fig. 3.15 (facing top)
Working on Lines
Vertical *(1960)*
Courtesy NFB

Fig. 3.16 (facing bottom) *Mosaic (1965)*
by Norman McLaren
Courtesy NFB

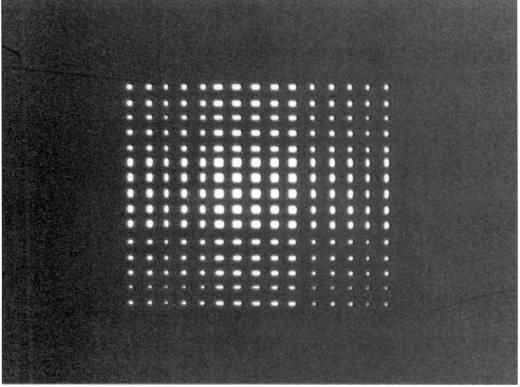

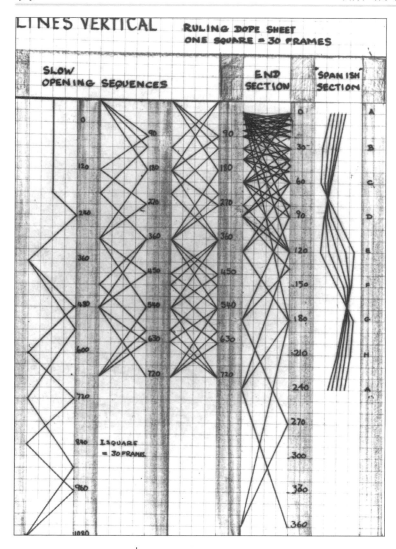

Actually, McLaren's two 'Lines' films and *Mosaic* are all the same film, in a manner of speaking. Two years after he completed *Lines Vertical*, he made *Lines Horizontal* by flipping each frame of the previously made film on its side. With a new soundtrack (composed by Pete Seeger), the film became an entirely new viewing experience. In 1965, the third film in the series, *Mosaic*, was created by running the other two films through an optical printer at the same time. In the new film, white dots appeared wherever the lines of the other works intersected. In this case, a live-action introduction and closing was added: a man walking on and off camera provides a frame for the abstract animations.

Throughout history, other artists have become known for their use of cameraless animation. New Zealander Len Lye was one of the masters of this technique. In fact, it is said that he influenced McLaren's work. Lye's film, *A Colour Box* (1936) (see CP 11), was created as an advertisement for the British General Post Office, and is thought to be the first cameraless animation to be publicly screened. Another of Lye's British-government-sponsored films, *Trade Tattoo* (1937), was created by working directly onto pieces of documentary film footage that show various workers at their jobs.

Fig. 3.17 *Preparation for Lines Vertical (1960) by Norman McLaren Courtesy NFB*

Harry Smith is another artist who worked directly on film in several of his earliest abstract works (which are titled as numbers in a series, from 1 to 7, and are presumed to have been created during the late 1940s and 1950s). Although Smith was secretive about his production techniques, it is apparent that he employed such methods as drawing, scraping, spray painting and bleaching.[24]

Another distinctive artist to work directly on live-action film footage is American Stan Brakhage, who manipulates the celluloid surface in all manner of ways: from scratching and drawing on it, to altering its appearance with chemicals and burning. *Dog Star Man* (1961–1964) and many of his other films were created using these and other means. Brakhage's film, *Mothlight* (1963), represents another type of cameraless animation. To make this film, Brakhage adhered bits of moth bodies, leaves and other natural materials to mylar splicing tape. When projected on the screen, these objects appear to be randomly placed semi-abstractions.

In recent years, Austrian filmmaker Bärbel Neubauer also has established a reputation for the creation of award winning cameraless animation, including *Algorithmen* (Algorithms, 1994) (see CP 12) and *Roots* (1996). Images from one of her most recent films, *Mondlicht* (Moonlight, 1997) (see CP 13), which was created by scratching on black leader, suggest the kind of energy that is characteristic of direct-on-film animation.[25]

Cut-outs and collage

There are two general techniques that fall under the heading of cut-out animation, the major difference being lighting. Like most animated images, cut-outs generally are top lit, allowing the viewer to see their colours, textures, and so forth. However, a few artists have specialised in silhouette animation, which is back lit, causing cut-out figures to have a solid black form. Both types of cut-out animation may involve hinged (or 'articulated') figures, to facilitate movement, or non-hinged figures. If no hinges are used, figures can be moved through a 'substitution method', meaning that an entire figure is cut out and used for each of the necessary incremental movements.

At the turn of the century, filmmakers such as J. Stuart Blackton found it was much easier to move a cut-out figure than to redraw a figure for every frame of film (i.e. his 1906 *Humorous Phases of Funny Faces* depicts a drawn man removing his hat with a cut-out arm). Emile Cohl, of France, also used articulated puppet figures in films such as the *Le peintre néo-impressionniste* (The Neo-Impressionist Painter, 1910).

Since that time, cut-outs have remained a relatively popular option among animators. Cut-outs can save time in preproduction, since one cut-out can be used throughout the entire production. However, the time saved in preproduction by using only one figure can be lost during the shooting stage, when that figure must be moved under the camera very carefully. To minimise time under the camera, an animator using cut-outs might turn to the substitution method, which requires that many variations of the primary cut-out figure be created during preproduction.

Chinese animators are well known for their use of articulated puppets. In the early 1950s, Wan Guchan began to think of using them for animated films and, in preparation, went to the province of Shanxi to study the shadow theatre and traditional decorative arts that used paper-cuts. He later collaborated with a number of other Chinese artists to create 'a new type of animation which was not only a major aesthetic success but also allowed for great economies of labour relative to traditional cartoons. In fact, it was enough to do one cut-out for all the scenery, then each character front on, profile and three-quarter, with a close-up, a mid-shot and a long-shot'.[26] The first film he made with the technique is *Zhu Baiji Eats the Watermelon* (1958).

The Russian animator Yuri Norstein is one of the most accomplished artists in the realm of cut-out animation. Norstein's first solo effort was *The Fox and the Hare* (1973). Subsequently, he has worked closely with his wife, Franceska Yarbusova, to create such films as *The Heron and the Crane* (1974) and *The Hedgehog in the Fog* (1975). However, his most celebrated work is the 27-minute film, *Tale of Tales* (1979), a lyrical, almost plotless, film that portrays the life of a lonesome young wolf.

In an interview conducted by Jo Jürgens, Norstein discusses the creation of his cut-out characters:

> The characters are made up of many small pieces of celluloid, which I animate with a pair of tweezers under the camera. On the other side of each piece of cel,

we've glued thin sheets of aluminum, since it doesn't shrink in the heat from the lights. The pieces are not attached to each other, as I prefer to be as free as possible and work as quickly as I can. When drawing the characters, the cel is first covered by a layer of white paint, which is then painted on with Aquarelle. We let the cut out pieces be transparent along the edges so that their outline isn't visible. That is important, because I sometimes use a lot more pieces to construct a cut out character than what is usual. The hedgehog and wolf cub are traditional cut out constructions, where the head and body are one piece each, while the legs and arms are three pieces.[27]

In his later work, characters have become even more complex.

Norstein explains that he works on a multiplane camera of his own design. It is 3.8 metres high, with a filming aperture of 2.6 metres by 1.5 metres. Although he typically shoots with four planes of glass, his camera can hold up to twelve. Spotlights on each side of every plane allow the projection of light onto any part of the image. In addition, the lowest plane can be under lit. Planes can move vertically and horizontally and the camera can move up and down within a range of 1.2 metres.[28]

About his filming process, Norstein adds:

I always do the animation myself – without video – but I cooperate with the cameraman when constructing the pictures. Of course all the ideas are mine, but the cameraman's work is so important and difficult that it would be impossible not to discuss them with him or to work without him at all. That includes the lighting, focus pulling, camera movements, how to avoid reflections in the glass plates, the quality of the film stock and developing the film.[29]

Norstein often combines his cut-outs with live-action footage. For example, this occurs in *Tale of Tales* when the wolf is roasting potatoes around an actual fire. Norstein explains:

... we project the live action directly on the background painting, frame by frame. The projector is on one side of the plane and projects the live action image on to a mirror on the opposite side. Then we adjust the position of the mirror so that the reflected image is projected on the drawing.[30]

In the film, Norstein also utilises a rear projection system, where live-action footage is projected 'on a special screen that lies horizontally underneath the lowest plane. We do that in the scene where the wolf cub is running along the highway ...'.[31]

Norstein gives a good deal of thought to the sound elements in his films. He sometimes talks to his composer well before he begins production; in the case of *The Hedgehog in the Fog*, all the music was composed before shooting commenced. However, he tends to think of a written script as 'a nuisance'. He says he likes to:

... improvise enormously and constantly change the screenplay during the production of the film. For *Tale of Tales* we had a complete script, which I had written together with Ludmila Petrushevskaya ... But only one-fifth of the script was used in the film. That is of course a dangerous way of working.[32]

Norstein's production process probably contributed to the very loose, almost non-narrative structure of the film, which seems more concerned with the feeling of any given moment than the continuity of actions.

While Norstein creates cut-out images to fit into his narrative films, a number of other animators have used 'found' images to create collage animation. American Frank Mouris did so in *Frank Film* (1976), an autobiographical work that combines

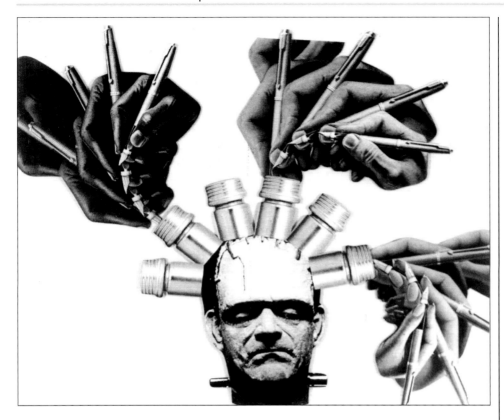

Fig. 3.18 Frank Film
(1976) by Frank Mouris
Courtesy the artist

a layering of visual images with a two-level soundtrack which challenges the audience member to be both a viewer and a listener simultaneously. A multitude of glossy magazine images bombard the viewer as the soundtrack pulls the listener in two other directions.

In contrast to Mouris's contemporary pictures, Larry Jordan and Harry Smith employ medieval images and other esoteric figures to confound the viewer in other ways (see CP 14). Jordan, who studied with filmmaker and collage-box maker Joseph Cornell, considers himself a Surrealist; therefore, it is not surprising that he says his films concern 'the unknown continents and landscapes of the mind'.[33] Jordan describes his production process as one of 'free association in combining images and constructing them'.[34] Although his use of nineteenth-century illustrations and engravings in collage boxes and such animated films as *Sophie's Place* (1983–1987) (see CP 10) are apparently motivated by 'visual preference' more than any other reason, he offers a few interesting aesthetic considerations in their regard. He says his images allow for a 'tension between the old (engravings) and the new (ideas and motifs in the film process)' and the ability to 'evoke stronger moods with material from that time'. In addition, he contends that 'the nineteenth-century imagery is already partly dislodged from mundane connotation, and gives me a head start on the Surrealism "freeing" process'.[35] While Mouris uses cut-outs because of their ability to evoke strong associations, Jordan seems to prefer images that are relatively free of signification.

Harry Smith, a painter who began his filmmaking career with direct-on-film animation, created several films with collage techniques. Smith's collage work has an affinity

with Jordan's in that it employs imagery that is firmly lodged in the ancient past. Also like Jordan, Smith's production process apparently can be considered more 'automatic' than logical and pre-planned.[36] Smith's longest complete film, *No. 12* (also known as *The Magic Feature*, or *Heaven and Earth Magic*, ca. 1958), is one of his most discussed. Although he says it was created with a script and a 'logical order', the film defies rational understanding. The disorientation might be the result of editing, since the script was created for a film that was to be at least four times as long, but it is perhaps more instructive to think of the irrationality as an aesthetic choice, in keeping with an experimental approach.[37]

American Terry Gilliam created many memorable collage animations for the British television series, 'Monty Python's Flying Circus' (1969–1974). Gilliam worked in a method that might be called 'stream of consciousness'; he explains that 'in animation terms I'm a jazz player ... and the lifeblood of jazz is improvisation'.[38] By some accounts, Gilliam chose to use cut-outs for their 'practicality and economy'.[39] His animation is fantastic, dryly humorous, and fairly surreal, not unlike his work as a live-action director of such films as *Brazil* (1985).

Related to collage animation is the photocollage, made with a series of still photos. This technique pushes the boundaries of animation because incremental movement of the subjects occur very slowly, or not at all; generally, it is the camera that is moved frame by frame, rather than the material in front of the camera. One of the best-known photocollages is *City of Gold* (1957), created by Tom Daly, Colin Low, and Wolf Koenig at the National Film Board of Canada. Glass-plate negatives from the late 1800s were used to create photos for the film, which portrays the effects of the gold rush on Dawson City in the Yukon.

Fig. 3.20 Die Abenteuer des Prinzen Achmed *(1926) by Lotte Reiniger*
Courtesy Cecile Starr

Chris Marker's science fiction film, *La jetée* (The Jetty, 1962), illustrates how animated movement can be suggested in a photocollage. In the film, a man is strapped to a chair while he undergoes time-travel experiments. The audience witnesses his writhing through a series of still photos, each one slightly different from the next, creating a very subtle animation of movement. Muffled voices and voice-over narration provide sound bridges throughout the scene.

As a whole, photocollages represent a very different set of aesthetic possibilities than cut-out animations. For one thing, their relatively static images – which cannot be overly energised, even with continuous camera movement – might tend to be tiresome to a viewer if used for any length of time. It is generally the case that photocollages rely heavily on sound to provide sustained interest and continuity. In *City of Gold*, the voice-over was provided by Pierre Berton, who has been praised for speaking the narration with 'perfection' because he is able to match 'the right voice to visual images'.[40]

The cut-out and collage techniques discussed so far are all top-lit methods. The German artist Lotte Reiniger specialised in silhouette animation, with delicately detailed cut-out figures that are under-lit. The fantasy of the artist's cut-outs compliment her subject matter – generally, adaptations of short children's tales such as 'Cinderella' and 'Red Riding Hood'. However, Reiniger also worked in very different contexts. For example, she contributed a celebrated sequence to Jean Renoir's live-action film, *La marseillaise* (1938). Reiniger's most famous film, *Die Abenteuer des Prinzen Achmed* (The Adventures of Prince Achmed, 1926), is a feature, running just over an hour in length.

Although Reiniger was unusually gifted as a cutter, it was not particularly unusual for women of her milieu to practice this art. William Moritz explains that the genre of silhouette cutting represented 'a kind of feminist validation of a women's folk art form'.[41] It was a skill that was commonly taught to women of the late 1800s and early 1900s, when 'it came to be practiced more and more by women who were not allowed access to other art training but who learned scissor-craft as part of their household duties'.[42]

In her films, Reiniger created subtle movement with jointed cut-outs and occasionally through substitution. Reiniger explains that she employed a combination of new and used cut-outs in her many films:

> The main characters would be cut fresh every time, whilst the secondary characters would get a change of costume. Then for the main characters I'd have to do new cut outs for the close-ups; these had to be quite large since otherwise you don't get any expressivity. Animals were so difficult to do that once I'd found a way to do one I'd use it over and over.[43]

Reiniger adds that she concentrated a lot of her motion on the hands of her characters because 'with silhouettes the hands are one of the few ways which can convey the characters' feelings'.[44] For the backgrounds of her works, she used various materials, including tissue paper, glass and sand. Artists working with under-lit cut-outs are not confined to working only in black and white. Colour can be achieved by placing gels, paper or paint under a sheet of glass supporting the images; the colour shines through in the space surrounding the cut-outs.

Under-lit sand

Although sand has not been widely used as a material for animation, it can offer an economical and creative alternative to other 2D techniques. To create the images, sand is placed on one or more horizontal planes of glass and under lit to create solid black images – a variation on the cut out silhouettes discussed previously (colour can be added in the same way, with gels, paper or paints placed under the glass). One of the biggest challenges to the under-lit sand technique is that relatively few of the visuals can be made in preproduction, since the sand must be manipulated directly under the camera. In addition, sand particles are easily displaced; they stick together due to static electricity and they blow around because of their lightness. On the other hand, the mobile grains result in a technique that facilitates fluid movement and metamorphosis.

Sand animation is very ephemeral; in most cases, there are no material objects left after the production has been completed, aside from the film itself and a pile of sand.[45] Even more than the modified-base technique of oil-painted animation, where some images might be retained in their final painted form, sand animation leaves no permanent traces. As with the modified-base technique, the artist has little or no reference to previous frames while he or she is working, with the possible exception of still photos or other recreations of the work. For that reason, the sand animator benefits from an ability to store past and future images in his or her head.[46]

The Swiss husband and wife animation team, Ernest ('Nag') and Gisèle Ansorge, used many different techniques, including marionettes and cut-outs, but they became best known for their works in sand. They had worked with powder as early as 1959, in a film entitled *Techniques d'animation* (Animation Techniques), but it was not until 1964 that they began to experiment with sand. A book produced by the Annecy International Animation Festival in 1994, to accompany a retrospective of the couple's work, explains:

It took them three years to perfect their technique. Nag had to adapt the table for animation and Gisèle had to perfect the technique ... *The Ravens* [in French, *Les corbeaux*] was presented in 1968 at the Tours Festival and [was] well received. ... Not only did sand suit the personality of Gisèle and produce exceptional results, but it also allowed them to enter the charmed circle of internationally recognised animators, something that no other Swiss had succeeded in doing. Consequently, they left behind all other techniques of animation and developed what they had created, jealously guarding their own independent way of seeing and thinking and artisanal working methods. But in spite of international recognition, sand animation was never very profitable.[47]

The animation stand that was used by Gisèle Ansorge is similar to other setups used for filming 2D animation, though the tabletop surface was altered to accommodate the sand. Above the primary level of under-lit, opalescent glass, two or three additional sheets of glass were placed approximately 20 cm apart, to allow for different levels of animation. Simple tools such as brushes, combs, bits of cardboard or cloth were used to move the sand – very fine quartz that was washed and strained to assure uniform quality and reduced dust.[48] By looking at an image of a film such as Les Enfants de Laine (The Children of Wool, 1984) or *Sabbat* (Sabbath, 1991), one can see how sand particles can be brushed and manicured on the surface to create softly delineated images.

Although the Ansorges were partial to black-and-white images, they also made films using colour. In *Le chat caméléon* (The Chameleon Cat, 1975), colour tints were achieved through cut-out pieces of acetate. Colour was employed in the television series, 'Si j'étais ... si j'avais ... ' ('If I were ... If I had ...', 1979), by painting the lower glass plate. Coloured sand also was used for very different effects. Subtlety is achieved by underlighting light green and sepia grains in *Anima* (1977) and red and black grains in *Alchemia* (1991). More intense effects are created by top lighting coloured sand in *Smile 1* (1975–1976) and *Das Veilchen* (1982). These films employ colour in intricate ways, perhaps causing the viewer to underestimate the difficulty of the process. Coloured sands are even more difficult to work with than regular sand because they tend to blend together, into what Gisèle Ansorg called a 'jam effect'.[49]

Caroline Leaf also is well known for her use of the under-lit sand technique; for example, in *The Owl Who Married a Goose* (1974). She began working with sand while she was a student at Radcliffe College, where she took an animation course from Derek Lamb and completed the sand film, *Peter and the Wolf* (1968), over a six-month period.[50] In her films, Leaf uses white beach sand, which turns dark when it is under lit. She uses various tools, such as stamps, combs, and forks, to achieve textures in her work, but relies mostly on her fingers.[51] Leaf animates her forms by carefully modifying the image of each recorded frame into its new form, saying:

> ... the trick is to draw each new position of the character before I erase the old one. I sprinkle sand down and carefully trace the outline of the character's position in the next frame. Then I clean away the sand outside the outline, and shove the sand into its place.[52]

She adds that her glass-painted animation also is done in that manner, except that 'it's more complicated and takes longer to do because the colours need to be kept separate and the images are more complex. But it's exactly the same idea'.[53]

Because it is so affordable, sand is an ideal medium for student work. Richard Quade produced his under-lit sand animation film, *Sand Dance* (1988), at the University of California at Los Angeles. In the film, Quade depicts a man dancing to a jazz score.

The soft delineation of the man's silhouette, which results from the wavy-lined edges that sand creates, is well suited to showing the figure's dance; thin traces of sand emphasise movement by trailing his arms in space. Although Quade's primary images are in almost constant metamorphosis, he creates somewhat static imagery in various ways. For example, the hat the man spins is made of a cut-out, which draws attention to itself because of its substantial form. Backgrounds sometimes are created on a sheet of glass below the one containing moving figures. When the man and a woman dance, for example, the surface of the ground remains intact as the figures pass over it.

Strata-cut and wax

Strata-cut and wax are modified-base techniques that toe the line between 2D and 3D. Both utilise mounds of a molded substance which is, in itself, three-dimensional; however, the transforming image occurs on the surface of the mound as it is cut away in thin layers, resulting in a flat, 2D surface.

Strata-cut is strongly associated with clay animator David Daniels because he has proven to be a master of the technique, which involves an intricate sculpting process. To create strata-cut animation, various colours of clay are used to make figures that are embedded within a clay 'background', forming a block of some sort. A camera is focused on the front of the clay mass, which is the surface where all the 'action' occurs. Very thin slices of clay are removed between exposures, with the effect that the image appears to move before the camera; follow-focus is used to keep the receding surface of the mound in focus.

Daniels explains the process this way:

> Strata-cut in its simplest form is this: if you take a cone and cut it away with the camera looking down from the top, a dot becomes a larger and larger circle ...

That is the first principle, and everything else follows from that. It's really the controlled use of shapes as opposed to animating shapes.[54]

The technique has been described as 'kinetic and yet highly efficient at the shooting stage' because, although it might take a long time to mold the clay block, it can be sliced up, or animated, in relatively little time. Daniels debuted his strata-cut technique in his thesis film, *Buzzbox* (1986), which took fourteen months to animate. Later, he used the technique for some commercial projects, including segments for 'Pee-Wee's Playhouse', Peter Gabriel's 'Big Time' music video (1987), a California Lottery commercial (1990) and a Honda commercial (1990).[55]

A 'Method of Producing Animated Motion Pictures' patented by Douglas Crockwell in 1948 illustrates the general concepts employed in the strata-cut method. Crockwell proposes that, rather than rely on drawn or painted objects, he would render in 'clay, or other suitable material, an elongated body extending between [two] patterns as bases, and then ... mold or model the surface of this body that it forms a smooth transition surface' between them.[56] He proposes to cut the form into 'a multiplicity of slices in the same way that a loaf of bread or a Bologna sausage is cut from end to end, and to photograph or otherwise to utilise the outlines of the slices, or of the end of the sliced body, in sequence, in depicting the proper outline of the subect' as more and more slices are removed.[57]

Figs 3.22 (a) & (b)
Pages from 'Method of Producing Animated Motion Pictures' (1948) patent by Douglas Crockwell

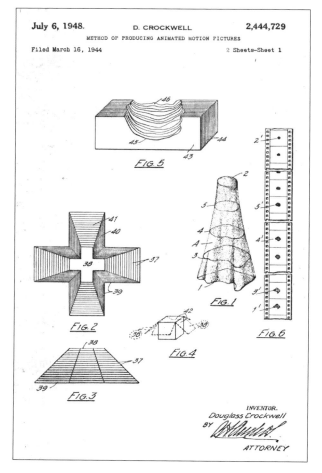

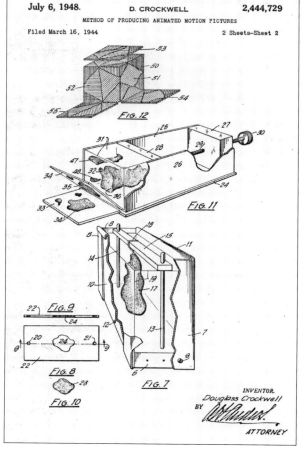

Using the strata-cut method, it is obvious that random movement can be created without much consideration given to the dimensional development (i.e. the 'molding') of shapes. But if any sort of narrative development is to occur, an artist employing the technique must have a fairly intuitive sense of movement as well as an ability to sculpt dimensionally. Like other modified-base techniques, the movement of strata-cut animation cannot be pretested. But, unlike other modified-base techniques, strata-cut offers little opportunity for spontaneity under the camera, except in the way that slicing occurs.

A related technique employs wax rather than clay. Wax animation was one of several production methods explored by German animator Oskar Fischinger. In 1970, William Moritz began restoring and cataloging the artist's work. In a filmography, he lists a number of 'wax experiments' that were created between 1920 and 1926. Moritz explains that Fischinger's wax films fall into 'two different types of technical experiments – those with wax modeling and those with wax slicing – and in both cases "wax" actually refers to a substance "kaolin" which was a commercial mixture of fine clay and wax'.[58] The wax-modelling films feature geometric forms such as pyramids that appear to grow larger and smaller, semi-abstract forms, and 'complex landscape or seascape surfaces with many ridges and furrows, probably made by pouring hot wax into cold water'.[59] Fischinger also created wax puppets for a bit of modelled wax animation called 'The Boxer'.

Fischinger's wax-slicing films were created with a 'labor-saving animation machine' of his own design, which:

> ... synchronised a slicing mechanism with a camera so that each time a slice was cut from the end of a prepared block of wax, the camera would photograph an image of the remaining end-surface of the block, thus rendering on film a time-lapse cross-section of the images formed in the wax.[60]

Fischinger's wax-slicing technique, as described by Moritz, has clear affinities with Daniels's strata-cut method.

Pinboard

The pinboard (*l'écran d'épingles*) technique is distinctive but rarely used. It requires the use of a specially designed piece of equipment, the pinboard, which is an upright, white, framed surface with about a million pins inserted into it. With the use of a roller or other tools, the pins are pushed in and out of the screen so that, when they are lit from an angle, the shadows create images that can be photographed. This modified-base technique, which is also known as pinscreen animation, was invented and developed by two individuals, the Russian Alexander Alexeïeff and the American Claire Parker.

Ideally, two people are needed to create images with the pinboard; Parker stood in back of the screen, pushing the pins outward, while Alexeïeff stood in front of the screen, making modifications to the shooting surface. Unlike most 2D animation, images on the pinboard are shot horizontally. Because of the slight depth created by the pins as they are pushed in and out, and the resulting shadow effect, this technique could be considered 3D; still, the actual spatial dimension of pinboard animation is small enough that it seems more relevant to a discussion of 2D animation.

A wide variety of image types is possible with the pinboard. Alexeïeff and Parker's *Tableaux d'une exposition* (Pictures at an Exhibition, 1972) include forms that range

Fig. 3.23 *Production of* Mindscape *(1976) by Jacques Drouin*
Courtesy NFB

from abstract to representational, from realistic to stylised and from firmly modelled to softly amorphous. For example, the recurring image of a black cat is at times a solidly composed flat figure, trotting across the screen. On the other hand, a spinning upper torso of a human figure is a wispy image that transforms as it moves in space. The figures in *La nuit sur le Mont Chauve* (The Night on Bald Mountain, 1933),

Fig. 3.24 *Close up of pinboard from Jacques Drouin's* Mindscape
Courtesy NFB

perhaps the couple's best-known film, tend to be more loosely constructed, blending into the dark background rather than being self-contained forms, to give the sensation of an irrational nightmare. Like sand, pinboards offer an artist a very malleable surface, making metamorphosis relatively easy. On the other hand, it allows a much greater level of detail than sand, since the pins are held rigidly by the screen.

Many of the visuals in Alexeîeff and Parker's pinboard films look somewhat like engravings – an outgrowth of Alexeîeff's career as an illustrator of books. Alexeîeff considered the pinboard to be 'somewhat analogous to the half tone process' of photography. One can see that *Le nez* (The Nose, 1963) and other works contain stippled images, not unlike the dotting found in halftones used for printing black-and-white photos.

The textures in Alexeîff and Parker's work were achieved through the use of found materials and various tools specially developed by the artists for use with the pinboard. A film on their work, *A propos de Jivago* (Alexeîeff at the Pinboard, 1960), explains how rollers with fine pins are used to make snow, how carved wooden rings are used to provide branches for various types of trees, and how the lid of a cold cream jar is used to make an apple.

Alexeîeff and Parker believed that their pinboard animation had limited commercial potential. They drew this conclusion based on the lengthy amount of time necessary to create each film, as well as their preference for chiaroscuro effects and dramatic storytelling, as opposed to the light and humorous stories so often associated with animation.[61] They did find some applications for the pinboard in book illustration, for classics such as Boris Pasternak's *Doctor Zhivago* and Dostoyevsky's *Notes from the Underground*. In addition, they made 33 pinboard pictures for the prologue and epilogue of Orson Welles's feature film, *The Trial* (1962).

Despite the somewhat limited applications of the technique, other animators have been influenced by Alexeîeff and Parker's work and have created pinscreen animations of their own. Another well-known example of pinboard animation is *Mindscape* (1976), by Canadian Jacques Drouin. Drouin learned the technique by working with Alexeîeff and Parker and made his film using their pinboard.

As this chapter has demonstrated, there is a wide range of techniques that can be considered within the category of 2D animation. Although each of them has a unique set of aesthetic qualities, there are some general concepts that can be used to discuss these and other forms of animation. The next chapter will overview some of the most important of them.

Notes

1. David James, *Allegories of Cinema: American Film in the Sixties* (Princeton: Princeton UP, 1989), 12.
2. Ibid., 21.
3. In 1987, I polled 21 independent animators and others working in the field. In response to a question 'How do you believe most independent animators support themselves and their productions?', 90 per cent cited 'freelance commercial work' (second only to 'teaching', at 95 per cent). 'Full-time commercial work' was noted by 60 per cent of the participants. In a survey of the participants own work, it was found that approximately half of these independent artists' work was within the realm of commercial animation. Maureen Furniss, 'The Current State of American Independent Animation and a Prediction for its Future', Masters Thesis, San Diego State University (1987).

Many pioneers of independent animation, such as Oskar Fischinger, Alexander Alexeîeff, Claire Parker, Norman McLaren, and Len Lye, as well as important contemporary figures, such as Joan Gratz and George Griffin, to name just two, have created advertising films in addition to their personal, independent work.

4. This model incorporates previous definitions of the term. For example, William Moritz asserts that 'no animation film that is *not* non-objective and/or non-linear can really qualify as true animation, since the conventional linear representational story film has long since been far better done in live-action'. Robert Russett and Cecile Starr have used the term 'experimental animation' to 'suggest individual techniques, personal dedication, and artistic daring', adding that the artists have generally 'avoided the standard animation stand and the production-line procedures of the commercial studio ... in varying degrees, they personalise their equipment and techniques, as does any fine artisan or craftsman'. Such definitions illustrate one or more tendency of an independent mode of production, but a more complete picture of independent animation is achieved when these definitions are combined. William Moritz, 'Some Observations on Non-objective and Non-linear Animation', in John Canemaker (ed.), *The Art of Animation*, (Los Angeles: AFI, 1988), 21–32, 21. Robert Russett and Cecile Starr, *Experimental Animation* (New York: Da Capo, 1988), 10.

5. See Charles Solomon, 'Animation Goes Down the Tube', *Los Angeles Times* (21 June 1981); Charles Solomon, 'Is There Life After Saturday Morning?', *Los Angeles Times* (27 June 1981). Leonard Maltin discusses the use of limited animation, which is predominant in television work, saying that it '... paved the way for a systematic destruction of the cartoon art form'. Leonard Maltin (1980), *Of Mice And Magic: A History Of American Animated Cartoons* (New York: Plume, 1987), 33.

6. For examples, see Jane Ann Dill, 'Jules Engel, Film Artist – A Painterly Aesthetic', *Animation Journal* 1, 2 (Spring 1993): 50–65; Giannalberto Bendazzi, 'The Italians Who Invented the Drawn-on-Film Technique', *Animation Journal* 4, 2 (Spring 1996): 69–77. Accompanying Bendazzi's article is a reprint of Corra's statement on 'Chromatic Music', 78–84.

7. *The Man Who Planted Trees* was produced by Hubert Tison of Radio-Canada, who had convinced Frédéric Back to work for him in 1968. *The Mighty River* was the final animated work produced by Radio-Canada.

8. Jo Jürgens, 'Frédéric Back: The Man Who Plants Hope', *The Art of Animation* 1, 1 (Spring 1994): 26.

9. Jürgens, 'Frédéric Back', 26.

10. Stanislav Ulver, 'Frédéric Back', *ASIFA International News* 6, 4 (1993): 10.

11. An interview with Piotr Dumala, in which he discusses his technique, is published on-line at http://www.absolutvodka.com/panushka/history/news/haff/i-dumala/index.html

12. Norman McLaren, 'Technical notes on *La Poulette Grise* (1947)', (1947; revised in 1984), 1. All of McLaren's technical notes are available from the National Film Board of Canada. By 'dissolves', or 'chain of mixes', McLaren refers to a technique whereby images are filmed on a series of frames, with the camera shutter moving from closed to open and back to closed again. For example, on a 24-frame chain of mixes, the filming of image A would begin with the shutter closed on frame one, fully open on frame twelve (allowing for full exposure of the image), and fully closed again on frame 24 (blacking out the image). Filming of the image B (which is dissolved to) begins on frame twelve, with the shutter closed. By the twenty-fourth frame (image A has gone black at that point), the shutter would be fully open (fully exposing image B), and by image 36, the shutter would be fully closed again (blacking out image B). The filming of image C begins on from 24, with the shutter closed – and the recording continues on in that manner, creating a chain of mixes. This technique is mentioned again in Chapter 4 of this book.

13. The 'Divertimenti 1991–1994' series contains six numbered films, each three minutes, fifteen seconds in length. These include *Winds and Changes*, *Love Song*, *Brushwork*, *Life Study*, *Slapstick*, and *Dark Matter*.

14. 'Divertimento no. 3 – Brushwork', Annecy '95 Festival catalogue, 54.

15. Id.

16. Clive Walley, correspondence with the author (25 Sept. 1997).

17. Dudok de Wit says it took him seven months to make the film, working with an assistant most of thetime; another animator and his assistant also worked with him for six weeks. Phillipe Moins, 'Michael Dudok de Wit: Between Chinese Brush and Roman Art', Annecy '95 daily festival program (3 June 1995): 5–6.

18. Talia Schenkel, 'Talking with Caroline Leaf', *Women and Animation: A Compendium* (London: BFI, 1992), 43.

19. John Canemaker, moderator, 'Walter Lantz Conference 1988: A Conversation with Caroline Leaf', *Storytelling in Animation: The Art of the Animated Image* (Los Angeles: AFI, 1988), 57.

20. Ibid., 58.

21. Caroline Leaf, interview with Jo Jürgens, unpublished manuscript.

22. Caroline Leaf, 'Two Sisters', from an interview with Denise Therrien, *Perforations* (April 1991), reprinted in *Women and Animation*, 47.

23. For more information, see Norman McLaren, 'Technical notes on *Lines Vertical* (1960)', 1. All of McLaren's technical notes are available from the National Film Board of Canada.

24. P. Adams Sitney, 'Interview with Harry Smith', *Experimental Animation*, 138.

25. More information on Bärbel Neubauer and illustrations of her work can be found on-line at the 'Absolut Panuska' site, http://www.absolutvodka.com/panushka/history/profiles/neubauer/index.html. A number of other artists discussed in this book are also represented on the site.

26. Marie Claire Quiquemelle, *The Wan Brothers and 60 Years of Animated Film in China* (Annecy: Annecy Film Festival, 1985), n.p. Papercuts and other aspects of Chinese animation are discussed in Ethan Gilsdorf, 'Chinese Animation's Past, Present, and Future: The Monkey King of Shanghai', *Animato!* 17 (Winter 1988): 20–23.

27. Yuri Norstein, interview with Jo Jürgens, unpublished manuscript.

28. Ibid.

29. Ibid.

30. Ibid.

31. Ibid.

32. Ibid.

33. Robert Russett and Cecile Starr, *Experimental Animation* (New York: Da Capo, 1988), 155–56.

34. Ibid., 157.

35. Id.

36. Ibid., 140.

37. Id. For more on Smith, see Paola Igliori, *American Magus: Harry Smith, A Modern Alchemist* (New York: Inanout, 1996). Larry Jordan denies afinities between Smith's work and his own. For more on Jordan, see G.T. Collins, 'Larry Jordan's Underworld', *Animation Journal* 6, 1 (Fall 1997): 54–69.

38. Les Paul Robey and Paul Wardle, 'Terry Gilliam: A Career Profile of One of the Cinema's Premier Fantasists', *Cinefantastique* (Feb. 1996): 24–37+, 26.

39. Giannalberto Bendazzi, *Cartoons: One Hundred Years of Cinema Animation* (Bloomington: Indiana UP, 1994), 278. For more on Gilliam's aesthetics, see Paul Wells, 'Terry Gilliam: On Being an Impish God', *Art & Design* 53 (1997): 61–65.

40. Richard M. Barsam, *Non-Fiction Film: A Critical History* (Bloomington: Indiana UP, 1992), 275.

41. William Moritz, 'Some Critical Perspectives on Lotte Reiniger', *Animation Journal* 5, 1 (Fall 1996): 40–51, 44.

42. Ibid., 44. For more information, see a source mentioned by Moritz: Rudolf Arnheim, 'Lotte Reinigers Schattenfilme', *Die Weltbühne* 52 (24 Dec. 1928): 961.

43. Lotte Reiniger, 'Lotte Reiniger: An Interview with Alfio Bastiancich', *Women & Animation: A Compendium* (London: BFI, 1992), 9–15, 13.

44. Ibid., 13.

45. Some artists, like Gisèle Ansorg, have preserved sand images by using a spray glue.

46. With the use of video-assist equipment, it is possible to get a better idea of how the action is progressing.

47. Anonymous, *Captured in Drifting Sand* (Annecy: Annecy International Festival of Animated Film, 1995), 20–21.

48. Quartz was chosen because generally the 'crystals are not electromagnetic and are heavy enough to be manipulated without having them blown away (as happens with ash for example); nor do they stick to the brushes'. Nonetheless, the quality of sand grains vary and the results of the sand animation tend to lack 'discipline'; for that reason, 'added to the effect of a draught of air or the slightest false move[, sand] can be difficult to work with'. Annecy, *Captured in Drifting Sand*, op. cit., 32.

49. Anonymous, *Captured in Drifting Sand*, 36. Original film titles are given with translations in English when different.

50. Schenkel, op. cit., 41.

51. Ibid., 44.

52. Leaf, interview with Jürgens, op. cit.

53. Ibid.

54. Michael Frierson, *Clay Animation* (New York: Twayne, 1994), 173.

55. Ibid., 175, 177.

56. Douglas Crockwell, 'Method of Producing Animated Motion Pictures', US Patent 2,444,729 (6 July 1948), col. 1–2.

57. Id.

58. William Moritz, 'The Films of Oskar Fischinger', *Film Culture* 58–59–60 (1974): 37–188, 83.

59. Ibid., 83.

60. Ibid., 41.

61. 'Alexander Alexeïeff and Claire Parker', notes inside the 'Visual Pathfinders' laserdisc of their work, *The World of Alexander Alexeïeff and Claire Parker* (Cecile Starr and LaserDisc Corporation, 1987).

General concepts: Mise-en-scène

COMPONENTS OF ANIMATION DESIGN

*A*nimation falls in the intersection of many artistic practices. This is because, to assess the aesthetics of animation with any level of expertise requires knowledge of not only history in general, but also the theory and history of drawing, painting, photography, sculpture, music, acting, dance and live-action motion pictures, for a start. Needless to say, such a prerequisite is daunting. What is perhaps most important is that analysts of animation at least recognise that there is an immense number of influences upon the aesthetics of animated works, even if they are unable to address them all.

This chapter, along with the next one, will outline fundamental issues concerning animation aesthetics, in order to provide a foundation for remaining chapters of the book. This chapter considers a number of elements related to the *mise-en-scène* of an animated work. In *Film Art*, David Bordwell and Kristin Thompson define the term quite clearly:

> In the original French, *mise-en-scène* (pronounced 'meez-ahn-sen') means 'staging an action', and it was first applied to the practice of directing plays. Film scholars, extending the term to film direction, use the term to signify the director's control over what appears in the film frame. As you would expect from the term's theatrical origins, mise-en-scène includes those aspects of film that overlap with the art of the theatre: setting, lighting, costume, and the behavior of the figures. In controlling the mise-en-scène, the director *stages the event* for the camera.[1]

Because the components of animation design obviously are not the same as those of live-action film, the aspects of mise-en-scène covered in this book are slightly different than those outlined by Bordwell and Thompson. This chapter covers the subjects of images, colour and line, and movement and kinetics, all of which can be considered components of the animated mise-en-scène.

The next chapter in this book, Chapter 5, focuses on non-visual elements that often work to give unity to an animated production as a whole: sound and (narrative or non-narrative) structure. While these chapters overview some of the production-related factors that affect the way that mise-en-scène, sound and structure tend to be produced, it is recommended that newcomers to the field also consult a number of 'how to animate' books, such as Shamus Culhane's *Animation From Script to Screen* and Kit Laybourne's *The Animation Book*, and try to become involved in creating an animated production.[2] Thorough knowledge of the production process is essential, since the procedures and materials used greatly affect the aesthetics of any animated work. When analysing a production, a researcher should always consider the effects of the particular media used, the crew size, the size and quantity of the original artwork, the way in which 'camera movement' is achieved, and other production-related factors. Likewise, it is advisable that analysts of animation become familiar with the aesthetics of motion picture making on a larger level; for example, one might consult Bordwell and Thompson's *Film Art* to learn more about the aesthetics of editing, cinematography, and a number of other aspects of film and video production that are not detailed in this book.[3]

It is also useful for the animation researcher to have a broad understanding of art production outside of motion pictures – that is, the production of 'still art'. This knowledge will help him or her to identify the characteristics of the many processes that can be used in rendering images for animation. Many different media can be used in creating animated imagery and every one of them has inherent qualities that significantly impact the production's final look.

For that reason, an analysis should begin by asking a number of questions about the tools used in creating the sounds and images. Was a computer employed? If so, which software applications were used? Was the work drawn or painted and shot entirely on paper? If so, was the paper smooth or textured? Were cels used? If so, were they clear, frosted and unvarnished, or frosted and varnished? What other media were used to render the images: pencils, Conté crayons, charcoals, oil paints, cel paints? Were images captured on video or on film, and which stock was used? These are just some of the questions that can be asked.

A person conducting an analysis of animation aesthetics should be concerned with all aspects of the materials used in the production, including the size and quantity of the artwork involved. It is common to hear the term 'field size' used in discussions of drawn or painted animation art. Standard field sizes for animation cels and papers include 12-field, 16-field, 24-field and larger sizes used for panning, or moving across a scene in a horizontal (or vertical) manner. A 'field chart' is used to determine the standardised measurements of an image rendered on paper or cels. Generally, the smallest image size used is 2-field, measuring approximately 2-inches wide by 1½-inches high. A 12-field measures approximately 12-inches wide by 8¾-inches high.

Field sizes provide a standardised measurement used by directors, artists, camera operators and others involved in the development and recording of animated images, but they also help the analyst. By merely looking at an image on a video monitor or

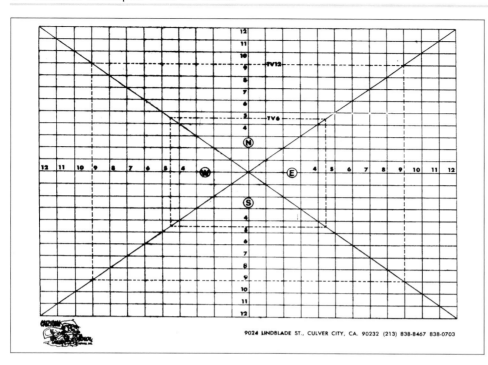

9024 LINDBLADE ST., CULVER CITY, CA. 90232 (213) 838-8467 838-0703

Fig. 4.1 *This is a field chart, used by artists to determine layout placement and to direct the camera operator. It is a standard tool – this one is from a leading distributor of animation supplies, Cartoon Colour Company Inc. It shows the TV-safe area, along with other standard field sizes*

projection screen, it is impossible to tell if it was created as 2-field or 12-field, since images of all sizes appear equivalent after they have been taped or filmed, assuming that they fill the screen and no reference object can be seen within the frame. However, the size of the original image affects the amount of detail that one sees in the film or video frame, including the resolution of lines and the density of coloured areas. When two images are captured in frames of the same format of video or film, the one that was drawn very small to begin with will have lower resolution (and so will appear more grainy) than the original image that was larger in size.

Throughout animation history, the limitations of cinematography also have affected the aesthetics of animation. As previously mentioned, animation cameras used to shoot 2D animation today generally are mounted on a vertical stand, allowing the camera to move toward or away from the artwork but not side to side. Live-action images are recorded horizontally, and close shots generally are achieved by dollying the camera in (physically moving it toward the subject) or by zooming in (altering the lens, but keeping the actual camera in one spot). In contrast, 'close-ups' in animation have been achieved either by moving the camera on its vertical stand (somewhat like a dolly) or by redrawing the artwork so that an image appears larger (i.e. 'closer') in each frame. The 'truck shot' is another common live-action camera move. In animation, it is not achieved by moving the camera left and right, as it is in live-action work, but by moving the surface of animated artwork past the camera (or, in the early years, by redrawing everything so the shot appeared to be moving). However, recently, 3D software that creates computer generated imagery has supplemented the animation camera or replaced it altogether, allowing for much more complex 'cinematic camera effects'. For example, the ballroom dancing sequence of Disney's feature *Beauty and the Beast* (directed by Gary Trousdale and Kirk Wise,

Fig. 4.2 *Janet Benn*
examining layouts, 1996
Collection of the author

1991) includes a 'flying' camera movement that would have been difficult (though technically not impossible) to render by traditional means.[4]

Needless to say, there are a number of factors that influence one's use of computer technologies or other means of production. Sometimes various media or technologies will be selected by an artist because he or she desires a certain quality in his or her work, but at other times an artist is required to work with materials that are controlled by his or her employer, or that are most economical. When discussing a work as a product of its creator's vision, it is very important to learn the extent to which his or her working conditions were dictated by outside sources.

Some indicators, such as the size of the production crew, may reveal the extent to which an artist's personal vision has been fully employed. If one individual is solely responsible for the conception, development, and recording of an animated work (one-person-one-film), it is relatively easy to assign creative responsibility to him or her. However, few animated works made at this time or in the past have been created with absolutely no outside interference. As the previous chapter notes, even independent artists have to rely on other people for some aspects of their work (e.g. the manufacturing of materials), which means that the creative endeavor is not completely controlled by the solitary creator.

In the case of large-scale commercial studio productions, it becomes increasingly difficult to assign creative control to one person. While most people know that individuals in the positions of producer, director and animator have great influence on a production, the contributions of employees in other roles, such as layout, is less often acknowledged. Grimm Natwick described the layout artist as a person who 'is supposed to edit the picture, to really change the drawing as it will appear when it goes onto the screen ... the function of the layout man [is] to plan a scene so it's ready to animate'.[5] As Natwick's observations suggest, layout clearly assumes an important

Fig. 4.3 *Sue Perrotto working with storyboards and exposure sheets, 1996 Collection of the author*

role, yet most analyses of animation production overlook the contribution of individuals in this position – and many others.

When discussing the aesthetics of a studio production, it is generally best to think of it as the result of many people working together, rather than a series of distinct developments. Again, Natwick's comments can be used as an example. Regarding character design for features at the Disney Studio, Natwick explained that the amount of creative control changed as the studio grew larger. During the early years, he says, 'the characters were usually designed by the animator', but that changed when 'the Disney Studio began to grow. They reached a point where they didn't want to use the animator's time, so the designer came into the picture'.[6] For example, after the design for *Snow White* was created, the animator and his assistants:

> ... kicked the character around. We were given two months at that time [for *Snow White*] just to play with the character, to do any kind of animation we wanted to see whether she worked, whether she animated, whether we could animate her. We made little changes we thought we could handle easily as artists.[7]

The scenario suggested by Natwick's comments is one in which a negotiation of creative elements occurs, making it virtually impossible to identify the contribution of any one person. Despite the fact that Disney supervised production of his films very closely, his features to some extent bear the imprint of the many people who contributed to them – not just an animator, or a character designer, or any other single person, but everyone involved with the production.

For many years, the work of major animation companies largely has been completed outside the central studio. This practice broadens the number of people who influence the aesthetics of an animated work. Today, many companies complete their work in Asian countries and other locations where labour is relatively inexpensive. Preliminary drawings generally are made by artists at the central studio, but the overseas company may be responsible for creating the majority of backgrounds, inbetween drawings and additional artwork.

Many of the overseas companies that American animation studios work with are located in Korea. In 1991, Gregg Vanzo founded two companies: Rough Draft Studios, located in Southern California, and Rough Draft Korea, a production facility staffed by 400 people capable of producing nine half-hour productions per month. Rough Draft was employed in Paramount's production of the feature, *Beavis and Butt-Head Do America* (1996), and it is also responsible for episodes of such television series as 'The Simpsons', 'King of the Hill', 'The Critic', 'Rocko's Modern Life', and 'Pinky and the Brain'.[8] Another company, Sunwoo Animation, was established in 1989 and in recent years also has contributed to many popular series, for such companies as Walt Disney, Klasky Csupo, Games Animation, Film Roman, and Hanna-Barbera. It employs 350 people who can produce six episodes per month, and also has offices in Hollywood.[9] Nelson Shin's Akom Productions is another successful Korean studio. It was established in 1985 and now employs 1500 workers in areas such as storyboard, sheet timing, layout, key animation, assistant animation, ink and paint, traditional and digitial effects, camera and editing. Akom has contributed to the production of 'Animaniacs', 'Pinky and the Brain', 'Batman', 'The Simpsons', 'The Tick' and 'X-Men', as well as a number of features. Its monthly capacity is twelve half-hour television episodes.[10] These are just a few of the 'completion' companies that currently contribute to the production of animated works.

With these general considerations of the production process in mind, the researcher will be better prepared to analyse what he or she sees and hears on the screen. This overview now will move into topics concerned more specifically with aesthetic qualities of the final production: image design, colour and line, and movement and kinetics.

Image design

In the majority of animated works, images can be discussed in two categories: characters and backgrounds. These areas are roughly differentiated by movement and centrality to the viewing experience. It is probably unnecessary to specify that characters attract the viewer's attention by moving about the screen and tend to be the central focus of animation, whereas backgrounds are relatively static and primarily provide the arena in which character action occurs. However, the fact that these two areas are equally important in an analysis of aesthetics may be less evident. Audiences generally remember characters the most, but background art greatly impacts the viewer's perception and cannot be overlooked in a discussion of image design.

In *Understanding Comics*, Scott McCloud describes a multitude of image types that are possible in art.[11] His points are made in the process of analysing print media, such as comic books and comic strips, but also are valid in regard to animation. McCloud provides a visual map to show how the rendering of an object can range from photorealist to iconic or abstract. Using a human face as an example, these terms would be illustrated by a drawing that comes close to a photo of a human face in its realism (photorealistic); a sign that clearly represents a human face but does not look realistic, such as a smiley face (iconic); and the total refiguring of a human face into a mere suggestion of its form (abstract).

McCloud contends that iconic images – those that are simplified to bare meaning, such as the smiley face – allow the viewer to identify with a character to a greater extent than realistically rendered images. His theory is that the realistic character takes on the attributes of a specific entity while iconic designs are more like an 'every man' or 'every woman', as the case may be.

Abstract forms may be hard-edged and geometric (a triangle or square, for example) or amorphous. Generally, abstract figures are not thought of as representing a 'character', although they can be discussed as possessing attributes that impart meaning to the viewer. Abstract images are rarely found in commercial animation today.[12] Whether they be for the purpose of entertainment or instruction, most commercial works strive for a clarity of meaning that can be achieved only with realistic or at least iconic imagery.

Character types in commercial animation generally are recognisable, real-world entities such as dogs, cats, boys and girls. To increase a studio's chances for success, these characters tend to be somewhat conventional. Although differentiation occurs from production to production, or series to series, there is a strong tendency to depict 'types' that conform to some popular formula of the past or are recognisable from some other context.

For example, some of the earliest characters to be featured in animated series were based on human figures found in print media. Perhaps the first animated stars of American animation were the characters of 'The Newlyweds', a series animated by Emile Cohl beginning in January 1913 that was based on a well-known comic strip by George McManus.[13] Other human-like characters of popular animated series, such as those in the 'Mutt and Jeff' (Pathé Frères, beg. 1913) and 'Colonel Heeza Liar' (Bray, beg. 1913) series, also were derived from comic strips, as were many others.[14] The origins of animation in other countries also have strong ties to print comics. Such is the case in Belgium, for example, where some of the first animation created was based on Belgian characters like Wrill, Tintin, the Smurfs, and Lucky Luke, beginning in the 1940s.[15]

Today, the practice of adapting cartoon concepts into animated works thrives in Japan, where the comic book industry is a hugely profitable enterprise. In the early 1960s, the successful Japanese comic book artist Osamu Tezuka moved into an animation career by creating adaptations of his popular comic books for television, 'Tetsuwan Atomu' (Mighty Atom; aka, Astro Boy, begun in 1963) and 'Jungle Taitei' (The Jungle Emperor; aka, Kimba the White Lion, begun in 1965). Other Japanese comic book artists have continued to produce successful animated works (known as *anime*) based on their print series (known as *manga*). Comic books still play a function in the development of animation produced in the United States and elsewhere, sometimes as part of a total merchandising package, where the series concept includes both animated programming and comic book versions of the product that are developed simultaneously.

It is sometimes the case that conventional character types have developed within the realm of animation. One example is Jessica Rabbit from the Disney feature, *Who Framed Roger Rabbit* (1988), directed by Robert Zemeckis. She is obviously a descendant of a 'female type' mentioned in Chapter 1 – the sexy singer animated by Preston Blair and made famous in *Red Hot Riding Hood* (1943), – and other Tex Avery films made at MGM.[16] In interviews, Zemeckis has acknowledged the strong influence Avery had upon *Who Framed Roger Rabbit*.[17]

Throughout the years, animal characters have been a favourite of production studios and many have been conventional types. A variety of popular cat characters that developed during the silent period of American animation (such as Krazy Kat, Felix, and Julius) are discussed in Chapter 2. Despite the diversity of animal stars that have appeared at various studios throughout the years, most have shared the quality of being anthropomorphic; that is, they have human characteristics such as the ability to walk upright and speak. Traditions of giving human characteristics to animals or inanimate objects have existed since the beginning of humanity, through practices such as animism (the belief that every thing on Earth possesses a spirit and impacts human life) and totism (the incorporation of natural entities into ritual behaviours). In these contexts, anthropomorphism functions as a means of allowing an animal or inanimate object to express the spirit thought to be inside it.

Oral and visual storytellers always have been intrigued by the idea that animals could be endowed with human-like thoughts and behaviours. Jean-Ignace-Isidore Gérard (under the name J.J. Grandville) and John Tenniel are just two of the influential artists who created fantastic and revolutionary images of anthropomorphic animals. Tenniel is perhaps best remembered for his illustrations of Lewis Carroll's *Alice's Adventures in Wonderland* and *Through the Looking Glass*.

Traditional stories featuring anthropomorphic animals, such as 'Little Red Riding Hood' and 'The Tortoise and the Hare', frequently have provided the premises for animated cartoons. The use of traditional stories has proven economical because, as public domain materials, they cost nothing to use. In addition, well-known stories cut down on the amount of work an animation writer needs to do. There is no need to spend time developing a character's personality or every detail of a traditional story, since the viewing public already knows the basic scenario.

However, even when telling traditional stories, some animated works are noted for including fully developed characters with unique personalities. A good example of this effort occurred in the 1933 Disney short film, the *Three Little Pigs* (directed by Burt Gillett). This film is often cited as one of the first efforts at 'personality animation', a term used to describe work that is concerned with delineating individual characters through the development of movement and voice.[18] Although the three pigs potentially could have been made to look and sound quite similar, each one was developed into a distinct character. For example, the character of the brick builder pig can be seen as much more serious just by his movement, especially when the other two pigs are shown dancing merrily in front of his house. Other noteworthy examples of personality animation in Disney films include the dwarfs of *Snow White and the Seven Dwarfs* (directed by David Hand, 1937) and the puppies of *One Hundred and One Dalmatians* (directed by Wolfgang Reitherman, Hamilton Luske, and Clyde Geronimi, 1961).

Although personality animation often is used in discussing groups of relatively similar characters who are differentiated, the general concept of 'personality' is of importance when any character is analysed. The development of fully rounded characters is valuable to all commercially oriented animators, since it expands marketing opportunities. Viewers are able to identify with characters who have a distinct and appealing personality that reminds us of someone we know (perhaps ourselves) or provides an idealised model of someone we would like to be. Identification increases a viewer's comfort level and loyalty, and makes him or her more likely to return for additional episodes and to purchase related merchandise.

A perfect example of viewer identification is found in the recent success of British director Nick Park of Aardman Animations, with his animated man and dog team of Wallace and Gromit. These characters have appeared in the short films *A Grand Day Out* (1990), *The Wrong Trousers* (1993) and *A Close Shave* (1995). Wallace is a self-assured but blundering inventor with an almost imperviously upbeat voice quality and somewhat restrained body movement. His constant use of phrases such as 'right then' reveal the character's obliviousness

Fig. 4.4 *Walt Disney's Snow White and the Seven Dwarfs (1937)* © *Disney Enterprises, Inc.*

to the chaos around him and help to make him endearing. Gromit, who does not speak, is the foil for all of Wallace's ideas and oversights and is defined through subtle but deftly rendered actions, such as rolling eyes, facial grimaces, and highly controlled body movements that allow him to react flawlessly in any given situation. Although Gromit is a voiceless dog, he clearly is the smarter of the twosome and the character with whom the viewer identifies most closely. Gromit easily falls into the tradition of silent film comedians such as Charlie Chaplin and Buster Keaton, who created pathos in their roles as 'underdogs' that ingenuously overcame their obstacle-filled lives.

Park's success with personality animation can be seen in his work before the 'Wallace and Gromit' series became successful. His short film *Creature Comforts* (1989) features a number of animals who are interviewed about living conditions at the zoo. Through body movements and voice, the animals are made into distinct personality types. A good example is the young bear, who raises his hand eagerly, trying to get a word in, and interrupts his parents in mid-speech. Each member of the bear family, and all the other characters in the film, are developed into interesting and greatly differentiated individuals through their voices and movements.

Some independent animators see their films as one-time creative expressions and so are not particularly interested in creating a series or spin-off marketing. For that reason, they might not invest so heavily in the development of personality in character animation. In fact, they might decide not to foreground human and animal characters through the use of distinctive body shapes, movements, and voices, but rather to blend them into the overall design of their work. Sometimes, these films tell highly personal stories. For example, Joanna Priestley's short film, *Grown Up* (1993), tells of her own experience of reaching the age of 40 and the ways in which passing time has affected her life. The film includes a number of figures that represent Priestley herself, as well as friends and family, but no attempt is made to define them as fully rounded characters.

Fig. 4.5 *From* Creature Comforts *by Nick Park, Aardman Animations, 1989*

Priestley's film provides an example of another aesthetic issue that should be considered in regard to character design: 'self figuration'. Donald Crafton is among those who has discussed the tendency toward self-figuration during the early years of animation history.[19] During the silent period, commercially produced animated shorts often included some reference to the artist of the film, either by depicting him or her at work or, eventually, through the convention of showing the artist's hand (sometimes a photograph of a hand) making preliminary sketches as a film began. By the 1920s, it had become relatively uncommon to see the artist (or even a hand) within commercial films. However, Crafton has suggested that self-figuration continues to occur on a much more subtle level.

Today, the tendency to tell highly personal stories and to include oneself in the animation is most apparent in animation produced by independent artists working outside the studio system. Both the early pioneers and the independents of recent years were able to be more overtly self-figurative because of the fact that they worked in a one-person or small-crew setting, which allows the artwork to retain a greater degree of creative control and personal meaning.

Although studio animation produced today might be somewhat less personal to the artist, the link between animated figure and animator in the industry remains a significant consideration. It is common practice for studio animators to keep mirrors by their drawing tables in order to view their own mouth, hand or other movements when rendering images (see Fig. 4.3). They also are encouraged to act out entire movements to get a sense of the way in which an action should occur. Sue Perotto, who worked as an animator on *Beavis and Butt-Head Do America* (directed by Mike Judge, 1996), said she had someone shoot polaroids while she and a third person had a mock fight, so she could better see how to render her two characters while they tussled on the ground.[20]

On a similar note, one of the great traditions of studio animation is to include 'inside jokes'. Phyllis Craig, who was in charge of the colour key department at the Film Roman studio, once provided the inspiration for a secretary in 'The Simpsons' series; she also says that a number of people in the crowd scenes of *One Hundred and One Dalmations* were based on Disney employees.[21] In *Who Framed Roger Rabbit*, a note on a bathroom wall saying 'For a good time, call Alison Wonderland' perportedly was included as an inside joke on a secretary at Baer Animation, Alison Rubin.[22] These sorts of references abound in the animation industry.

As mentioned previously, backgrounds play a very important part in the aesthetics of any animated work. During the early years of animation history, backgrounds were kept to a minimum to avoid problems of retracing but, after cels were put into wide usage, more elaborate environments started to develop. Like other aspects of animation production, the design of backgrounds is influenced by a number of people in departments such as layout and background painting.

Tim Beihold, who works in layout for Disney animated features, explains that 'every composition you see in an animated film has been designed in layout'.[23] He likens his role to that of a Director of Photography in live-action production, saying that he works closely with the film's director in planning the look of backgrounds, the placement of characters, the editing of scenes and the types of camera moves used.

Walt Peregoy worked as a background stylist at both the Disney and Hanna-Barbera Studios. In an interview with Bob Miller, he pointed out that elements of background design differ substantially depending on what era one is discussing, as well as whether the production in question is a theatrical feature or made for television; one should keep in mind that, in his words, 'There's the ideal situation and there's the reality of the styling situation'. It is not surprising to find that, at Hanna-Barbera, where Peregoy headed the background department between 1968 and 1973, he worked much more rapidly than he did at Disney, when he designed the backgrounds for *One Hundred and One Dalmatians* (1961). Although he feels that many of the backgrounds he created at Hanna-Barbera reflect a sense of individual style, he believes the company's practice of sending animation to overseas studios eventually made the backgrounds more 'interchangable' than unique.[24]

Colour and line

The use of colour in animation can be difficult to discuss in an analytical way because even trained graphic artists tend to attribute their use of colour to something along the lines of 'instinct' and 'inspiration' rather than any strict formula that can be expressed in words. Jules Engel, who worked as a colour designer for United Productions of America (UPA) and Disney, has stated that a sense of how to use colour is something 'you're born with – you either have it or you don't'.[25] While it is undoubtedly true that many intangible factors affect the application of colour in animated imagery, or artwork of any kind, it is important to keep in mind that some artists study colour theory and apply it in their work. Colour theory can help an artist to think in terms of how colours work individually or in combination to affect the viewer.

Many basic textbooks on drawing and painting contain some discussion of colour and its aesthetics. Daniel M. Mendelowitz's *A Guide to Drawing* contains the following description of the way in which colour is created:

> Color is an optical sensation produced by the various wavelengths of visible light that form a narrow band on the known spectrum of radiant energy. White (or apparently colorless) light, such as that emitted from the sun at noon, contains all the colors of the spectrum – violet, blue green, yellow, orange, red, and their innumerable intermediate gradations – so balanced and blended that they become isolated only when a beam of white light is passed through a prism ... When light strikes an object, some of the component rays are absorbed and others reflected. The reflected rays determine the color we perceive. Thus, a lemon absorbs almost all light rays except those for yellow, which reflected to our eyes give the lemon its characteristic color. Leaves reflect mostly green rays, and therefore we say that leaves are green.[26]

In a discussion of animation aesthetics, the analyst primarily is concerned with reflected colour rather than the colour of light itself.

Reflected colour has certain qualities, or dimensions, that help to create meaning: hue, value, and intensity. The term 'hue' refers to intervals in the colour spectrum that are known as violet, blue, green, yellow, orange and red. These hues are divided into primary, secondary and tertiary colours depending on the way they are derived (see CP 15). Red, yellow and blue are primary colours; they cannot be made by mixing any other colours and therefore they serve as a primary foundation for other hues. Secondary colours are created by mixing two primary colours together; thus one arrives at orange (from red and yellow), green (from yellow and blue), and violet (from red and blue). Tertiary colours represent combinations of the primary and secondary colours. They are hyphenated, with the primary colour appearing first, as in the case of red-orange or blue-green (the order may be reversed, as in green-blue, to suggest dominance of the secondary colour).

Technically, black, white and the gradations of gray are not colours; they are 'values'. Within the realm of art, they often are used as conventions to indicate various levels of light. The term value refers to the amount of the relative lightness or darkness of a hue, or its likeness to white, black or a some intermediate point. Values can be affected by the amount of light that is reflected from a surface, so that a colour of part of an item resting in a shadow will appear to have a darker value than that same colour on another area of the object. Mendelowitz provides a good example to clarify the meaning of value:

> Perception of value depends upon a number of factors: (1) the actual coloration of the subject; (2) its lightness or darkness relative to its surroundings; and (3) the degree to which the subject is illuminated or in shadow. Beginners tend to see color as distinct from lightness or darkness ... Similarly, the novice often thinks of an entire white form as light, although certain areas of it are in shadow and consequently of medium or even dark value; and of a black surface as dark even when it is brilliantly illuminated.[27]

The term 'intensity' is used to describe the saturation of colour and the extent to which it is pure or altered by the addition of white, black, gray or another hue that can affect its brilliance. A complimentary hue, or the colour that appears across a colour wheel from any given colour, can be added to lower its intensity (e.g. the complement of yellow is the meeting point of red and blue, or violet; violet lowers the intensity of yellow and vice versa). The term 'low intensity' is used to describe a relatively gray, or dull, colour. 'High intensity' is used to describe a colour that is highly saturated, or pure.

A few other concepts will help the colour analyst to assess and describe the aesthetics of a work. One of these is the way in which hues function as warm or cool. Warm colours include yellow, orange, red and the colours inbetween them, while cool colours include green, blue and violent and the colours inbetween them. It is said that warm colours move forward in space and stimulate the viewer. Cool colours, on the other hand, tend to move away from a viewer and are calming in nature. Mendelowitz suggests that the affects of colours are conditioned by the environment: warm colours might subtly suggest the danger of blood and heat or fire, but cool colours are more familiar in the soothing contexts of the sky, water and plants in nature.

It is sometimes useful to consider the way in which colour schemes can be employed in a work of art. The three most commonly employed colour schemes are monochromatic, analogous, and complementary (see CP 15). Monochromatic colour schemes are built around one hue that is modified with the addition of black and white. An analogous colour scheme typically is built around the colours on one side of a single primary colour; for example, blue, blue-violet, violet, and red-violet (pure red would not be used). Complementary colour schemes primarily are built around complements: yellow and violet, blue and orange, or red and green. The psychological impact of a type of colour scheme will vary depending on the colours used in it, but monochromatic schemes may be more unified and thus calming in nature than a complementary scheme, which contains a range of opposing colours.

Jules Engel suggests that colour has a number of functions in animated work.[28] First, it can create space – a sense of openness and serenity or, perhaps, claustrophobia and anxiety. He uses the example of the UPA short, *Gerald McBoing Boing* (directed by Robert 'Bobe' Cannon, 1951), as an example. At the beginning of the film, colour and design are used to create a light and simple background, but eventually they become darker and more complex. Background hues become bolder and more pervasive as the tension grows, and blackness envelopes the height of drama, as Gerald leaves home and a train enters the scene. Accordingly, Engel underscores his second point: that colour can be used to create *any* effect, whether it be dramatic, sombre, joyous or otherwise. Finally, he explains that colours can be 'heard', in the sense that they emit a feeling that can affect viewers in a way that parallels music. It could help the analyst to think of a production's colours as taking on a musical form, since he or she might be more accustomed to interpreting the effects of music than visuals on the screen. One might ask: If these colours were music, how would they sound? This general idea will be discussed further in upcoming chapters of this book.

In order to determine the way in which colour works in animation, the analyst must understand something of the psychological impact of colours, but also the effects of materials used in recording a work. Trained colourists within the animation industry take into account the ways in which various film and video stocks reproduce colours. Likewise, media analysts also should keep in mind that stocks have distinct characteristics; however, they also must remember that the colour quality of a particular film or video copy of animation can change over time, due to a variety of reasons that range from chemical change and fading, to marketing considerations.

To illustrate the latter, one can use the example of the Warner Bros. 'Looney Tunes' shorts, a series that is familiar to many people. A number of colour stocks were in use during the 1910s and colour animation became relatively common during the 1930s.[29] Nonetheless, a significant amount of animation made in the United States and elsewhere continued to be produced in black and white, including the 'Looney Tunes' series. After the television industry converted to colour in the 1960s, Hollywood studios (both live-action and animated) almost exclusively began to make productions in colour, to facilitate their use on the 'small screen' (i.e. television).[30]

In the early 1970s, the 'Looney Tunes' series, which had been produced in black and white from their beginning in 1930 until 1943, were converted into colour. Leonard Maltin describes the changes that occurred when Warner Bros. had the shorts redone:

> The process, executed in Korea, involved tracing over frames of film. (The studio had burned all its original artwork some years earlier in order to make storage space.) ... At first glimpse, the colours are quite pleasing, but one soon discovers that details have been dropped in the tracing, mechanical errors have been made, and not every frame has been traced.[31]

From his description, one can see that an analysis of the aesthetics of these animated shorts is complicated by many factors.

Today, many aging colour film prints have taken on a reddish cast as various dyes in the stock have begun to fade, making an analysis of colour almost impossible. Black and white films do not suffer from the same kind of fading, which can make an analysis of their 'colour' a bit simpler. It may seem strange to think of black and white films as having colour, when they are composed of the values of black, white and shades of gray. However, these values greatly impact a viewer's perceptions, in just like variations in full colour. Darkness and lightness can be used to create mood and atmosphere, and to delineate features of the visual layout, all of which create meaning for the viewer.

When analysing colour, writers should understand the way the application of colour occurs within a large studio production process. Throughout the animation industry, colour and line primarily have been the domain of colour key, inking and painting departments. Typically, the colour key artist receives a 'model sheet' containing various images (characters, props, and so on) and is responsible for selecting the particular colours that will be applied to them. Phyllis Craig, who worked for a variety of companies, including Disney, Hanna-Barbera and Film Roman, relied on an intuitive sense of colour, as well as a perception of what the director would desire, indicating that colour key artists often are given a great deal of leeway in their selection of colours.[32] However, the role of colour key varies greatly by studio. While working at Disney during the 1950s, Craig found herself painting models over and over, until the director found the precise shade that suited his taste. When she moved to Hanna-Barbera in the 1960s, she found that the company's rate of production was much faster than Disney's, so that she moved through a set of models rather rapidly, painting each image once and rarely being asked to make adjustments.

Craig explains that exhibition formats also influenced the way in which she selected colour. Generally, television characters are composed of solid, highly contrasting colours; tiny details and subtle shading are not used because they will be completely lost on television, which historically has had relatively poor resolution. Animation produced for projection in theatres usually contains much finer detail in terms of colour. Subtle shading is desirable because film has finer resolution. In addition, the images projected in a theatre will be quite large, so shading will make them much more visually appealing. Craig's work for Hanna-Barbera was aimed at television exhibition, while her work for Disney was for theatrical release, which accounts for some of the differences in her working methods.

Traditionally, when cels have been used to create animation, colour has been affected by the number of cel layers (typically, up to five) used at any one time. The cel on top gets the most light, with light diminishing progressively for each subsequent cel in the stack. Long ago, the yellowish colour of the cel material also was a significant consideration, but today's cels are relatively colourless.

In any case, to compensate for the varying levels of light or the yellowness of the older cels, different shades of the same paint colour, or 'let-downs', are used on different cel layers. The variations in colours should be evident to the historian who is studying a stack of cels as a 'set up' or complete production unit, with the background and all the cel layers necessary to make a single exposure. When let downs are not used for some reason, patches of lighter or darker colours generally appear on moving parts of a character in the film or video recording.

When examining original cels of large studio productions, it is possible to note differences in the quality of lines in artwork made before the 1960s, particularly. At the Disney Studio, before the advent of photocopying, studio inkers were strictly trained to hold pens correctly and to trace animators' images with a high degree of accuracy. Another group of employees, called 'line checkers', later measured the thickness of the inkers' lines to assure uniformity. The individuals in these positions were very skillful. Craig notes that, during the 1950s at Disney, 'an animator wouldn't even need to clean up his drawings, because a good inker knew what lines to pick up'; she stresses that 'inking was a skill and an art, and not just a production-line job'.[33]

After the 1950s, inkers began to play a much smaller role in the studio's productions. Beginning with *One Hundred and One Dalmatians*, the Disney Studio created its 'inked' lines on cels by using a Xerox process (not like the ones studios use today – the initial set up was very large and complicated). As a result, the lines within the film are of a much different quality. If it had not been for the photocopy process, it is unlikely that the studio would have considered the idea of a film in which a hundred-plus spotted puppies must be drawn over and over. The advent of colour copiers brought more versatility to the animation process, allowing photocopied outlines to match the colour fields they define.

However, in the words of one software manufacturer, 'technology has come a long way since the days when copiers were considered cutting edge'.[34] Now, most major studios are turning to animation software that controls not only inking and painting but also aspects of animated movement. Consequently, let downs are no longer necessary since there are no levels to be affected by light variations, and in any case, a computer can be programmed to make whatever adjustments are necessary. Human artists are still needed to render some of the more difficult images.

Although the nature of lines in commercial studio productions has become somewhat less remarkable, some independent artists have continued to foreground the quality of lines in their work. Interesting examples of a bold graphic style can be found in Joanna Quinn's *Girls Night Out* (1987) and *Britannia* (1994) (see Figs 3.2 (a) and (b)), and in Marcel Jankovics's *Sisyphus* (1974). These films are suited to the use of bold lines because they deal with issues related to power and physical strength.

Movement and kinetics

Animation is the art of creating movement, generally employing inanimate objects but sometimes through the use of live figures whose movements are posed on a frame-by-frame basis. In any case, the characteristics of created movements can vary significantly: an object can move fluidly and rhythmically; in short incremental bursts; slowly and hesitantly (as if working against gravity); or in a multitude of other ways that all suggest meaning to the viewer.

When motion pictures began to develop at the end of the 1800s, a number of fine artists who had been working in painting or other still arts, such as Marcel Duchamp and Hans Richter, were attracted to the new medium for its ability to depict movement. Since that time, students of animation have continued to devote much of their time to the study of motion. Animators study the laws of physics, to learn how gravity impacts the way in which an object travels through space. They consider the factors of acceleration and deceleration on a figure in movement, which affect the spacing of images in sequential frames. They also learn about the way in which weight holds objects down, so that walking characters do not 'float' but rather make contact with the ground in a realistic manner.

Animators also learn different ways of thinking about the creation of animated imagery and movement. Most commonly, animators work in what is called the 'pose-to-pose' method, which means that the most significant 'key poses' in a sequence of movements are drawn first, so that the 'inbetween' poses that make up the action can be filled in later, by an assistant or 'inbetweener' on the staff. However, another well-known method is 'straight-ahead' animation, meaning that every drawing is rendered in the order in which it will be shot. This style is associated with the modified-base technique, 3D animation, and any other animated production where movements are created under the camera in the order they occur; of course, cel or drawn animation can be created in this manner as well. Straight-ahead animation generally is considered more spontaneous than pose-to-pose animation, since it is more difficult to regulate exactly how or where a set of drawings will end up, unless careful storyboarding or another form of documentation is created. Tex Avery is one of the notable Hollywood animators who liked to work in the straight ahead style; as Tom Klein has explained, 'it is as if he preferred the uncharted course that would lead him to personal discovery, rather than the safety of a mapped out endeavor'.[35]

Some people continue to use this method today. For example, in an interview with Jo Jürgens, Andreas Deja says his 'animation is pretty much straight ahead, although it's a combination', adding that he does not really like pose-to-pose animation because 'it's usually a little stiffer', although he was required to work that way on *Who Framed Roger Rabbit*[36] However, most commercial enterprises cannot risk the imprecision that can come with straight-ahead animation. Indeed, considering the investment of time and money that is entailed in animation production and the need for many people to work in unison, pose-to-pose animation would seem much more suitable from a producer's point of view, at least.

Another means of controlling the outcome of animated imagery is by the use of reference footage. In the late 1800s, figure studies made by photographers such as Eadweard Muybridge and Jean Marey paved the way for the study of movement on a frame-by-frame basis. Since their time, many animators have used the technique of filming a live-action 'reference' to provide a real-life basis from which animated drawings can be composed. Sometimes, this reference footage provides only inspi-

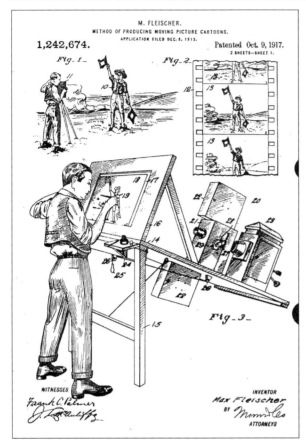

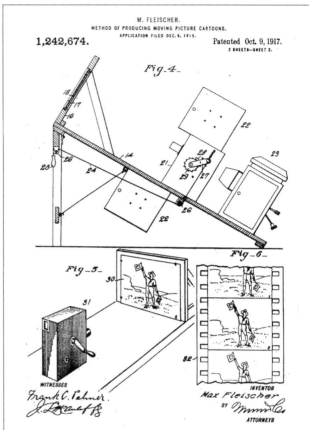

ration, but other times it is actually retraced frame by frame in a process known as rotoscoping.

The Rotoscope was patented by Max Fleischer in 1917. From his patent illustrations, one can see that the technique employs film footage that is traced by an artist whose illustrations are then refilmed. Rotoscoping allows for the creation of animated images that move with a high degree of realism. Ko-Ko the Clown (used in a series of films from 1917–1929) provides an early example of rotoscoping; another distinctive example is Gulliver of Fleischer's feature, *Gulliver's Travels* (1939).

While rotoscoping helps to produce animated movement that is relatively realistic in its appearance, other techniques lend a much more 'cartoony' look to a production. One of these techniques is called 'squash and stretch'. Most beginning animation students are given a squash and stretch exercise to render a bouncing ball that 'squashes' when it hits the ground and 'stretches' when it reaches mid-air on its cycle. This technique can be used to animate a character's walk, so that its form is flattened when it steps down and elongated when it steps upward. Because the technique requires the use of exaggeration, its results are somewhat humorous.

The squash and stretch of character animation relies heavily on metamorphosis, or the transitioning of one shape into another. Metamorphosis also allows inanimate objects, such as a table and chairs, to shift their shapes in order to sing, dance or do

Figs 4.6 (a) & (b)
Rotoscope patent of Max Fleischer, 1917

Public domain

other fantastic things. In a discussion of Disney animation, Russian film theorist Sergei Eisenstein said that the metamorphic – what he called 'plasmatic' – quality of some of the studio's early animated figures appealed to some primordial components of the human psyche. To him, the shape-shifting of metamorphosis created 'attractiveness' in a work.[37] He suggested that metamorphosis can provide a means of connecting to areas of the subconscious, increasing our enjoyment of animated imagery.

In the late 1980s, the computer animation term 'morphing' was introduced into the public's vocabulary, to describe the seamless transitioning of one live-action figure into another. The feature film *The Abyss* (directed by James Cameron, 1989, with effects by Industrial Light & Magic) and singer Michael Jackson's 'Black or White?' music video (directed by John Landis, 1991, with effects by Pacific Data Images) are among the influential live-action productions that helped to popularise the technique.[38] But, metamorphosis has been a quality of animation since its earliest years: Felix the Cat is one character who is famous for shifting shape throughout his films. In *Felix in Hollywood* (1923), he turns himself into a travelling case in order to trick his owner into taking him along. Long before, Emile Cohl's *Fantasmagorie* (1908) intrigued its viewers with characters whose shapes metamorphosed through a dream-like sequence of events.

Clearly, metamorphosis is a tool that lends itself to the development of fantasy in animation. However, metamorphosis also is apparent to some extent in more realistic scenarios, including rotoscoped animation sequences and even live-action films and videos. Consider the way a human face reforms when a person is talking, or the way that weight shifts on a body depending on whether a person is standing, sitting or lying down. Studying motion picture film frame by frame reveals the contortions that the body goes through in any act of movement.

The way in which an object moves in space also affects the extent to which metamorphosis of drawings must occur, since artists use this technique to depict changes in perspective. Movement in space is said to occur along three axes: x, y, and z. These letters are used to represent back-and-forth motion from left to right, top to bottom, and near to far, respectively. In terms of drawn animation, movement along the x- and y-axis is relatively easier to render than z-axis movement, because side-to-side or up-and-down movement does not require a figure to change substantially in its proportions. On the other hand, z-axis movement requires perspective drawing because a figure must be altered in dimensions to give the appearance of getting nearer to or farther from the viewer.[39] Despite the added difficulty of movement along the z-axis, generally it is seen as an aesthetically desirable type of action. Z-axis movement pulls the viewer's focus into the frame and helps to create a sense of depth through the use of foreground, middle-ground, and background planes of action.

Some studios have created techniques to enhance this dimensionality. For example, the Disney Studio employed a multiplane camera in the scary forest scene of *Snow White and the Seven Dwarfs* and other films. Because there is space between the cels placed under the multiplane camera, there is a realistic sense of perspective change as the camera records movement. The foreground, middle ground and background appear to move at different speeds, replicating human perception of movement. The Fleischer Studio developed a different device for creating a realistic sense of space; the Stereoptical process employed a set back that was placed behind cel artwork, which was photographed horizontally rather than vertically.

Regardless of how it is rendered, movement is widely considered to be of key importance to all 'motion pictures'. In his textbook on live-action scriptwriting, Dwain V. Swain warns the writer to:

> ... beware of static situations. A moving picture should move, should tell its story in action ... Unfortunately, all too often, writers write scripts in which people merely sit around and *talk about* past, present, or future action. Even worse, they choose topics which offer little opportunity for things to happen: for the story to develop in terms of people doing things.[40]

Since part of the appeal of animation lies in the illusion that inanimate objects have 'come to life', it is understandable that many people have considered constant movement to be of central importance to animation aesthetics.

Throughout animation history, many animation studios have employed what is known as a 'full animation' style, which involves the constant movement of characters. A number of studios have set up training courses in order to help their artists understand the mechanics of real life and animated movement. In the 1930s, Walt Disney initiated a series of 'Action Analysis' classes, which were taught by Don Graham for the benefit of the artists. According to Graham, the courses were created because Disney was concerned with the lack of analysis that animators were employing in their work. Graham explained that the three most common weaknesses concerned the entrance of a character into a scene, the exit of a character from a scene, and 'knowing how to vary the different actions in order to interpret moods'.[41]

In order to prepare themselves better, he suggested that artists study a combination of actual movement in live-action films as well as animated movement from previous works. He stressed that 'the kind of mood or feeling to be portrayed should determine the type of action, not the action to portray the mood'.[42] In other words, he discouraged the use of stock movements and stressed that animators should interpret the actions by identifying with the mindset of the character being depicted. In order to do so, an artist may have to act out the movements him or herself. Consequently, it is beneficial for that individual to be trained as a performer or at least to be uninhibited enough to take on various personas.

The ability of any studio or individual to depict constant movement in his or her work is related to economics, since it is time-consuming and, as a result, costly to render constant movement throughout an animated production. It is sometimes the case that studios use money-saving techniques such as the re-use of actions from previous episodes or the 'cycling' of actions within a given animated production to make their work stretch further. Cycling is the practice of reusing a set of drawings that make up a complete movement (such as a walk cycle) or a single rendering of background images (e.g. a bunch of trees that a character can walk past more than once). In either case, the viewer sees the same series of images over and over for a short span of time. Cycled movements are generic in nature and therefore create more generalised meaning to a character's movements than personality animation.

Despite the cost of creating movement, it is relatively uncommon to find absolute stillness in an animated work. When it does occur, stillness – referred to as 'a hold' – generally is used for emphasis. For example, a hold is employed when the wolf character ogles the sexy singer, 'Red', on stage in *Red Hot Riding Hood*; the exaggeration of seeing his body freezing horizontally adds humour to the scene.

In real life, living beings are never completely still because bodily functions such as breathing and heartbeats cause at least minute amounts of movement at all times.

Fig. 4.7 *The Janitor (1993), by Vanessa Schwartz*
Courtesy Jules Engel

Seeing an animated figure that is completely still – that is, to see a single image that is photographed for more than, say, half a second – might strike the viewer as being unrealistic. Most animation contains constant motion, even if only at the level of blinking eyes and moving lips, or a camera movement across a still background. In more experimental works, 'still' poses are sometimes indicated by photographing two or three slight variations on the same drawing in a sequence, or cycle. The result is a slightly shaky, or kinetic, pose. Absolute stillness can work against one of the central attractions of animation, the illusion that inanimate objects have been 'endowed with life'; it could be said that, when an image within an animated production becomes still, its lifelessness is readily apparent.

John Lasseter contends that computer-generated imagery has even less tolerance for stillness than other types of animated imagery. He explains:

> ... as soon as you go into a held pose, the action dies immediately ... To combat this, use a 'moving hold'. Instead of having every part of the character stop, have some part continue to move slightly, like an arm, a head, or even have the whole body move in the same direction ever so much.[43]

However, Jules Engel holds a very different opinion about the quality of stillness in a work. He contends that computer animation may have little tolerance for holds because of the quality of its images. He explains, 'a good drawing is never dead. Good drawings have texture in the lines and a beauty of their own. Computer animation doesn't have that. Computer generated imagery is plastic.'[44] He believes that animators actually tend to err on the side of 'overanimating' rather than underanimating; he suggests that constant movement might be employed to cover up the fact that the original artwork has no fascination of its own.[45] In contrast, he holds up the example *The Janitor* (1993), an Academy Award-nominated short created by Vanessa Schwartz while she was one of his students at the California Institute of the Arts. He says he encouraged her to linger on images to make use of the strength of her individual renderings.

Clearly, there are many considerations in designing animated imagery. Many individuals who are attracted to the field of animation have focused their education and art background on the development of characters and the means of creating movement. However, artists who excel in these aspects of animation might find they know less about the issues of sound and structure, which also are key ingredients in making an animated production a success. While an attractive mise-en-scène is impressive, an audience is likely to lose interest unless there has been attention given to the way in which figures and their movements develop throughout the course of the work, and the cohesiveness of the production on a global level. Sound and structure are two elements that can provide a sense of overall unity and are important considerations in both the creation and the analysis of animated works. The next chapter will be devoted to a discussion of them.

Notes

1. David Bordwell and Kristin Thompson, *Film Art: An Introduction* (New York: McGraw-Hill, 1997), 169.

2. Shamus Culhane, *Animation from Script to Screen* (New York: St. Martin's, 1988); Kit Laybourne, *The Animation Book: A Complete Guide to Animation Filmmaking, from Flipbooks to Sound Cartoons* (New York: Crown, 1972).

3. Bordwell and Thompson, op. cit., x.

4. Debra Kaufman explains that the scene represents the first time a 3D computer-animated background was used in a Disney film. She reports that 'the set was completely built in the computer, using Alias Research software for modeling, Pixar's RenderMan for rendering, and Wavefront to fly the camera around three-dimensionally. The characters were "retroset" within the ballroom, with their movements following the computerised camera moves'. Debra Kaufman, 'Computer as Paintbrush', *Hollywood Reporter* (21 Jan. 1992): S36–S40.

5. Grim Natwick, 'An Interview with Grim Natwick', conducted by Bethlehem Tsemayu, edited by Phil Denslow (May 1980), in *Animatrix* 1, 4 (1987–1988): 51–60, 56–57.

6. Ibid., 57.

7. Id.

8. 'Rough Draft Studios: company bios', promotional material from the company (ca. March 1997).

9. 'Sunwood Entertainwood' brochure, promotional material from the company (ca. March 1997). There are two other arms of the company as well. Sunwoo Productions, which produces commercials, has existed since 1974 and Anivision Korea, which also creates animation, was established in 1991. The Hollywood office, which represents all three Sunwoo companies, is called Anivision America.

10. 'Akom Production Co.' brochure, promotional material from the company (ca. March 1997).

11. Scott McCloud, *Understanding Comics* (Northampton, MA: Kitchen Sink, 1993).

12. However, abstract forms did figure into commercial advertising in the past. For example, both Norman McLaren and Len Lye incorporated abstract figures into their work for the British Post Office in the 1930s. Oskar Fischinger's film, *Kriese* (Circles, 1933), provides another example.

13. For more information on early animated films, see Denis Gifford, *American Animated Films: The Silent Era, 1897–1929* (Jefferson, NC: McFarland, 1990).

14. Other examples include the Katzenjammer Kids (Hearst/La Cava, beg. 1916), Farmer Al Falfa (Bray/Terry, beg. 1916), Bobby Bumps (Bray/Hurd, beg. 1915), Sammie Johnsin (Sullivan, beg. 1916), Jerry (from 'Jerry on the Job', Hearst/La Cava, beg. 1916), and Dreamy Dud (Carlson, beg. 1915). Animated stars emerged in the Hollywood film industry at around the same time that live-action stars began to make a name for themselves. (It was not until the 1910s that the Hollywood live-action film industry regularly began to give screen credits to its popular performers and a 'star system' developed.)

15. Philippe Moins, 'Comic Strips and Animation: The Belgian Tradition', *Animation World Magazine* 2, 4 (July 1997).

16. In an interview with Kathryn Kramer, Richard Williams, who was the director of animation for *Who Framed Roger Rabbit*, acknowledged that he 'overdosed' on watching old animated shorts, including 'all the Tex Avery cartoons'. He explained: '[T]he rabbit's got Droopy's red hair. Droopy sort of had this cashew nut-shaped head so I put that on the rabbit. It's got Brer Rabbit's pants and feet. It's a Frankenstein monster. All the characters were Frankenstein monsters. Jessica was based on a thing in a Donald Duck cartoon called *Duck Pimples* and they had a woman that wasn't as zaftig but it was the same colours. I call it a "hip rehash".' Richard Williams, interview with Kathryn Kramer (1 August 1991), London. See also, Frederick Patten, 'Roger Rabbit: A Family Tree', *Animation Magazine* (Summer 1988): 27. Patten notes that Jessica Rabbit 'could be a twin sister to the star of Tex Avery's *Red Hot Riding Hood*'.

17. Linda Baer, whose company (Baer Animation) was responsible for creating a portion of the film's animation, discusses Zemeckis's influences in an unpublished interview with Jonathan Schwartz, conducted 21 June 1991. In the interview, she also mentions the re-use of Disney material: 'Dave Pecheko was the morgue expert, and he would go down to the Disney morgue [materials depository] and go through tons of stuff. We looked at film, old film, reviewed everything, and he would go down and dig it up and then we used what we could, and what we couldn't use, we re-pasted, or re-animated a lot of it. But we tried to use as much as we could from the morgue.'

18. The components of personality animation are detailed in Frank Tomas and Ollie Johnson, *Disney Animation: The Illusion of Life* (New York: Abbeville, 1983).

19. Donald Crafton (1982), *Before Mickey: The Animated Film, 1898–1928* (Cambridge, MA: MIT, 1987).

20. Sue Perrotto, interview with the author, New York (Jan. 1997).

21. Phyllis Craig, interview with the author (ca. August 1995). Information from this interview was used as the basis for an article, Maureen Furniss, 'Animation and Color Key: The Career of Phyllis Craig', *Animation Journal* 5, 1 (Fall 1996): 58–70.

22. Baer, interview with Schwartz, op. cit.

23. Tim Beihold, 'Layout and Background' seminar, World Animation Celebration, Los Angeles (29 March 1997).

24. Bob Miller, 'Designer of Worlds: An Interview with Stylist Walt Peregoy', *Animato!* 22 (Winter 1992): 14–19.

25. Jules Engel, interview with the author (ca. Sept. 1995).

26. Daniel M. Mendelowitz, *A Guide to Drawing* (New York: Holt, Rinehart and Winston, 1976), 121. The overview of colour terminology used in the next several paragraphs draws on Mendelowitz's chapter on colour, though the terms he covers are widely understood as basic 'introduction to art' concepts.

27. Ibid., 77.

28. Jules Engel, conversation with the author (17 Aug. 1997).

29. Jere Guldin has overviewed some of the processes that existed prior to World War II, including Kinemacolor, Prisma, Brewstercolor, Raycol Color, Multicolor, Cinecolor, Gasparcolor and Technicolor. Jere Guldin, 'Photographing Animated Motion Pictures in Early Color Film Processes', *Animatrix* 7 (1993): 20–30, 21.

30. For information on the American film industry's relationship with television, see Christopher Anderson, *Hollywood TV: The Studio System in the Fifties* (Austin: University of Texas Press,

1994). Discussions of both the Disney and Warner Bros. studios are included in the book, although they do not necessarily pertain to animation production.

31. Leonard Maltin (1980), *Of Mice and Magic: A History of American Animated Cartoons* (New York: NAL, 1987), 229.
32. Craig, interview with the author, op. cit.
33. Id.
34. Jim Kristoff, president of Metrolight, quoted in Paula Parisi, 'Tools of the Trade: Computer Keyboards are Replacing the Traditional Paint and Brush', *Hollywood Reporter* (26 Jan. 1993): S24+, S24.
35. Tom Klein, 'Apprenticing the Master: Tex Avery at Universal (1929–1935), *Animation Journal* 6, 1 (Fall 1997): 4–20.
36. In discussing the two animation styles, Deja compares the work of Chuck Jones, which he calls 'very posey', to Art Babbit which is 'very straight ahead'.
37. Sergei Eisenstein, *Eisenstein on Disney* (London: Methuen, 1988), 21. Andreas Deja, in Jo Jürgens, 'Getting Its Own Life', *The Art of Animation* (Spring 1994): 14–21, 17, 18.
38. In 1992, Doug Smythe and Tom Bigham, who had done significant research in the area of morphing while he was a student at the Massachusettes Institute of Technology, were given an Academy Award for Technical Acheivement. For more on morphing and *Willow*, see Mark Cotta Vaz and Patricia Rose Duignan, *Industrial Light & Magic* (New York: Ballantine, 1996), 132–135.
39. The situation is different in respect to 3D animation because in that context the main consideration in *z*-axis animation is following focus on a character as it moves nearer to and farther from the camera. Of course, the use of deep focus avoids that problem, since the foreground, middle ground and background are all in focus simultaneously.
40. Dwight V. Swain, *Film Scriptwriting: A Practical Manual* (New York: Hastings House, 1977), 125.
41. Don Graham, 'Class on Action Analysis' (22 Feb. 1937), 1.
42. Ibid., 18.
43. John Lasseter, 'Viewpoint', *Animation Magazine* (March/April 1994): 44–45, 45.
44. Engel, conversation with the author (17 Aug. 1997).
45. Id.

General concepts: Sound and structural design

ELEMENTS OF SOUND

One of the biggest differences between amateur and professional animation often lies in the way that sound is employed. It is common for beginners to be enamoured with the visual components of animation and give very little attention to the soundtrack.[1] However, most people will find that the secret to success for many award-winning films is the care with which aural elements – voices, sound effects and music – have been handled.

These components of the soundtrack are blended in a hierarchy that gives meaning to the production. Typically, the sounds deemed most important are made to be the loudest; in most cases, the dialogue is loudest in the hierarchy in order to effectively deliver narrative information, with effects and music recorded at a lower level as supporting elements. However, by changing the hierarchy, perhaps by swelling the music or by including sound effects that are so loud that the dialogue cannot be heard, one can manipulate the listener's perception of what is occurring within a scene.

In *Film Art*, Bordwell and Thompson identify the acoustic properties of motion picture sound as loudness, pitch and timbre.[2] They note that the loudness, or volume, of a given sound is affected by the amplitude, or breadth, of vibrations in the air. The loudness of a sound affects our perception of distance, so that 'often the louder the sound, the closer we take it to be'.[3] Pitch, on the other hand, is related to the frequency of sound vibrations. Generally, we think of the pitch of a sound in terms of 'highness' (e.g. tinkling bells) or 'lowness' (e.g. a thud). Timbre is a more abstract concept and, consequently, a bit more difficult to define. Bordwell and Thompson write that:

> ... the harmonic components of a sound give it a certain 'color' or tone quality – what musicians call timbre. Timbre is actually a less fundamental acoustic parameter than amplitude or frequency, but it is indispensable in describing the texture or 'feel' of a sound. When we call someone's voice nasal or a certain musical tone mellow, we are referring to timbre.[4]

These acoustic properties of loudness, pitch and timbre affect the way in which sound produces meaning in a work. However, these terms provide only a basic vocabulary with which to describe the quality of a sound. The previous chapter recommends that newcomers to the field seek information on production techniques in specialised books; similarly, it is advisable that additional sources be consulted in order to fully understand recording techniques and the aesthetic complexity of sound in motion pictures.[5] However, in doing so, one should be aware that the recording and function of sound in animation can be quite different than that in live-action productions.

Dialogue in animation

In his essay on 'The Sound of the Early Warner Bros. Cartoons', Scott Curtis suggests some of the ways in which sound components in animation and live-action work can vary.[6] For example, in live-action productions, voices generally are recorded at the same time that visuals are shot or, when necessary, are dubbed in after the production is completed. Although practices vary throughout the world, in the American animation industry it is most common to record voices (and sometimes other sound elements) before the visuals are finalised. The advantages of this practice, which has existed since the early years of animation history, include the ability to achieve greater synchronisation of lip movements to dialogue and the ability to use voice tracks for inspiration in character design and movement.

At the Fleischer Studio, a manual given to employees spelled out the technicalities of synchronising lip movements to recorded dialogue. Although every studio had its own methods, this manual illustrates some general procedures in the development of actions from the soundtrack. It explains that, after the selected 'takes' of dialogue have been assembled into the general order in which they are to appear in the film, the 'head animator will then underline those *syllables* which he judges the most suited for *accents in animation*. The most emphatic accents will be underlined with red pencil and the secondary accents will be underlined with a brown pencil'[7] (emphasis in original).

The manual also stresses that the voices and visual elements should be interrelated. It advises artists that:

> ... in animating a bit of dialogue or singing, the mouth actions are really secondary. To make it convincing, the action itself is the important thing. This does not mean that mouth actions should be slighted. They *must* be on the 'nose' (accurate) and convincing, but perfect mouth-actions mean nothing if the action itself is not convincing.[8]

The manual gives the example of using a 'preparatory gesture', which is 'a supple-mentary action preceding an emphatic action': 'A girl stomps her foot and says, "No!"! If she stamped her foot and said "No!" at the same time, it would weaken her attitude; but if she first stamped her foot and *then* accented the word "no" about $^{1}/_{12}$ feet later, it would carry more weight.'[9]

Voice recordings are important not only for the development of action within animation; they also greatly affect characterisation. As a result, the delivery of lines constitutes a valuable area of study. Within the broad category of animation, there is much more variation in the range of voices used than in live-action media. Although there are certainly examples of relatively 'realistic' voices being used in animation, particularly in work produced outside the commercial arena, to a great extent dialogue is spoken in a stylised way.[10]

However, in his article, 'Voice Acting 101', voice actor Joe Bevilacqua says that most trained professionals believe 'first and foremost that voice acting is *real* acting, not just "doing funny voices" ... Characters should be real, no matter how cartoony the style is'.[11] Another voice actor, Bob Bergen (who today plays the voice of Porky Pig) says that anyone who has the attitude of 'I want to work in cartoons but ... I don't want to be an actor ... will never work. In this business, they could care less if you can do great voices. It's the acting that gets the job. It is definitely a skill and a craft that takes time to cultivate'.[12]

Performing voices for animation is a specialised job that differs substantially from other voice-talent occupations such as dubbing foreign films or providing voice-overs for commercials or instructional media. To play the role of an animated character, voice artists generally must alter their normal speaking voices substantially in terms of both sound (adopting unusual speaking voices) and volume (yelling and crying out is relatively common). Voice actor Vern Louden recalled working for Jay Ward, who would bring in a storyboard drawing of a character and 'say "Give me a hokey voice!" Well, you'd look at that animal and turn your vocal chords inside out trying to find something that Jay would like. And eventually you'd please him'.[13] It is sometimes the case that animation voice talent is required to read lines in a wide variety of ways, so that directors have a range of choices when building their tracks.

However, what the director is looking for is sometimes a particular speaking voice that already has proven marketable. The previous chapter discusses the use of conventional characters to help guarantee popularity and sales. Bevilacqua notes that, today, animation studios often 'want the familiar, not the new. Most of the great voice actors, such as Mel Blanc, Daws Butler, and Paul Frees are gone now, and the studios need sound-alikes to keep their cartoon franchises going'.[14]

Another major trend in recent American animation production is the casting of live-action film and television stars to play the parts of animated characters. Large salaries have been paid to such well-known performers as Robin Williams and Tom Hanks to speak the lines of characters in *Aladdin*, *Toy Story* and other animated features. Although 'Beavis and ButtHead' creator Mike Judge has done many voices for the television series as well as the feature he has directed (*Beavis and Butt-Head Do America*, 1996), the voices of Robert Stack and Cloris Leachman, are among the others, also are heard in the film. The Klasky-Csupo studio is known for employing celebrity voices in the television series it animates, which have included 'The Simpsons' (the first three years, before it moved to the Film Roman studio), 'Rugrats', 'Duckman' and 'Aaahh!!! Real Monsters'.[15] Among the stars who have voiced dialogue for their animated series are Kirk Douglas, David Duchovny, Andrew Dice Clay, Cheech Marin, Ice-T and Taj Mahal.

Performing for animation can be particularly fulfilling for a performer because of the versatility animation can provide. Barbara Wright, director of talent and casting for Klasky-Csupo comments that performers are asked to:

> ... do things that they are not often or never asked to do [for live-action productions]. You know they have wonderful abilities in them and it's fun to hear what they can do with the resonance and texture of their voices, and how character can be commmunicated through voice as opposed to the entire actor ...

She adds, 'without their bodies and faces, it's a challenge to bring richness and meaning into solely the voice performance'.[16]

In the case of animated features, particularly, one reason why celebrity voices are used is because a star has 'already developed a persona' the production team 'can draw from to fill out the character'.[17] In addition, the use of celebrities is thought to appeal to adult audiences, which are apt to be more familiar with the performer than young children would be; as a result, the animation can be successfully marketed to a broader range of viewers.[18] Other marketing opportunities afforded by the use of live-action celebrities include increased exposure in the media. Voice performer Corey Burton laments, 'they get someone like Don Rickles coming in to Toy Story and say, "OK, Don, you're Mr Potatohead", and they get to use his personality ... they see it as a big marketing plus. That way they get little bits on "Entertainment Tonight" and other "behind the scenes" TV shows'.[19]

Once the cast of voices has been selected, performers can be recorded in various types of recording sessions. Bevilacqua explains:

> Sometimes every character is recorded separately, then edited and mixed together later by a sound engineer. This can be a very difficult way to perform, as the actor does not have the opportunity to hear how the other actors say their lines and respond naturally. Most of Mel Blanc's work on the Warner Bros. cartoons was done this way.

> Another type of recording session is done by dubbing the voices during post-production, when the animation is already completed. This is perhaps the most difficult of all for an actor. Most cartoons imported from Japan are recorded this way for the English market. Stephanie Morganstern, who plays Sailor Venus on 'Sailor Moon', is an expert at this type of work ...

> The best recording sessions usually are the ones in which all the actors are in the same room performing together as if it were a radio play. All of Jay Ward's cartoons, such as 'Rocky and Bullwinkle', were done this way. Mark Evanier, who wrote and voice-directed 'Garfield', also works this way. I remember sitting in on many recording sessions of 'The Jetsons', when Daws Butler, Penny Singleton, Mel Blanc, Howard Morris, and the whole cast sat in a circle and worked off each other. They encouraged, prodded, and provoked one another into great performances.[20]

No matter how a recording session is done, once it is over, voices for animated works are subject to continued alteration. Voice recordings for animation might require more or at least a different kind of post production work than other recording sessions because directors sometimes request that lines be electronically 'vari-speeded', or altered in pace, in order to match the tempo of a desired action.

Like other aspects of aesthetics, voices are affected by production context. For example, every version of an animated work that is dubbed for use in various countries includes a different performance; this fact must be taken into consideration when making broad statements regarding voice tracks.[21] In addition, the analyst should keep in mind that sometimes the sound elements of a production, including voices, are changed over time. For example, the voice of the Mammy Two-Shoes character in the 'Tom and Jerry' series (at MGM, directed by William Hanna and Joseph Barbera, 1940–1958) was changed when June Foray re-recorded the dialogue originally spoken by Lillian Randolph.[22] This alteration, from a 'black' accent to an 'Irish' one probably occurred as a result of changing values in society – in this case, sensitivity to the stereotyping of black Americans.

Sound effects

Some of the most famous animated characters of studio animation – Tom and Jerry, the Pink Panther, the Roadrunner, Wile E. Coyote, and Gromit the Dog – have had no voices at all (at least for most of their careers). Like many comedians of the silent era of film, these characters tend to rely on physical comedy and facial expression to a great extent. In addition, music and sound effects also are vital to these characters' comedy routines. Sound effects in animation often are applied in an exaggerated manner, with no realistic congruity between an action and the noise created from it.

A rather unique example can be found in the short film, *Gerald McBoing Boing* (directed by Robert 'Bobe' Cannon), which was released by United Productions of America (UPA) in 1951. This Academy Award-winning animated short capitalises on the humorous possibilities of sound effects: a little boy cannot speak in a regular language but instead makes various noises, including a springy 'boing' sound, for which he is named. Finally, his 'defect' pays off when he hits it big in radio.

Tregoweth 'Treg' Brown was one of the most influential sound effects artists in Hollywood (although on Warner Bros. cartoons, he is credited as 'film editor'). A tribute to Brown appears in the Warner Bros. film, *One Froggy Evening* (1955), directed by Chuck Jones; near the end of the film, the cornerstone of a building bears his name. Jones explains that Brown:

> ... was one of the few great comic sound cutters; I told him to look for incongruities, and he did. Once we had a coyote and sheep-dog film and we showed boulders rolling towards the wolf. Instead of using the regular sound effect, he used the sound of a locomotive – and it worked.[23]

Regarding Brown's work in *Zoom and Bored* (1957), on a scene where the Coyote gets his foot caught in a Captain Ahab hook, Jones says:

> Treg used every sound effect except the proper ones for this scene – he had horns, and oinks, and all kinds of things – and I'll tell you something, people have looked at that thing, people who know about film, and they don't notice it ... which is wonderful, of course. His sound effects gave the cartoons a great deal of subconscious humor.[24]

Throughout *Zoom and Bored*, one can hear jet engines, cow bells, and all manner of exaggerated noises, which are easily understood as conventional comic effects.

Sound effects need not be layered and complex – or humorous – to provide a deep level of meaning and greatly impact the visuals of a film. On the contrary, a relatively simple mix of sounds can serve to heighten the drama or suspense of a scenario. The Academy Award-winning film *Balance* (1989), by the German brothers Christoph and Wolfgang Lauenstein, provides a good example. In *Balance*, visual elements are stripped to a minimum: a group of almost identical, basically non-descript, silent figures move about on a barren platform that is suspended in mid-air. While fishing off the side of their small and delicately balanced habitat, one of the figures reels in a box that serves as the catalyst in the film, ultimately bringing chaos to their world. The teetering sounds emitted by the platform, the sliding of the box across its surface, and the faint bit of music emitted by the box underscores the sparseness of the film's environment while providing it with dimensionality. The audience certainly can see the desolation of the space but the limited range of sounds one hears helps to define it.

Musical scores

Of all the components of sound, music is the category that has attracted the most critical attention, perhaps because it is also the aspect that has most concerned major producers of motion pictures, both live-action and animated. Throughout much of film history, studios have viewed motion pictures as an important way to showcase – and subsequently sell – music.

However, commercial producers are not the only ones who have been attracted to the musical components of animation. Many people who would be considered fine artists from outside the field of animation, as well as experimental animators, have valued music above voice recordings and sound effects. In his essay, 'A Sound Idea: Music for Animated Films', Jon Newsom discusses the sound design of a number of experimental animated productions.[25] One of them is *La joie de vivre* (The Joy of Life, 1934), created by English artist Anthony Gross, who had studied and exhibited work in Paris, and Hector Hoppin, an American financier and former classmate of Hoppin's.[26] The film reflects the influence of Futurism and modern dance, as whimsical female figures frolic within an industrial landscape of buildings and electrical equipment. Its score was composed by Tibor Harsányi prior to the creation of its images, to allow close integration of sound and visuals.[27] Newsom explains that the score was 'separately published for concert performance with the title "*La joie de vivre*: divertissement cinématographique" '.[28] He adds that, in the preface to the sheet music, Harsányi stated that the score has a:

> ... special musical structure, which corresponds to that of cinematic works: the unconscious gliding of scenery, the linking of changes of view, the mobility of clear outlines, the constant movement of the frame itself ... [The piece's] char-acteristics are in opposition to the purely 'scenic' structure of symphonically conceived works.[29]

Norman McLaren was another of the many individuals to experiment with the relationship between music and animated imagery. One of his central interests was the way that different sensory components of a film could be seen as interdependent; he, like Sergei Eisenstein, Oskar Fischinger and many other artists, was intrigued by the concept of synaesthesia, or the overlapping of the senses.[30] McLaren's interest in sensory overlaps began when he was young. He recalled:

> ... when I was a teenager, I used to collect smells. I had a wooden box with holes drilled in it, and with test-tubes in the holes. I'd go around collecting smells and making arrangements of those tubes. I'd arrange them like a melody – like a

pan-pipe. I'd run it across my nose and get one smell after another – a little melody with ten notes of smell. I'd rearrange them and try them in a different way.[31]

Throughout his life, McLaren continued to experiment with different types of sensory overlaps, such as sound and image, or sound and colour, with varying degrees of satisfaction. He once remarked, 'ever since I was eighteen years old I have searched a great deal for correlations between sound and image ... and finally I decided that there can be no precise correlation'; in conclusion, he states, 'correlations between

pitch and colour are, in my experience, highly subjective. All the theories I've read about, and thought of myself, are arbitrary'.[32]

Nonetheless, McLaren was able to formulate a general relationship between colour and sound, which he used in his own work but 'didn't stick to all the time':

> Low pitches I relate to colour of low-light values, irrespective of hue and chroma; high pitches to high-light values, irrespective of hue and chroma. In other words, I let *dark* browns, olives, reds, purples, blues predominate on the screen during a low-pitch passage, and use yellows, pale greens, pale oranges, very pale reds, purples, and blues during a high-pitched passage.
>
> The timbre of the sound might sometimes determine which of these colours [is used]. To me it seems related to hue and possibly more so to the saturation or chroma of the colour. With a *full-bodied* passage I would tend to select a low-light-value colour, with a high chroma such as a deep rich red, purple or blue; for a *thin*-bodied low-pitch passage I would choose a low-light-value colour with a low chroma, such as a deep brown, khaki or mustard. In other words, the fewer harmonies there are in the sound, the less saturation or chroma I tend to use; and the richer and more strident the sound the more intense the saturation.[33] (Emphasis in original.)

Just as important to McLaren was the correlation between the music and the movement of visual imagery. He says he 'almost instinctively' tended to 'translate fortissimo with the movement of a very *large* image and pianissimo of a very *small* image or a large image far away ... the amount one stimulates the ear-drums (dynamic-range) correlates with the degree to which one stimulates the retina'.[34]

McLaren tended to avoid voices in his work because he wanted to prevent language barriers. Music posed no such problem, and he employed a wide range of it. He used folk, jazz, popular, and classical soundtracks, in some cases having music specially composed for his films.[35]

One of the ways McLaren created music for his films was relatively unusual. He was intrigued by the idea that shapes produce particular sounds when placed on an optical soundtrack – another aspect of his interest in synaesthesia. As a result, he conducted experiments with 'animated sound', to see how sound elements could be created by drawing (or otherwise fabricating) synthetic soundtracks. He wrote about his processes in 'Technical Notes on the Card Method of Optical Animated Sound' and 'Handmade Sound Track for Beginners' guidelines that are available from the National Film Board of Canada.[36] A good example of his work in this area appears in his film *Neighbors* (1952), where synthetic sound complements the narrative by creating a mechanistic-sounding musical accompaniment to the fantastic, mechanised movement of characters across the screen.

Sometimes attempts have been made within the commercial animation industry to experiment with the relationship between visuals and sounds. The most famous of these experiments is *Fantasia* (production supervisor Ben Sharpsteen, 1940). The original title of this film, 'The Concert Feature', reveals Walt Disney's conception of the work: it would be a film that would marry animated images with classical symphonic works into a concert of visuals and music. A stereo-sound system, Fantasound, was even developed to create a dimensional sound environment, breaking new ground in the use of multiple audio tracks for film.[37]

In creating this experimental feature, abstract artists such as Jules Engel and Oskar Fischinger were employed along with composer Leopold Stokowsky. For a variety of reasons, the film was not a commercial success; one problem with the original film was the fact that many theatres were not equipped to play the Fantasound soundtrack. Nonetheless, *Fantasia* has continued to attract attention as a fairly unique experiment within the animation industry.[38]

For the most part, studios have relied on conventions of sound based on the proven success of the short humorous cartoon. As one might expect, the constraints of such a formula have made some creators unhappy. In an article entitled 'Music and the Animated Cartoon', written in the mid 1940s, Chuck Jones argued that 'only one serious danger confronts the animator: an under-evaluation of his medium'.[39] In this essay, Jones contends that:

> ... all cartoons use music as an integral element in their format. Nearly all cartoons use it badly, confining it as they do to the hackneyed, the time-worn, the proverbial ... many cartoon musicians are more concerned with exact synchronisation or 'mickey mousing' than with the originality of their contribution or the variety of their arrangement.[40]

The term to which Jones refers, 'mickey mousing', is a reference to a practice associated with the Disney Studio, as one might suspect. In the first 'Mickey Mouse' film, *Steamboat Willie* (directed by Walt Disney, with a score by Carl Stalling, 1928), one can see that the score is largely motivated by actions that occur on the screen: we see a variety of animal 'instruments' (such as an unfortunate cat) being played throughout much of the film and, consequently, hear the sounds these items make. This film made quite an impact as the first animated film to be exhibited with a sound-on-film process. In 1928, close synchronisation was an incredible novelty to be capitalised upon – so it is no wonder that sound is linked so closely with the film's visuals. However, the novelty wore off and, as Jones suggests, over the years the term 'mickey

Fig. 5.3 Steamboat Willie *(1928) by Walt Disney*
© *Disney Enterprises, Inc.*

mousing' has acquired somewhat of a negative connotation, being used to describe a situation when sound and visual elements are deemed to be too tightly matched.

According to Jones, creative applications of music did not proliferate in the mid-1940s because of 'the thing known in some quarters as "box office" ' – wide audience approval or, in other words, profits. He says that, at the time, there was 'a wave of reaction against the type of cartoons known as "Rembrandts"; that is, any type of cartoon except those based on the "boff" or belly laugh'.[41]

Undoubtedly, the development of animation music was greatly limited by the dominant form of Hollywood animation, the humorous cartoon short, as well as production practices. Curtis writes that it was a priority to use music that fell into regular eight-bar phrases, which gave the animator an easy pattern to use in structuring his or her work.[42]

However, these points should not suggest that music was thought of as inconsequential. As early as the 1930s, Hollywood studios were well aware that music used in animated shorts and features could be a source of great profit. Indeed, animation was used as a tool for marketing two types of music – the popular songs of musical performers whose work was owned by the parent studio and original scores created specifically for the animated work.

Curtis notes that musical directors at Warner Bros. were 'heavily encouraged to use compositions owned by the studio'. He finds that, typically, each of the studio's animated shorts employed portions of five to fifteen separate compositions; these selections came from up to five music companies that generally, though not always, were studio-owned.[43] On the other hand, the Disney Studio was in a different situation.

After the coming of sound, the Disney Studio began producing both the character-driven 'Mickey Mouse' shorts and music-driven 'Silly Symphony' shorts.[44] At first, the studio composed its own music to cut down on costs. J.B. Kaufman notes that, in 1929, Disney:

> ... had no music catalog, and the use of copyrighted music in his films meant the added expense of royalty payments – at a time when his meager budget was already stretched thin. Stalling and his musical successors were usually discouraged from using such material in their scores.[45]

However, Disney was all the more encouraged to produce original music by the overwhelming success of one of its songs in 1933, 'Who's Afraid of the Big Bad Wolf?' from the 'Silly Symphony' film, *Three Little Pigs* (directed by Burt Gillett). Kaufman notes that, by the end of that year, 'at least a dozen recordings of "Who's Afraid" had been issued by various record labels, and several of those recordings were further "milked" by recoupling with alternate B-sides or on subsidiary labels'.[46]

In subsequent years, original songs were produced for many films in Disney's 'Silly Symphony' series, but some of the most memorable have come from the studio's feature productions. For example, Disney's first feature, *Snow White and the Sesven Dwarfs*, contains such classics as 'Someday My Prince Will Come' and 'Whistle While You Work'. These melodies were written by Frank Churchill, who composed the score of *Three Little Pigs* and a number of other 'Silly Symphony' shorts, as well as that of *Bambi* (directed by David Hand, 1942). Another valuable musician at the Disney Studio was Leigh Harline, who scored the music of many 'Silly Symphony' shorts, as well as *Pinocchio* (directed by Ben Sharpsteen and Hamilton Luske, 1940).

Increasingly, Disney's marketing of film music became more focused. In 1949, the first offering of the newly established Walt Disney Music Company was from the yet-to-be-released feature film, *Cinderella* (directed by Wilfred Jackson, 1950). After developing other music-related companies, in 1990 the Walt Disney Company consolidated all of its labels under the name of Walt Disney Records. Many of its releases have been immensely successful: to take but one example, the soundtrack of *The Lion King* (directed by Roger Allers, 1994), with more than seven million copies sold, was the best-selling album of 1994. During the 1990s, some of the company's most popular music was written by Alan Menken, Howard Ashman, and Tim Rice.

Danny Elfman, who gained fame as the leader of the band Oingo Boingo, is one of the most successful musicians to venture into the production of animation soundtracks. Elfman is well known for creating the theme music for 'The Simpsons', as well as the songs and scores for a number of feature films. His work on *The Nightmare Before Christmas* (directed by Henry Selick, 1993) marked his fifth collaboration with the film's director, Tim Burton. Elfman also provided voices for characters in the film and produced the film's album.

Like other aspects of animation production, sound composition and recording varies greatly depending on its production context. During the 1930s and 1940s, budgets and time schedules were nowhere near as generous as they have been for such composers as Menken, Ashman, Rice and Elfman. The Fleischer Studios (and later the Famous Studios) employed a musical director named Sammy Timberg, who said he 'worked with the artists from the first drawings to the end. I would do maybe forty pictures a year ... it was a challenge'[47] (ellipses in original). Timberg worked on short films, including the 'Betty Boop', 'Popeye', and 'Superman' series, as well as such features as *Gulliver's Travels* (directed by Dave Fleischer, 1939) and *Mr. Bug Goes to Town* (aka: Hoppity Goes to Town, directed by Dave Fleischer, 1941). Later in his career, he spent four years working for Columbia's animation studio, Screen Gems.

The situation was not much different for Carl Stalling at Warner Bros. After a few years at the Disney and Iwerks Studios, Stalling moved to Warner Bros. and composed scores for hundreds of animated shorts, generally working within a very short time frame. His work in animation was aided by his experience as a silent movie accompanist. As Daniel Goldmark notes:

> Accompanists, more often than not, had to create spontaneous scores for films, assisted only by thematic musical catalogs. These books would have well-known material arranged for piano and indexed according to the mood or ideas with which they were most often associated. Stalling's job was more of a pastiche artist [someone who pastes things together in an artistic way] than a composer, as he had to create a musical narrative with a wide array of genres, including folk, classical, Tin Pan Alley, and big band, among others. When he went to Warner Bros., this skill came in very handy.[48]

Today, television series continue to be produced under smaller budgets and shorter working schedules than those of feature films; naturally, the restrictions of the production context affect the way in which their sound elements are produced as well.

One way in which producers have been able to minimise costs and production time is through an increased reliance on computer technologies. In a 1997 article on 'The Ink and Paint of Music', composer Amin Bhatia explained the way in which he employs digital audio, samplers and a musical instrument digital interface (MIDI) system to create music for animated productions.[49] He explains:

> The process of initial writing is a slow and laborious process. It begins with meetings and spotting sessions with the producers, who determine the overall style of the music, be it orchestral, rock, ethnic, country ... From these meetings, one runs back to the hovel of a MIDI studio and experiments with themes, variations, ideas and anything that strikes a fancy.[50]

Bhatia says that, after playing these trials back to the producer and receiving his or her consent on the style and themes:

> ... the actual writing of music to picture begins. In live action, one waits until the picture is 'locked' and there are no more edits in show timing. In animation, the picture is usually the last thing to show up! In my work with Nelvana, I start by reading storyboards and listening to a prerecorded dialogue track that has beeps to tell me where in the storyboard I am. From this I can time out my scenes and organise my computer metronome track to block out the beats and bars of music I have to write to. The picture itself is being rendered and colored in another department across town, or sometimes overseas. I don't get to check my work against picture until two days before the final mix of music, dialogue and sound effects.[51]

Within this general work mode, there are many smaller steps. For example, Bhatia begins with a 'skeleton sketch', which he says is equivalent to an animator's pencil-sketch line drawings: he uses 'only one or two synthesizers to flesh out the actual melody and make sure it works to the picture timings. Working with a MIDI sequencer is akin to a word processor. You can juggle notes and tempo about, just like words and fonts, and never commit to anything till you finally "print" it to tape'.[52] After the skeleton sketch is satisfactory, he adds woodwinds, strings, brass and percussion – taking hours to add all the necessary instruments.

Bhatia explains that he does not do his work alone. In fact, a company he works with, Magnetic Music, takes over the final mixing of the music. He says:

> ... after I've finished writing, I entrust the staff at Magnetic to do the final mix of all the various audio tracks (never mix your own music), which can have as many as 40 different synthesizer sources. Nelvana's producers are present during this ... if something 'feels wrong' to them, everything grinds to a halt. I dash to the computer to rewrite sections of music ...[53]

The final step in the process is the music mix, when sound effects, dialogue and music are blended together.

Bhatia's employment of the latest technologies might make his work seem quite removed from that of composers during the 1930s and 1940s. However, he acknowledges strong ties with that period, specifically to the work of Carl Stalling. Bhatia writes that Stalling:

> ... defined the all too well-known musical style of playing every visual gag with a musical sound effect. Whether it be a group of plucked violins tiptoeing across the screen in perfect sync, or the suprise 'oh no' orchestral phrases that preceded every exploding Acme device, Carl and his peers created a set of musical rules ... I've seen cases where producers of a new series ... will plan for an audio track that uses sound effects and underscore in a conventional live-action approach. Yet, when the show is previewed, the inevitable request comes through to 'make the

music busier' ... 'play the gags' ... 'it's missing something' ... All this is Carl's fault![54]

What Bhatia's remarks make clear is that an aesthetic analysis must take into account not only the current state of production processes, but also the history that has affected dominant conventions. Like the visuals of a film, many people influence the development of a soundtrack – people not only of the present but also of the past.

Undoubtedly Stalling's 'gag' musical notations have had such a lasting impact due to the fact that one of the enduring narrative structures of animation is also the gag structure. The remaining portion of this chapter will overview variations in narrative and non-narrative structures which, along with music, greatly influence the cohesiveness of an animated production as a whole work.

STRUCTURAL DESIGN

Live-action performance and animation can be employed for a variety of purposes. For the most part, this book focuses on one category of animated production, films and videos made primarily for entertainment or as some form of personal expression. Most of these productions employ a narrative structure; that is, they tell stories with a beginning, middle and end. However, the structure of an animation production can be quite different if its primary purpose is to advertise a product or serve as a documentary or instructional aid.

Any analysis of the structural design of a work should consider first its primary function. Is it to entertain a wide audience? Is it to experiment and uncover new techniques or ways of thinking? Is it to relate information in a clear, methodical manner? Each of these functions can affect the extent to which narrative or non-narrative structures are used within a work.

During the silent era of animation, a gag structure – one funny incident after another, with little or no plot development – already was considered the most commercially desirable formula for entertainment purposes. Margaret Winkler, the successful distributor of 'Felix the Cat', 'Out of the Inkwell', and 'Alice Comedy' films, saw humour as being the ingredient of primary importance – a philosophy that was carried on by her husband, Charles Mintz, who took over the business.[55] For example, Russell Merritt and J.B. Kaufman have noted that the distributor threatened to reject Disney's *Alice Chops the Suey* (1926) because 'it has too much story and lacks in gags'.[56]

Gags provide small units of action that do not require sustained concentration on the part of audience members or the retention of narrative information over a long duration of time. Instead, gags bombard audiences with aural and visual information intended to sustain laughter. The gags appearing in animation can be seen as an equivalent to the slapstick comedies of the Mack Sennet studio or individuals known for their physical humour, such as Charlie Chaplin and Buster Keaton. Eventually, storylines made a stronger presence at Disney and throughout the animation industry, following the norm set by live-action films; however, gags have continued to provide a popular format for animated productions.

Even when a motion picture is heavily reliant on a gag structure, almost without exception it also will include some kind of 'narrative thread', or story, that holds the gags together. In live-action and animated productions, this structure is most often linear in nature, with a beginning, middle, and end that progresses in a forward trajectory. In *The Classical Hollywood Cinema: Film Style and Mode of Production to*

1960, David Bordwell explains that the classical model of cinema requires all actions to be united through a cause-and-effect relationship, and to lead toward a unified conclusion, or closure of the plot.[57]

In a textbook on scriptwriting, Dwight V. Swain argues that every film story must have a:

> ... beginning, middle and end ... The *beginning* establishes your character within the framework of his predicament ... The *middle* reveals the various steps of Character's struggle to defeat the danger that threatens him ... The *end* sees the Character win or lose the battle. Remember, in this regard, the story doesn't truly end until the struggle between desire and danger is resolved, with some kind of clear-cut triumph.[58] (emphasis in original)

Although Swain's book refers to live-action films, the same principles can be applied to commercial animation, which also follows the classical formula.[59] Conventionally structured films are enjoyable to most people because they allow viewers to anticipate events and their outcomes, and feel gratified when they occur.[60] Additionally, linear structures are enjoyable because they conform to the ideology of a work ethic: moving forward, achieving goals and making progress.

A number of individuals have developed methods to illustrate storytelling formulas at an even more detailed level. Vladimir Propp is among those who suggested that all stories can be described as derivations of a set number of conventional scenarios.[61] Taking folktales as his focus, he identified 31 functions performed within a narrative that, when they occur, can be found in a fixed sequence. He also described seven 'spheres of action' in the form of character attributes, such as 'the villain' or 'the helper'. Although Propp's method of structural analysis has not had a deep impact on media analysis, his theories have been employed in some studies of narrative structure, particularly in terms of live-action feature films.[62]

Some filmmakers have developed methods of analysing narrative elements within their own work. For example, the Fleischer Studio created a 'Story Mood Chart' to

Fig. 5.4 Mr. Bug Goes to Town *promotional material* Bugville Buzz Roto Section, *courtesy the Museum of Modern Art, New York*

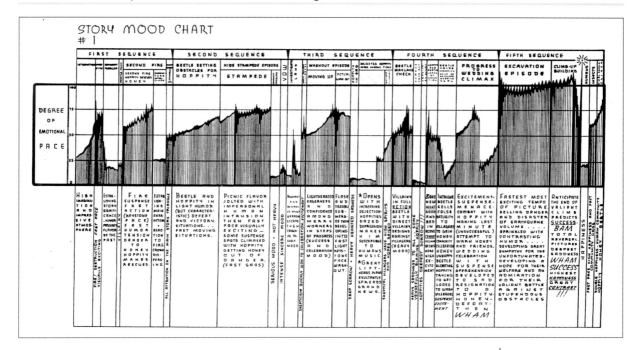

Fig. 5.5 Mr. Bug Goes
to Town *story mood chart*
Courtesy William Moritz

illustrate the 'degree of emotional pace' in its feature, *Mr. Bug Goes to Town*. A sort
of bar chart reflects the rise and fall of emotion throughout the film, with the high
point occurring in fifth sequence's 'Excavation Episode' and subsequent 'Climb Up
Building', which is followed by a rapid *denouement*, or decline in dramatic action.
Norman McLaren used a different kind of visual chart to illustrate the development
of action and emotion in *A Chairy Tale* (1957). A series of abstract images represent
these and other acts: '... chair blocks man, sustained tension while man searches for
solution, the solution strikes, happiness, certainty, ceremonious squat, chair joyous,
then doubtful, man is worried ...'[63]

The dominance of linear narratives worldwide has been so extreme that it can be
difficult to conceive of alternative modes of expression as having any widespread
appeal. Nonetheless, a number of alternatives exist. An artist can utilise an alternate
structure for the purpose of disturbing a viewer's sense of equilibrium, or perhaps
because he or she believes it is difficult to portray an alternative vision of the world
by using dominant forms of communication. Two terms, 'cyclical' and 'thematic',
are useful for describing some alternatives to a linear structure.

A cyclical structure does not reach a conclusion but rather comes back to its beginning.
This type of structure sometimes is employed in works that deal with traditional
myths or natural occurrences, such as life and death or the changing of seasons. A
cyclical structure does not provide pleasure in the way that a linear one does: there
is no goal to achieve, less emphasis on expectation and fulfillment, and no closure to
signify an end to the experience. Its strength is in showing unity and renewal, as
opposed to consumption.

One artist who is known for employing cyclical structures is Faith Hubley. Joanna
Priestly explains that Hubley's work is 'based in myth, poetry, music, dance and
reverence for all life. Pictographic, iconographic humans, animals and dreamshapes
cavort in organic, watercolor environments. There are no plots'.[64] Hubley depicts

cycles in her work because it reflects something she finds in nature, and in connection with:

> ... ancient traditions of loving and honoring the Earth ... the tribal fragments that form her films coalesce like the simple patterns of our lives: sleep, eat, work, eat, work, exercise, eat, relax, sleep. Our lives are cycles of weeks, months, years, of traffic, of friendship, of menstruation, of weather, of depression and of joy. They never become the linear, Hollywood narratives that some of us fantasize about.[65]

A highly unusual structure that provides a variation on cyclical storytelling can be found in the work of Dutch animator Paul Driessen. His film *The End of the World in Four Seasons* (1995), made at the National Film Board of Canada, contains a number of windows in which actions occur largely in repeated patterns. As its title suggests, the film moves through four separate seasons of the year, each with its own series of humorous events. Sometimes the viewer realises that

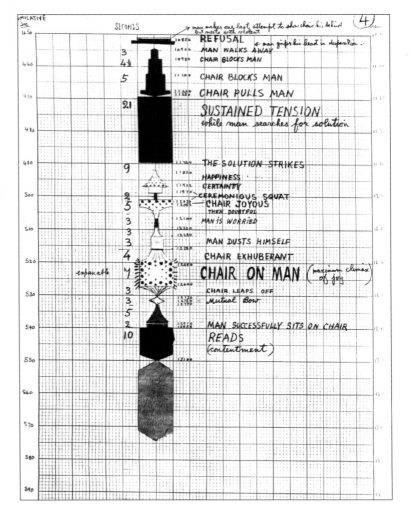

Fig. 5.6 (facing left)
Multiple frames from A
Chairy Tale *(1957) by
Norman McLaren*
Courtesy NFB

**Fig. 5.7 (facing
bottom)** *Chart from*
A Chairy Tale
Courtesy NFB

Fig. 5.8 (left) The End
of the World in Four
Seasons *(1995) by Paul
Driessen*
Courtesy NFB

an incident occurring in one window in fact has a relationship to something in another window; for example, an apple falling from a tree in one frame is seen, drawn in a different scale, hitting the ground within another frame. However, the relationship between the nine or so simultaneous events often is ambiguous. Sound elements and the timing of action subtly direct the viewer to images on the screen, but largely each of the frames vie for attention at the same time. Nonetheless, all actions are united by the cyclical concept of the seasons.

In a similar vein, a number of artists have created 'compilation films' uniting a series of vignettes created by different artists into a single work. Falling within this category is American David Ehrlich's *Academy Leader Variations* (1987), a 6½-minute film composed of artists' variations on the standard 'countdown' leader found on a reel of film. Among the other animators who participated in this ASIFA-sponsored project are Jane Aaron, Skip Battaglia, Paul Glabicki, George Griffin, and Al Jarnow of the United States; Jerszy Kucia, Piotre Dumala, Krzysztof Kiwerski, and Stanislaw Lenartowicz of Poland; George Schwizgebel, Claude Luyet, Daniel Suter, and Martial Wannaz of Switzerland; and A Da, Yan Ding Xian, Hu Jing Qing, Lin Wen Xiao, He Yu Men and Chang Guang Xi of China.

A thematic structure creates an experience that can be quite different than that of a linear or cyclical production. Rather than moving forward, or even in a repeated pattern, thematic works tend toward stasis. In that respect, they can be described as meditative or poetic in nature, exploring an experience, emotion or other abstract concept in depth. They also tend to be highly subjective and often rely on abstract imagery, which might provide the only means of expressing an ineffable notion. However, even in relatively thematic works, there can be a sense of building toward a final moment in the film; for example, the meditational, relatively abstract films

Fig. 5.9 (top) *Design for*
Allures (1961) and
Fig. 5.10 (bottom) *from*
Caravan (1952) by
Jordan Belson, depicting
circular mandala images
Collection of the artist

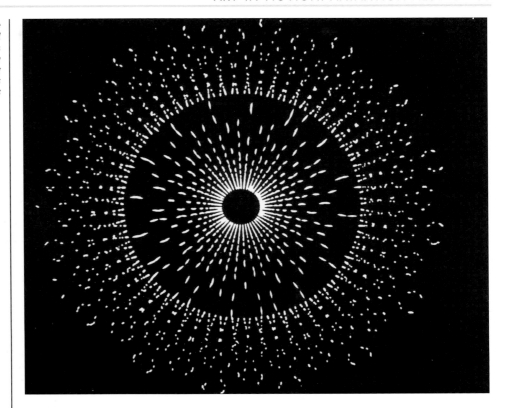

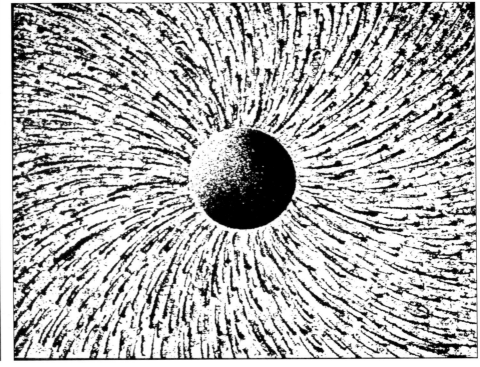

of Jordan Belson generally conclude with a circular mandala image that can be said to depict a state of enlightenment (see also CP 16).

The variations in structural models described here sometimes can be seen as operating in conjunction with one another. For example, McLaren's *A Chairy Tale* is in most respects a linear tale, because it tells the story of how a man deals with the problem of a renegade chair; he confronts the problem and ultimately reaches his goal. On the other hand, the concept of the film can be said to revolve around a central act or idea: an attempt to sit in a chair, which involves both 'frustration' and 'the need to understand one another'. In following this rather narrow subject matter, *A Chairy Tale* could be considered somewhat thematic in its structure. Compilation films, too, often display attributes of more than one type of structure, since segments may be cyclical or linear, but typically they are unified by one particular theme around which all segments are all based.

The real benefit of identifying the structural model(s) operating in a film is that it reveals the general way in which information is organised. Linear, cyclical and thematic models provide different means of relating information and, consequently, require the viewer to participate in different kinds of perceptual experiences. Depending on one's background and expectations, these models can be viewed as aesthetically pleasing or undesirable; however, they all represent viable ways of structuring a motion picture.

The structure employed in a work is affected by its purpose, as well as many other aspects of its production context, such as the year in which it was made and the exhibition requirements of that time. During the mid- to late-1940s, advertisements used on television might have run for three minutes, but soon they were standardised to one minute in length. It was not until the early 1980s that shorter formats, running from ten seconds to thirty seconds, became more the norm. Changes in length affect the speed at which information must be presented and, therefore, the structure of the work.

Whether an animated series is made for television or for theatrical release also affects the running time and the way in which a plot must be structured. American animated shorts shown in theatres averaged seven minutes throughout the 1930s and 1940s. However, the lengths of American made-for-televison productions of the late 1950s varied due to differences in exhibition practices. For example, 'Crusader Rabbit' (1949–1951) cartoons were made into four-minute segments that could be combined in one day's programming or run separately on different days, depending on a station's programming needs.[66]

The somewhat longer episodes shown on American television today are generally structured so that commercial breaks can be worked in. For that reason, a 'half hour' show actually runs about twenty-two minutes in length. To accomodate commercials, a series of plot build-ups and resuming actions are included in the script; dramatic peaks must occur before the breaks to assure that the viewer will return to watch the program.

Other circumstances result in very different structural requirements. For instance, made-for-television animated programs created where television is state sponsored might be free of commercial breaks that otherwise affect the development of narratives. Another consideration is that broadcast times across the world are not standardised. In the United States, television programs appear in half-hour and one-hour time increments (including commercial breaks), but in England, broadcasters air ten-minute animated shorts, true half-hour programs (fitting into 30-minute windows, without room for commercial breaks), or shows of other lengths.

These differences can complicate international distribution. For example, the immensely popular British series of 'Wallace & Gromit' films produced by Aardman Animations run just under 30 minutes in length, which means they work well for British television but not for American broadcasting. It is relatively difficult to show the films in the United States because they are not 22-minutes long, the length required in order to fit in commercials.

There are of course an infinite number of factors that can affect the mise-en-scène, the sound, and the structure of animated productions. However, it is now time to turn to more focused aesthetic analyses. The next chapter will examine one company that has been extremely influential in the realm of commercially produced animation. Having a broad background in aesthetics will allow the reader to see better how this organisation, The Walt Disney Company, has impacted the aesthetics of animation.

Notes

1. Part of the reason that sound is overlooked is due to some long-standing prejudices that have prioritised visuals over sound. In a 1988 article entitled 'Animation is a Visual Medium', Charles Solomon articulated this point of view when he said 'perhaps the greatest weakness of many recent animated features and television programs has been the failure of the writers and directors to recognise the essentially visual nature of the medium'. Charles Solomon, 'Animation is a Visual Medium', in John Canemaker (ed.) *Storytelling in Animation: The Art of the Animated Image* (Los Angeles: The American Film Institute, 1988), 93.
2. David Bordwell and Kristin Thompson, *Film Art: An Introduction* (New York: McGraw-Hill, 1997), 318–319.
3. Ibid., 318.
4. Ibid., 319.
5. For practical and theoretical discussions related to sound recording and aesthetics, see Rick Altman, editor of *Sound Theory/Sound Practice* (London: Routledge, 1992).
6. Scott Curtis, 'The Sound of the Early Warner Bros. Cartoons', in Rick Altman (ed.) *Sound Theory/Sound Practice* (New York: Routledge, 1992), 191–203.
7. *Fleischer Manual*, 42. A copy of the manual is located the Museum of Modern Art. The author's copy was given to her by J.J. Sedelmaier.
8. Ibid., 46.
9. Ibid., 47.
10. Curtis suggests that the unnatural voices of cartoon characters can be thought of as analogous to the characters' 'distorted' and 'elastic' bodies. Curtis, op cit., 202.
11. Joe Bevilacqua, 'Voice Acting 101', *Animation World Magazine* 2, 1 (April 1997).
12. Bob Bergen, quoted in Bevilacqua, 'Voice Acting 101', op cit.
13. Vern Louden, quoted in Fred Patton, 'Some Notes on "Crusader Rabbit" ', *Animatrix* 6 (1990–1992): 29–36, 33.
14. Bevilacqua, op. cit.
15. Jerry Roberts, 'Thesps are Drawn to Toontown', *Variety* (19–25 May 1997): 40+.
16. Barbara Wright, quoted in Roberts, op. cit., 40.
17. Corey Buron, quoted in Bevilacqua, op. cit. He notes that multi-voiced performers draw inspiration from the script. In other words, in the traditional approach, voice talent creates characters based on the writing, whereas the practice of using established live-action stars reverses the process; writers instead rely on the voice talent for the development of characters.
18. Lee Harris, quoted in Bevilacqua, op. cit.

19. Corey Buron, quoted in Bevilacqua, 'Voice Acting 101', *Animation World Magazine* 2, 1 (April 1997).

20. Bevilacqua, op. cit.

21. Practices related to the dubbing of Japanese animation into English-language versions is discussed Bob Miller, 'U.S. Renditions: Dubbing for Dollars', *Animato!* 27 (Fall/Winter 1993): 16–17+.

22. Karl Cohen, 'Racism and Resistance: Black Stereotypes in Animation', *Animation Journal* (Spring 1996): 43–68. For information on the career of June Foray, see Michelle Klein-Häss, 'Faces Behind the Voice: June Foray – Queen of Cartoons', *Animato!* 30 (Fall 1994): 18–20. Later, the 'Tom and Jerry' series was taken over by Rembrandt Releases (1961–1962) and Sib-Tower 12 Productions Releases (1963–1967). For details, see Jeff Lenburg, *The Encyclopedia of Animated Cartoons* (New York: Facts on File, 1991), 131–133.

23. Chuck Jones, quoted in Leonard Maltin (1980), *Of Mice and Magic: A History of American Animated Cartoons* (New York: New American Library, 1987), 266.

24. Id.

25. Jon Newsom, 'A Sound Idea: Music for Animated Films', *The Quarterly Journal of the Library of Congress* 37, 3–4 (Summer–Fall 1980): 283–309, 284.

26. In an unpublished essay on the film, Christine Ferriter asserts, 'even though Hoppin was given equal billing with Gross on all the films they made together, it becomes evident by looking at the surviving sketches and storyboards that Gross was the creative half of the partnership, while Hoppin contributed to the mass-production of drawings, and had a working knowledge of still and movie cameras'. In making this remark, she cites David Curtis, 'The Animated Films', *Anthony Gross* (Hampshire, England: Scholar Press, 1992). Christine Ferriter, '*La Joie de vivre*: Animation within an Artistic Historical Context', unpublished essay written at California Institute of the Arts (11 Feb. 1993).

27. Ferriter, ibid.

28. Tibor Harsányi, '*La Joie de vivre*: divertissement cinématographique' (Paris: Editions Maurice Senart, 1934), noted in Newsom, op. cit., xx.

29. Ibid.

30. Two articles by Richard E. Cytowic explain synaesthesia in more detail. See Richard E. Cytowic, 'What Shape is that Taste?', *The Independent on Sunday* (13 Feb. 1994): 52, 54; and Cytowic, 'Tasting Colors, Smelling Sounds: Neurological Clues to a Confounding Condition', *The Sciences* (Sept./Oct. 1988): 32–37.

31. Norman McLaren, quoted in Donald McWilliams (ed.), *Norman McLaren on the Creative Process* (Montreal: National Film Board of Canada, 1991), 34. This 1968 quote is included in a section of the book entitled 'A Synaesthetic Story', 34–35.

32. Norman McLaren, in personal papers provided by Donald McWilliams.

33. Id.

34. Id.

35. In 1984, Norman McLaren completed technical notes for his productions while he was at the National Film Board of Canada, which continues to distribute them today. McLaren categorises his use of music in these notes. He includes 'films with music', 'music came before pix', 'music came after pix', 'music & pix together', and 'films without music'.

36. The German animator Oskar Fischinger is another individual who conducted early experiments with animated sound.

37. An *International Sound Technician* article recalls that 'the Fantasound track contained three 200-mil push–pull program tracks and one 200-mil push–pull control track. These were all printed on a separate 35 mm photographic film and run in interlock with the projector. Each of the three program tracks was transmitted through a variable gain amplifier. The gain of each of these amplifiers was automatically controlled by one of the three frequencies recorded on the control track', which ran next to the sprocket holes. C.O. Slyfield, 'Sound in Animated Motion Pictures', *International Sound Technician* (ca. 1952): 2–5.

38. During the early 1990s the studio began work on a new version of the film, which contains a combination of footage from the original *Fantasia* as well as newly created material. The plan is to release the film, *Fantasia 2000*, on the New Year's Eve of the new century.

39. Although it is relatively rare to find experimental uses of music within the commerical Hollywood industry, occasional references to experimental techniques can be found. For example, Scott Bradley, who composed scores for the 'Tom and Jerry' series, discusses one solution to his search for 'funny music' to accompany a humorous sequence involving the cat and mouse team. He says: 'I was stuck for a new way of describing the action musically, and for a whole day I worried about a two-measure phrase. Everything I tired seemed weak and common. Finally, I tried the twelve-tone scale [i.e. a row], and *there it was!* ... I hope Dr. Schoenberg will forgive me for using *his system* to produce funny music, but even the boys in the orchestra laughed when we were recording it.' The twelve-tone system developed by Schoenberg was considered an avant-garde approach to 'serious' music composition. Scott Bradly, quoted from 'Music in Cartoons: Excerpts from a talk given at the Music Forum, October 28, 1944', *Film Music Notes* 4 (Dec. 1944): n.p., in Newsom, 'A Sound Idea: Music for Animated Films', op cit., 293. For more on Bradley, see 'Scoring for Cartoons: An Interview with Scott Bradley', *Pacific Coast Musician* (15 May 1937); Chuck Jones, 'Music and the Animated Cartoon', *Hollywood Quarterly* (1945–1946): 364–370, 370.

40. Jones, 'Music and the Animated Cartoon', op cit., 365. In Jones's view, one of the most successful weddings of sound and image can be found in *Fantasia*: in 1945, he described what he believed might be 'the happiest, most perfect single sequence ever done in animated cartoons, perhaps in motion pictures: the little mushroom dance from the *Nutcracker Suite*. Here was an instance of almost pure delight; again, an entrancing blend of the eye and the ear in which I found the music itself personified on the screen'.

41. Ibid., 364.

42. Curtis, op. cit. The Fleischer manual also encourages such rhythmic animation, noting that every foot of film contains 16 frames, which is convenient for measuring music that runs in phrases of 8 and 16 beats. Every 1½ feet in length, which is one second at sound speed, contains 24 frames.

43. Curtis also explains that technological limitations greatly influenced the way in which sound was used. The Vitaphone sound-on-disk system in use at Warner Bros. until 1933 did not allow for various tracks to be used, so all sound elements had to be recorded at one time. If sound and dialogue were to occur simultaneously, they had to be recorded through the 'playback' system of placing music in the background while dialogue was being spoken. However, this system did not result in a high-enough quality of music for use in music-driven motion pictures. As a result, one can hear that music will take a pause when dialogue or a sound effect occurs. Curtis notes that, in the manner of silent film production, effects often were performed by musicians. Curtis, op. cit., 193.

44. In the Warner Bros. studio, the 'Looney Tunes' and 'Merry Melodies' series often are thought to be similarly distinguishable, although Curtis makes interesting observations related to the actual recording of music for the two series, concluding that there were actually quite a few similarities in the ways music fit into the production process of both series. He finds that 'ostensibly, the Warner Bros. series split worked on the same principle as Disney's, that is, action taking precedence in the "Looney Tunes" and music guiding action in the "Merrie Melodies". But the actual scoring of the cartoons (and close listening) blurs the distinction between them'.

 He also indicates that, while most of the music for the 'Looney Tunes' series was recorded after the production of images, the music director was still consulted at the beginning of the process, so that timing could be indicated on sheets of written music, 'indicating so many frames for each action. This action was coordinated with the bars of music and the timing was then transferred from the music sheets to exposure sheets, from which animators drew and exposed the requisite number of pictures'. Curtis, op cit., 194–195.

45. J.B. Kaufman, 'Who's Afraid of ASCAP? Popular Songs in the Silly Symphonies', *Animation World Magazine* 2, 1 (April 1997).

46. Ibid. Sheet music for this song and subsequent Disney melodies was published by the Irving Berlin Music Corporation.

47. Anonymous, 'A Tribute to Sammy Timberg, 1903–1992', *The World Animation Celebration* program (24–30 March 1997): 70–71; see also G. Michael Dobbs, 'Sammy Timberg: From Tin Pan Alley to Aniation Cel', *Animato!* 33 (Fall 1995): 42–43.

48. Daniel Goldmark, 'Carl Stalling and Humor in Cartoons', *Animation World Magazine* 2, 1 (April 1997).

49. Amin Bhatia, 'The Ink and Paint of Music', *Animation World Magazine* 2, 1 (April 1997).

50. Id.

51. Id.

52. Id.

53. Id.

54. Id.

55. See Russell Merritt and J.B. Kaufman (1992), *Walt in Wonderland: The Silent Films of Walt Disney* (Baltimore: Johns Hopkins, 1993), 15.

56. Charles Mintz, quoted in Merritt and Kaufman, op. cit., 16.

57. David Bordwell, Janet Staiger and Kristin Thompson, *The Classical Hollywood Cinema: Film Style and Mode of Production to 1960* (New York: Columbia UP, 1985), 13.

58. Dwight V. Swain, *Film Scriptwriting: A Practical Manual* (NY: Hastings House, 1977), 90.

59. David Bordwell and Janet Staiger write: 'The classical style extends its influence to other filmmaking domains as well. It has changed the history of animation; Walt Disney build his career upon transposing the narrative and stylistic principles of classical cinema into animated film.' Bordwell and Staiger, 'Alternative Modes of Film Practice', *The Classical Hollywood Cinema*, op. cit., 379.

60. People constantly classify information in order to make sense of their experiences. Joanna Macy explains this process in terms of positive and negative feedback by writing, 'where percepts match code, that is where the incoming data is meaningful in terms of the constructs by which we organise our experience, we respond in such a way as to perpetuate this match. That is, in effect, the operation of negative feedback, and by means of that the cognitive system stabilises itself – the world makes sense'. Joanna Macy, *Mutual Causality in Buddhism and General Systems Theory: The Dharma of Natural Systems* (Albany, NY: State University of New York, 1991), 83.

61. Vladimor Propp, *The Morphology of the Folktale* (Austin: University of Texas Press, 1973). For another example, in 1921, George Polti described 36 basic dramatic situations, based on fundamental human emotions, that he believed underlie all literary works. George Polti (1921), *The Thirty-Six Dramatic Situations* (Boston: The Writer, 1986).

62. For example, see Peter Wollen, 'North by Northwest: A Morphological Analysis', *Readings and Writings* (London: Verso, 1982). This essay and its use of Propp's model is discussed in Robert Lapsley and Michael Westlake, *Film Theory: An Introduction* (Manchester: Manchester University Press, 1994), 131–134.

63. Norman McLaren, visual chart of action in *A Chairy Tale* (1957), available from the National Film Board of Canada.

64. Joanna Priestley, 'Creating a Healing Mythology: The Art of Faith Hubley', *Animation Journal* 2, 2 (Spring 1994): 23–31, 25.

65. Ibid., 28.

66. Additional 'Crusader Rabbit' shorts were produced between 1957 and 1959.

6

Classical-era Disney Studio

OVERVIEW OF DISNEY'S EARLY YEARS

When most people think of animation, one of the first names that comes to mind is The Walt Disney Company. Although Disney animation makes up only a small percentage of animation created internationally throughout history, it is imperative to study this studio and understand how widespread its influence has been. Regarding the live-action Hollywood film industry, David James has observed that 'in no other medium has a single practice been able to produce itself so entirely normatively';[1] however, Disney can top that in the realm of animation. It is safe to say that in no other medium has a single *company's* practices been able to dominate aesthetic norms to the extent that Disney's has.

This chapter will overview aesthetic and promotional strategies employed by The Walt Disney Company, focusing primarily on the company's early years, from the 1920s through the 1930s. In addition, some attention will be given to a transitional period in the studio's history, which occurred during the 1940s. There have been many books and articles written about The Walt Disney Company, so readers should have no trouble finding additonal information on the studio to supplement the relatively limited amount of material presented here.

A number of sources have recounted the ways in which Walt Disney got started in the animation business. He was born in Chicago, but grew up in Kansas City. After beginning a job at Kansas City Film Ad Service in 1920, Disney set up his own studio to begin animating 'Newman Laugh-O-gram' films for a local theatre chain; the

**Figs 6.1 (a) & (b) (right
& opposite)** *Disney
opened his own studio
in 1920 to begin
animating the 'Newman
Laugh-O-gram' series*

series featured animated advertisements in addition to short subjects of topical
interest. In 1922, he quit Kansas City Film Ad Service and opened his own studio,
which he named Laugh-O-gram Films, Inc. At this studio, he employed a number
of individuals who eventually would be big names in the animation industry,
including Hugh Harman, Rudolf Ising, and Ub Iwerks.[2] Among the animation
produced there were a number of films based on traditional stories, such as *Little Red
Riding Hood*, *Puss in Boots*, and *Cinderella* (all 1922).

By the early 1920s, the American animation industry was relatively well established.
Despite the fact that animation was largely dismissed as 'filler items' on a theatre
program, a number of series began to set themselves apart, the most significant being
the 'Felix the Cat' and 'Out of the Inkwell' (starring Koko the Clown) films produced
by Pat Sullivan and Max Fleischer, respectively. Both series were produced under
contract with the most successful animation distributor at that time, Margaret
Winkler, whose office was located in New York City. At this point, virtually all the
major motion picture studios (including those producing animation) were located
in New York and New Jersey, although many of them eventually moved to Southern
California.

The film that really helped Walt Disney to make a name for himself was *Alice's
Wonderland* (1923; aka: Alice in Slumberland, 1926). It was completed in 1923, shortly
before he moved to California, where his brother Roy was living. This film featured
Virginia Davis in the role of Alice, a live-action girl who lives in an animated

environment; in later episodes, she was joined by an animated side-kick cat, Julius. Disney's scenario provided a variation on the Fleischer Studio's 'Out of the Inkwell' series, in which an animated character, Koko the Clown, lives in the real world. *Alice's Wonderland* and subsequent films in the 'Alice Comedies' series also varied in that they starred a female character, while virtually all other series centred on males. Disney produced *Alice's Wonderland* with the hope of securing representation by Winkler, which apparently came after she had a disagreement with Sullivan and felt it wise to take on another property.[3] Disney signed a contract for a series of 'Alice Comedies' on 16 October 1923. His company had been in financial trouble and Winkler's contract provided him with some much-needed support.

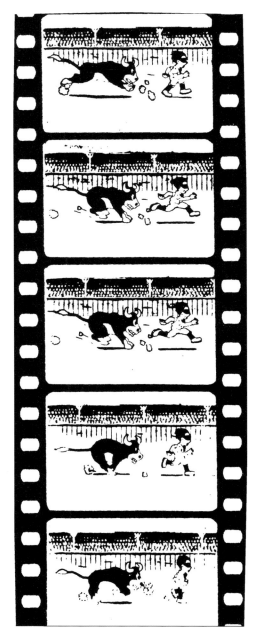

Aesthetically, the 'Alice Comedies' series (1924–1927) have much to tell about the times in which they were made. Their structure reflects what Winkler saw as a successful formula of the day, constant gags with little emphasis on plot development. Apparently, a statement made in reference to the first film in the series, *Alice's Day at Sea* (1924), is typical of her attitude: 'I would suggest you inject as much humor as you can. Humor is the first requisite of short subjects such as Felix, Out of the Inkwell, and Alice.'[4] Winkler is credited as editor on the first five 'Alice Comedies' because she decided to recut Disney's version of them at her New York office, ostensibly to tighten the gag structure.

Winkler's influence on the series is clearly indicated through a number of contacts she made with Disney. For example, after she saw a print of *Alice's Day at Sea* in December 1923, she sent Disney a telegram, asking 'him to ship all of his positive and negative raw footage. "We believe same can possibly be improved by re-editing here ... All our films are recut in New York".'[5] On 21 January 1924, Disney wrote to Winkler, saying that the negative and print of *Alice Hunting in Africa* had been shipped 'together with all cut-outs, both negative and positive'; he added, 'I sincerely believe I have made a great deal of improvement on this subject in the line of humorous situations and I assure you that I will make it a point to inject as many funny gags and comical situations into future productions as possible.'[6]

However, the next month Disney was again writing, 'I am trying to comply with your instructions by injecting as much humor as possible and believe I have done better on this production'.[7] He notes that his work had been viewed by 'professional critics' and optimistically adds that it is his 'desire to be a little different from the usual run of slapstick and hold them to a more dignified line of comedy.'[8] By 'dignified', Disney probably was referring to his desire for increased plot development, which would not come for a number of years – not until he had broken ties with Winkler's company, some time after the 'Alice Comedies' series had ended.

Nonetheless, a viewer can find that there are changes in narrative elements as the series progresses. In later years, Alice becomes increasingly marginalised within the films, revealing that the incorporation of the live-action girl into the storyline and visuals was more problematic than creating the animated environment on its own. Russell Merritt and J.B. Kaufman speculate that the live-action and animated material was combined in various ways, sometimes through a matte process and other times through double exposure, but in any case, that the procedure was difficult and often unsatisfactory. They also suggest that subsequent Alice performers (there were four altogether) lacked the talent of the original actress, Virginia Davis, so in later films there was added incentive to keep the part of Alice to a minimum.[9]

Given the marginalisation of Alice within the narratives and the Disney Studio's increased emphasis on animated content, it is not surprising that, in 1927, the 'Alice Comedies' began to loose steam. To replace the series, Disney designed another original character, Oswald the Lucky Rabbit, who would appear in a wholly animated series (1928 under Disney; 1928–1938 under Walter Lantz); this character has been described as a transition between Julius (from the 'Alice Comedies') and Mickey Mouse.[10] Oswald was an overnight success as a film star and proved profitable for spin-off merchandising as well.

This turn of events proved to have both good and bad consequences for Disney. The series' distributor, Charles Mintz, who had married Margaret Winkler and taken over the business, had become more powerful and was able to begin releasing Disney's work through Universal, one of Hollywood's larger studios. In 1928, the 'Oswald' property proved so attractive that Mintz edged Disney out of the business and continued producing the series for Universal himself. Disney had not owned the rights to the character, so he was in no position to contest demands made by Mintz, who had managed to lure Hugh Harman and a number of other animators away from the studio to work on the series for him. Although this situation seemed to be rather unfortunate, the separation from Mintz and Disney's subsequent need for a new product line had very, very good results.

Ub Iwerks proved to be a loyal partner, staying to help Walt and Roy Disney to re-establish their animation studio and develop a new star. Out of this collaboration came what is the most famous animated character in history, Mickey Mouse. Together with composer Carl Stalling, who also came from Kansas City, they created Mickey's debut film, *Steamboat Willie* (1928): although it was the third film starring the mouse to be produced, it was the first of the series to employ the new sound-on-film process and, therefore, it was selected to be the first 'Mickey Mouse' release. Given the film's debut when sound-on-film processes were taking Hollywood by storm, it is not surprising that *Steamboat Willie* uses every opportunity to foreground an element of sound; even a passing cat becomes a musical instrument of sorts.

Despite the film's apparent novelty in terms of sound, it strongly draws upon past Disney material. For example, the scene of Mickey peeling big potatoes down to a tiny nub comes straight out of an 'Alice Comedy', *Alice the Whaler* (1927), in which a generic mouse performs almost exactly the same gag. As Merritt and Kaufman explain:

> ... as early as 1925, Disney was already remaking earlier films and recycling gags. When Disney found a joke or comic routine that was successful, he hung onto it tenaciously, and working to deliver one cartoon per month, he constantly repeated himself ... The Alices and the Oswalds are in every way apprentice films, witty and frequently charming, providing Disney with a storehouse of gags, plot

ideas, and secondary characters that he could reintroduce and refine in his 1930s' shorts.[11]

Merritt and Kaufman also note that, even during the silent era, Disney often employed scenarios centred around musical events.[12] For example, in the silent 'Oswald' film, *Rival Romeos* (1928), a goat eats sheet music and is played like an instrument – the same gag one finds in *Steamboat Willie*. One can easily see that *Steamboat Willie* represents a continuation of Disney's past formulas more than a wholly new concept.

In the early years, the Disney Studio also garnered inspiration from the live-action cinema and its performers; Merritt and Kaufman demonstrate the indebtedness of Disney's early films in this regard. Among the many important influences on Walt Disney and Ub Iwerks was Buster Keaton, whose physical comedy and inventive spirit showed up in numerous animated shorts.[13] The authors explain that the influences of comedians such as Harold Lloyd, Laurel and Hardy, and Charlie Chaplin, as well as swashbuckler Douglas Fairbanks, can also be found in early Disney productions.

The authors also note more general influences from the live-action cinema, explaining that 'by the time he started his Oswald series [in 1927], Disney had already gone a long way in incorporating and adapting live-action Hollywood conventions. But the Oswald series marked an unprecedented intensification of the effort'.[14] The relationship to live-action cinema can be seen in the more intricate staging of scenes, the number of shots used, the way in which material was edited, an increase in complex camera movements, and increasingly complicated character movements.

Los Angeles Times
MONDAY MORNING, APRIL 19, 1965

The Greatest Pedagogue of All
BY DR. MAX RAFFERTY

If he earns your praise, bestow it; if you like him let him know it;
Let the words of true encouragement be said;
Do not wait till life is over and he's underneath the clover,
For he cannot read his tombstone when he's dead.
                        —BRALEY

We educators are a close-knit clan, proud of our pedagogy, devoted to our degrees, covetous of our credentials. Outsiders like Adm. Rickover who come nosing around our hunting preserves usually get the kind of treatment reserved for an umpire at a South American soccer match. The admiral, fortunately, is tough and doesn't care, but it's pretty rugged on the average fellow whom we find trespassing on our premises.

★

There is one shining, tremendous exception to this rule. He's a quiet fellow with no great shucks of a formal education, as I recall. He hasn't written any books that I have heard of. He's never been a college president or a professor or even a state superintendent of schools. Yet he is the greatest educator of this century — greater than John Dewey or James Conant or all the rest of us put together.

His name is Walt Disney, and he operates out of Hollywood, of all places.

Like a lot of people, he came up once, long ago, with a gimmick. It was a highly unlikely mouse

Rafferty

with a twisted grin and a squeaking falsetto which was Walt's very own. It made him, and it was followed by other gimmicks: an irascible duck, a dopey dog and a cow named Clarabell. The money rolled in. This would have been enough for most of us.

Not for Walt. The gimmicks gave him the wherewithal to build a springboard from which he launched into something unprecedented on this or any other continent—compensatory education for a whole generation of America's children. The classics written by the towering geniuses out of the past who had loved children enough to write immortal stories for them began to live and breathe again in the midst of a cynical, sin-seeking society which had allowed them to pass almost completely into the limbo of the forgotten.

Before the enchanted ken of the little ones Pinnochio danced once more on unsteady wooden legs. Snow White fled the

witch's envy. Little Alice talked with rabbits and went into a land which only children can really understand. And most like Walt himself, of course, there was that boy who never grew up, who never lost the wonder and the glamour of childhood, Peter Pan.

His live movies have become lone sanctuaries of decency and health in the jungle of sex and sadism created by the Hollywood producers of pornography. Walt's pictures don't dwell on dirt. They show life as something a little finer than drunken wallowing in some gutter of self-pity. The beatniks and degenerates think his films are square.

I think they're wonderful.

★

One of his most recent ones, they say, will make a pretty penny — Academy Awards and all that. I hope it makes him $100 million. It's about time, for all our sakes, that a picture like this came along and cleaned up, in more ways than one.

Many, many years from now — decades, I hope — when this magical Pied Piper of our time wanders out of this imperfect world which he has done so much to brighten and adorn, millions of laughing, shouting little ghosts will follow in his train— the children that you and I once were, so long ago, when first a gentle magician showed us Wonderland.

Fig. 6.2 *Media praise for Walt Disney's achievements in the 1960s* Los Angeles Times *(19 April 1965)*

By the time the studio was producing its 'Mickey Mouse' series, it clearly had moved toward the development of linear storylines. After he broke his ties with Charles Mintz, who championed gags just as his wife had, Disney had more freedom to structure his films in whatever way he wished. Another factor in favour of narrative development was that, with the end of silent film, the popularity of physical humour waned to a great extent and was replaced by comedy of the spoken word. Certainly, the 'Mickey' films continued to be influenced by the gags of silent comedians but, as Robin Allan has noted, Disney's concern with continuous narrative 'set him apart from his rivals'.[15] Eventually, the narratives of 'Mickey' shorts were developed even further with the addition of several new starring characters: Donald Duck, Pluto, and other characters provided versatility in the plots because each had a unique personality and thus could be depicted in different kinds of activities.

But the 'Mickey Mouse' series was just one of two successful series of short films that were produced by the Disney Studio after the coming of sound. The studio's other series, the 'Silly Symphonies', were very different in nature. Instead of relying on a set of stock characters, each film was considered a 'one-shot', meaning that it employed characters and scenarios that did not recur. The 'Silly Symphonies' tended to be less plot-driven than the 'Mickey's but certainly they were not structured around gags to the extent of Disney's earlier works. An important function of the 'Silly Symphonies' was to provide a place for experimentation, where new techniques or equipment could be employed without risking the popularity of a set of developed characters. The Disney Studio tested Technicolor in *Flowers and Trees* (1932), used the multiplane camera in *The Old Mill* (1937), and experimented with drawing the human form (in preparation for *Snow White and the Seven Dwarfs*) in *The Goddess of Spring* (1934).

In 1937, the Disney Studio accomplished one of its best-known technical feats, the release of the first feature-length cel animation film, *Snow White and the Seven Dwarfs*. Disney began to think about a feature film sometime around 1933. Despite the great success of *Three Little Pigs* and its theme song, 'Who's Afraid of the Big Bad Wolf?', in general shorts were expensive to produce relative to their ability to make a profit. Features could demand a high rental price, but exhibitors were not willing to pay more for short animated films, despite the fact that animation was a costly production technique.

In an article entitled 'Before Snow White', J.B. Kaufman explains that 'the original impetus to produce a feature with Disney animation came in 1933, from outside the studio', when Mary Pickford approached Disney with the idea of starring in a live-action/animation version of 'Alice in Wonderland'.[16] At the time, Disney was distributing his work through Pickford's company, United Artists. Unfortunately, Paramount secured a deal for a feature based on the Alice tale at about the same time, dispelling both Disney's and Pickford's hopes for the project. Kaufman also discusses the Disney Studio's collaborations with MGM and Fox during 1933 and 1934, in which it provided animated sequences for live-action feature films. Undoubtedly, these experiences also fuelled Disney's desire to make a long-format film. The studio considered several other ideas for a feature, including 'Rip van Winkle' and 'Babes in Toyland', before making its final decision. The concept of 'Snow White' was being discussed as a 'Silly Symphony' when finally it was selected as the feature concept. In 1934–1935, the story adaptation of *Snow White and the Seven Dwarfs* was completed and, in 1936, the animation phase was started.

At the time of *Snow White*'s production, the studio was undergoing some changes. In order to complete the film, many new employees were needed. In the past, the majority of animation artists had worked their ways up through the ranks, learning on the job. However, the Disney Studio suddenly found itself in need of a formal training program after it experienced a period of rapid growth during the early 1930s. According to Robin Allan, 'the staff number had grown from a handful ... to 750 by the time Disney was making *Snow White*'.[17] Disney began its formal training program at the studio in 1932, with Don Graham at the helm; Graham had been an art instructor at Chouinard Art Institute, which later merged with a music school to become California Institute of the Arts. Graham's 'action analysis' classes profoundly influenced the look of Disney animation.

In an action analysis class of 22 February 1937, Graham addressed some problems Disney had been concerned with 'for a long time': that animators did not know how to handle characters entering or exiting a scene, and that they were weak at knowing 'how to vary the different action[s] in order to interpret moods'.[18] He provides an example of the latter, saying:

> ... for instance, Pluto walks into a scene briskly or angrily, or he walks in happily or tired. The animator must visualise any number of different types of walks, all expressing different feelings, and yet express these by Pluto's actions ... the ability to portray feeling or sensation or mood by a walk or run, or some simple act of these characters is, at present, very much a guesswork proposition, particularly among the younger animators, for there is a tendency to overlook the mood or sensation and just look at the problem as a piece of action.[19]

To learn how to animate the feelings properly, Graham suggested that the animators watch films of live-action movement as well animated movement, to see how actions occur in real life and how other animators had solved the problem of depicting it.

In *Snow White and the Seven Dwarfs*, animators had to deal with not only the personality animation of seven similar cartoonish dwarfs, but also several relatively realistic human figures. To help solve the problem of animating Snow White, live-action footage of dancer Marjorie Belcher was used as a reference throughout the film.

Elisabeth Bell argues that the design and animation of Snow White's character was so influential that it resulted in the establishment of a conventional look for Disney heroines. She contends that 'classical dance carriage and royal bearing are inter-changeable in Disney animation ... The language of ballet, and its coded conventions for spectatorship of "high" art, are embedded in the bodies of young Disney women' who are modelled on the figures of highly-toned dancers.[20]

On the other hand, the studio was not as prepared to handle a realistic male character; *Snow White* has been criticised for the overly realistic rendering of the Prince, who moves stiffly and suffers from a lack of stylisation. Writing on the representation of gender in Disney films, Sean Griffin has noted that, while it is often commented that the studio's female characters have 'appeal', the studio has been less successful in its 'attempts to create a "realistic" human *male* form who has "appeal" '.[21] He adds that 'until *Aladdin*, only *Pinocchio* (1940) and *Peter Pan* (1953) had been successful in presenting male figures that came close to the "appeal" of Snow White or her counterparts ...'[22]

It is sometimes suggested that *Snow White* was the first feature-length animated film to be made. However, by the end of 1937, at least three long animations already had been created outside the United States: *El Apóstol* (The Apostle, 1917) by the Argentinean Quirino Cristiani, *Die Geschichte des Prinzen Achmed* (The Adventures of Prince Achmed, 1926) by the German Lotte Reiniger, and *Reinicke Fuchs* (aka Le Roman de Renard; Reynard the Fox, 1937) by Russian Ladislas Starevich.[23]

Nonetheless, the Disney film was both more profitable and influential than any of its predecessors. *Snow White and the Seven Dwarfs*, which was first budgeted at $250,000 and ended up costing $1.5 million, gained an immediate international reputation and made a huge profit for the struggling Disney company. In 1938, it earned an estimated $4.2 million in the United States and Canada alone; of course, the film and its merchandising has earned hundreds of millions more since then.

The success of the film not only fuelled competition domestically between the Disney and Fleischer Studios, but also inspired subsequent versions from filmmakers in other countries. According to William Moritz, as a result of its popularity, Joseph Goebbels issued 'a general call to German animators to step up their production of colour animated films for children, and specifically commissioned a live-action feature film of *Snow White* (Schneeweisschen, 1939)' he hoped would surpass Disney's animated feature in quality.[24] The first animated feature produced in Italy, Anton Gino Domeneghini's *La Rosa di Bagdad* (1949), is clearly modelled on Disney's *Snow White*. Giannalberto Bendazzi has explained that the film's producer began the feature-length project during World War II, when there was a slow-down in the production of his company's mainstay, advertising films.[25]

In some respects, it is not surprising that *Snow White and the Seven Dwarfs* would have such great impact, particularly in Europe. Disney scholar Robin Allan has shown how the film reflects a distinctly European sensibility, particularly due to the influence of the Swiss-born inspirational artist Albert Hurter, who joined the studio in 1932 and began working on *Snow White and the Seven Dwarfs* by 1936.[26] In 1935, Disney had journeyed to Europe, picking up materials for the model department, numerous books containing illustrations, and mechanical toys. But, of course, the strongest link to European culture is in the film's origin: the German tale of Snow White, taken from the Brothers Grimm.

Traditional storytelling

When popular stories are remade, either by adapting a literary source for a motion picture or remaking a motion picture, it can be interesting to consider the differences that have occurred during the adaptation process. Sometimes, the tendencies of an individual or the culture in which he or she works are made clear by looking at the way in which ideas have been modified. In terms of the Disney Studio, one can examine the adaptation process with relative ease because so many of the studio's features, particularly, have been based on well-known stories: folktales (also called fairytales), fables, myths, and legends. Sometimes, people unfamiliar with traditional literature will use these terms interchangably, but in fact each represents a unique form. Anyone who will be analysing Disney features (or, for that matter, much of animation history) probably will find him or herself in the position of discussing these sources of material, so it will be useful to briefly define them here.

In her writing on children's literature, Donna E. Norton describes the above four types of traditional tales.[27] Both folktales and fables can involve human and animals characters, and both are set in a non-specific time and place. However, fables have a clearly defined instructive purpose and include a moral implication or lesson to be learned. 'Snow White and the Seven Dwarfs' (which Disney released as a feature in 1937) falls under the classification of folktale, while 'The Tortoise and the Hare' (which was released as a 'Silly Symphony' short in 1935) is an example of a fable, with its moral that 'slow and steady wins the race'.

The function of myths is to explain the great mysteries of the world: the creation of the Earth, the reasons for the weather and other daily occurrences, human emotions, and so on. Just as one sees within the realms of Greek or Norse mythology, scenarios often take place in a world beyond our own. Disney's production of *Hercules* (1997) has a basis in myth. Legends, on the other hand, are based on historical events, although are greatly exaggerated stories. The legend of Robin Hood provides a clear example; Disney produced an animated feature based on it in 1973.

Because traditional tales were passed on by storytellers throughout much of history, they generally were simple and direct but structured to hold interest. Oral storytelling lends itself to conflict and typecasting, which is used to avoid verbose character development that might decrease the listener's interest. Folktales, in particular, tend to be cross cultural and have direct equivalents in various cultures, though some are commonly associated with a central disseminating source.

Aesop's Fables is one of the major sources of traditional literature used in animation production; stories from this collection were employed by many animation producers during the early years of the cinema, in particular. It has been said that these tales were made up by a Greek slave who lived during the sixth century. He told the stories as a means of offering 'advice' to his master, using animals to avoid the retribution of specific individuals who might be named. In actuality, the fables probably came from many sources, but they were published collectively by William Caxton in 1484 under the title, *The Book of the Subtyl Historyes and Fables of Esope*.[28] At the time the fables were published, books were rare and expensive; those published for children tended to be instructive, offering advice for behaviour and thinking. Aesop's fables are stories about the weaknesses of people and animals, and their morals contain a lesson to be learned. For example, children learn that the weak and strong must help each other in 'The Lion and the Mouse' and that persistence pays off in 'The Tortoise and the Hare'.

Another popular source of traditional literature is *The Tales of Mother Goose*, which was first published in the mid-1600s by Charles Perrault. These stories are taken from the French oral storytelling tradition and include 'Cinderella', 'Sleeping Beauty', 'Puss in Boots', and 'Little Red Riding Hood'. By the mid-1700s, children's books were becoming more popular in Europe and North America, in part because the middle class was growing and becoming more powerful. At that time, both *Aesop's Fables* and *The Tales of Mother Goose* were reprinted by John Newberry (subsequently, a prize for literature was named after him) and sold successfully, proving the marketability of children's literature.

Some years later, in 1812, the first edition of stories by the Brothers Grimm was published. The brothers were two German scholars named Jacob and Wilhelm who were interested in how folktales reflected the ancient German language and traditions. Their stories include 'Cinderella', 'Hansel and Gretel', 'Little Red Riding Hood', 'The Frog Prince', 'Snow White and Rose Red' and 'Snow White'. The brothers obtained the stories in different ways; some of them were told by several acquaintances, others were collected when the Brothers travelled to various locations. Accounts of the amount of editing that occurred from telling to printing vary. Apparently, one of the brothers was a scholar and the other was more of a poet, so the two made compromises between the original integrity of a tale and revisions that would increase the stories' suitability for young readers.

Bruno Bettelheim has analysed the functions of fairytales and other forms of traditional literature. He suggests that fairytales are perfectly suited to helping a child deal with the traumas of growing up. He writes that fairytales, unlike most literature, are apt to 'stimulate his imagination; help him to develop his intellect and to clarify his emotions; be attuned to his anxieties and aspirations; give full recognition to his difficulties, while at the same time suggesting solutions to the problems which perturb him'.[29] In their original forms, many traditional stories are violent and fear-producing, yet Bettelheim contends that these elements very much represent the experiences of children. By presenting solutions to these situations, the fairytale provides a child with a model for coping with his or her fears.

An article by Jack Zipes, 'Breaking the Disney Spell', outlines major differences between the original story of Snow White and its adaptation in Disney's animated feature.[30] In the film:

- Snow White is an orphan; in Grimm her mother dies in childbirth, her father remains alive, and she is not forced to do the work of commoners

- the prince plays a larger role; in Grimm he is negligible

- the queen is jealous of Snow White's beauty and envious of her handsome beau; in Grimm this does not occur

- the animals are anthropomorphised; in Grimm this does not occur

- the characters of the dwarfs are fully explicated as rich and hardworking individuals; in Grimm they are anonymous and are not foregrounded

- the queen only comes once and dies because of her failed plan to injure the dwarfs with a huge rock; in Grimm she comes three times and dies when she is forced to dance in red-hot shoes at Snow White's wedding

- Snow White returns to life when she is kissed by the prince; in Grimm she returns to life when one of the dwarfs stumbles while carrying her coffin.

Zipes contends that Disney retains key ideological features of the original tale, especially those that relate to the domestication of women and patriarchal order. However, he says that Disney builds in an Horatio Alger-type of story, based on the filmmaker's own rise to success: 'a male myth about perseverance, hard work, dedication, loyalty, and justice'.[31] These ethics can be seen in the dwarfs who are both hard working and, as a result, wealthy. However, due to their inability to function as credible love interests (they are diminutive, cartoonish and characterised as children) they do not interfere with the love-relationship subplot that is developed between the Prince and the Princess. The inclusion of a heterosexual coupling parallels a convention of the Hollywood cinema on a much larger scale – it is almost mandatory that films of the classical period (and beyond) contain a subplot involving romantic attraction between a man and a woman. Mainstream media tend to reflect an 'ideal' view of dominant sectors of the culture. In American society, this perspective tends to be built around a white, heterosexual, and partriarchal social organisation.

Due to the pervasiveness of this formula in the mainstream Hollywood cinema, it is not suprising that analysts have found the tendency in films produced by the Disney Studio. For example, Harry Benshoff has identified such a pattern in a number of the 'Silly Symphony' shorts, including *Flowers and Trees* (1932), *The China Shop* (1934), and *The Moth and Flame* (1934), which depict heterosexual courtship rituals operating 'within the ideology of bourgeois white male propriety'.[32] Laura Sells also has found the pattern in Disney's adaptation of the Hans Christian Andersen tale of 'The Little Mermaid', written in 1837, for the Disney film released in 1989. She identifies a number of crucial differences surrounding the story's portrayal of roles for women, suggesting that, in part, it 'teaches us that we can achieve access and mobility in the white male system if we remain silent, and if we sacrifice our connection to "the feminine".'[33] By analysing the similarities and differences in additional Disney productions or works from other studios, one could obtain a better understanding of the extent to which these attitudes pervade animated media.

Censorship

To some extent the storylines of Hollywood films, including the nature of romantic relationships, have been affected by pressures originating outside the studios themselves. For example, for many years, censorship was employed to control the depictions that were shown in American film theatres. This area of research has been increasingly popular as censorship-related documentation has become more available to the public. In his book, *Hollywood Censored: Morality Codes, Catholics, and the Movies*, Gregory D. Black overviews the development of organised censorship bodies within the United States.[34] In *Forbidden Animation: Censored Cartoons and Blacklisted Animators*, Karl Cohen focuses a chapter specifically on the 'Censorship of Theatrical Animation'.[35]

During the early years of film history, the cinema developed a mixed reputation. While people from all social groups were drawn to watch the novelty, it was widely perceived that theatres often provided unwholesome entertainment for children and women and tended to attract criminal elements. On 24 December 1908, when New York's mayor, George B. McClellan ordered the city's movie theatres to be closed, many welcomed the action. Naturally, members of the film industry were not among them.

One reaction within the industry was to support the formation of the New York Board of Motion Picture Censorship, later called the National Board of Review (NBR), which would standardise the approval and censorship of films nationally. It was hoped that this action would prevent censorship at local levels. As Black explains, 'a proliferation of state censorship boards, each with different standards, would make it next to impossible for producers to make films accessible to the huge, diverse American audience' with its range of moral standards; the best option seemed to be self-censorship, which 'was just good business'.[36] As a result, the major film producers at the time agreed to submit their films to the NBR, which began its reviews in March 1909.

Unfortunately, the NBR was deemed ineffective by many, resulting in the formation of a number of municipal and state censorship boards by 1915.[37] Black reports that 'industry problems intensified when over a hundred antimovie bills were introduced in state legislatures in 1921'.[38] After trying other measures, the major film studios formed a trade association, the Motion Picture Producers and Distributors of America (MPPDA), and hired a spokesperson, William Harrison 'Will' Hays, to campaign against censorship while encouraging studios to clean up their acts. He formed a Studio Relations Department (SRD), which drew up guidelines called the 'Don'ts and Be Carefuls'. Since the SRD lacked real enforcement power, studios interpreted its rules in different ways and abided by them to varying degrees.[39]

Community and religious groups across the country continued to lobby against Hollywood. However, the organisation that most intimidated the industry was the National Catholic Legion of Decency, which represented a well-organised faction of movie viewers who might boycott and bring great financial hardship upon the film studios. The Legion of Decency, like a number of other groups, wanted 'entertainment films to emphasise that the church, the government, and the family were the cornerstones of an orderly society; that success and happiness resulted from respecting and working within this system'.[40]

The SRD, like its predecessors within the industry, was seen as ineffective. Pressure from the Legion of Decency, particularly, continued to build and, eventually, the

Fig. 6.3 Look *magazine article (1939), Part 1*

much more authoritative Production Code Administration (PCA) was put into place. It was established in 1934, replacing the SRD as the primary censoring body in Hollywood, with outspoken Catholic leader Joseph I. Breen hired as its administrator.[41] Leonard J. Leff and Jerold L. Simmons, in their book on Hollywood censorship, *The Dame in the Kimono*, write about the significance of this change:

> When Hays converted the Studio Relations office into the Production Code Administration, he altered more than the name. He ordered member studios to submit all treatments and scripts to Breen; to direct all appeals not to a [generally sympathetic] Hollywood Jury ... but to the Association board in New York; and to pay a $25,000 fine for releasing a picture that violated the Code. More important, Association members would bar from their theaters all pictures that lacked the Production Code Seal. After 1934, no picture without the Seal could secure a decent theatrical release or profit.[42]

Between 1934 and 1968, when a ratings system was put into place, the PCA was charged with regulating the films produced within the Hollywood film industry. It had considerable power for many years, although after World War II its effectiveness began to diminish for a variety of reasons.[43]

Some of the most famous elements of the PCA-enforced 'Production Code' are mandates that the bedrooms of married couples contain twin beds and that one foot must stay on the ground at all times (minimising the possibility of 'sexual misconduct'). Another famous element of the Production Code is the requirement for 'compensating moral values' demanded by Breen. Essentially, he required that anyone who committed a socially unacceptable act – adultery, murder, robbery, and so forth – pay for his or her transgressions by the end of the film. Jail time or even death was required for the worst of the perpetrators.

Apparently, the format that most concerned the PCA was the live-action feature. Detailed files can be found on virtually all the live-action features produced between the early 1930s and the mid-1940s. Short films, including film trailers, also were subject to censorship.[44] However, there are some indications that animation – even animated features – were seen as somewhat less consequential than live-action works. It is not uncommon to see something similar to the phrase 'animated cartoon' written across PCA documentation of animated features, suggesting that its status as animation made it relatively harmless.

However, as animation preservationist Jere Guldin suggests, the content of animated shorts of the 'pre-Code period' (he focuses on 1930–1934 in particular) was every bit as risque as that of its live-action counterparts. He writes:

> ... whatever morally dubious goings-on were depicted in the live-action films of Paramount, Warners, and Columbia generally were duplicated in the cartoons produced by those same studios. There was sex, implied and otherwise ... drug usage ... nudity, swearing, stereotypes, flagrant homosexuality, extreme violence, toilet humor, gags done in downright bad taste – you name it, the cartoons revelled in it.[45]

Guldin notes that, while some animated works produced after the formation of the PCA 'managed to contain objectionable elements', they were in the minority.[46]

One does not need documentation to see how censorship – or the lack of it – might have affected storytelling practices at the Disney Studio and elsewhere. Just by comparing films from the periods before and after the formation of the PCA, one can see changes that easily can be attributed to censorship pressures. Looking at some of Disney's early animated works, one can find gags based on material that surely would have been deemed unsuitable when the Production Code was in effect. For example, the fact that rather violent actions occur – for example, when puppies are imprisoned and ground up to be made into hotdogs in *Alice's Mysterious Mystery* (1926) – is one indication that Disney (and the entire film industry) was operating with relative freedom in terms of film content. In *Steamboat Willie*, Minnie is picked up by her underpants and a cow's udders are not only plainly visible, but also figure in gags. Guldin explains that this was not so uncommon at that time: 'Before losing their mammary glands to censorship, cows paraded through cartoons with heavy- swinging udders that scraped the ground on occasion.'[47]

Although *Snow White and the Seven Dwarfs* was produced during the period of heightened censorship, its status as animation seems to have lessened the perceived need for attention. A memo in the PCA file, dated 4 March 1936, indicates that 'production has started' although 'shooting has not yet begun'.[48] The memo-writer might have been responding to a letter sent by William Garity of the Disney Studio two days earlier. In this letter, Garity states: 'As you are aware, this picture is an experiment on our part and we do not have, at the present time, a completed script, such as would be used with a live action production'; adding, 'I cannot see, from my knowledge of what is intended, any censorable parts in the picture'.[49]

Fig. 6.4 Look *magazine article (1939), Part 2*

A script was sent to the PCA in early November 1937, and it seems that Garity's feelings were mirrored by the censors. Reviewers wrote the following remarks on their review of the film in early 1937: 'feature length cartoon', 'fairy story', 'first feature length cartoon in Technicolor. Done superbly'.[50] Charts used by these reviewers contain a series of categories that could be used to record plot content. Although such categories as 'Type of Criminal?', 'Type of Crime?', 'Any Killing?' and 'Violence?' appear on the form, nothing was noted in regard to *Snow White and the Seven Dwarfs* – despite the fact that the evil queen and her actions easily could be considered relevant. Other countries were perhaps more sensitive to the subject matter of the film and imposed some type of censorship on it. For example, in England, children under the age of sixteen were not admitted to screenings, and in Australia an incident involving the witch and a skeleton in the dungeon were removed from the eighth reel.[51]

Most Disney features were subject to relatively little, if any, intervention by the PCA. For most films, there is no evidence that script changes or edits to the final film were required, although both demands are found throughout the files of most live-action features produced during the 1930s and much of the 1940s. Karl Cohen contends that the lack of intervention was the result of voluntary compliance. He writes, 'the studios avoided troubles through self-censorship ... animators simply didn't challange the system except in rare cases'.[52]

However, there are some instances in which censors felt compelled to make remarks. For example, *Fantasia* (1940) is cited for some suggestive behaviour. Joseph Breen warned that the centaurettes used in the film 'should not be part the body of a horse and part a beautiful female body showing breasts' and that the film should 'avoid anything sensually suggestive in the action of the Bacchus chasing one of the

THE NATIONAL ASSOCIATION FOR THE ADVANCEMENT OF COLORED

PEOPLE RECOGNIZES IN "SONG OF THE SOUTH" REMARKABLE ARTISTIC MERIT

IN THE MUSIC AND IN THE COMBINATION OF LIVING ACTORS AND THE CARTOON

TECHNIQUE. IT REGRETS, HOWEVER, THAT IN AN EFFORT NEITHER TO OFFEND

AUDIENCES IN THE NORTH OR SOUTH, THE PRODUCTION HELPS TO PERPETUATE

A DANGEROUSLY GLORIFIED PICTURE OF SLAVERY. MAKING USE OF THE BEAUTIFUL

UNCLE REMUS FOLKLORE, "SONG OF THE SOUTH" UNFORTUNATELY GIVES THE IM-

PRESSION OF AN IDYLLIC MASTER-SLAVE RELATIONSHIP WHICH IS A DISTORTION

OF THE FACTS.

                                        WALTER WHITE
                                        AACP
                                        EXECUTIVE SECRETARY

Fig. 6.6 *Telegram from Walter White NAACP (1946) regarding* Song of the South
Courtesy Karl Cohen

centaurettes'.[53] The same letter warns against showing 'forward or excessive body movement' in 'the portrayal of the shy harem girls, and in their Oriental dance'.[54] *Song of the South* (1946) also received a relatively large amount of criticism from the

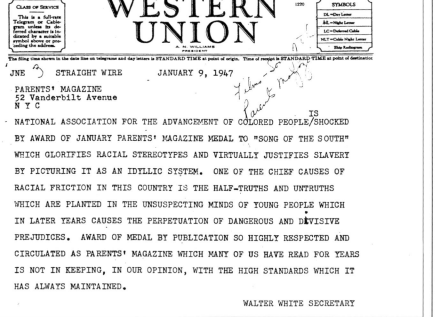

NATIONAL ASSOCIATION FOR THE ADVANCEMENT OF COLORED PEOPLE/SHOCKED IS

BY AWARD OF JANUARY PARENTS' MAGAZINE MEDAL TO "SONG OF THE SOUTH"

WHICH GLORIFIES RACIAL STEREOTYPES AND VIRTUALLY JUSTIFIES SLAVERY

BY PICTURING IT AS AN IDYLLIC SYSTEM. ONE OF THE CHIEF CAUSES OF

RACIAL FRICTION IN THIS COUNTRY IS THE HALF-TRUTHS AND UNTRUTHS

WHICH ARE PLANTED IN THE UNSUSPECTING MINDS OF YOUNG PEOPLE WHICH

IN LATER YEARS CAUSES THE PERPETUATION OF DANGEROUS AND DIVISIVE

PREJUDICES. AWARD OF MEDAL BY PUBLICATION SO HIGHLY RESPECTED AND

CIRCULATED AS PARENTS' MAGAZINE WHICH MANY OF US HAVE READ FOR YEARS

IS NOT IN KEEPING, IN OUR OPINION, WITH THE HIGH STANDARDS WHICH IT

HAS ALWAYS MAINTAINED.

                                        WALTER WHITE SECRETARY

Fig. 6.7 *Telegram from Walter White NAACP (1947) regarding* Song of the South
Courtesy Karl Cohen

PCA. Reviewers of the live-action/animation feature were particularly critical of language used in the script. For example, Joseph Breen noted that the word 'Bloody' would be found objectionable by British censors. He also suggested that Disney 'take counsel with some responsible negro authorities ... As I have already presumed to suggest to you, our negro friends appear to be a bit critical of all motion picture stories which [depict] their people, and it may be that they will find in this story some material which may not be acceptable to them'.[55] A memo from a reviewer to Breen provides several suggestions 'with a view to minimising adverse reactions from certain negro groups': the establishment of the film's period as the 1870s; the replacement of the phrase 'ole darky' with 'old man' and the name 'Marse John' with 'Mister John'; as well as sensitivity to scenes showing the 'Negro groups singing happily. It is the characterisation of these groups to which certain types of Negro leaders are most likely to take exception'.[56]

By the 1950s, PCA files began to reflect the organisation's waning influence with a decreased amount of correspondence. However, the Disney animated features produced during this time were met with a variety of interesting responses. In regard to *Alice in Wonderland* (1951), a film analyis form remarks 'violence and courtroom scene involve anthropomorphic characters, not humans. Probably should not be listed for statistical purposes'.[57] Both alcohol consumption and violence (swordplay) are noted in *Peter Pan*, although no need for script changes are indicated. Likewise, a comment made in regard to *Lady and the Tramp* (1955), that 'the battle between the dogs and the rat is so realistically vicious that it might terrify children', seems to have illicited no changes; in fact, the 'violence' section of the film's analysis chart is marked 'no'.[58] One can speculate (but at this point only speculate) that these comments reflect the reviewers' feelings that animation was less influential on audiences than live-action.

Despite the fact that there is relatively little documentation of formal censorship in terms of Disney films (or other animated productions), it is essential to understand that this kind of pressure existed. As Cohen suggests, self-censorship likely played a significant part in molding the content of films long before they passed by the censor's eye. That is, most censorship probably occurred internally, rather than outside the studio, while formal regulation was in effect.

PROMOTIONAL STRATEGIES

Disney's aggressive development of new projects and employment of the latest in technological achievements contributed greatly to the reputation of his studio. However, Disney also was wise to find public relations opportunities in various arenas. This section will overview some of Disney's strategies for developing his reputation within different levels of society and different age groups.

By the early 1930s the Disney Studio was receiving acclaim not only among the general public, but also within fine art circles. Bill Mikulak's research on gallery and museum exhibitions has demonstrated that, although there were some exhibitions of animated artwork from other studios during the 1930s, by far the most extensive effort in this regard concerned the Disney Studio.[59] Mikulak notes that, prior to World War II, exhibitions of Disney artwork took place at a number of sites, including the Philadelphia Art Alliance in 1932, the Art Institute of Chicago in 1933, the

Museum of Modern Art in 1938, and the Los Angeles Museum of Contemporary Art in 1940. Disney's sense of promotion obviously was very keen, as he assured his high profile by affiliating himself with cultural institutions across the country.

In 1939, Disney used his stature and widespread popularity to launch a program of gallery sales, featuring a limited number of cels from films. By then, he had gained fame as the producer of 'Mickey Mouse' and 'Silly Symphony' shorts, as well as the first animated feature to come from an American studio. He already had started merchandising products containing the image of Mickey Mouse, and he had experienced great success with the soundtrack of *Three Little Pigs* in 1933. In this context, it does not seem surprising that Disney would take advantage of another spin-off product, production art, to make some extra profit. At the time, most studios, including Disney, considered the cels used for creating animation to be disposable materials and routinely washed them so they could be re-used. If the public wanted to buy them, so much the better!

In this case, extra profit might not have been the only motivation for the sale of production art. Mikulak quotes a report that says Disney actually began his art marketing program with the Courvoisier Gallery to maintain staff levels when other work had ended:

> He began making his composite drawings for the galleries so he wouldn't have to lay off any of his employees during the slack season. Instead of cutting his staff, he made work – assigned people to cut up the celluloid drawings, mount them on backgrounds and wrap them with cellophane. Most of these composites utilised hand-prepared backgrounds to highlight the cels. Only a few of them matched cels with their original background paintings as seen in the films.[60]

Of course, at that time, cel collecting was nowhere near the big business it is today.

As Disney continued his push into fine art circles, one of the most savvy alliances he created was with the Museum of Modern Art (MoMA). Since 1935, MoMA had been collecting motion pictures that its librarian, Iris Barry, deemed to be of historical merit. Among the animation included in various programs distributed by MoMA, Disney films were by far the most common. This relationship undoubtedly helped to assure Disney's place in film history. MoMA's film library has been an important factor in defining the canon of filmmaking in the United States, since it was the primary circulating collection available within the country for many years.

But, Mikulak indicates that the relationship between Disney and MoMA was mutually beneficial: Barry's collection was formed through donations by Hollywood studios and Disney was among those who answered her call, both by providing copies of some 'Mickey Mouse' and 'Silly Symphony' films, and by attending fundraisers to assist the museum. The Disney films turned out to be relatively important to the museum's reputation. After *Snow White*'s release, with World War II raging, Americans increasingly looked for culture inside its borders. Mikulak explains that:

> ... in the early 1940s, MoMA was in the midst of aesthetic and political cross-pressures that pitted elite tastes in European modernist painting styles against nativist American populism. While the Museum had a longstanding interest in Disney, in the midst of World War II, the studio provided MoMA with an art that helped counter accusations that its Eurocentrism was un-American.[61]

Disney balanced his upward-spiralling reputation with anchors in middle America. For instance, between 1934 and 1944, the studio took out a series of 'Disney Pages' in *Good Housekeeping* that generally served as promotions for films currently being

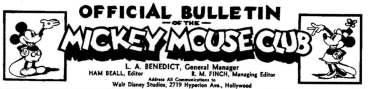

NOW IS THE TIME TO TAKE STOCK OF YOUR MICKEY MOUSE CLUB AND STUDY OUT WAYS AND MEANS TO MAKE IT BIGGER AND BETTER IN 1932 THAT THE BOX OFFICE MAY PROFIT THEREBY.

OFFICIAL BULLETIN
— OF THE —
MICKEY MOUSE CLUB

L. A. BENEDICT, General Manager
HAM BEALL, Editor   R. M. FINCH, Managing Editor
Address All Communications to
Walt Disney Studios, 2719 Hyperion Ave., Hollywood

VOL. II, No. 1   JANUARY 1, 1932

START A MEMBERSHIP DRIVE!

MICKEY APPEARS IN RECORD SHOW

Mickey Mouse was the featured cartoon on what is believed to be the world's record endurance show recently staged at Lakemba, Australia. Eight features were presented on the bill, which ran from 10:30 in the morning until 5:30 o'clock in the afternoon for one admission.

Publicity matter invited patrons to "Come early—Bring your lunch—Stop all day—No extra charge." The admission price was a quarter with half price for the children. And the bill was staged on a holiday at that!

Airplane Gifts

Proof that Young America is still air-minded is given by the stimulation of attendance at the Fox Egyptian Mickey Mouse Club in Long Beach, California, through the giving away of Thunderbird monoplanes, arranged through the cooperation of 22 Long Beach merchants. One plane is being given away each Saturday for a 10 weeks' period.

The manager has found the giving away of the miniature aircraft not only stimulates the attendance of regular members of the club, but it attracts many other youngsters to sign up for membership.

Now Is the Time to Get Busy Enrolling Children To Help Your Box-Office

This issue of the Mickey Mouse Bulletin marks the inauguration of a new volume of the publication and the advent of a new year for the hundreds of Mickey Mouse Clubs throughout the length and breadth of the land.

During the twelve-month past, scores of new Mickey Mouse Clubs have been added to the roster, and indications are that before another new year rolls around, the number will be doubled.

Mickey Mouse Is Winning Fun Film

Mickey Mouse tops the comedy field for both adults and children to judge by the results of a recent poll conducted at the Vilas theatre at Eagle Rock, Wisconsin. He polled more than half the votes.

Second place went to Laurel and Hardy with "Our Gang" a close third. The most popular male star was Richard Dix, while Greta Garbo, despite the legion of imitators, holds her place as first lady of the screen. Robert Montgomery and Joan Crawford tied for second place. The manager conducted the contest in the form of a questionnaire to determine the desires of his audiences. He has arranged to show several "demand pictures."

There is no time like the present to build up your club and put your theatre in a position to cash in at the box-office on the future of this juvenile organization that is sweeping the country.

Put on an active membership drive now! Several of the clubs are already doing it and are being astonished at the results they are achieving. An account of these activities is printed elsewhere in the Bulletin.

It should not be hard for an aggressive manager to realize that right now the children offer the best means of bringing adult patronage to the theatre, when finances in general are at a low ebb and the box-office suffering.

Parents will deny themselves for their children and will strain their budgets to permit the youngsters to attend the theatre, even if they

(Continued on Page Three)

MICKEY MOUSE'S MUSINGS

♦ ♦ ♦

The glorious holidays are over and Yours Truly with Minnie and the rest of our company have buckled down to work again, with a firm resolve to give you the finest sound cartoons possible in 1932.

I note with great pleasure that Liberty Weekly has put the Mickey Mouse cartoons at the head of its list of 1931 achievements in short subjects, but I assure you that it hasn't gone to my head or Walt Disney's and we know we have hard work cut out for us during the coming year.

Again I want to congratulate the managers on the great progress made in building up the Mickey Mouse Clubs to their present top position among juvenile organizations of the kind in the country.

Fig. 6.8 *Page from the* Mickey Mouse Club Bulletin, *1932*

© *Disney Enterprises, Inc.*

exhibited or about to be released. J.B. Kaufman has explained that these pages 'served to acquaint a wider audience with new Disney characters and stories, much as the Disney television programs of two decades later would do – and, like those programs, create a wider demand for the studio's films and related merchandise'.[62] Informative but largely promotional articles on Disney appear in other popular magazines. For example, in 1947 *American Cinematographer* carried a two-part story on 'The Men Behind the Mouse'.[63] In the early 1950s, *International Sound Technician* ran an article on Disney's 'Sound in Animated Motion Pictures', written by Disney Sound Director C.O. Slyfield. The article contains a sidebar on 'Walt Disney', which glorifies his ability to 'materialise a dream'; according to the article, 'not many people have the faith, or the understanding, or the ability to inspire others to go along with them to achieve that dream. Walt Disney has'.[64] These are just two of many homages to Walt Disney and his studio that can be found throughout a variety of publications at the time.

Many of the Disney Studio's marketing strategies were aimed at adults, but certainly children constituted a major target audience. One of the strategies used to develop young viewers was the formation of Mickey Mouse Clubs. Writing on 'Disney Animation and the Business of Childhood', David Forgacs suggests that the success of character licensing and merchandising in the late 1920s probably 'played a part in shifting Disney animation towards both cuteness and a more "family"-oriented product because it demonstrated the potential of the toys and gadgets market as a source of additional income'.[65] He also remarks on the importance that the syndication of cartoon strips to newspapers and magazines and licensing with foreign publishers has had in maintaining the popularity of Disney characters among a broad family audience.

Richard deCordova has written about Disney's relationship with child audiences in an article entitled 'The Mickey in Macy's Window: Childhood, Consumerism, and Disney Animation'.[66] Drawing upon the work of Cecil Munsey, deCordova describes three events that constituted the beginnings of Mickey Mouse merchandising: the sale of rights to use Mickey's image on school tablets in 1929, the small-scale production of Mickey Mouse dolls in 1930, and the signing of a contract for international licensing of Mickey Mouse merchandise later that year.[67] By 1931,

Fig. 6.9 *The Disney Studios' ink and paint department, early 1950s*
Courtesy Phyllis Craig

'theaters across the country had begun to receive a stream of Mickey Mouse dolls and toys for diplay and giveaways', which were sometimes supplied by department stores.[68] These stores participated in what deCordova calls 'the most elegant scheme of Mickey Mouse merchandising of the period, the Mickey Mouse Clubs', the campaign for which was outlined in a 1930 booklet published by the Disney Company.[69] J.B. Kaufman points out that that 'the idea of the Mickey Mouse Clubs was started independently by an exhibitor, then discovered by Disney and picked up by the studio'.[70]

Essentially, the Mickey Mouse Clubs were part of a Saturday afternoon theatre matinee, an event that included a number of cultural and social activities and concluded with a screening of films. As deCordova describes the clubs, one of their functions also was to connect children to local businesses, which would sponsor the club and its activities. He reveals that 'the growth of the Mickey Mouse Clubs was impressive. By the end of 1930, a hundred and fifty theatres across the country had clubs and, according to Disney's estimates, there were a hundred and fifty to two hundred thousand members. By 1932, *Photoplay* magazine claimed that the clubs had one million members. Although these figures may exaggerate actual membership, they are credible', judging by the number of reports on club activities that appeared in the media nationwide. He adds that, 'in 1932, new club chapters were being formed at the rate of thirty per month'.[71]

SHIFTS IN THE STUDIO'S STRUCTURE

As a number of analysts have remarked, Disney's studio operated as a model of patriarchal order. More than any other motion picture studio of the 1920s and beyond, its productions have been identified as the creations of a sole individual: Walt Disney, aka 'Uncle Walt.' While accounts of individuals at the studio stress that Disney did, indeed, play a central role in most of the animation produced while he was heading the studio, it is nonetheless important to recognise the many influences on the films. Recent work on inspirational artists such as Sylvia Holland and Albert Hurter, partner Ub Iwerks, the inker and painters, and other studio employees has helped to broaden our understanding of the Disney production process.[72]

To this day the Disney company encourages unity and singularity of purpose among its employees. For example, theme park workers are called 'cast members' as if they were part of a large production rather than autonomous employees. However, at some times, cracks of discontent appear within every organisation. In terms of the Disney animation studio, one of the most pivotal of these experiences was the strike of 1941. This event represented a decisive moment not only for Disney as a studio owner, but also for many of his studio's employees and the art of animation on a larger scale.

The Disney Studio experienced its success with the 'Mickey Mouse' and 'Silly Symphonies' series at the beginning of the Depression years. After a period of rapid growth, the company remained financially unstable, but nonetheless pulled through the economic crisis without bordering on bankruptcy (as had most other studios in Hollywood). The studio staff remained relatively small during the early 1930s. and most newly hired people received training in-house.

One can imagine that, although Disney paid fairly low wages, people were happy to be working – especially for a newly prosperous company that had worldwide recognition. Certainly, Disney provided better equipment than most other studios and a learning environment that far exceeded other facilities as well. No effort was spared to achieve the desired results and creative artists were encouraged to experiment. An unheard-of luxury, pencil tests (films of the artists' pencil drawings), were used to check the flow of the characters' movement. More time was spent planning the production as a whole; the Disney Studio was the first to use storyboards to chart out action, allowing for the development of a distinct beginning, middle and end, as well as more even pacing. However, these luxuries came about because of Disney's philosophy to put profits back into the productions, as opposed to paying employees higher wages.

When provisions of the New Deal helped create an economic up-turn in 1933, the Disney Studio (and industry throughout the United States) began to renew its strength. During the next four years, the studio added large numbers of new employees, many of whom had a different attitude than the older studio workers. The position of the new-hires was strengthened by a growing job market and economy, as well as a national movement toward unionisation to improve working conditions across the country.

In the 1930s, unionisation began to occur throughout the animation industry. The Disney Studio held off unionisation longer than most other animation companies but, by 1941, organisers had made a presence there as well. On 27 May 1941, Walt Disney addressed a gathering of employees, saying: 'Threats and rumors of a strike are again circulating within the studio ... I desire that it be made plain to all my employees that they are free to join any union which they may select or prefer.'[73] Despite these comments, Disney's anti-union sentiment was widely known. The next day, 28 May 1941, several hundred picketers stood outside the studio.

In February of that year, Walt had addressed his employees regarding a drop in production that had been occurring over the past four months. He began the talk by assuring that he recognised the right of employees to join a labour organisation, but contended that his statement actually had 'nothing whatever to do with union matters'.[74] Indeed, his talk soon turned to his personal outlook for studio production and general comments regarding the studio work ethic: 'In the twenty years I have spent in this business, I have weathered many storms. It has been far from easy sailing. It has required a great deal of hard work, struggle, determination, confidence, faith and above all, unselfishness. Perhaps the greatest single factor has been our unselfish attitude toward our work.' In his talk, Disney also addressed concerns that profits were not being distributed to employees, noting that bonuses as high as $153,000 had been distributed between 1934 and 1941.

Later in the speech, Disney explained that he believed 'a lot of the younger men are not appreciative enough of the help that is being given to them by the many loyal, unselfish men in the organisation ... The men who have pioneered in this business with me have had a much tougher time than any of you who are newcomers here now. It may be that we are making it too easy for you'. It is clear that Disney aimed his hostility at the newly hired workers who in recent years had filled the studio in great numbers. His criticism of them became more harsh when he added that 'the stumbling and fumbling of green, inexperienced people has cost this studio millions of dollars'. He contended that the answer to the company's crisis would be a 'good honest day's work. Believe me, that will be a cure for all our problems. You can't deny that it is individual efficiency that leads to collective efficiency'. Although Disney suggested that he was open to unionisation, his call for 'collective efficiency' seems to reflect his true feelings: that his new employees should stand by the studio with the same loyalty felt by his long-time workers.

Disney fired some union organisers before the official picketing occurred and lost many of his most talented artists during the ensuing strike. Government arbitrators were called in to settle the matter while Disney himself was sent on a diplomatic tour of South America, to spread a 'Good Neighbor' policy for the government and the film industry (i.e. to encourage good relations between the United States and South American countries at a time when World War II was raging and political alliances were being formed internationally).[75] Even after the strike was settled, there was a great deal of uneasiness throughout the studio. The wife of animator Vladimir 'Bill' Tytla, Adrienne, said that her husband returned to work at the studio but 'there was too much tension and electricity in the air'; with Vladimir, 'everything was instinctive and intuitive, and now the vibes were all wrong'.[76]

Tytla was among the artists who left the Disney Studio during the early 1940s, as a result of the work situation, unionisation and striking; he went to Terrytoons in 1943. Among the many other artists who departed were Art Babbitt, John Hubley, Dave Hilberman, Steve Bosustow, Adrian Woolery and Bill Hurtz. Some were hired off the picket line by Frank Tashlin, who was heading the newly formed animation unit at Columbia Pictures. After World War II, many of these same artists worked together at a new production company, United Productions of America (UPA).

Of course, the Disney Studio continued to function, but changes were under way. During the 1940s, Disney produced a number of wholly animated features, including *Pinocchio* (1940), *Fantasia* (1940), *Dumbo* (1941), *Bambi* (1942) and *The Adventures of Ichabod and Mr. Toad* (1949). However, the studio's interest began to turn more and more toward live-action filmmaking. It began by producing a number of films that in some manner combined live-action and animated imagery, including *The Reluctant Dragon* (1941), *Saludos Amigos* (1942 in South America; 1943 in the USA), *Victory through Airpower* (1943), *The Three Caballeros* (1944 in Mexico; 1945 in the USA), *Song of the South* (1946), *Fun and Fancy Free* (1947), *Melody Time* (1948) and *So Dear to My*

Heart (1949). Of course, the idea of combination films was nothing new to the studio, having produced the 'Alice Comedies' during the 1920s and having considered the idea of a live-action/animation 'Alice' feature starring Mary Pickford in 1933.

By the end of the 1940s, Disney had embraced live-action features whole-heartedly, though the studio continued to draw inspiration from previously produced storylines and characterisations. Derek Bousé has demonstrated the connection between Disney's first live-action series, the 'True Life Adventures' wildlife films (which began with *Seal Island* in 1948 and ended with *Jungle Cat* in 1960), and the animation it already had produced. Bousé explains the correlation in part by noting that key animation personnel, including James Algar and Ben Sharpsteen, crossed over to work on the 'True Life' films. He notes that the connection between the animated and live-action films was purposeful:

> ... each of the films opened with an animated introductory sequence, reminding audiences that these 'documentaries' were closely related to, if not creative extensions of, the Disney cartoon features they already knew and loved.[77]

The Disney Studio ceased production of animated shorts in 1955, at a time when many studios were abandoning their short film units. Television, government anti-trust cases, and other factors had changed the film industry drastically, and theatrical shorts, animated or otherwise, were no longer in demand. In the 1950s, Disney expanded into theme parks, opening Disneyland in Anaheim.

During this time, Disney faced competition from a new and very different force in animation, the UPA Studio, which was founded in part by strikers who left Disney during the early 1940s. The next chapter focuses on the UPA Studio's aesthetics of 'limited animation', a term now used to describe a great range of works within the scope of animation production. As the next chapter will show, UPA and its limited animation provided not only an economical alternative to 'Disney-style animation' but sometimes a social and political alternative as well.

Notes

1. David James, *Allegories of Cinema: American Film in the Sixties* (Princeton: Princeton UP, 1989), 20.
2. Russell Merritt and J.B. Kaufman note that names of the artists known to us now as Rudolf Ising and Ub Iwerk spelled their names differently throughout much of the 1920s: Rudolph Ising and Ubbe Ert Iwwerks. Russell Merritt and J.B. Kaufman, *Walt in Wonderland: The Silent Films of Walt Disney* (Baltimore, MD: Johns Hopkins, 1993), 12.
3. Ibid., 53.
4. Ibid., 15.
5. Ibid., 57.
6. Walt Disney, letter to M.J. Winkler (21 Jan. 1924). Copy located in the M.J. Winkler Collection at the Film Study Center, Museum of Modern Art, New York.
7. Walt Disney, letter to M.J. Winkler (26 Feb. 1924). Copy located in the M.J. Winkler Collection at the Film Study Center, Museum of Modern Art, New York.
8. Ibid.
9. Merritt and Kaufman, op. cit., 14.
10. Ibid., 87.
11. Ibid., 15.
12. Ibid., 20.
13. Ibid., 22, 24, 29.

14. Ibid., 29.
15. Robin Allan, 'European Influences on Early Disney Feature Films', in Jayne Pilling (ed.) *A Reader in Animation Studies* (London: John Libbey, 1997), 241–260, 243.
16. J.B. Kaufman, 'Before Snow White', *Film History* 5, 2 (June 1993): 158–175, 158.
17. Allan, op. cit., 250.
18. Don Graham, 'Class on Action Analysis: Introduction to Study of Action: Primary Actions' (22 Feb. 1937).
19. Id.
20. Elizabeth Bell, 'Somatexts at the Disney Shop: Constructing the Pentimentos of Women's Animated Bodies', in Elizabeth Bell, Lynda Hass and Laura Sells (eds) *From Mouse to Mermaid: The Politics of Film, Gender, and Culture* (Bloomington: University of Indiana Press, 1995), 107–24, 111.
21. Sean Griffin, 'The Illusion of "Identity": Gender and Racial Representation in *Aladdin*', *Animation Journal* 3, 1 (Fall 1994): 64–73, 65.
22. Id.
23. In the United States, two films by the Fleischer Studio contained animation, *The Einstein Theory of Relativity* and *Evolution*, which appeared in 1923 and 1925, respectively.
24. Bill Moritz, 'Resistance and Subversion in Animated Films of the Nazi Era: The Case of Hans Fischerkoesen', *Animation Journal* 1, 1 (Fall 1992): 4–33, 12.
25. Giannalberto Bendazzi, 'The First Italian Animated Feature Film and Its Producer: *La Rosa di Bagdad* and Anton Gino Domeneghini', *Animation Journal* 3, 2 (Spring 1995): 4–18.
26. Allan, op. cit., 248.
27. Donna E. Norton, *Through the Eyes of a Child: An Introduction to Children's Literature* (New York: Merrill, 1991), 227.
28. Ibid., 257–258.
29. Bruno Bettelheim (1975), *The Uses of Enchantment: The Meaning and Importance of Fairy Tales* (New York: Vintage, 1989), 5.
30. Jack Zipes, 'Breaking the Disney Spell', in Elizabeth Bell, Lynda Hass and Laura Sells (eds) *From Mouse to Mermaid: The Politics of Film, Gender, and Culture* (Bloomington: University of Indiana Press, 1995), 107–24, 111, 36.
31. Ibid., 37.
32. Harry Benshoff, 'Heigh-ho, Heigh-ho, Is Disney High or Low? From Silly Cartoons to Postmodern Politics', *Animation Journal* 1, 1 (Fall 1992): 62–85, 68.
33. Laura Sells, 'Where do the Mermaids Stand? Voice and Body in *The Little Mermaid*', in Elizabeth Bell, Lynda Hass and Laura Sells, op. cit., 175–92, 181.
34. Gregory D. Black, *Hollywood Censored: Morality Codes, Catholics, and the Movies* (Cambridge: Cambridge UP, 1994).
35. Karl Cohen, *Forbidden Animation: Censored Cartoons and Blacklisted Animators* (Jefferson, NC: McFarland, 1997).
36. Black, op. cit., 14.
37. Ibid., 15.
38. Ibid., 30.
39. Ibid., 33.
40. Ibid., 39.
41. For details specific to the Production Code Administration, see Gregory D. Black, 'Hollywood Censored: The Production Code Administration and the Hollywood Film Industry, 1930–1940', *Film History* 3 (1989): 167–189.
42. Leonard J. Leff and Jerold L. Simmons, *The Dame in the Kimono: Hollywood, Censorship & the Production Code from the 1920s to the 1960s* (New York: Grove Weidenfeld, 1990), 52–53.
43. For example, following the decision of *United States v. Paramount Pictures*, studios were forced to sell of their theatres, which 'were vital to Code enforcement because they dominated the film rental business ... In January 1950, with the process of divorcement just under way, even *Variety* speculated about the demise of the Breen office'. This situation and others are discussed in Leff and Simmons, *The Dame in the Kimono*, op. cit., 155.

44. An article in *Look* magazine overviews some issues related to the censorship of short animated films. 'Hollywood Censors Its Animated Cartoons', *Look* (17 Jan. 1939): 17+. This article is discussed in 'Studio Strategies: Sexuality, the Law, and Corporate Competition', a chapter in Eric Smoodin, *Animating Culture: Hollywood Cartoons from the Sound Era* (New Brunswick, NJ: Rutgers, 1993).

45. Jere Guldin, 'Risque Not New', *Animato!* 24 (Winter 1993): 31–38, 32.

46. Ibid., 37.

47. Id. J.B. Kaufman points out that today 'there are variant prints of *Steamboat Willie* in existence, some reflecting censorship cuts. Several "Mickeys" of 1929–1930 had trouble with state censor boards'. J.B. Kaufman, correspondence to the author (5 Aug. 1997).

48. D.M. (probably Douglas McKinnon), 'Memorandum for the files' (4 March 1936), in the '*Snow White* Disney 1937' file, PCA Special Collections, Margaret Herrick Library, Beverly Hills, CA. PCA Special Collections files mentioned in future reference are housed in this archive unless otherwise incidated.

49. Wm. E. Garity, letter to Mr. Douglas McKinnon (2 March 1936), in the '*Snow White* Disney 1937' file, PCA Special Collections.

50. MacKinnon & Metzger CRM, Reviewers, analysis chart (9 Dec. 1937), in the '*Snow White* Disney 1937' file, PCA Special Collections.

51. Joseph I. Breen, letter to Mrs. Thomas A. Hearn (West Coast Committee, National Legion of Decency) (7 March 1938), in the '*Snow White* Disney 1937' file, PCA Special Collections; Joseph I. Breen, report from AMPP (26 Feb. 1938), in the '*Snow White* Disney 1937' file, PCA Special Collections.

52. Karl Cohen, correspondence to the author (Sept. 1997).

53. Joseph I. Breen, letter to Walt Disney (24 Nov. 1939), in the '*Fantasia* RKO-Disney 1940' file, PCA Special Collections.

54. In regard to the 'shy harem girls', Karl Cohen writes: 'The line in the script that was questioned is absurd as the dancers of the bubble dance are elephants – are there suggestive movements that an elephant can make? Who is a sexy elephant going to turn on? Another dancing girl mentioned in the script that was questioned is a goldfish! In my book, I note the reviewer for the PCA was probably skimming the text and when they saw words that flagged their attention they circled them and later commented on them without noting the dancers were animals. I'm sure reviewing scripts all day was a dull job and people fell asleep at the wheel.' Cohen, correspondence to the author (Sept. 1997).

55. Joseph I. Breen, letter to Walt Disney (13 Dec. 1944), in the 'Disney 1944 *Song of the South*' file, PCA Special Collections.

56. F.S.H. (probably Francis Harmon), letter to J.I.B. (Joseph I. Breen) (31 July 1944), in the 'Disney 1944 *Song of the South*' file, PCA Special Collections.

57. Author unknown, analysis chart (ca. 1947), in the '*Alice in Wonderland* Disney 1947 (rel. 1951)' file, PCA Special Collections.

58. Healy, film analysis, in the '*Lady and the Tramp* Disney 1954' file, PCA Special Collections, Margaret Herrick Library, Beverly Hills, CA.

59. Bill Mikulak, 'Disney and the Art World: The Early Years', *Animation Journal* 4, 2 (Spring 1996): 18–42.

60. Ibid., 36. Mikulak quotes Frank S. Nugent, 'Disney is Now Art But He Wonders', *New York Times Magazine* (26 Feb. 1939): 4.

61. Mikulak, op. cit., 34.

62. J.B. Kaufman, 'Good Mousekeeping: Family-oriented Publicity in Disney's Golden Age', *Animation Journal* 3, 2: 78–85.

63. Herb A. Lightman, 'The Men Behind the Mouse: Part 1. A Day at Disney's', *American Cinematographer* (Oct. 1947): 354–355+; Herb A. Lightman, 'The Men Behind the Mouse: Part 2. How Animated Cartoons are Made', *American Cinematographer* (November 1947): 394–395+.

64. C.O. Slyfield, 'Sound in Animated Motion Pictures', *International Sound Technician* (ca. 1952): 2–5.

65. David Forgacs, 'Disney Animation and the Business of Childhood', *Screen* 33, 4 (Winter 1992): 361–374, 366.

66. Richard deCordova, 'The Mickey in Macy's Window: Childhood, Consumerism, and Disney Animation, in Eric Smoodin (ed.) *Disney Discourse: Producing the Magic Kingdom* (New York: Routledge, 1994): 203–213.

67. Cecil Munsey, *Disneyana: Walt Disney Collectibles* (New York: Hawthorne Books, 1974), 85–105, cited in deCordova, 'The Mickey in Macy's Window', 205.

68. deCordova, op. cit., 206.

69. Id.

70. J.B. Kaufman writes that the first club was started by California exhibitor Harry Woodin and apparently was in place by July 1929. Kaufman has notes on a letter Disney wrote to Charlie Giegerich (from the Powers office) on 30 July of that year, which included press clippings on the club, and a copy of another letter from Disney to Giegerich dated 16 September that expresses great enthusiasm for the concept. J.B. Kaufman, correspondence to the author (5 Aug. 1997 and 19 Aug. 1997).

71. deCordova, op. cit., 209.

72. Robin Allan, 'Sylvia Holland: Disney Artist', *Animation Journal* 2, 2 (Spring 1994): 32–41; Kaufman, 'Before Snow White', op. cit; and Maureen Furniss, 'Phyllis Craig: Ink and Paint', *Animation Journal* 5, 1 (Fall 1996).

73. Walt Disney, 'Walt's Talk to Studio Personnel in the Theater', 27 May 1941 (dated 14 Oct. 1942), Walt Disney Archives.

74. Walt Disney, untitled speech to employees, 10 and 11 Feb. 1941, Walt Disney Archives. All references to this speech in subsequent paragraphs were taken from the same manuscript.

75. For more on this period and the films that resulted from the trip, see J.B. Kaufman, 'Norm Ferguson and the Latin American Films of Walt Disney', in Jayne Pilling (ed.), *A Reader in Animation Studies* (London: John Libbey, 1997), 261–267.

76. Adrienne Tytla Gibb, *Disney Giant*, unpublished and undated manuscript quoted in 'John Canemaker, Vladimir Tytla – Master Animator', *Animation Journal* 3, 1 (Fall 1994): 4–30, 23.

77. Derek Bousé, 'True Life Fantasies: Storytelling Traditions in Animated Features and Wildlife Films', *Animation Journal* 3, 2 (Spring 1995): 19–39.

7

Full and limited animation

AESTHETICS OF FULL AND LIMITED ANIMATION

Two-dimensional (2D) animation can be described as fluctuating between two aesthetic poles: full animation and limited animation. These terms – which generally are not applied to puppets or other three-dimensional (3D) techniques – are basically quantitative measures, but they have acquired misleading qualitative connotations. Full and limited animation are two stylistic tendencies that can achieve different aesthetic results, with neither being inherently pleasing nor repellent, but both being subject to creative or uninspired applications.

A comparison of full and limited animation styles primarily will be concerned with four criteria: the movement of images, the metamorphosis of images, the number of images, and the dominance of visual and aural components.

Full animation employs constant movement with a minimum of cycles, while limited animation tends to utilise cycles or be devoid of movement to a great extent. Since the early years of animation history, virtually every studio has used cycles, largely as a way to reduce the total number of drawings that need to be made for a film, thus saving time and money. In some cases, cycles have been used somewhat creatively, as in Disney's first 'Alice Comedy', *Alice's Wonderland* (1923), where the cycled running of a group of lions is 'hidden' within varied backgrounds and a small number of repetitions. Sometimes cycles or sets of motions have been so generic that they can be used with little or no modification in more than one episode in a series of productions. However, the re-use of drawings is anathema to full animation.

In true full animation, every drawing in a production is used only once. Complicating the drawing process is that, in full animation, images tend to be highly metamorphic. Often, shapes are altered to reflect something about the character's feelings or reactions (personality animation, which relies heavily on movement, is associated with a full animation aesthetic). Also, characters in full animation frequently change proportions due to movements on the z-axis, toward and away from the foreground or 'camera'. In limited animation, one finds that there is much less shape-shifting of characters.

Because full animation involves constant movement and metamorphosis of shapes, with (theoretically) no cycling or re-use of drawings, a great amount of artwork is needed. The actual photography process of full animation also increases the need for drawings. When it comes time to record images with the animation camera, full animation requires more images per increment of the recording medium (film will be used as an example here) than limited animation. In animation, it is common to find any given pose used for one, two or even three frames of film. Using an image for only one frame of film, otherwise called filming 'on ones', provides much smoother movement of images than using an image for three frames of film, or filming 'on threes'. If an animated work is filmed on ones, it requires three times as many images than animation filmed on threes. Animation filmed on ones and twos is consistent with full animation, whereas threes, fours, fives or even sixes are associated with a limited animation style (filming on higher numbers produces a 'stepped' feeling of movement, which might be desirable to achieve a certain effect).

Camera movement also affects the amount of artwork used in animation. Limited animation tends to include extensive camera movements; for example, it is common for the camera to pan over a background to create a sense of motion. Sometimes, before the camera starts a pan, it will hold on the beginning and ending images for a few extra frames in order to use up more time, perhaps in an effort to save on drawings. The camera also might hold on characters for a relatively long period of time, possibly while only a very simple gesture occurs (such as blinking eyes).

So far, only visual elements have been discussed in terms of full and limited animation, but sound plays a role as well. While full animation has an emphasis on visuals, limited animation is dominated by its sound, typically in the form of voice-over narration or dialogue between characters. It is sometimes the case that limited animation uses a device to cover a character's mouth (such as a mask, or perhaps the character will turn his or her back to the viewer); that way, there are fewer complex drawings needed to synchronise lip movements to dialogue.

The best way to illustrate the differences between full and limited animation is to view two representative examples side by side; for example, a 'Mickey Mouse' short, such as *Clock Cleaners* (directed by Ben Sharpsteen, 1937), and an episode of 'Tetsuwan Atomu' ('Astro Boy'), *The Birth of Astro Boy* (directed by Osamu Tezuka, 1963).[1] In some ways, it is ideal to compare the aesthetics of 'Mickey Mouse' and 'Astro Boy' shorts because of the prominence of their two creators. The historical significance of Disney and the 'Mickey Mouse' series already has been discussed.

'Astro Boy' was created by the historically most important animator in Japan, Osamu Tezuka, a man who has influenced many in the field of animation, as well as print comics (as a previous chapter indicated, Japanese animation is known as *anime*, while Japanese comics are known as *manga*). In regard to the current Japanese manga industry, Frederik L. Schodt has stated that 'none of the major artists today has escaped his influence. Many have specifically said that they chose their career when they first read Tezuka's comics'.[2]

Although Tezuka trained to be a doctor, he was unsatisfied with that career. His real love was drawing and eventually Tezuka established himself as a major print

Fig. 7.1 *Disney Studios'*
Clock Cleaners *(1937)*
© *Disney Enterprises, Inc.*

cartoonist. He created comics that were stylistically unique because they adopted a very 'cinematic' approach, using the equivalent of close-ups and camera angles. Tezuka's comics tend to be very long, sometimes between 500 to 1000 pages in length. Pages are used without economy; a movement or facial expression might be shown in many frames, rather than in one. Today, manga artwork continues to reflect many of the characteristics of Tezuka's groundbreaking work.[3] Tezuka's influence also spread to the motion picture industry, particularly in respect to character design. For example, the 'big eyes' of his characters, originally influenced by the character designs of American and European animators, are now quite typical in anime.[4]

In 1963, Tezuka created 'Astro Boy' as the first made-for-television series in Japan. The series is based on Tezuka's successful print comics series, which had been launched in the early 1950s. Incidentally, Tezuka did not limit his animation work to television series. Later in his career, he made a number of interesting independent short films, including the popular *Onboro Film* (Broken Down Film, 1985), which contains a number of visual gags related to the mishaps of projecting an old film: while a simple love story is told, the audience sees shifting frame lines, an inverted title card, scratches and even a stray hair that gets into the frame.

By viewing the first few minutes of *The Birth of Astro Boy*, one can see the characteristics of limited animation quite clearly. As Astor Boynton III races down the super highway, cycles are used to repeat the action of cars passing by. Camera movements are used extensively to depict the 'drama' of the crash: a zoom in on faces reacting (without movement) in horror, a zoom out on the car crash itself, a pan along the rubble created by the accident. Often, shots linger on an image a moment before cutting. As Astor's father reacts to his son's accident, the characters in the crowd behind him are perfectly still. Back in his office, some rather generic mouth movements are the primary actions that accompany the doctor's speech about his plan to build a robot to replace his son.

Another mainstay of limited animation, voice-over narration, provides important plot information.

While *Clock Cleaners* opens with a zoom and contains a few cycled movements, in general it adheres to the principles of full animation. The actions of Mickey, Donald and Goofy cleaning their respective portions of the clock are varied and seldom repeated more than twice. The sleepy stork, an incidental character, seems to be included largely for the action it can cause in the film. While struggling with the bird, Mickey's shape squashes and stretches in an effort to push the intruder outside. To an even greater extent, Donald's body metamorphoses as he battles the renegade coil that springs up and mocks his every move. In this case, too, extra actions are thrown in, despite the fact that they do not advance the story in a significant way; for example, Donald's body 'tick tocks' back and forth for several seconds, while he tries to control the movement. A great deal of motion is created when Goofy is surprised while cleaning a bell. After it is struck, his legs squirm about like a bunch of wet spaghetti noodles, reacting to the shock. Here and elsewhere (e.g. as he attempts to punch the bell ringer) humour is created through the elongation of his body and other metamorphic changes. Later, when Goofy is knocked into a dizzy state, he dances along the edge of the structure and other precarious sites, accompanied by a musical score. Overall, dialogue plays a very small part in the film. In that respect, alone, it is clearly different from the episode of 'Astroboy'.

Once again, it should be stressed that the term 'limited animation' does not necessarily mean 'bad animation' – it merely indicates that a certain style has been employed. Sometimes, people tend to label limited animation as relatively bad because it looks 'easier' to do than full animation, the perception of worth being tied to a work ethic, or the value of labour.

Perhaps the term 'limited' is ill-conceived because it suggests that something is missing, or is of a 'limited' degree of quality. Jules Engel has said that there is really 'no such thing as limited animation, only limited talent ... Each style of graphic and each kind of gesture has its own requirements for motion'.[5] Engel's words provide the proper perspective from which to begin any analysis of full or, for lack of a better term, limited animation. In evaluating their use, ultimately, the question that must be asked is, does the use of full or limited animation seem consistent with the objectives of the work as a whole?

The previous chapter focused on The Walt Disney Company, which historically has dominated animation production and helped to naturalise the superiority of full animation. But, the power of the Disney Studio has not been absolute. Its strongest challenge came in the late 1940s and early 1950s, with the rise of limited animation and a studio called United Productions of America (UPA).

UNITED PRODUCTIONS OF AMERICA (UPA)

UPA was founded after World War II by three former employees of Disney named Dave Hilberman, Zachary Schwartz and Stephen Bosustow. Interested in modern art and liberal in their political leanings, these artists were determined to create a new style of animation, both in form and content. Using minimalist designs and stylised colour, UPA garnered great critical acclaim.[6]

UPA should be discussed as an alternative to the Disney Studio ideologically as well as aesthetically. The studio's founders and several other prominent artists who worked

Fig. 7.2 *UPA artists*
Courtesy Jules Engel

there departed from Disney in the early 1940s, largely as the result of the strike (discussed in Chapter 6). Former Disney employee Frank Tashlin was head of the Columbia animation unit at that time and hired a number of these Disney strikers off the picket line. A short time later, the United States entered World War II and many of the future UPA animators joined the Army's First Motion Picture Unit, which was stationed at Fort Roach in Culver City, California.

During the war, Hilberman, Schwartz, and Bosustow formed a company named Industrial Films and Poster Service, to create a film for the United Auto Workers (UAW), *Hell Bent for Election* (1944), which supported Franklin Delano Roosevelt in his presidential campaign. The liberal attitudes of company members also can be seen in another animated production made early in its history, *The Brotherhood of Man* (1946), a film about race relations, which also was sponsored by the UAW. These films were well received and helped to establish the studio's reputation.

The studio changed its name to United Productions of America and, after Schwartz and Hilberman sold their shares to Bosustow in 1946, again established a tie with Columbia. UPA's first two films for its new distributor, *Robin Hoodlum* (1948) and *The Magic Fluke* (1949), employed established characters from Columbia's 'The Fox and the Crow' series. The two films, which reflect the influence of modern art in their angular figures and use of flattened space, were well received, earning Academy Award nominations.

UPA's success rested on the talents of a diverse range of artists: director/animators Pete Burness, Bobe Cannon, John Hubley, Paul Julian, Bill Hurtz, and Ted Parmelee; colourist Jules Engel; designer Herb Klynn; and writers Bill Scott and Phil Eastman. They were joined for a period of time by experimental filmmakers John Whitney

Figs 7.3 & 7.4 *Jules Engel at work at UPA*
Courtesy Jules Engel

Figs 7.5 & 7.6 *UPA's*
Gerald McBoing Boing
(1951)
Courtesy Jules Engel

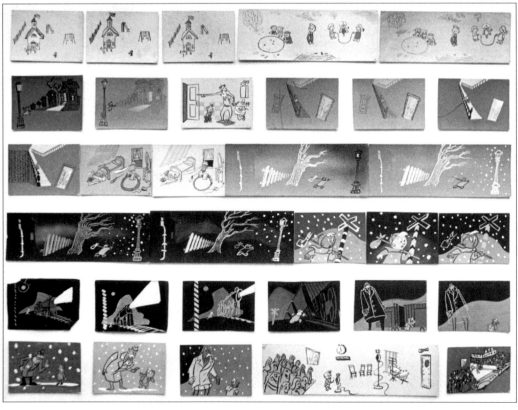

and Sidney Peterson, as well as animation director and jazz trumpeter Ernie Pintoff. These individuals worked together in a spirit Engel calls:

> ... democratic. Everyone was respected as an artist in his own field, and we all had the same presence. Everyone – even the ink & paint, which is usually the bottom of the heap – everyone was invited to the story conferences. We were all on the same level – no second class ... I think this was the first time in the industry that someone tried a system with no hierarchy – and no lowerarchy.[7]

Despite its ideological differences, Engel insists that 'UPA was not anti-Disney. Most of the key people had come from Disney, and we had left during times of strike and business difficulties ... UPA looked for new avenues. We used many devices of modern art in the graphic design and color'.[8] (See CPs 18 and 19.)

UPA's films reflect a concern with formal design and minimalism. Colour played a significant role in the creative process, with large, sometimes patterned, colour fields being used to suggest a simplified background space. One can see that the interior of the home in the Academy Award-winning *Gerald McBoing Boing* (directed by Bobe Cannon, 1951) has no perspective lines to indicate depth. To an even greater extent, the interiors of *The Tell-Tale Heart* (directed by Ted Parmalee, 1953) appear to be set in an ambiguous space. In addition, objects are not shaded to give them dimensionality but rather are rendered very flatly. These films are united by their foundation in modern art practices, though they reflect the diverse aesthetic sensibilities of the artists working at UPA.

UPA's new looks differed dramatically from that of other studios and garnered critical attention – even Disney productions were influenced by them. During the early 1950s, Disney produced two shorts that clearly reflect the UPA style: *Toot, Whistle, Plunk and Boom* (directed by Ward Kimball and Charles Nichols, 1953) and *Pigs is Pigs* (directed by Jack Kinney, 1954).

Aside from its modern design practices, UPA also was set apart from Disney, Warner Bros. and other animation studios by the storylines of its work. In turning to the

Fig. 7.8 *Disney Studios'*
Pigs is Pigs (1954)
© *Disney Enterprises, Inc.*

classic works of authors such as Theodore Geisel (also known as Dr. Seuss), Edgar
Allen Poe and James Thurber, the studio tended to develop plots involving human
characters, as opposed to humanised animal characters. For that reason, anthropo-
morphism is not apparent in the best-known work of UPA, such as *Gerald McBoing
Boing*, *Rooty-Toot-Toot* (dir. John Hubley, 1952), *Madeline* (dir. Bobe Cannon, 1952),
The Tell Tale Heart and the 'Mr. Magoo' series of films (directed largely by Pete
Burness, 1949–1959). Also unique is the studio's reluctance to use 'hurt gags', or
violence employed for the sake of humour. Instead of aiming for broad comedy,
UPA's productions were more oriented towards enrichment and the pursuit of culture,
which appealed to the expanding middle class of the 1950s. UPA aligned itself with
everything modern – in its art style, in its adaptation of contemporary literature, and
in its progressive social views.

During the 1950s, the nature of the film industry changed drastically, especially in
relation to the production of animation and other short films. One of the key points
cited in the demise of shorts units at Hollywood studios is the end of block booking,
which had forced exhibitors to purchase short films along with features and so-called
low-budget 'B pictures' in order to get the relatively few star-filled, prestige 'A
pictures'. For UPA, this factor and others, such as the investigation of communist
activities within the film industry, caused the studio to weaken during the mid-1950s.
The experience of one of the studio's animation directors, John Hubley, remains an
example of a worst-case scenario because, after being identified as a former member
of the communist party, he was blacklisted from the industry and had to continue
his work using a 'front man' to conduct business.

During that decade, there was an industry-wide shift in the dominant mode of
animation production in the United States. Rather than producing films for the 'big
screen', animation studios began creating work for a new exhibition venue: the 'small

screen' – television. In 1959, after all the branches of UPA (Los Angeles, New York and London) had closed, a number of its employees followed the trend and went into the new made-for-television animation industry.

MADE-FOR-TELEVISION ANIMATION

UPA gained critical acclaim in part due to the stylisation of its productions, which included the use of limited animation. Although UPA's work originally was created for theatrical screenings, the use of limited animation shortly became associated with television to a much greater extent. Limited animation was embraced by many studios as a way to create animation quickly and at relatively low prices, which worked well with the restricted production time and the small budgets of the fledgling television industry.

Unionisation had contributed toward the greatly increased price of creating animation during the 1940s, so the entire industry was feeling the effects of higher costs. Since the viability and widespread acceptance of television was still uncertain until the mid-1950s, few people were willing to invest large sums of money in it. Clearly, television programs featuring full animation were the last thing on anyone's mind. As an alternative, limited animation was used in children's programs and sometimes in television commercials.

Aesthetics of early television animation

Karl Cohen has researched a number of early studios that created animated advertisements for television. He notes that television ads in the United States date from 1941, 'when the government allowed NBC to go commercial (to charge for ads) on 1 July of that year'.[9] At first, ads were presented live, but it did not take long for filmed ads – including animated spots – to appear. Cohen sites four companies as being the major producers of animated advertising for television at the end of the 1940s: Fletcher Smith Studios, Tempo, Transfilm, and Shamus Culhane Productions. He notes that 'all had animation directors who had worked for Metro-Goldwyn-Mayer, Disney, and/or Fleischer during the 1930s'.[10]

An article in the May 1945 issue of *Television* describes an example of an extremely limited animated work: 'a three-minute film commercial designed to fill in the air-time between programs', which 'was successfully tried out for the first time in television recently on WBKB (Balaban & Katz), Chicago'.[11] The article explains that the spot, which was for Red Heart Dog Food, 'consisted of 36 cartoons and headlines. These were alternately filmed onto two 35 mm-slide film strips and projected directly onto the face of the iconoscope using lap dissolves. The sound was a narration in rhyme, recorded over a musical background'.[12]

This example stretches the boundaries of what most people would call 'animation'. The ad is composed of a series of still shots that are linked together by camera effects. If 36 frames are used over three minutes, the average screen time for any image would be five seconds. As a result, the transitions from image to image would have to be a great deal slower than the average speed of animation, in which (film) images typically change imperceptibly every one-eighth, one-twelfth, or one-twenty-fourth of a sec-

Herkimer, the Red Heart dog cries when he thinks he cannot win the award. He cheers up when he learns that he will win the Red Heart medal.

Herkimer and his Red Heart award. These stills were taken from the three-minute film commercial.

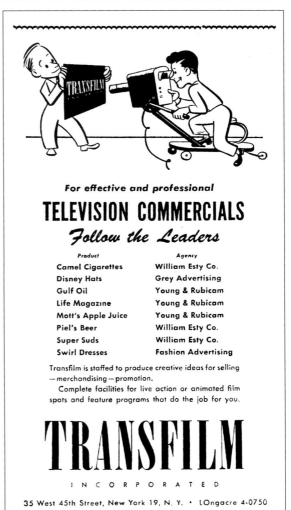

For effective and professional

TELEVISION COMMERCIALS
Follow the Leaders

Product	Agency
Camel Cigarettes	William Esty Co.
Disney Hats	Grey Advertising
Gulf Oil	Young & Rubicam
Life Magazine	Young & Rubicam
Mott's Apple Juice	Young & Rubicam
Piel's Beer	William Esty Co.
Super Suds	William Esty Co.
Swirl Dresses	Fashion Advertising

Transfilm is staffed to produce creative ideas for selling — merchandising — promotion.
Complete facilities for live action or animated film spots and feature programs that do the job for you.

TRANSFILM
INCORPORATED

35 West 45th Street, New York 19, N. Y. • LOngacre 4-0750

ond. Nonetheless, this example demonstrates the situation into which early made-for-television animation was introduced. The article notes that the cost of the commercial was approximately $325, adding that 'other producers and advertisers anxious to tee-off with an economical but still effective commercial will find this technique an excellent pattern to follow'.[13]

By the late 1960s, television advertising had become a well-established endeavour. However, as Leonard Glasser explains, limited animation techniques and general money-saving tactics continued to be employed to a great extent. Glasser's studio, Stars and Stripes Productions Forever Productions [sic], with offices in New York, Chicago and Toronto, created over 300 popular wholly animated or animation and live-action combined commercials for major clients between 1963 and 1971. Despite his success, Glasser says he often had to find ways of making creative productions on relatively low budgets. One way he lowered costs was by composing lyrics himself and by recording his own voice for a number of commercials.[14]

One of the first jobs Glasser ever accepted was to make an advertisement for a battery charger on a budget of $1100. Glasser knew that there was no way he could produce a one-minute commercial on that budget, but he accepted the contract and had to come up with a way to produce the spot. Eventually, he got the idea to have the lights

Fig. 7.9 (left) *Red Heart Dog Food ad (ca. 1945),* and **Fig. 7.10** (right) *an advertisement for an early television advertiser, Transfilm Incorporated (late 1940s)*
Courtesy Karl Cohen

go out almost as soon as the commercial started. As a result, he could use black leader for most of the running time; only at the very end, after a light was found, did the lights (and the images) come back on.

Despite the amount of business that Stars and Stripes attracted, budgets remained under $10,000 for a one-minute ad (which was the standard length through the 1970s). Glasser estimates that production schedules for animated shorts ranged from eight to twelve weeks. In order to save time and money, the ads sometimes were shot on fours or sixes, although he preferred to shoot on twos.[15]

By the 1980s, production values in animated advertising had risen, along with budgets. Eventually, a few studios began to set new standards for television advertising. Such was the case with Kurtz & Friends, founded by Bob Kurtz in 1972, which used full animation techniques to produce ads for major clients such as Chevron Oil, Levi jeans, and AT&T. However, limited animation remained very much the mainstay of other aspects of the made-for-television industry.

Many changes were made in the structure of the Hollywood film industry because of consent decrees that followed the Paramount anti-trust case in 1947. One consequence of the restructured system was the widespread closing of studio animation units during the 1950s and the sale of existing animated product to the expanding television market; thus, the 'golden age' of Hollywood studio animation ended by the mid 1950s, while the 'made-for-television' era began at about the same time.

In his discussion of 'Crusader Rabbit' (1949–1951), the first animated series to be made for television, Karl Cohen demonstrates that being economical was a very important consideration.[16] The process used by the series's creators, Alexander Anderson and Jay Ward, encapsulates the techniques of limited animation:

> ... to keep the series within its tight budget, Anderson let the soundtrack carry the momentum. He limited the amount of cel art by using a good deal of cut-outs. He also made use of a lot of camera movement over the static or almost-static images. Details, such as mouth movements, were standardised and limited ... A stock image library was set up that included standard cycle movements, reaction shots and other artwork that could be used or copied quickly ...[17]

The stories, starring a smart rabbit and his big, dumb tiger sidekick, Rags, were divided into short episodes with cliff-hanger endings, in a format similar to radio adventure serials.[18] Once a week, Anderson and Ward completed a week's worth of voice recordings and animation at their company, Television Arts Productions, Inc. They recorded between the hours of 9 p.m. and 4 a.m. In the words of voice artist Lucille Bliss, they worked 'grueling hours, but the studio time was cheaper then'.[19]

The series was produced by Jerry Fairbanks, who completed post-production at his own studio. Fred Patten notes that the producer attempted 'to present limited animation as a dynamic technological advance. As *Daily Variety* put it: "Newly developed Teletoon animation technique will be used in filming the series. Method eliminates many of the costly features of theatrical animation, yet retains the illusion of movement and life, according to Fairbanks." '[20]

After he stopped making 'Crusader Rabbit' shorts, Anderson went into advertising and Ward temporarily left the animation business. In the late 1950s, Ward went back into television, founding Jay Ward Productions. He started production on 'Rocky and his Friends' in 1958, with the help of Bill Scott and other UPA veterans who were looking for work after that studio closed its doors. 'Rocky and his Friends' made its debut on the ABC Television Network in November 1959, but never received high ratings and was cancelled in 1961; from 1961 to 1964, it ran as 'The Bullwinkle Show' on NBC, hosted by a moose puppet that was voiced and moved by Scott, who wrote and produced the show as well.

Despite the series' mixed success, it nonetheless remains a cult favourite today, in large measure due to its writing. The humorous dialogue is sophisticated and sometimes subtle with a reflexive quality woven throughout, as characters acknowledge their status as performers in an animated world. Typical of limited animation techniques, one finds that sound, rather than action, propels the story.

When one discusses the use of limited animation on American television, yet another studio inevitably comes to mind: Hanna-Barbera, which had a huge influence on the practices of American made-for-television animation. The studio was founded by Bill Hanna and Joe Barbera in 1957, after the closing of the MGM studio, where they both had worked. They proposed to make short films for television for around $3000 per episode, or approximately one-tenth of what the average studio-produced animation was costing at that time. The studio's first series was 'Ruff and Ready' (1957–1964), which Charles Solomon notes 'owed a great deal to "Crusader Rabbit" '.[21] It was introduced by a live host who used puppets.

The studio's next series was the popular 'The Huckleberry Hound Show' (1958–1962), which introduced the Yogi Bear character in 1960. One of the studio's most successful series was 'The Flintstones', which debuted on ABC in 1960. The series is particularly noteworthy because it was aired successfully in a prime time evening slot, which no other show until 'The Simpsons' in the late 1980s managed to do for any length of time.[22] Despite the popular and economic success of the Hanna-Barbera studio, critics were not kind, blaming it for spreading the wildfire of limited animation, which led to the perceived artistic stagnation of the American animation industry.

By the mid-1960s, the concept of 'Saturday morning cartoons' was well established within the American television industry. The CBS network led the way with nine half-hour shows that proved to be extremely attractive to advertisers (aiming product at children). The other networks followed in the same footsteps, demanding more animated product and, as a result, causing a flood of cheaply and rapidly produced series to appear.

Increasingly, complaints were aimed at the artistic integrity of the series; Jeff Lenburg finds that 'one recurring criticism of television animation was that the work often appeared rushed, thus dramatically undermining the quality'.[23] In the opinion of veteran animator Friz Freleng, the networks cared little about aesthetic issues:

> The networks go for the numbers (or viewers). They don't care what the quality of the show is – I don't think they even watch the shows. As long as it's got high numbers, it doesn't matter whether the show is good or not.[24]

Writing in the 1980s, Leonard Maltin explained how he believed that the series produced by Hanna-Barbera had contributed to the situation:

> ... at first Hanna-Barbera cartoons compensated for their visual shortcomings with excellent comedy scripts, but before long all the good intentions were defeated by the sheer volume of work. Repetition – of character design and development as well as of stories – became stultifying in the studio's enormous output. However, kids didn't seem to mind, so advertisers and television executives had no cause for complaint. Other studios followed Hanna-Barbera's lead, and soon this kind of assembly-line product was considered the norm.[25]

As a result of the increased load of production for 'Saturday morning', more and more work began to be shipped overseas, to low-paid labourers who would do the inking and painting, among other things. As American artists saw more and more jobs leaving the country, they became increasingly hostile to the animation that was being produced for television.

During this period, the animation industry became increasingly commercialised, particularly in the early 1980s, when there were significant changes in government regulations concerning children's programming (they are discussed in detail in Chapter ten). However, later in that decade, particularly after the great success of the innovative Disney feature *Who Framed Roger Rabbit* (1988), Hollywood once again became interested in the potential of animated features to attract not only children, but adult viewers. Shortly thereafter, the made-for-television industry in the United States also became re-energised – by the remarkable success of the Fox Network's primetime series, 'The Simpsons' (beg. 1989).

Contemporary uses of limited animation

During the 1990s, made-for-television animation in the United States has been undergoing a creative rebirth, with more popular and successful shows on the air than ever before. Limited animation still plays a significant role in the aesthetics of the new shows; however, one finds much less obvious criticism of the technique than existed in previous years. How can this be explained? Perhaps the expectations and sensibilities of the critical establishment and viewers are changing. On the other hand, it could be that limited animation is being used in a more creative and aesthetically pleasing manner. In fact, it is likely that both possibilities are true.

The increased acceptance of limited animation has arisen partly as a result of a changing cultural context. Today's viewer has more than likely grown up watching limited animation techniques on television, rather than the full animation typically found in films screened in a theatre. Of course, Disney features and other theatrical works continue to employ full animation and it is likely that many people still have a preference for and place value on the techniques of full animation in the classical style. Nonetheless, it seems that, in general, there is now more tolerance for limited animation, a fact that is probably due to the dominance of made-for-television series in the animation industry during recent years.

One also can argue that there has been an increasingly creative use of limited animation, which has hastened its acceptance. The remainder of this chapter will explore this notion, focusing on two primetime series, 'The Simpsons' and 'King of the Hill' (begun in 1997), both of which air on the Fox Network and both of which are animated by the Film Roman studio in Hollywood (with additional work done offshore).[26]

While both series are created with relatively high-production values, they employ limited animation. However, limited animation techniques are used within the series in a creative way, so that the animation style seems to enhance the depiction of characters and their activities. Limited animation is employed in a somewhat stylised manner, and is set within backgrounds that tend to be quite elaborate and detailed, drawing attention away from the simplicity of the movement. Creative editing and camera movements are used to some extent, in keeping with the aesthetic of limited animation, but they are used as storytelling devices rather than merely efforts at saving time and money (which of course they are as well). The episodes that will be examined in this chapter are *Hurricane Neddy* (1996) from 'The Simpsons' and *King of the Ant Hill* (1997) from 'King of the Hill'.[27] However, any number of other episodes could be used just as well.

Typical of limited animation, the two shows are very dialogue driven and characters tend to be relatively still. In most cases, the only part of a speaking character that moves to any degree is his or her mouth. One notices that, when crowds – or even just one or two listeners – are present, those characters tend to stand perfectly still or move very little, usually only blinking their eyes. In both episodes, more than one example of this kind of 'still crowd' occur. In *Hurricane Neddy*, a large group of people gather outside Ned Flanders's home after it has been rebuilt and subsequently falls apart; as he breaks into a rampage, no one in the crowd moves a muscle. Similarly, in *King of the Ant Hill*, when Dale is standing on the lawn, speaking to Hank and the others about fire ants, he is the only one who moves.

Even when characters do move, the animation does not reflect some of the primary characteristics of full animation, such as squash and stretch. However, the lack of squash and stretch seems in keeping with the development of a relatively realistic diegesis concerning human(-like) characters. However, care is given to synchronise the mouth movements with the (English) dialogue – another realistic touch.

On the other hand, the actual characters are not rendered with much of an attempt to create realism. The characters in 'The Simpsons' are clearly caricatures and the characters of 'King of the Hill' are purposely created to be flat and somewhat rough in design, parallelling the style one finds in Mike Judge's 'Beavis and Butt-Head' series. In both 'The Simpsons' and 'King of the Hill', the characters are for the most part drawn without shading or the suggestion of dimensionality, a technique that is relatively common among animated series.[28]

While the characters are fairly simple in terms of design and movement, backgrounds are visually compelling.[29] In the 'Simpsons', visual interest is created by the design of the scenes, which often employ a vast array of colours within a single shot. For example, the large crowd outside Flanders's home – as well as the rubble that had been there previously – is painted with a rainbow of colours, which hardly allows the viewers' eyes to rest on any one spot. The diversity of the colours seems to help keep the eye 'in movement', though the characters themselves are relatively still.

Sometimes, gray imagery provides a contrast with the characters' brightly coloured universe. One example in *Hurricane Neddy* is the scene in which ominous storm clouds appear. They are painted in variations of gray and move in a rapid, precisely even pace across the sky. The use of gray imagery also is used in depicting kitschy old movie footage of the 'Juvenile Aggression Study'. In this case, the 'black and white' design also works as a convention to signify 'old' film stock.

In 'The Simpsons', coloured areas generally are painted very 'flatly', with little or no attempt at shading. As a result, there is no development of a realistic spatial quality; although perspective lines are drawn in, the flatness of the coloured regions work against a dimensional reading. In contrast, backgrounds in 'King of the Hill' seem to be rendered with a concern for dimensionality. One can see that trees and other environmental objects are painted with variations in colour to suggest that they have substance and depth. While they, too, provide visual interest, they obviously do so in a way that is different from than the flattened, busy patches of colour in 'The Simpsons' environment. On the whole, 'King of the Hill' is more subdued than 'The

Simpsons' in terms of character action and visual design. More similarity can be found in the way that images are captured.

In both episodes, camera movements are used in a manner that is consistent with limited animation techniques, with pans or tilts moving over still artwork. For example, in *Hurricane Neddy*, the camera zooms out after Ned climbs on top of the rubble that once was his home. In *King of the Ant Hill*, the camera pans down the Eco-Kill instructions in Peggy's hand and later pans down the incriminating maps that hang in Dale's home. More visually engaging is a stepped zoom that occurs when Dale finds Peggy in his basement.

However, the camera movements – and editing – also are used creatively within both episodes, breaking up the stillness of the limited animation with various techniques: segments of relatively fast action, rapid cutting, relatively unusual perspectives and *z*-axis movement. For example, in *Hurricane Neddy*, bad weather necessitates rapid action in some scenes, as the wind whips through the town, causing objects to fly around rapidly. In part of the episode, relatively quick scene changes occur through a series of dissolves, while Ned is undergoing the eight-month 'University of Minnesota Spankological Protocol'. An optical illusion creates visual interest elsewhere, when the community shows Ned his new house. What looks like a long, curved hallway turns out to be a mistake: a badly constructed space that narrows and ends in mid-air. Barney's full-size face peering through a small door, reminiscent of an image from *Alice in Wonderland*, adds humour to the scene. True *z*-axis movement, another device that adds visual interest, is included when Flanders walks down the aisle in his church and when he is dragged into the mental hospital.

In *King of the Ant Hill*, *z*-axis movement is used to depict Hank and Peggy driving into the garden shop. Later, Peggy enters on the *z*-axis in a scene where Hank is shot from a low angle as he runs his hands through the soil. In both shots, movement toward the foreground creates complexity in the animated figures and movements. This episode of 'King of the Hill' also employs quick cutting, typical of a chase scene in a live-action production. As Hank follows Dale around his truck, rapid editing and character movement adds excitement to the pursuit.

Cycling is another significant component of limited animation that can be found in both episodes. In *Hurricane Neddy*, cycles are used somewhat subtly to depict wind and rain. They also are used more obviously to show the background as Ned drives to the Calmwood mental hospital after his breakdown. Certainly, there is no attempt to fool the viewer into thinking that the background images are anything but cycles. These kinds of repetitions become part of the kitsch – so bad that they are good, as the saying goes. Kitsch value also appears in the grainy black-and-white film of the aggression study sponsored by 1950s-style 'Angry Man Dinners', a parody of the 'Hungry Man' TV dinners sold in the United States.[30]

Cycling sometimes is used quite purposefully to provide humour – for example, at the end of *King of the Ant Hill*, when Hank drives around and around his small patch of sod, tracing the exact same path. It is difficult to imagine this action occurring within a live-action production. If a live character were to go around and around without deviation, the viewer might assume that the character's perception was impaired for some reason (why else would he or she trace the same route?). But here, within the context of animation, the cycle functions as a comic device.

One can see that limited animation is used throughout the episodes analysed here, as well as in the rest of the two series. But, rather than detracting from the overall quality of the work, its use actually adds a positive element in terms of storytelling.

Limited animation is in keeping with a kind of middle-class sensibility that is central to the two series, creating a 'flatness' in the families' daily lives. 'The Simpsons' is set in Springfield, which is perhaps the most common name among cities in the United States. 'King of the Hill' is set in Arlen, Texas, and is based on an amalgam of personalities that creator Mike Judge knew from his experience growing up in New Mexico and Texas. These two series are not about people who move fast or have overly exciting lives; limited animation helps to reinforce this fact visually.

In an article written in 1989, 'The Simpsons' animation director, David Silverman, stressed it was important that 'the animation remains in character. We describe it as robotic, frenetic. Maybe funky is the word ...'.[31] Although 'The Simpsons' has changed considerably since 1989, the point to be taken here is that, whether the techniques can be classified within the tradition of full or limited animation, they should remain in keeping with the overall intentions of the production. In a series about quirky, maladjusted people, the smooth, cartoony look of full animation could work against the content. By embracing limited animation, these series to some extent mark themselves as being outside the mainstream, or representing a different vision of life. If full animation represents the *status quo*, perhaps limited animation can be interpreted as an alternative practice, allowing for more effective expression of marginal points of view (making it a potentially subversive practice that has economic benefits as well).

Whereas this chapter and the majority of the previous chapters have focused on aspects of two-dimensional animation almost exclusively, the next chapter of the book will examine the aesthetics of three-dimensional animation, including clay, puppets and the pixilation of living things. Throughout history, these techniques have been used by animators across the world. Within recent years, the creation of three-dimensional animation and the popularity of the resulting work has grown rapidly, furthering the commercial and aesthetic possibilities of animation production as a whole.

Notes

1. The English-language version of the episode, not the original Japanese version, is used in this comparison. The intention is to discuss the aesthetics of limited animation in a general sense, so the relevance of the example does not rest on the faithfulness of the adaptation for English-speaking audiences.

2. Frederik L. Schodt, *Manga! Manga! The World of Japanese Comics* (New York: Kodansha, 1986), 64. Despite Tezuka's historical importance, another animator, Hayao Miyazaki, is considered to be the most successful animation director in Japan today, with many extremely popular works, including *Nausicaa of the Valley of the Wind* (1984) and *My Neighbor Totoro* (1988), among others. Miyazaki began his career as an assistant animator at Tezuka's company, Mushi Productions. For an introduction to the Japanese animation industry, see John Beam, 'An Animato! Introduction to Anime', *Animato!* 30 (Fall 1994): 60–61.

3. For more on Tezuka's comic book work, or Japanese manga in general, see Frederik L. Schodt, *Dreamland Japan: Writings on Modern Manga* (Berkeley: Stone Bridge, 1996).

4. See Philip Brophy, 'Ocular Excess: A Semiotic Morphology of Cartoon Eyes', *Art & Design* profile 53 (March 1997): 26–33.

5. Jules Engel in William Moritz, 'The United Productions of America: Reminiscing Thirty Years Later', *ASIFA Canada* 12, 3 (Dec. 1984): 14–22, 17.

6. An overview of UPA can be found in Charles Solomon, *The History of Animation: Enchanted Drawings* (New York: Wings, 1994), 207–227.
7. Engel, quoted in Moritz, op. cit., 16.
8. Ibid., 17.
9. He adds, 'some promotions were even shown before that date, but they were not paid commercials: they were experiments created so potential sponsors could see how ads might look on TV once it went commercial'. Karl Cohen, 'The Development of Animated TV Commercials in the 1940s', *Animation Journal* 1, 1 (Fall 1992): 34–54, 36. Following the article, Cohen lists a number of studios that were operating at the time.
10. Karl Cohen, op. cit., 40.
11. Anonymous, 'Commercials', *Television* (May 1945): 22–23, 22. This article was given to the author by Karl Cohen.
12. Id.
13. Id. The article mentions that the $325 cost was the price of the experimental ad, but suggests that the price on a commercial basis would be nearer to $450.
14. Leonard Glasser, interview with the author in Studio City, CA (25 March 1997).
15. Id.
16. Karl Cohen, 'The Origins of TV Animation: "Crusader Rabbit" and "Rocky and Bullwinkle"', *Animatrix* 1, 4 (1987–1988): 1–8, 1. In its initial run, 195 episodes of 'Crusader Rabbit' were produced. Several years later (1957–1959), the production of an additional 260 colour episodes were produced by other individuals.
17. Ibid., 2–3.
18. Fred Patten, 'Some Notes on "Crusader Rabbit"', *Animatrix* 6 (1990–1992): 29–36, 30.
19. Lucille Bliss, quoted in Patten, op. cit., 32. See also Karl Cohen, 'Lucille Bliss: From Crusader Rabbit to Smurfette', *Animato!* 28 (Spring 1994): 30–31+.
20. Patten refers to a *Daily Variety* article of 17 Jan. 1949. Fred Patten, op. cit., 30.
21. Charles Solomon, op. cit., 237.
22. A number of series have been tried in prime time slots. See Bill Givens, ' "The Simpsons" Marks the Return of Prime Time Adult Animation', *Animation Magazine* (Fall 1989): 22–25.
23. Jeff Lenburg, *The Encyclopedia of Animated Cartoons* (New York: Facts on File, 1991), 13.
24. Fris Freleng, quoted in Lenburg, op. cit., 13.
25. Leonard Maltin, *Of Mice and Magic: A History of American Animated Cartoons* (New York: NAL, 1987), 344.
26. These two series are related in a number of ways, not the least of which is their proximity in programming. 'King of the Hill' made its debut on 12 January 1997, in the Sunday 8.30 p.m. slot directly following 'The Simpsons', which helps to assure it a large audience (especially considering that the next show in the line-up at 9.00 p.m. is another incredible hit, 'The X-Files').
27. The first US air date of *Hurricane Neddy* was 29 December 1996 and the first US air date of *King of the Ant Hill* was 4 May 1997. In the United States, these two episodes aired as reruns on the Fox Network on 29 June 1997.
28. However, the convention of the action-adventure series, including comedy-adventures such as 'The Mighty Ducks' and 'Pinky and the Brain', is to render characters with one-tone modelling. A dimensional effect is created by painting a shadow along the edge of the character to give it a kind of dimensional form and a sense of a 'drama'. In series that are not action based, such as 'The Muppet Babies' or 'Lulu', one tends to see a lack of dimensionality, similar to what one finds throughout most of 'The Simpsons' and 'King of the Hill'.
29. At the Film Roman Studio, each episode of 'The Simpsons' is treated as though it is a 'special', according to Phyllis Craig, who worked in the Studio's Color Key department. She explains that each episode is given its own set of directors and artists, and is treated with more care than most series receive. One of the special treatments given to the series is in the rendering of backgrounds. Craig says, 'we do the background on cels ... that's what gives it that good graphic look. For every other show, the backgrounds are done by background artists on background boards'; she adds, 'the people that work in the Color Key department for "The Simpsons" all have a very strong graphic art background. It's urgent in their case. We tried

putting a regular color key person in there and she just couldn't do it. It really takes a good graphic art background and a whole different sense'. Phyllis Craig, interview with the author (ca. August 1995). For more information, see Maureen Furniss, 'Animation and Color Key: The Career of Phyllis Craig', *Animation Journal* 5, 1 (Fall 1996): 58–70.

30. The bad art/good art opposition occurs throughout the series, whether the series is referencing its own roots in comic books, pandering to the commericialism of Crusty, or revelling in the ultra-violence of its made-for-television series, 'The Itchy and Scratchy Show'. How can one blame the series for having these attributes when it quite candidly admits to them?

31. Givens, op. cit., 23.

8

Three-dimensional animation

AESTHETICS OF THREE-DIMENSIONAL ANIMATION

So far, much of this book has focused on two-dimensional (2D) animation techniques; for example, the use of paper, cels or other surfaces on which images can be drawn or painted. These media are called two-dimensional because they only have the dimensions of height and width; any depth must be created through techniques of rendering perspective. This chapter will overview a completely different category of animation techniques. It focuses on animation made with objects that have body and form in themselves. These media have height, width and depth – that is, three dimensions (3D).

As this book has pointed out already, 3D animation has a long history. However, for many years 2D animation techniques (particularly cel animation) have overshadowed 3D animation both in terms of commercial success and scholarly discussion. Today, the situation has changed to some extent because there is more 3D animation production worldwide and increased critical attention to it. This chapter will focus on three particular types of 3D animation: clay, puppets, and pixilation.

Overview of the techniques

Each of the three techniques discussed here has persevered throughout motion picture history, developing prominence at certain moments and in different locations. In

the United States, clay animation has become increasingly popular in recent years
largely due to the creative efforts of Will Vinton and his studio's patented Claymation
process. Vinton achieved fame with such works as the 1975 Academy Award-winning
short *Closed Mondays* and the Oscar-nominated *The Great Cognito* from 1982, as well
as a series of popular television commercials featuring 'The California Raisins' (1989)
(see CPs 20 and 21). Giannalberto Bendazzi explains that, with the success of *Closed
Mondays*, 'for the first time after many unsuccessful attempts and limited uses, clay
found a place in animation', particularly in terms of commercial practices.[1]

One of the most memorable of these early attempts was 'The Gumby Show' (see CP
22), produced by Art Clokey and NBC in 1956–1957.[2] The Gumby theme song claims
that the character 'was once a little green slab of clay'; however, it would be more
accurate to describe him as a slab of 'Plasticine', which is the name of the oil-based
clay substance most commonly used in clay animation. The clay generally used for
fine-art sculpture is water based and it dries out too easily to be used for animation.[3]

For many years, the practice of puppet animation was strongly connected with Eastern
Europe. Many consider the Czech artist Jirí Trnka, creator of such works as *Song of
the Prairie* (1949) and *Ruka* (The Hand, 1965) (see CP 23), to be a master of this genre.
A traditionally trained puppeteer, he directed a Prague studio that has released many
of his country's most celebrated puppet films; during this time, he worked closely
with animators such as Bretislav Pojar, who contributed greatly to Trnka's work.
Another well-known representative of this tradition is George Pal, who was born in
Hungary and lived in various places before settling into a career in Hollywood. There
he created the 'Puppetoons' series for Paramount and later became known for his
special effects as a producer of science fiction feature films, such as *Destination Moon*
(directed by Irving Pichel, 1950) and *War of the Worlds* (directed by Byron Haskin,
1953). Russian-born Lou Bunin is yet another well-known puppet animator. He
directed a puppet theatre in Chicago and later worked in Hollywood, creating
sequences for the MGM feature *Ziegfeld Follies* (directed by Vincent Minnelli, 1946)

Fig. 8.2 *Jirí Trnka adjusting the set from* Song of the Prairie *(1949)*

Courtesy Trnka Studio

and a live-action/animation feature *Alice in Wonderland* (directed by Dallas Bower, 1950).

These and other Eastern European animators have had great influence on puppet animation around the world. For example, it is said that Japanese artist Kihachiro Kawamoto, who had a strong interest in his country's traditional marionette and puppet theatre, became interested in animation after viewing Trnka's *Cisaruv Slavík* (The Emperor's Nightingale, 1948). He studied with Trnka, among others, for two years and in 1965 returned to Japan to work in television and make such puppet films as *Dojoji* (The Dojoji Temple, 1976) and *Kataku* (The House of Flames, 1979).[4]

Today, puppet animation has been re-invigorated by a number of people working outside Eastern Europe. For example, American Henry Selick, owner of Twitching Image Inc., gained renown as the director of *Slow Bob in the Lower Dimensions* (1991), *The Nightmare Before Christmas*

Fig. 8.3 Alice in Wonderland *(1950) includes sequences created by Lou Bunin* From Le quotidian 5, Centre International du Cinéma d'Animation *(3 June 1995): I*

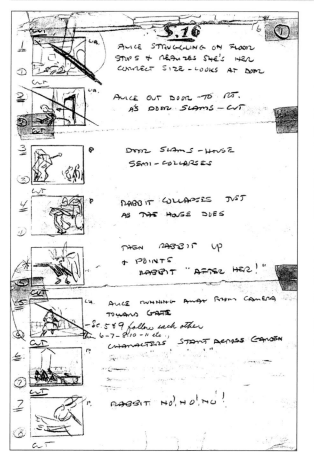

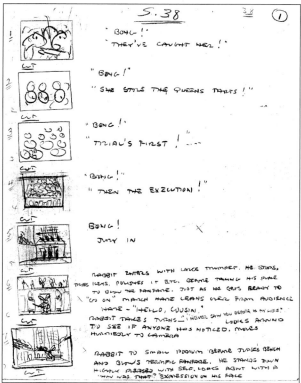

(1993) and *James and the Giant Peach* (1996).[5] British animator Barry Purves has won acclaim for his sophisticated puppet animations, including *Screenplay* (1991) and *Rigoletto* (1993). And the American Brothers Quay (Stephen and Timothy), who work out of a London studio, are well-known figures in the realm of puppet animation, due in large measure to the popularity of their 1986 film, *Street of Crocodiles*.

Related to puppet animation is the use of hand-controlled puppets or marionettes that are filmed in real time. Because the objects are made to 'act' in front of the camera and are not moved incrementally for frame-by-frame recording, these techniques are more akin to live-action work than animation. Nonetheless, they merit a bit of attention here.

One individual whose work falls into this category is Gerry Anderson, who created several popular made-for-television series in Britain, including 'Stingray' (1964), 'The Thunderbirds' (1965) and 'Captain Scarlett' (1967). To make his characters move realistically, he employed a technique he called 'super-marionation', which involves the use of wires and machinery that synchronise mouth movements to the dialogue being spoken.[6] Better known on a larger scale is the 'muppeteering' of American Jim Hensen and his studio, which has appeared in the 'Sesame Street' and 'The Muppet Show' television series, as well as in feature films. Henson's studio has designed many animal puppets, including Kermit the Frog and Miss Piggy, that are controlled by the hand of a 'muppeteer' who is hidden below the stage or otherwise manipulated in real time.

Pixilation is another technique that closely borders on live-action practice, although it clearly falls within the realm of animation. Whereas clay and puppet animators move inanimate objects incrementally before a camera and shoot them frame by frame, the pixilation animator shoots 'live' objects – essentially, people – frame by frame. Some of the best examples of pixilation are found in the work of Norman McLaren in films such as *A Chairy Tale* (1957) (see Fig. 5.6), *Two Bagatelles* (1952) and *Neighbors* (1952) (see Figs 5.1 and 5.2). Probably because of the difficulty of directing live performers in terms of individual frame movements, as well as the highly stylised look of the performance, pixilation has not been a widely used technique in commercial animation.[7]

However, the Bolex Brothers used the technique in a feature-length film entitled *The Secret Adventures of Tom Thumb*, which was released in 1993. The studio is based in Bristol, England, and is headed by Dave Borthwick and Richard Hutchinson. They explain that pixilation was employed in the film partly as a result of budgetary concerns, saying:

It goes back to short films we were making from the mid-eighties onward; four, five minutes long ... We couldn't afford to make models so we tended to work with ready-mades, anything we could find around the house; Action Men and things like that. And of course one of the best ready-mades you can get is the human body. In terms of joints, all the stuff is already there.[8]

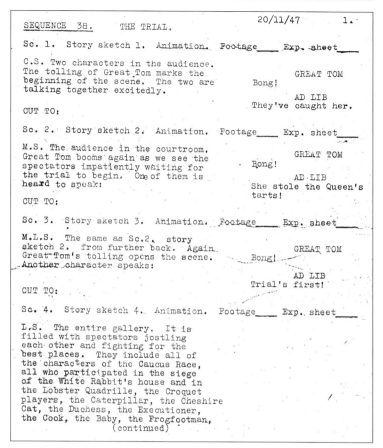

Fig. 8.8 *Scene from 'The Thunderbirds' (1960) by Gerry Anderson 'The Thunderbirds' is the property of Polygram Television. Postcard © & TM 1993 ITC Entertainment Group Limited. All rights reserved*

Fig. 8.9 *A Chairy Tale (1957) by Norman McLaren Courtesy NFB*

Backgrounds and characters

Clearly, the technique of pixilation has a lot in common with live-action motion picture making. However, all relationships being relative, one actually might find that clay and puppet animation also are quite similar to live-action cinema, at least in comparison with 2D animation techniques. For example, almost all 3D animation is shot horizontally on a set of some sort, just like live-action motion pictures. In contrast, 2D animation generally is recorded from a camera placed overhead – that is, vertically. The use of sets for 3D animation makes it possible to get a number of angles on the action with relative ease.

However, the scale of 3D animation can impede one's ability to get certain kinds of shots (e.g. low ones) or to place the camera within elements on the set, particularly if a very small scale is being used. When little objects are being used in 3D animation, it sometimes is necessary to build alternate models or sets in order to obtain difficult angles or shot sizes. For example, it might be necessary to create a duplicate object that is much larger than the one used on the primary set in order to create the effect of a close shot.

The sets for 3D animation can be designed in a variety of ways, creating diegetic spaces, or 'film worlds', that range from relatively realistic to highly stylised. Films that employ pixilation or live-action/animation often are shot in real spaces and at full (1:1) scale. This practices can be described as the equivalent of 'location' shooting in live-action production. For example, Jan Svankmajer shot his live-action/animation film *Alice* (1988) at full scale, placing his live actress and animated characters within what appears to be real rooms, or outside on a rocky terrain. Even completely animated works sometimes use sets that create a very realistic diegetic space. In *Street of Crocodiles*, the central puppet figure of the film walks through a setting that is realistic for its time and place – also very much like a 'location'.

The sets of *The Wrong Trousers* is designed with miniatures. Employing objects that look like they would appear in an actual house or other space, the backgrounds emulate a real environment. Nonetheless, the audience clearly can see that the set pieces are miniatures. This practice might be compared to the construction of 'studio sets' used in live-action production. In some cases, audiences can recognise the constructed nature of live-action sets – perhaps the rear projection used during 'driving' scenes or an 'outdoor shot' that clearly has been created inside a sound stage. Still, viewers generally accept them as part of the story's diegetic space. In a similar fashion, we are able to accept the miniatures of the 'Wallace and Gromit' film sets as relatively real spaces. Since everything about animation (the characters, the movement, the environment) is fantasy based, the acceptance of its constructed sets might come to a viewer even more easily.

Some animated works do not attempt to closely emulate reality in their settings. For example, Gumby's home base is a surrealistic toyland.[9] Although Art Clokey often employed real objects at full scale in 'The Gumby Show' (including children's toys such as trains, cars, and dolls), these items only imparted a general sense of a space, rather than a detailed 'realistic' background. The effect is fantastic, due to the fact that the 'Gumby world', or diegesis, is a much more simplified version of what the average viewer would read as a real-world environment – and because Gumby and his pals slide between environments (e.g. into a 'book world') so easily. In the pixilated film *Neighbors*, Norman McLaren also has set up a simplified environmental space. Although the film is shot 'on location' outdoors and employs actual lawn chairs and

a full-scale picket fence, the homes that appear behind the two men quite obviously are created of small-scale painted boards (see Figs 5.1 and 5.2).[10] Another Canadian film, *La basse cour* (A Feather Tale, 1993), by Michéle Cournoyer, creates an even more incongruous relationship between images on the screen. As a woman who is rendered in 2D symbolically turns into a bird that is defeathered by her mate, she sheds real (3D) feathers.

The backgrounds of Will Vinton's *Closed Mondays* go in another direction, seeming to aim for a more unified diegetic space; its environments are made of clay, the same substance used to create the characters themselves. Although clay backgrounds might be modelled to look very similar to 'real life' environments, the Plasticine is a further step away from the replication of actuality than a background made of miniatures and, of course, an actual location. In some respects the 'clay on clay' aesthetic (i.e. using clay backgrounds with clay figures) is similar to the effect of using painted backgrounds with cel animation and the aesthetics of most other 2D techniques. Of course, the clay backgrounds are dimensional, have surface texture and natural shadowing, so there are also differences between a unified clay production and a unified painted or drawn production. Still, these kinds of works are similar in providing audiences with a sense of a total fantasy world, which is a consideration for anyone studying audiences and perception.

The elements used within an environment not only affect the development of a diegetic space, but also can influence lighting and colour. Lighting can become an important consideration in the production design of 3D animation, just as it can be in live-action work. Natural shadows are created when the sets are lit, and the depiction of flat, naturalistic or expressionistic lighting has the potential to greatly affect the viewer's understanding of character and narrative elements. However, different types of materials receive light in different ways; for example, clay objects tend to absorb light, while hard wooden or metal surfaces are much more reflective. As a result of light absorption and the nature of the material itself, the colours in clay animation tend to be of relatively low saturation, whereas hard surfaces might be much more brightly coloured in appearance.

Like backgrounds, the characters of 3D animation are affected by the materials used to create them. All 3D figures have inherent surface texture and are subject to the laws of gravity, but variations in terms of movement and the display of emotion can occur when different types of puppets, clay figures or pixilated beings are used. Consider, for example, that a wooden puppet generally has a rigid face, incapable of stretching to show a smile or speak. It has been suggested that the mastery of Trnka's films is evident in his ability to create expression through subtleties of movement, environment, and lighting, as well as camera angle and framing, despite the inflexibility of his puppet figures. Trnka explained:

> From the beginning, I had my own idea of the style of the puppets. Each one of them should have his or her fixed expression, as opposed to other puppets that could change expression via various technical devices achieving greater realism. However, we have seen that in practice this expression does not become more realistic, merely more naturalistic.[11]

Although the restrictions of a solid wooden puppet might at first seem to create a drawback, Trnka interprets this so-called 'limitation' as a creative attribute which forces the artist to find a narrative solution more creative than merely showing a smile or a frown.

While puppets made by Eastern European animators often have been made of wood, each carved by hand, a variety of other materials have also been used by 3D animators. For example, Art and Ruth Clokey used foam rubber to create the bodies of the characters animated in the made-for-television series 'Davey and Goliath' (1960–1962; 1969–1971; with various specials, 1965–1975), and the heads were made of epoxy. Today, the Prague-based Trnka studio is among those that use latex puppets, among other types.[12] Seventy of them were moulded for the studio's made-for-television series, 'Silverwing' (based on Jan Karafiat's children's tale, *Brucci*, which means 'Firefly' in Czech, 1995) (see CP 17). Moulded latex figures also were employed in *The Nightmare Before Christmas*, directed by Henry Selick in the United States.

The surface of puppets made from these materials are flexible, yet they are typically designed so they cannot be significantly altered in appearance (whether that means metamorphosed or accidentally pushed out of shape) during the animation process. However, the attributes of clay animation are quite different. Plasticine is soft and malleable, which allows for easy metamorphosis of shapes. Sometimes this flexible quality is advantageous, allowing for a kind of 'squash and stretch' technique or other aspects of shape shifting that cannot be achieved with wooden or latex puppets, or pixilated humans.

However, the softness of clay also presents problems. Under hot lights especially, figures made of clay tend to sag. They also are easily pushed out of shape during the animation process. How does one move a leg or an arm of a Plasticine figure without leaving fingerprints or accidentally pressing on another part of the body? Nick Park recognises these problems when he explains, 'while puppet animators only need to move the joints of their puppet to animate it, Plasticine animators have to resculpt the moving parts of the character for every new frame'.[13] Of course, puppet animators also have to worry about disrupting exterior components of a figure to some extent, especially if it involves loose clothing or flexible latex that should remain in position from shot to shot. Nonetheless, Park's statement suggests the relative difficulty of manipulating clay figures that are softer than other 3D characters.

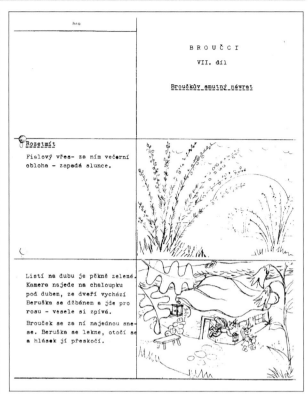

z	vt.	střih	techn.	poznámka	hudba
1.	Rozetmít	Komentář: Vypravěč: A byl srpen. Tam dole v pšenici zněly srpy a ten vřes byl v plném květu.			
2.		Beruška: "Tralala, la la la ...." Vypravěč: Brouček se zastavil u kmotříčků, aby se pochlubil, že už létá sám.			

hra
B R O U Č C I VII. díl Broučkův smutný návrat
Rozetmít Fialový vřes- za ním večerní obloha - zapadá slunce.
Listí na dubu je pěkně zelené. Kamera najede na chaloupku pod dubem, ze dveří vychází Beruška se džbánem a jde pro rosu - vesele si zpívá. Brouček se za ní najednou snese. Beruška se lekne, otočí se a hlásek jí přeskočí.

Figs 8.11 (a) & (b)
Script and storyboard for the Trnka studio's 'Silverwing' series, based on Jan Karafiat's children's tale, Brucci, *or* 'Firefly', *1995*

When 3D characters are moved frame by frame, it is necessary to build figures that are well supported and flexible. On the outside, these figures might be made of latex, plasticine, or other materials, but underneath they generally are composed of an 'armature', which is a kind of skeleton. The most sophisticated (and expensive) of these armatures are made of coated steel or aluminium (sometimes supplemented with plastic and other materials) and include specially machined, highly flexible ball-and-socket joints.

The complex characters used in the 'Wallace and Gromit' series are made with this kind of underlying structure, assuring flexibility and durability. The bodies of figures used in Art Clokey's 'Davey and Goliath' series also were supported by armatures with ball-and-socket joints. In contrast, the characters used in 'The Gumby Show' were shaped around an armature of simple twisted aluminium or copper wire. The series' creator, Art Clokey, figures that each animator began the day with 20 to 30 Gumby figures.[14]

Puppets, too, can rely on armatures for support. In *The Film, The Art, The Vision: Tim Burton's Nightmare Before Christmas*, Frank Thompson explains how the puppets used in that feature were created.[15] First, models of the characters were sculpted so a mould could be created around them. The armatures, mostly designed by Tom St. Amand, were placed inside the completed moulds, which were then injected with foam latex. After the latex had solidified, the puppet was removed from the mold and cleaned up in the studio's fabrication department. The surfaces of some puppets were covered with urethane-based paint and others were treated with a rubber cement and solvent mixture that would open the surface of the foam, allowing pigments to adhere firmly.

Of course, not all types of 3D animations rely on characters that are supported by armatures. The figures used in pixilation are human, which creates different considerations. Obviously, they do not need reinforcement to keep them upright; nor do they easily get bent out of shape. Nonetheless, the animation of humans can be very challenging.

Movement in 3D animation

In pixilated work, the expressions and movements of characters tend to be highly stylised. In his film notes, McLaren comments that the technique can be used to create:

> ... a caricature type of movement ... In much the same way as a pictorial caricature can make comment on character and situation by distorting the static form of a drawing, so live-action-animation can create a caricature by tampering with the tempo of human action, by creating hyper-natural exaggerations and distortions of the normal behavior, by manipulating the acceleration and deceleration of any given human movement.[16]

Borthwick and Hutchinson find that the development of this caricature requires a special skill on the part of the performers, as well as the animators. In an interview with Andrew Osmond, they explain that the performers in *The Secret Adventures of Tom Thumb* had to act in the same way as the animated objects, so they 'had to 'split up' an action into increments of 12 or 24 per second'.[17] They say that it might have taken three to hours to shoot four or five seconds of footage. Because most trained actors 'found it difficult to grasp idea of working in increments ... [the filmmakers] ended up working with colleagues who understood the technique'.[18]

However, 3D animators who do not deal with live 'objects' are confronted with a different set of problems. How to keep 3D figures from falling over or anchored firmly to the ground during a walk cycle or series of off-balance movements is a question most 3D animators have to answer. In *The Wrong Trousers* (1993), Plasticine figures were stabilised in their positions with rare earth magnets, which held the feet through perforations in the metal floor of the sets.[19] Making figures leave the floor of sets – when jumping, for example – presents another set of problems for all 3D animators. Wires and other tricks must be used to create the illusion that a character is suspended in the air.[20] Karl Cohen explains that, 'to animate Gumby, a variety of tools and materials are used. He is held in place with T-shaped pins, or thin wires if he is called upon to fly'.[21] In *Neighbors*, two pixilated characters appear to fly about their yards. This action required the performers, Grant Munro and Jean-Paul Ladouceur, to repeatedly jump into the air, so that a frame of film could be exposed each time they were off the ground.

Whether a 3D character is walking, running or jumping, it is difficult to recreate an absolutely realistic sense of movement when working frame by frame. Footage created with frame-by-frame photography lacks the 'motion blur' that occurs naturally when a figure moving in real time performs before a live-action camera. One solution to this problem was developed by Phil Tippett and Jon Berg while they were working on *The Empire Strikes Back* (directed by Irvin Kershner, 1980). The process they called 'Go-Motion' employs computer-controlled motors that actually blur the motion of frame-by-frame animated figures during photography.[22]

Adding to the difficulty of the photography process in 3D animation is a certain amount of inherent uncertainty. Whereas the majority of movement in cel animated works and many other 2D productions is finalised prior to the photography stage, 3D images are animated under the camera. Although elaborate storyboards and exposure sheets can be created and pre-tests done, it often is the case that, during the actual recording of images, the object animator must use intuition to guide his or her choice of incremental movements that will become part of the final production. British puppet animator Barry Purves contends that 'model animation, by its very process, has a slight unpredictability and spontaneous feel to it – even the animators cannot exactly predict where the puppet will go'.[23] In general, the same can be said for most other types of 3D animation.

Jane Aaron's *Traveling Light* (1985), which involved the animation of small pieces of paper on a set composed of household furniture, serves as an example. Although Aaron planned the two-minute film for about a year, much of the final decision making during filming was spontaneous. The moving ray of 'sunlight' in the film was created by hundreds of pieces of ripped paper in various colours, which were rearranged by Aaron and her small crew largely on the basis of intuition.

In regard to the production process, Aaron says:

> ... it's nerve-wracking, because the camera can't move for days at a time, and you have to be careful and remember how and where you moved everything. Another problem is hitting the right timing. Sometimes it gets really tense on the set just from the concentration.[24]

She also says:

> We'd get footage back, sometimes only thirty feet of film after five days of intensive shooting. We'd look at the dailies and someone would say, 'I love the way the blue goes down and under the rug.' I'd forgotten it happened, it was not planned out.[25]

Of course, every animator varies in his or her degree of planning and spontaneous creation but, in any case, as Purves suggests, 3D animation cannot be as completely regulated during the production process as some 2D animation techniques, particularly cel animation.

For the movement of 3D figures to remain consistent, generally it is necessary to limit the number of animators to one or two individuals who may work in conjunction with a small crew of assistants. For example, Nick Park had the primary responsibility of animating the Wallace and Gromit figures in *The Wrong Trousers*, while another animator, Steve Box, mostly moved the villainous penguin.[26] However, this is not to say that 3D animation is always limited to the work of a very small crew.

When completing *The Nightmare Before Christmas*, director Henry Selick ran as many as twenty stages with fifteen animators working at once. In order to retain consistency in the animation, Selick carefully rehearsed movements with the animators before they began shooting an action. In addition, tight storyboarding that suggested poses and exposure sheets that specified frame numbers minimised the amount of arbitrary movement that an individual animator might add to a sequence.[27] The characters' movements were detailed in 50 storyboards, each containing 66 drawings.[28] That makes 3300 total storyboard images for the 75-minute film – roughly 42 per minute or about 1 sketch for every 1.5 seconds of film. Selick explains that the storyboards provided a means to sketch out the film very clearly before the expensive process of animation began.[29]

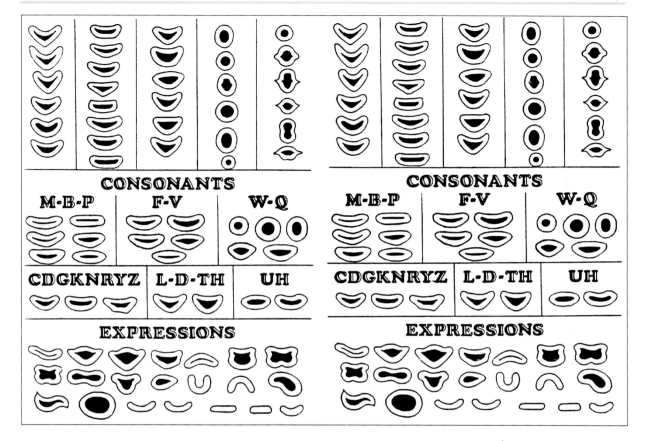

Fig. 8.12 *Mouth replacements for 'Gumby', created by Art Clokey*

Courtesy Karl Cohen

Ray Harryhausen described a similar process used to match his dimensional animation with an already filmed live-action performance in *Mighty Joe Young* (directed by Ernest B. Schoedsack, 1949), which he worked on with the legendary animator of *King Kong* (directed by Merian C. Cooper, 1933), Willis O'Brien. Harryhausen explained that it was necessary to carefully time the live-action footage:

> How many frames does it take the sword to go from Point A to Point B? That dictates how many frames you have to get the skeleton up, so when the actor's hand is in a certain place the skeleton's sword will block it. You have to break it down into analysing every frame.[30]

Nonetheless, he adds that, despite the need to be at a certain point at a specific frame, there is some ambiguity in the movements. He explains, 'you sort of judge it from experience. A lot of it depends on experience'.[31]

The 'replacement' method of animation is another means by which some standardisation of movement can be achieved in 3D animation. Rather than distort the original figure by reshaping it under the camera (e.g. gradually bending an arm and then straightening it out), with this method an animator will use a series of prefabricated parts in various positions (a straight arm, a slightly bent arm, a sharply bent arm, and so forth) that replace each other in consecutive frames. Art Clokey used the replacement method to create mouth movements for his character, Gumby – a 'mouth chart' shows the number of positions used.[32] Karl Cohen explains: 'Petroleum jelly is used to hold the irises in place so eye movements can be made quickly. Paper mouths are used to create the 60–70 mouth positions used.'[33]

The mouth movements of characters in *The Nightmare Before Christmas*, such as Jack and Sally, also were animated through the replacement method. During the animation process, Jack's entire head was replaced, while only Sally's face 'mask' was removed, in order to preserve the order of her long red hair. Sally had ten types of faces, each made with a series of eleven expressions (e.g. eyes open and closed, and various facial poses) and synchronised mouth movements.[34]

Using the replacement method, a crew of individuals can be employed to create the moving parts during the pre-production process, so that the 'creative' work of animation under the camera is kept to a minimum. However, it is rarely the case that animation is carried out only through the replacement system. In creating *The Nightmare Before Christmas*, animators followed an exposure sheet that dictated which replacement parts to use in terms of head movement and speech synchronisation. This controlled the quality of the action and the amount of time it took on screen.[35] However, body movements, including elaborate dances, were animated through manipulation of the models themselves. Selick contends that:

> ... the use of the replacement faces freed up the animator to concentrate on other aspects of the movement. The faces make up only a small part of the animation process, and lip synchronisation is actually somewhat mechanical. The animators are active on the set and create a performance while they work, animating the body, hands, arms and other moving parts.[36]

He adds that 'each character is judged separately' and the choice to use the replacement method or to manipulate the puppet has a lot to do with the desired effect.[37] Selick decided to use the replacement system for Jack in *The Nightmare Before Christmas* because the character is very expressive, whereas animation of the model was employed for the character of James in *James and the Giant Peach*, because he is a more naturalistic character, being based on a real boy.

Intricate commercial productions such as *The Nightmare Before Christmas* have employed video assist systems that store at least the last two frames that were shot on a set, allowing an animator to better align his or her movements with those already recorded. Back in the days of the 'Gumby' production, video assist did not exist. Instead, metal gauges were used to mark the position of the 'Gumby' characters on the set. After a shot was taken, a gauge would be moved in to hold a spot until the character was successfully reshaped; before the next shot was taken, the gauge would be removed.[38] Borthwick and Hutchinson say that, in making *The Secret Adventures of Tom Thumb*, a video assist unit was used toward the end of production to help keep a record of the last positions shot. Nonetheless, they say that most of the work on the set entailed 'making sure the actors' positions were right, as well as checking the model being animated'.[39]

Not all 3D animators have welcomed the use of video assist systems. At one time Barry Purves did his work without the use of video playback, commenting:

> I probably did my best animation under those conditions. My concentration was more focused, and I made sure that I was certain of every movement, or believed in every gesture, before I animated it, and I would do a shot in a complete session without breaking and losing attention.[40]

He feels that, by using video assist, sometimes 'the original spirit and instinct can be lost'.[41]

It is interesting to consider how the manner in which animation is created might affect the overall aesthetics of a work. If an animator uses video assist, or instead chooses to store everything in his or her mind, is there a qualitative difference in the end product? If there is a very close relationship between one artist and the actual movement of figures in a production, how does that impact the aesthetics of a work and the way in which it is evaluated, if at all? This book already has discussed the concept of self-figuration, in which an artist in some respects depicts himself or herself within a work. While this tendency is arguably strongest in terms of the early years of the animation industry, as well as small-scale (one person, one film) independent productions, perhaps this concept has special applications in respect to 3D productions animated under the camera primarily by one individual.

Another interesting consideration in respect to 3D animation relates to spectatorship. What is the effect of seeing objects we 'know' to be inanimate suddenly become endowed with life? How does this experience compare with the viewing of drawn animation, which more clearly are marked as being fabricated, rather than something of the 'real world'? Some of these issues are discussed within a book on animation theory, *The Illusion of Life: Essays on Animation*, an anthology edited by Alan Cholodenko.[42]

Uncanny object

Some essays in Cholodenko's book argue that there can be something disturbing or even horrifying in the realisation that inanimate objects could be endowed with life and intelligence. For example, Robyn Ferrell discusses this kind of reaction, writing:

> ... animated figures are capable of seeming uncanny. The doll that comes to life, the friendly robot and the dog that makes a fellow adventurer are not frightening but desirable; the revival of a childhood wish, suggests Freud. But the sly turn of a doll's head, the imperceptible flicker of a statue's stone eyelids, the animal whose expression is for a moment almost human, these can be uncanny. The uncanny must be fleeting, peripheral, threatened. It is a type of moment rather than a class of objects; an effect of a process of perceiving rather than of an image perceived.[43]

As Ferrell suggests, not all animation creates the sense of the 'uncanny' in the viewer, but it seems as though 3D animation is apt to provoke that experience to a greater extent than 2D animation. The reason is that, unlike 2D figures, 3D objects – clay, wooden, latex or (pixilated) human – already have a 'real life' status, even before they are set in motion. Although the notion of the uncanny is a bit too theoretical for an in-depth investigation within this book, it might be of interest to individuals who are writing on spectator issues related to 3D animation. The remainder of this chapter will at least suggest some related concerns by illustrating a number of works that contain images that can be described as uncanny.

Mary Shelley's *Frankenstein*, a story about the re-animation of dead human tissue, is often cited as a pivotal text in the formation of the horror (or Gothic) genre, in terms of both literature and motion pictures. Within the realm of animation, many artists have been attracted to tales of horror and, in the process of telling them, often bring to life some 'dead objects' of their own.

Some examples can be found in a series of films by British animator David Anderson, which includes *Deadsy* (1989) and *Door* (1990), films that employ a combination of

2D and 3D animation techniques. An element of horror is even more pronounced within such puppet films as *Nocturna Artificialia* (1979), *Street of Crocodiles* and other works by the Brothers Quay. In the words of animator Joan Gratz, these animators' films 'are at times frightening, ambiguous, obscure and astonishing'.[44]

In a *Sight and Sound* article, Jonathan Romney writes: 'The Quays do not so much animate dead matter as dramatise the deadness of matter.'[45] *Street of Crocodiles*, which was inspired by the writing of Polish author Bruno Schulz, is darkly poetic and often disturbing to the first time viewer. Because it lacks narrative, being an exercise in visualising the descriptions in Schulz's book, viewers have very few means of interpreting the actions of the empty-headed dolls, rotating screws, and maniacal clapping bear, among other creepy things that populate the film. This lack of understanding adds to the uneasiness one feels as he or she watches the eerie figures, confirming our darkest fears that, deep in the shadows, inanimate objects do in fact live. The filmmakers' distributor, Zeitgeist Films, comments that the 'masters of miniaturisation, [the Quays] turn their tiny sets into unforgettable worlds, suggestive of long-repressed childhood dreams'.[46] In *Street of Crocodiles*, we find horror and yet with that feeling can come fascination and even pleasure.

Without a doubt, some of the most intriguing work in 3D animation has been produced by Czech animator Jan Svankmajer, who is known for such diverse films as *Moznosti dialogu* (Dimensions of Dialogue, 1982), *Alice*, and *The Conspirators of Pleasure* (1997), which employ a wide range of 3D objects, including puppets, clay, and pixilated humans. Despite this diversity, deep within all of these works lies an aesthetic that seems deeply rooted in horror – the kind of horror one associates with an unsettling nightmare, rather than outright violence.

The content of Svankmajer's films tend to be highly symbolic and complex, creating a challenge for the viewer as well as the analyst. There are, however, a number of possible reasons for the elusiveness of Svankmajer's meaning. On the one hand, Svankmajer's statements have been somewhat (although certainly not to a great extent) veiled by the pressure of government censorship in Czechoslovakia. On the other, the artist's alliance with surrealism results in work that is characterised by dreamlike imagery and irrational events.

An analysis of Svankmajer's work, like that of Trnka, Pal, and other Eastern European puppet animators, is facilitated by an understanding of the political climate of their home countries, which for many years were under communist regimes that included strict censorship of all forms of expression. Under such rule, the direct questioning of the government or society was forbidden, and vagueness of narratives or complete abstraction were looked upon as highly suspect. The most favoured films were uplifting or educational, with clearly delineated plots. However, animators found ways to work around political constraints.

Acclaimed Zagreb animator Borivoj 'Bordo' Dovnikovic has discussed this issue in regard to his experience at Zagreb Film beginning in the late 1950s. Although he felt no outside pressure to conform to political objectives, a certain obligation was 'understood':

> We had no problem with censorship in Zagreb Film or with the Government. However, you must know that we had 'a policeman in our brains', as we've described it, and that we knew what subject matter should be avoided, which included anything against politicians, the Communist Party and the Federal State of Yugoslavia.[47]

As Amy Lawrence has noted, Eastern European artists 'became adept at the use of irony, indirection, and the double-voicedness of allegory. The subversive potential of animation was often successfully disguised by its use of genres and styles traditionally associated with children (fairytales, fantasy, folk stories, etc.)'.[48]

When artists did challenge their governments overtly, they generally found themselves – at the very least – unable to work. Trnka, for example, made films with the government's approval for most of his career and reaped such benefits as a better-than-average home and nice cars. However, in the 1960s, one sees that his art takes on a decidedly subversive tone; the contrast is evident when *Song of the Prairie* (1949) and *The Hand* (1965) are compared. *Song of the Prairie* is a light (although sophisticated in design) parody of Western films and their conventions, with a predominant theme of 'true love wins all'. However, *The Hand* shows a man who tries unsuccessfully to escape from the golden cage in which he is forced to toil; in other words, imprisoned under the oppressive 'hand' of the government. By the time the film was released, Trnka had became more publicly outspoken regarding his country's politics. Perhaps not surprisingly, his career all but ended (then Trnka became ill and died in 1969). Jan Svankmajer, too, has been pressured to stop creating subversive artwork, but nonetheless he has continued to produce outspoken statements that have won acclaim throughout the world.

Affiliated with the Prague Surrealist Group since the late 1960s, Svankmajer has worked in many art forms, including live-action film, painting, sculpture, etching and design work. Although he has explored various themes in his films, ranging from politics to kinky sexual perversions, his interest in objects (often bizarre or grotesque objects, such as bloody meat or the skeletons of strange creatures) has remained constant. Svankmajer invites the viewer to re-examine items that are generally discarded or overlooked as trivial in our real world, and to consider both their meaning as objects within our environments and our reactions to them. Wendy Jackson has commented that:

> ... one could almost make a dictionary of objects as symbols in Svankmajer's films, something akin to Freud's *Interpretation of Dreams*. From fish to rolling pins, to keys, stones and wardrobe closets, objects usually trapped in the banality of life take on new meanings as metaphors for emotions and ideas.[49]

Svankmajer thinks of objects as being creatures with a will of their own, with independent movement, and even a history.[50] In 1982, Svankmajer stated:

> To my eyes, objects have always been livelier than human beings. More static but also more telling. More moving because of their concealed meanings and their memory, which beats human memory. Objects are keepers of the events they have witnessed ... In my films I have always tried to extract content from the objects, to listen to [the object themselves] and to put their stories into images.[51]

This philosophy greatly impacts Svankmajer's interpretation of the 'Alice in Wonderland' tale in his film *Alice*, which depicts a live-action girl who interacts with animated objects.[52] The film took over two years to create, with six months devoted to building props and models, one year for shooting, and one year for editing. It was supported with funding by the British Channel 4, a West German television station, and a private investor in Switzerland (Condor Features), and made during a time when Svankmajer was discouraged from filmmaking in his own country. After he created *Dimensions of Dialogue*, which received critical acclaim outside Czechoslovakia, the communist state-run studios 'made it clear that Svankmajer's "pessimism" wouldn't be tolerated'.[53] Nonetheless, with the assistance of international backers, Svankmajer was able to work on *Alice* autonomously, without state support.

Lewis Carroll's story is, by nature, a subjective one, since it represents the dream of a young girl. This subjectivity is embraced by Svankmajer's version, which is told solely through the voice of a single child, with lines read in English by Camilla Power, who speaks the words of different characters. When each of these characters' lines are read, the viewer is reminded of the storyteller's presence by a close shot of Alice's lips, voicing 'said the white rabbit', or whatever phrase is appropriate for the character. This somewhat jarring effect constantly forces the viewer to re-evaluate his or her relationship with the images presented on the screen; rather than being absorbed into the diegesis in a seamless way, the observer is constantly reminded of the film-viewing experience. In terms of spectator positioning, this creates an interesting juxtaposition. Although it would seem that using real spaces and recognisable (albeit obscure and often unpleasant) objects from real life throughout the film would tend to tie a viewer into the diegesis, the constant breaks in the narrative assure a distancing of that individual from the film.

There are many instances where the viewer of Svankmajer's film probably feels sympathy for the young actress who plays Alice, if not for the character herself, in part because her world is so violent. Svankmajer's Alice is hit on the head by a rake, which plops her into a mechanical device moving downward (the rabbit hole). Repeatedly, she struggles with the handle of a drawer, which always comes off and often throws her to the ground. This poor Alice is continually getting hit by or throwing 'bad objects', especially drawer handles, taking everything in stride. After falling onto a bed of leaves and after her adventure in the rabbit hole, she calmly watches as the hole in the ceiling above her mends itself – then it is on to the next experience.

It is interesting to note that much of what Svankmajer's Alice confronts is far from the stereotype of a 'little girl's' experience. Not only is she physically resilient and willing to get dirty, but she also shows no fear of ugly lizards, bugs, mice (who build fires on her head), or any other element of her strange realm, including macabre creatures made of bones and other lifeless materials. Compare this world with the more widely known adaptation of the Carroll story, the 1951 *Alice in Wonderland* feature made by The Walt Disney Studio, and the elements of horror in Svankmajer's version become very clear. Disney's world is whimsical and clean throughout. Even the death of the charming oyster babies is handled in a light and humorous way. Disney's Alice could never survive in Svankmajer's universe.

Svankmajer has created a world in which fantasy and reality are one in the same; when Alice is hurt, she licks her blood, just as the stuffed white rabbit licks and eats the shavings that fall out of his body. Eventually, she awakens from her 'dream', only to find the glass case in her room really is broken, that the stuffed rabbit is nowhere to be found, and that its hidden drawer does exist.

It is clear that Svankmajer's impression of the ways in which dream states and reality overlap guided the making of *Alice*. He explains: 'If I were to compare the dream with something, I would compare it with childhood ... [*Alice*] as I filmed it and how, of course, Lewis Carroll conceived it on paper, is an infantile dream. I strictly adhered to its "logic" when making the film.'[54]

However, *Alice* is not really a 'film for children'. As Karl Cohen writes in a review: '[A]ny parent taking a young child to see Jan Svankmajer's *Alice* is in for trouble – despite the assurance of the film's opening line: "Alice thought to herself, now you will see a film made for children".[55] The next thing said by the narrator, after a pause, is the word 'perhaps', which might be best read as a reflection on the suitability of the film for a young viewer: '... [N]ow you will see a film made for children – perhaps ...' In this eerie passage, one is given a warning of things to come; the promise of the uncanny experiences that lie ahead.

It is difficult to say just what makes the images in the film somewhat uncanny, but clearly the linking of the 'real world' and animated imagery tends to encourage the effect. Svankmajer increases our identification with the Alice character by depicting a variety of actions that evoke discomfort in the viewer, such as when she pricks her finger on a protractor or gets bits of wood nailed into her head by a renegade mouse. In addition, a number of other elements work to connect the audience with the action. The use of rapid editing, close shots and sound effects all draw the viewer into the movements on the screen. Without being given enough time or space to evaluate the reality of the actions, one tends to be swept along by them. The close-ups of the white rabbit's eerily thrashing, ugly yellowed teeth are reminiscent of something at least mildly fear-evoking or repulsive that most people have seen in the real world. A certain wiping noise accompanies the rabbit's closely photographed, rapid action of clearing sawdust off his pocket watch; for being a simple sound and a succinct movement, they are resoundingly realistic. Our responses are also controlled to some extent by identification with the wide-eyed stares of actress Kristyna Kohoutova, intently focused on the marvellously disturbing actions that occur before her. Her belief in the characters is so convincing that perhaps we, too, feel a certain compulsion to believe.

One can further evaluate the uncanny images of *Alice* by comparing them with figures in some of Svankmajer's other works. For example, the clay body parts of *Tma, Svetlo, Tma* (Darkness, Light, Darkness, 1989) or the cutouts of *Muzne Hry* (Manly Games, 1988) remain at the level of animated figures, rather than crossing into the realm of anything approaching a living being. In these two films, Svankmajer apparently makes no attempt to link the images to a real world context – for example, the backgrounds in both are clearly fabricated. The figures could hardly be mistaken for anything existing in real life; everyone can see that they are clay sculptures or paper cutouts whose movements are very stylised, rather than being even remotely realistic.

Whether or not an uncanny quality is created, bringing figures to life remains a central concern of animation. Nowhere is this more apparent than in the realm of computer animation, where many strive to create the illusion of reality with the use of new technologies. The next chapter will explore some of the key issues in 2D and 3D computer animation, including one of the most challenging problems in the field: creating a convincing human form – what one might call the 'Frankenstein' of the new century.

Notes

1. Giannalberto Bendazzi, *Cartoons: One Hundred Years of Cinema Animation* (Bloomington: Indiana UP, 1994), 258.

2. In 1956, the show appeared briefly as a test on the American children's program 'Howdy Doody'. Incidentally, in September 1997, Art Clokey reported that tests were under way for a computer animation feature using Gumby and Pokey. Art Clokey, conversation with the author (25 Sept. 1997).

3. For more on the development of Plasticine and other issues concerning clay animation, see Michael Frierson, *Clay Animation* (New York: Twayne, 1994).

4. Charles Samu, 'Contemporary Japanese Animators, Part 2', *Plateau* 8, 2 (1987): 21; Bendazzi, op. cit., 415–416.

5. During the production of *The Nightmare Before Christmas* and *James and the Giant Peach*, Selick's company was known as Skellington Productions.

6. In addition to realistic lip synchronisation, Anderson utilised futuristic vehicles to minimise the problems with making characters walk in a realistic way. His special effects team included Brian Johnson, who later created effects for the feature film *Aliens*, and Derek Meddings, who worked on features in the James Bond and Superman series. Incidentally, early models were built with electronic units in the head region, resulting in disproportionately large heads for the bodies and a fairly abnormal appearance; later dolls contained the wiring in their bodies, so heads were no longer required to be so large.

7. However, variations on the technique, such as the stop-motion recording of various live-action 'scenes' can be seen in the work of avant-garde filmmakers such as Stan Brakhage and even Oskar Fischinger, in his 'Munchen-Berlin Wandering' film diary (1927) of images recorded frame by frame. Time-lapse photography is a related technique, the major difference being that pixilation is associated with 'enacted' scenes while time-lapse deals with naturally occurring phenomena.

8. Dave Borthwick and Richard Hutchinson, in an interview by Andrew Osmond, 'Making *The Secret Adventures of Tom Thumb*: Interview with the Bolex Brothers', *Animato!* 31 (Winter 1995): 45–50, 45. In an introduction to the interview, Osmond explains that 'Borthwick did most of the talking with Hutchinson occasionally adding remarks', although he does not indicate which person is speaking within the article itself. As a result, I have chosen to refer to the two individuals' remarks as though they responded together.

9. Art Clokey, correspondence with the author (30 Sept. 1997). Clokey says that in producing his first feature, *Gumby 1*, he used 65 sets. He discussed his aesthetics in an on-line interview with Editor at Large of *Omni* magazine, Keith Harary. Art Clokey, interview with Keith Harary, 3 Jan. 1997 (Internet site address unknown).

10. Some of Art Clokey's earliest animation was influenced by Norman McLaren. Clokey writes: 'In 1952, I made a pixilated commercial for Budweiser, animating a lawn mower and other items, including human beings. Then in 1954 I produced a ten-minute film titled *Lawn Party*. They were both influenced by McLaren, whom I admired.' Clokey, correspondence with the author (30 Sept. 1997).

11. Jirí Trnka, quoted in Philip Moins, 'Jirí Trnka – A Puppeteer Without Strings', *Annecy 95* festival catalogue (Annecy: Annecy International Animation Festival, 1995): 213–14, 214.

12. Studio literature lists several techniques under its production methods, including puppets, cutouts, objects, and Plasticine. Woodcarvers, puppeteers and a full range of other production personnel are employed at the studio. Anonymous, 'Studio Jiriho Trnky' publicity material (1997).

13. Jo Jürgens, 'Cute Icebears and Crazy Penguins', *The Art of Animation* (Spring 1994): 9–11, 10.

14. Richard Pursel, 'Art Clokey is Gumby – Gumby is Love', *Wild Cartoon Kingdom* (n.d. – ca. 1993): 16–25, 21. Art Clokey explains: 'The first clay Gumby puppet was created in 1955. Between 1956 and 1960, in a Hollywood studio located on Santa Monica Boulevard and Hudson, I formed, or modeled, Gumby, Pokey, Gumbo (the father), Gumba (the mother) and the Blockheads by hand, or with a rolling pin and guide rack. Slabs of clay would be rolled out like a thick pie crust dough. Then for Gumby and the father, Gumbo, the clay was rolled into a wedge shape $5/16$-inch thick at the head end and $1\frac{1}{4}$-inch thick at the foot end. Then, with a cheese cutter wire, the slab of clay was cut around a cardboard pattern to form a Gumby silhouette in clay. The next step was to cut slits in the back and press in the wire armature, and smooth over the slits like a clay surgeon. Then cylinders of clay were rolled out by hand to form arms $\frac{1}{4}$-inch in diameter. They also were slit, pressed around wires and smoothed out. By 1960, we were melting the oil-based clay and pouring it into molds in which armatures previously had been set. Eyes were cut out of ping pong balls; the pupils were made out of black photo paper. In 1956, we had made the eyes of white clay discs and red beads. In producing

the new Gumby series, in Sausalito, California, we employed eighteen animators and twenty-one artists to make set, props and figures.' Clokey, correspondence with the author (30 Sept. 1997).

15. Frank Thompson, *The Film, The Art, The Vision: Tim Burton's Nightmare Before Christmas* (New York: Hyperion, 1993), 128, 136.

16. The 'hyper-natural' expressions to which McLaren refers were created in *Neighbors* by having actors move at slower than normal speeds, while filming at an equivalent slower than normal speed. For example, if a performer moved half as fast as normal, the camera would be run at half the normal speed, or twelve frames per second rather than twenty-four frames per second. When the resulting scene is projected, the action appears at a 'normal' rate, but the movement itself is unnatural. McLaren recalls that the movement/shooting was sometimes twelve times slower than normal.

17. Borthwick and Hutchinson, op. cit., 45.

18. Id.

19. Jürgens, op. cit., 10.

20. Barry Purves, British puppet animator, makes a comparison between the images of computer and puppet animation that could be applied in general to 2D and 3D animation: he explains that 'they do not have to be secured to the floor; they do not have to be suspended by wires when they jump; wearing of clothes or a long cloak do not get in the way of the animation process; a move can be erased if the animator is less than happy ... and so on ...' Barry Purves, 'The Emperor's New Clothes', *Animation World Magazine* (June 1996).

21. Karl Cohen, 'Gumby', *Animation Magazine* (Summer 1988): 8.

22. Stephen R. Bissette, 'The Life and Times of Phil Tippett', *Animato!* 35 (Summer 1996): 30–40, 31.

23. Purves, op. cit.

24. John Canemaker, 'Jane Aaron', in Jayne Pilling (ed.), *Women and Animation* (London: BFI, 1992), 55–56, 55.

25. Ibid., 56.

26. Jürgens, op. cit., 10.

27. Production information presented on 'Tim Burton's *The Nightmare Before Christmas* Deluxe CAV Laserdisc Edition', Touchstone Home Video.

28. Frank Thompson, op. cit., 93.

29. Henry Selick, telephone conversation with the author (29 Aug. 1997).

30. Ray Harryhausen, in an interview by Scott MacQueen, 'Ray Harryhausen: From Fan to Technician', *Animato!* 24 (Winter 1993): 12+, 18. In the same issue, an interview by Stephen R. Bissette, '... From Creator to Artist', covers different aspects of Harryhausen's career. The Bissette interview is continued in the next issue, *Animato!* 25 (Spring 1993): 46–60.

31. Harryhausen, in an interview by MacQueen, op. cit., 18.

32. 'Gumby Mouth Chart', reproduced in Cohen, op. cit., 8.

33. Id.

34. Thompson, op. cit., 140.

35. At times, reference footage of models also will be used to guide the production of 3D animation. For example, in the Vinton Studio's *Closed Mondays*, actors were filmed reading lines to provide frame-by-frame guidelines for exactly synching the character's mouth movements to the dialogue.

36. Selick, telephone conversation with the author (29 Aug. 1997).

37. Id.

38. Cohen, op. cit., 8.

39. Borthwick and Hutchinson, op. cit., 45.

40. Purves, op. cit.

41. Id.

42. Alan Cholodenko (ed.), *The Illusion of Life* (Sydney: Power, 1991).

43. Robyn Ferrell, 'Life Threatening Life: Angela Carter and the Uncanny', in Cholodenko, op. cit., 131–44, 132.

44. Gratz screened the two Anderson films and the Quay film in her 'My Choice' screening at the Zagreb 1994 World Festival of Animated Films. Joan Gratz, *Zagreb 94* festival catalogue (Zagreb: Zagreb 1994 World Festival of Animated Films, 1994), 41.

45. Jonathan Romney, 'The Same Dark Drift', *Sight and Sound* (March 1992), n.p., excerpted in publicity materials for Zeitgeist Films, ca. 1992.

46. Author unknown, 'Zeitgeist Films Presents The Brothers Quay', Zeitgeist Films publicity information.

47. Bordo Dovnikovic, quoted in Steve Montal, 'The Master from Zagreb: Bordo Dovnikovic', *Animation Journal* 5, 2 (Spring 1997): 52–63, 55.

48. Amy Lawrence, 'Masculinity in Eastern European Animation', *Animation Journal* 3, 1 (Fall 1994): 32–43, 32.

49. Wendy Jackson, 'The Surrealist Conspirator: An Interview with Jan Svankmajer', *Animation World Magazine* (June 1997).

50. Bendazzi, op. cit., 364.

51. Jan Svankmajer, quoted in Bendazzi, op. cit., 364. The comment appears in footnote one, which refers to an interview that appears in a Czech magazine, *Film a doba*.

52. *Alice* was not the first of Svankmajer's films inspired by Carroll; in 1971, he created an object-animation film based on *The Jabberwocky*.

53. Karl Cohen, 'The Czech's Alice Come to America', *Animation Magazine* (Summer 1988): 46–47+, 47.

54. Jan Svankmajer, quoted in Peter Hames, 'Interview with Jan Svankmajer', *Dark Alchemy: The Films of Jan Svankmajer* (Westport, CT: Praeger, 1995), 106.

55. Cohen, 'The Czech's Alice Come to America', op. cit., 46.

Animation and new technologies

INTRODUCTION TO NEW TECHNOLOGIES

*I*n January 1997, it was estimated that nearly 75 per cent of all live-action feature films being produced included some type of digital effect or computer-animation techniques.[1] Wholly animated features and made-for-television series also are being created with a great deal of help from computers. Without a doubt, new technologies will become an even more important force in the production of entertainment media within the next few years. As a result, it is vital for both production personnel and analysts to understand at least the basic terms and concepts related to computer animation.

Only a few years ago, computer hardware and software was not as 'user friendly' as it is today, so artists trained in traditional methods found it difficult to use. In addition, the technology itself was incapable of rendering a wide variety of images, so artistic expression was rather limited. These issues are becoming resolved – the technology is both easier to use and more versatile – so more and more animators are finding it easy to learn about computer animation and to trade in a pencil and paper for mouse and monitor.

The job of the analyst remains somewhat complex when it comes to a discussion of digital effects and animation. One reason for the difficulty is the fact that computer animation within live-action films is becoming less and less visible. In 1993, Tim McGovern of Sony Pictures Imageworks already was able to say that 'visual effects technology has become so powerful, you can remake almost any part of any character with a computer-generated image, and the viewer could never tell the difference'.[2] New technologies writer Bill Hilf echoed these sentiments in 1997, explaining that digital images have been used to create anything:

> ... from high-profile stars, such as T-Rex, Woody, and Babe, to virtually indistinguishable illusions, such as virtual stunt doubles, removing celluloid blemishes, and animating a wind-blown cape on a live actor ... The rapidly growing use and application of digital effects in film has made it very difficult for the audience to determine what is 'real'.[3]

Another difficulty facing writers in this area is the rapidity of change. Technology evolves so quickly that it is virtually impossible to provide an up-to-date account of the state of the industry; by the time something is printed and distributed (even electronically), it seems another change has occurred. Despite these impedances, it is vital that writers possess an understanding of the processes of computer animation and special effects, and attempt to keep up with new developments in these fields. This chapter will begin with a discussion of basic terms and concepts that are applicable to a discussion of new technologies. It will then provide an historical overview of relatively recent developments within the industry, concluding with a discussion of general aesthetic issues that are still being resolved.

Basic terms and concepts

Throughout its history, computer animation has been employed in many contexts, including space exploration, defence projects, medical research, forensics, education, Internet development and entertainment. Within today's entertainment industy, it is sometimes used to create three-dimensional (3D) animated projects that are completely computer generated (such as the feature *Toy Story* in 1995), but it prevails in assisting hand-drawn animation and creating special effects that enhance live-action imagery (see CP 24).

Any student of the media realises that special effects have been used throughout the history of motion pictures. In recent years computers have added significantly to the possibilities, but many older techniques continue to exist side by side with computer effects, still creating illusions that delight and amaze audiences. Some companies, like Industrial Light & Magic (ILM) and Digital Domain, provide a full range of services, including compositing, matte painting, models and miniatures, only some of which are computer assisted. Other production houses, such as Pacific Data Images (PDI), have concentrated almost exclusively on computer-generated imagery, creating special effects for live-action work as well as commercials and other products.

Much of the vocabulary used in a discussion of computer animation will be familiar to people who have an understanding of 'traditional' animation techniques. For example, 'computer-generated imagery' (referred to as CGI – or CG), like traditional animation techniques, falls into the two general categories of two-dimensional (2D) and three-dimensional (3D).[4] The work created with 3D software – like the images of *Toy Story* (directed by John Lasseter, 1995) and many of the special effects in *Jurassic Park* (directed by Steven Spielberg, 1993), to name just two examples – is sometimes called 'modelled animation'. Many people think of 3D images when they hear the term 'computer animation', but in fact the realm of 2D production also represents a very significant component of the industry.

Software in the 2D category generally is known as 'digital ink and paint' (or DIP). The images created with 2D software sometimes are referred to as 'computer-assisted animation' or 'key-framed animation', but they can look very much like traditional cel animation that is produced without the aid of a computer. The advantages of using 2D software are numerous, but among the most important is increased productivity.[5] Steven Chadwick, Manager of Digital Research and Development for Nelvana, a Canadian production house, says that the use of the software eliminates problems with dirt, cel flare (light coming off the surface), and drawings out of order; as a result, it has cut the studio's number of retakes by 85 per cent.[6] In addition, the computer allows Nelvana to create special effects that would be too time consuming to produce manually. Nelvana uses DIP software produced by Cambridge Animation Systems in Great Britain, which is the world's leading manufacturer of 2D software.

In his article, 'Developing a Digital Aesthetic', Hilf overviews a number of key concepts and terms related to a discussion of computer animation. He writes:

> ... at the very heart of CGI is the 'pixel', which is essentially a small dot. It is created by manipulating electron light beams that are emitted by a cathode ray tube housed within a computer. Pixels are used to create the forms of computer animation; 'digital imaging' is the name given to this process.[7]

In respect to 3D imagery, Hilf explains that 'most CGI is accomplished through the orchestration of geometric forms – spheres, triangles, squares, cones, cylinders, and so on'.[8] Animators use the resulting groupings of geometric forms as frameworks, or 'wire-frame models', which can be rearranged or reformed:

> ... into whatever shape or figure is desired. This manipulation of geometric models is often called 'tweaking', referring to the ability of the computer animator to configure small details and change the appearance of a particular animation. The process of adding texture, lighting, and depth effects to a computer-generated model is called 'rendering', [a term] commonly used when discussing the process of adding finishing details to a computer animation.[9]

The exact methods used to model, render and animate at any given studio vary because most of them modify their purchased 'off the shelf' software in some manner. In June 1997, Wendy Aylsworth, Vice President of Technology and Facilities at Warner Bros. Feature Animation, reported that the studio maintained a team of thirteen in-house codewriters, who modified off-the-shelf software in order to integrate the products together, add features that those products did not have in them, and adjust existing features to increase their ease of use and rate of output.[10]

Typically, the purchased programs have an 'open architecture' that allows companies to add (or 'plug in') proprietary software (tools created in-house). When software is designed by studio employees, the variations become 'proprietary' – in other words, the exclusive property of that studio. Carl Rosendahl, who founded PDI in 1980, explains that most of the top digital studios write a lot of their own software in order to meet their own creative needs.[11] He says that, in the case of PDI, 'commercials drive most of the R&D [research and development]; at any given moment, the company is typically working on eight or ten commercials that must be completed in only six to eight weeks'.[12] Commercials and other short works provide opportunities for development because they do not take long to complete and typically are quite different from one another; companies that work long term on a single concept probably are not in as good a position to try out new things.

The product modifications made by PDI and other studios in turn affects the development of off-the-shelf software. Rosendahl contends that software produced by such industry leaders as Wavefront and Softimage is 'incredibly influenced by companies like PDI because we're pushing and defining the high end of the graphic tools market'.[13] As an example, he discusses 'morphing', a technique developed at the New York Institute of Technology which allows the seamless transformation of one object into another. Rosendahl explains that:

> ... morphing became a mainstream production technique only after Industrial Light & Magic started applying it in a few of their film projects, like *Terminator 2* [directed by James Cameron, 1991]. When [PDI] produced Michael Jackson's 'Black or White' video [directed by John Landis, 1991], the morphing technique really took off. It's a tool you can now buy for $100, and it can run on your PC.[14]

Sometimes a studio will license (sell the rights to) its proprietary software. However, some keep their developments secret, in order to gain an edge on the competition in terms of creativity or productivity, which can translate into lowered costs. These kinds of advantages are necessary in the highly competitive environment that exists today, where a number of companies are bidding for work and the price of computer-generated images is still quite high.

Indeed, images produced with computer technology generally are far more expensive than their live-action counterparts or even more traditionally produced special effects. In reference to *Terminator 2: Judgment Day*, director James Cameron estimated that, per second of screen time, 'it cost more to cast the digital T-1000 than to hire Arnold Schwarzenegger'.[15]

In an effort to save money, the Australian live-action feature *Babe* (directed by Chris Noonan, 1994) employed both animatronic models of animals (created by the Henson Creature Shop) and CGI (created by Rhythm & Hues), depending on the situation. Charlie Gibson, who co-founded Rhythm & Hues in 1989, explains that 'there are distinct advantages to both techniques. With animatronics, once you've built the models, the execution of the shot becomes fairly economical ... But if you need to do certain kinds of quick action, digital will be better'.[16] He adds, ' "Babe" (the pig) was in the film so much that they used the animatronics for cost reasons. When there were fewer shots of animals, like the puppies, digital was cheaper'.[17] In addition, the use of animatronics has the advantage of allowing interaction on the set between live performers and models.

Another money-saving strategy employed in the realm of CGI – as in the practice of traditional animation – is the re-use of imagery: the use of cycled movements and the development of libraries of character designs, backgrounds, and so forth. According to Tim Sarnoff, Senior Vice President of Warner Digital Studios, 'The digital revolution will obviously allow us to re-use anything – backgrounds, props, potentially animation itself'. He notes: 'We have clear plans to re-use and access the images we create from one project to another.'[18]

Former Vice President of Feature Film Production at Pixar, Ralph Guggenheim, discussed the use of the 'digital backlot' in *Toy Story*, explaining that the studio kept a database of images from the film, including textures, models, and shaders, much of which has continued to be used. He says:

> We re-use all that stuff endlessly because we're making interactive products based on *Toy Story*. Since modeling is a very large portion of all the effort that goes into one of these things, subsequent ancillary projects get the benefit of that effort ...[19]

He adds that the re-use of objects is sometimes 'unrecognisable from one piece of work to the next. In *Toy Story*, one would never recognise that the mutant baby toy has the head of Andy's sister, re-used and reconfigured'.[20]

Having sketched out the basic terms and concepts of computer animation, this chapter will now discuss some of the significant contributions of various production houses in recent years. An overview of these establishments will lay the foundation for a discussion of the aesthetic issues that continue to confront the field, providing challenges for artists and areas of analysis for historians and theorists of animation.

Industry in its second wave

Histories of computer animation often refer to a first and second wave of developments. The first wave primarily consisted of experiments created by artists and developers working within the government, educational institutions, and private enterprises, mostly located within the United States. In *The Visualisation Quest*, Valliere Richard Auzenne identifies seven American institutions whose developments 'formed the foundation' for computer animation: Massachusetts Institute of Technology (MIT), the University of Utah, Ohio State University, Lawrence Livermore National Laboratory, the Jet Propulsion Laboratory (JPL), Boeing, and Bell Telephone Laboratories.[21]

Auzenne explains that government research greatly aided the development of computer animation. He says that the close involvement of the military in computer graphics and animation during the 1940s and 1950s can be explained by two factors: timing and economics. He elaborates by explaining that early developments 'took place during World War II or immediately following and were related to radar detection; at that time there was still great concern over national security', and computer animation was developed for defence purposes. In addition, 'these systems were very expensive; private resources could not afford them. However, the government, via tax dollars, could'.[22]

During this first wave, some companies created computer-animation techniques for use in feature films, though in a relatively limited manner. Significant among the early efforts are *Westworld* (directed by Michael Crichton, 1973) and *Futureworld* (directed by Richard T. Heffron, 1976), with computer animation by Information International, Inc. (Triple I). Triple I was one of the studios that helped to provide a model for future work. According to pioneer software developer Turner Whitted, the company 'defined the state of the art. It was mainly a place that made really glitzy stuff, but it was the first time anybody had been able to make anything quite that glitzy'.[23]

During the 1980s, a so-called 'second wave' of developments occurred within the field of computer animation. Auzenne describes the core of 'second-generation computer animation houses' as being composed of PDI (established in 1980) (see CPs 25 & 26), Cranston-Csuri (estab. 1981), Lucasfilm's computer-animation division (estab. 1980 and later renamed Pixar), and Digital Production (estab. 1981).[24]

Some of the most significant contributions at that time were made by George Lucas. In 1979, he hired Ed Catmull to head a computer division within his company, Lucasfilm. However, film studios were not convinced of the feasibility of using computer-animation techniques, due to the expense and the aesthetic limitations.

Many of the animators themselves also were reluctant to work with the new technologies. Robi Roncarelli writes:

> ... despite major advancements between 1978 and 1982, computer animation's mathematical structure, based on rigid geometric shapes, still made it a poor means for character animation production. Traditional animators continued to view computer animation with great skepticism. It was not the personal type of expressive medium they were used to working with.[25]

Catmull was among those who tried to solve this problem. His Pixar Image computer was designed 'specifically for the artist'. He explains: 'We had to get to a point where artists could design the models and their appearances. It required a great deal of technical expertise to use the equipment, so we began to design systems that artists could use, not just technical people.'[26] One finds that the emphasis on making 'artist friendly' equipment has continued to be a significant concern in the creation of hardware and software products.

Despite the efforts of many people to encourage computer animation within the film industry, the 'revolution' was somewhat slow in coming. Contributing to this situation was the release of the ill-fated live-action feature *TRON* (dir. Steven Lisberger, 1982), which contained animation by MAGI (which completed the majority of the work), Triple I (with the second largest contribution), Digital Effects, and Robert Abel and Associates.[27]

In some respects, the film was a breakthrough for computer animation within motion pictures, including 235 computer-produced scenes totalling over fifteen minutes of CGI, more than any previous film.[28] Historian Robin Baker writes that *TRON* 'was the movie that intended to prove the full range of creative visual effects computers could produce'.[29] However, the results were different than expected. The film's financial and critical failure has been attributed to unexpectedly high costs and a weak storyline, but in any case its effect was to weaken the immediate prospects for using extensive CGI in feature films.

Despite the generally bad effects of *TRON*'s release, Hilf contends that the film's 'value as a historical and cultural artifact is immense'.[30] Certainly, it played a part in sparking the imagination of at least one individual who would become extremely important in revitalising the computer-animation industry during its second wave. In an interview with Jo Jürgens, John Lasseter explains:

> When I was working on *Mickey's Christmas Carol* (1983) at Disney, *TRON* was being produced at the studio. Two of my friends, Jerry Rees and Bill Kroyer, were doing storyboards and choreography of the computer animation in the movie. They invited me to see some of the first footage they had just got back of the light-cycle sequence from MAGI, one of the companies that did the animation in the movie. I was blown away ... When I saw this computer animation, it was like a door opened in my mind. I thought, 'this is the future'.[31]

Shortly thereafter, Lasseter worked with Glen Keane to create a 30-second 'Wild Things Test' using MAGI Synthavision, basing their work on Maurice Sendak's book, *Where the Wild Things Are*.[32] By 1984, Lasseter had been offered a short-term position at Lucasfilm, which made him leave Disney for Northern California, where he could persue his vision for the future.

During the early 1980s, Lucasfilm began to establish its place as a leader in the development of CG special effects. Its first commercial CGI material appeared in *Star Trek: The Wrath of Khan* (directed by Nicholas Meyer, 1982), in an effect directed by

Alvy Ray Smith that runs just over one minute in length. Characters in the film watch the CG 'Genesis Demo', which shows the revitalisation of a dead planet.[33]

The first production that Lasseter worked on at Lucasfilm, *The Adventures of Andre and Wally B.* (1984), also was directed by Smith.[34] The short work was screened at festivals and won acclaim for its aesthetics. Critics applauded the realism of its forest imagery, its inclusion of 'motion blur' (the blurring that occurs in live-action motion pictures), and its personality animation effects.[35]

Within the next few years, Lasseter wrote and directed a series of other successful shorts: *Luxo Jr.* (1986), *Red's Dream* (1987), *Tin Toy* (1988), and *Knickknack* (1989). These works were made to demonstrate the quality of the hardware and software products created at the company, which was purchased by Steve Jobs in 1986 and renamed Pixar, after the computer developed there.[36] Lasseter used Pixar's 3D graphics software, RenderMan, which helped to create an increased sense of realism in the images. But what really seemed to excite the critics was the way in which these CG works came alive with personality and told stories in a cinematic way. They disproved the general belief that a computer could only produce cold and unengaging imagery.

In his interview with Jürgens, Lasseter says he was inspired to create a storyline for *Luxo Jr.* after meeting with animator Raoul Servais at a Belgian animation festival:

> I showed him my footage of the two lamps moving around and he asked me what the story was. I said there was no story, it was just a little character study, but he told me that every film, no matter how short, must have a story. So having that in mind, I went back and came up with this idea of the ball.[37]

He adds that *Luxo Jr.* constitutes:

> ... a very important milestone from the standpoint that it was the first computer animated film that was accepted outside the computer graphics community ... It was very obvious to me that you can't just throw out all the principles of traditional animation that have been developed over fifty years as soon as you go into computers.[38]

Craig Good, Post-production Supervisor at Pixar, explains how *Tin Toy* – the first computer-animated short to win an Academy Award – achieved 'a polished, cinematic feel', which has become characteristic of Lasseter's work. He recalls:

> ... we did very careful staging, editing (of storyboards, animatics and even the final footage), and tried to move the camera the way live-action filmmakers do. Too many computer animated films fly the camera all over the place just because they can. We wanted the audience to respond to traditional dolly and crane movements, not to make them dizzy.[39]

Meanwhile, Lucasfilm's ILM was making its own contribution to computer-animation history with its work on *Who Framed Roger Rabbit* (directed by Robert Zemeckis) in 1988. And, it continued to develop its reputation for special effects expertise with work on such films as *Willow* (1988), *Indiana Jones and the Last Crusade* (1989), *The Abyss* (1989), *Back to the Future* (1989), *Akira Kurosawa's Dreams* (1990), *Backdraft* (1991), *Terminator 2: Judgment Day* (1991), *Death Becomes Her* (1992), *Jurassic Park* (1993), *Forrest Gump* (1994), *The Mask* (1994), *Jumanji* (1995), *Twister* (1996), *Jurassic Park: The Lost World* (1997) and many other productions.[40]

During this time, PDI also was developing its reputation as a leader in computer animation. During the early 1980s, it created a revolution when it designed computer-generated flying logos for the American television series 'Entertainment

Tonight'. Carl Rosendahl explains that his work for that client, as well as a number of other projects, led to great success: 'By 1985, we basically owned broadcast graphics ... If you turned on your TV at 8 o'clock, the main logo IDs for two of the three networks were PDI products ... I figured at one point we had about a 60% share of the high-end of that market ...'[41]

PDI has changed directions over the years, moving into television commercials, music videos, special effects for theatrical films, made-for-television work, and animated shorts. Some of the company's most memorable animation appears in Michael Jackson's 'Black or White' music video and the 3½-minute *Homer3*, which was created in 1995 for an episode of 'The Simpsons'.[42]

As computer technologies advanced, more and more special effects were employed within live-action films. At first, the use of CGI in the film industry seemed to parallel the practices of the early cinema, with a live-action frame used to surround the special techniques. An often quoted statistic about *Jurassic Park*, that the film includes only 6½ minutes of actual computer-generated imagery, serves as an example.[43] Because the animation in this film is so naturalistic, the viewer does not sense the use of a live-action frame, as one is bound to do when watching Winsor McCay's *Little Nemo* (1911).

Today, the use of CGI has been extended into full-length animated productions. It also has become an international phenomenon, with major production houses located in Canada, England, France and other countries throughout the world. It could be said that, during the late 1980s and early 1990s, the computer-animation industry experienced a surge in its second wave, which was characterised by the increased rate of production and internationalism that occurred at that time within the animation industry as a whole.

One of the most pivotal years for change seems to have been 1993. That year, Drew Takahasi, who co-founded Colossal Pictures in 1976, explained that '3D computer animation was not really considered a viable special effects tool until 1991 with *The Abyss* [1989] and *Terminator 2* [1991]', both directed by James Cameron. He adds that after the 1993 release of '*Jurassic Park* the whole business really kicked off' its success.[44] In 1993, Charlie Gibson, of Rhythm & Hues, said that the industry was closely watching *The Nightmare Before Christmas* (directed by Henry Selick), which was released that year. He claimed:

> We are very interested to see how that movie is going to pay off, because it wasn't done using traditional Disney-style cel animation but used an alternative form of storytelling ... [employing] puppets shot one frame at a time. If that movie really flies, the bigger studios will feel a lot warmer to the idea of funding a computer-generated movie.[45]

Although Gibson described the computer-animation industry of 1993 as still being 'in the novelty stage', an article in *The Hollywood Reporter* of that year began, 'once shunned by artisans, computers have worked their way into the industry's mainstream'.[46] During the previous few years, a number of significant studios had appeared on the scene. For example, the British effects house Computer Film Company was established in London in 1987, followed by the American firms Rhythm & Hues (in 1989), Sony Pictures Imageworks (1992), and Digital Domain (in 1993, co-founded by Canadian James Cameron), among others. And, about this time, the ever-traditional Disney Studio joined the fray, winning an Academy Award for Scientific and Technical Achievement jointly with Pixar in 1991, for the development of its proprietary CAPS animation software.

Certainly, by 1993, developments in computer animation already could be seen within the realm of made-for-television production. By that time, the French production house Fantôme Animation (founded in 1985) had created a wholly CGI made-for-television series, with 50 three-minute episodes of 'Les fables géométriques' (Geometric Fables) (see also CP 27), released between 1989 and 1992. These episodes are loose adaptations of Aesop's fables. A longer-format series, 50 five-minute episodes, are educational in nature. They were created in packages based on five themes: Geometry, Colours, Numbers, Opposites, and Music.[47]

Then, in 1993 and 1994, two other wholly CGI made-for-television series appeared on the air: 'Insektors', also from Fantôme, and 'ReBoot', from the Vancouver-based studio, Mainframe Entertainment.[48] The 'Insektors' series, which centres around opposing forces within the insect world, is directed by Renato and Georges Lacroix (see CPs 28 & 30). It is broadcast on the French television stations Canal+ and France 3, and is distributed to more than 160 other countries worldwide. It received an international Emmy in 1994, among 30 other awards.[49]

'ReBoot' is an action series featuring characters who inhabit a computer world. The series' concept originated in the late 1980s, within a group of individuals that included Ian Pearson, Gavin Blair and Phil Mitchell. All are British, but they decided to establish their studio in Canada for financial reasons. Rogier van Bakel reports that 'the reason the "ReBoot" team ended up in Vancouver in early 1993 is simple: money. Importing pricey computer workstations and high-end video equipment to England to start up the show was not an option. The gear would have been twice as expensive as in North America', and office space in London also proved to be more costly.[50]

According to Pearson, the character designs were greatly influenced by the fact that, when they 'first discussed creating a series that was entirely animated by computer, the technology was in its infancy. We decided to set the characters inside of a computer so that we could get away with looking "blocky" and moving with a mechanical motion'.[51]

Fig. 9.1 Le berger et les poissons (*The Shepherd and the Fish*) from 'Les fables géométriques' series (1989–1992) by Fantôme Animation
© Fantôme

Fig. 9.2 Le coq et la perle *(The Rooster and the Pearl) from 'Les fables géométriques' series (1989–1992) by Fantôme Animation*
© *Fantôme*

The 'ReBoot' series is animated with a combination of Softimage 3D and in-house software created at Mainframe, running on UNIX-based Silicon Graphics workstations. One of the company's software developers, Phil Peterson, contends that 'Softimage is still the fastest, and probably the best commercial package out there for animating characters'.[52] Animator Phil Mitchell also attests to the rapidity of the production schedule, noting that one season (sixteen episodes) of 'ReBoot' contains almost 320 minutes of CGI. He suggests that people make a comparison with '*Toy Story*', which runs about 80 minutes. That movie took years to do ... We can now do

Fig. 9.3 Les grenouilles qui demandent un roi *(The Frogs Who Demanded a King) from 'Les fables géométriques' series (1989–1992) by Fantôme Animation*
© *Fantôme*

Fig. 9.4 *'Insektors' series (1993–1994), from Fantôme Animation* © *Fantôme*

two episodes in under six weeks'. Like 'Insektors', 'ReBoot' has received critical acclaim, for both technical achievement and content (see CPs 29 and 31).[53]

It was not until 1995 that the first completely CGI theatrical feature, *Toy Story*, was brought to the screen. Before *Toy Story* was released, Pixar's director of Engineering,

Fig. 9.5 Le pont de la konkorde *(1993–1994) by Fantôme Animation* © *Fantôme*

Fig. 9.6 *'Binome'*
characters from the
critically acclaimed
'ReBoot' series, a
Mainframe/Alliance
Production
ReBoot is a registered
trademark of Mainframe
Entertainment, Inc.
ReBoot^TM and ReBoot^TM
characters ©1998 Mainframe
Entertainment, Inc. All
Rights Reserved.

Tony Apodaca, predicted: 'This is not gonna be a repeat of *TRON*.'[54] And, indeed, it was not. Due in part to *Toy Story*'s remarkable success, any ill effects of the previous film seem to have dissipated, with plans put in the works for expanded production of CGI theatrical features. In her 1997 article entitled 'Firms Plan CGI Pix for Infinity and Beyond', new technologies reporter Ellen Wolff contends that 'the success of *Toy Story* helped make this development possible on an industry wide basis'.[55] As a result, the public will be seeing even more computer-generated imagery in the years to come, despite the fact that developers are still working out a number of production-related issues. The remainder of this chapter will discuss some of the industrial and aesthetic hurdles facing computer animation today, focusing in particular on issues related to the depiction of human characters.

Aesthetic issues

The increased rate of production within the realm of computer animation has led to an unlikely problem: an infestation of insects! Given the difficulty of rendering truly realistic human characters even today, it should come as no surprise that they are not taking center stage in *Toy Story* or other feature CGI concepts. Much more viable are characters designed with hard structures which lack hair; consequently, insects seem to have become a very popular subject. Already, this chapter has discussed one example of a made-for-television production featuring insects has been discussed: the French 'Insektors' series. Fantôme co-founder Georges Lacroix explains:

> ... one of the reasons we chose insects is simply because they were easier to animate. For instance, they did not require muscles and they made lip synch simpler; it's easier just to have the mouth move like a box, without having to purse their lips to whistle or to smile and show their teeth ... Essentially, we decided not to ask the computer to do more than it could do.[56]

A memorable sequence involving CGI insects appears in the 1996 feature *Joe's Apartment* (directed by John Payson, with animation by Blue Sky Studios), as cockroaches perform a Busby Berkeley-style dance routine around a toilet bowl and other amusing feats. For the first production of a multi-picture deal made with Disney after the success of *Toy Story*, Pixar is featuring a variety of the tiny creatures in a film entitled *A Bug's Life*, while DreamWorks SKG is in production on a feature with the working title Antz.[57] Ellen Wolff echoes Lacroix's observation when she says:

> It's notable that both companies are tackling naturalistic motion by animating insects – creatures that aren't too complex and that computers can easily replicate to produce the hordes required. Lasseter says a key to success in this emerging medium is 'choosing the subject matter that lends itself to the medium well'.[58]

Hair and fur are textures that continue to present aesthetic challenges to computer animators. During the 1960s, MAGI developed the technique of 'ray tracing', which could be used to 'create reflections, transparency, shadows and refractions' to allow 'a close approximation of real photography, or photoreality'.[59] Ray tracing excelled in the depiction of hard and shiny surfaces, but was not effective in realistic depictions of hair and fur. And, solutions to this problem have not been readily available.

Indeed, one of the most common points made in any discussion of computer animation today is the way in which these textures and other aspects of human and animal forms have continued to complicate the computer animator's work. A 1992 article in *The Hollywood Reporter* pointed out that 'cutting edge R&D [research and development] focuses on realistic motion, hair and facial expressions'.[60]Three years later, in 1995, an article in *Wired* reported that:

> ... for many, the ability to generate a photorealistic human, an artifactor, remains the elusive goal. While animators have been developing a lively tradition of computer-generated 'characters' in the form of animals, aliens and others, the ability to conjure a convincing human from a synthetic source has hovered tantalisingly out of reach. But that's changing.[61]

However, in 1996, articles continued to emphasise the difficulty of creating a human figure. About the recently released, highly successful CGI film, *Toy Story*, a newspaper article reports:

> At top speed, Pixar could produce only about 3½ minutes of completed animation each week. For nine months, technicians and animators trained their talents on one critical point, the colour and texture of a [child's] hair. This element is still remembered as one of the toughest single parts of *Toy Story*.[62]

John Lasseter seems to back up this observation, saying:

> ... there is no doubt that the humans and the dog were the most difficult things to do. Their stylisation was a way to make them achievable. As time goes on, there is a lot of research going into hair, clothing and skin, so within a few years, you'll see much more convincing human characters.[63]

Some of the most significant problems related to the depiction of the human form are movement and imperfection. Beverly J. Jones reports that:

> ... early technical attempts to simulate human motion and facial expression were quite disappointing ... the resulting images [were] boring because the movements [were] smooth and lack[ed] variety. Unique and dramatic variety in human motion have traditionally held the attention of the entertainment industry. Consider, for example, John Wayne's walk and Marilyn Monroe's [walk].[64]

The variations in an individual's walk can be considered 'imperfections', since they are non-standard elements. While this kind of difference creates realistic characters, it also greatly complicates the artist's job. Paula Parisi writes, 'the absolute imperfection of living things is a renderer's nightmare'.[65] In a *Wired* article, she includes an example from *Jumanji* (1995), provided by director Joe Johnston. He says:

> The big challenge was fur ... It needed to be matted down, with knots in it, burrs and things animals would have. When our first tests came back on the lion, he was totally groomed with this big mane of perfect hair. He looked like Tina Turner. They spent quite a bit of time dirtying it down.[66]

Among the early attempts to tackle a computer-animated human was *Tony de Peltrie* (1985), which was created by a team of artists at the Centre de Calcul of the University of Montreal; it has been acclaimed as 'one of the first persuasive human figures in computer animation'.[67] In a synopsis of a presentation given by one of the creators, P. Bergeron, Valerie Hall overviews some of the techniques employed in the work. She explains that 'the animation was done on a 3D interactive graphics system, TAARNA, which [was] designed for use by people with no computer background'.[68] She explains that the 'two major things' that had to be done involved defining the facial expressions (muscle) and laying out the body motions (skeleton).[69] To achieve 'the required realism in the facial expressions', a grid of dark lines was drawn onto the face of a real person, matching control points on the animated figure.[70] A total of twenty photographs of this face were digitised. In addition, a clay model of the character's face and body were created; a control grid was drawn on them, and they were photographed and digitised as well. The character's speech was pre-recorded and timed out onto an exposure sheet, so that synchronisation could be done 'using techniques very similar to traditional cel animation'.[71] The 7½-minute film took three years to produce and cost $1.5 million.[72]

Tin Toy, which was released in 1988, is considered to be the first (publicly exhibited) attempt at using Pixar's RenderMan software to animate a human character (the same software was used to create *Toy Story* in 1995). In this case, a model was used as a basis for the animation. At first, Lasseter tried to digitise a toy doll but, when that proved unsatisfactory, a clay figure was constructed. The clay model was digitised using a Polhemus 3-Space Digitiser, which tracked the position of a wand over its surface.[73]

As the examples of *Tony de Peltrie* and *Tin Toy* suggest, live and inanimate models can be used to provide a basis for CGI through the use of some kind of digitiser, which translates the dimensions of a real object into computerised data. Paula Parisi writes that such scanning:

... involves running a laser beam over a person or object, feeding the minutest details of shape, texture, and color into a computer. The digital data set of an actor can then be manipulated at will. A mainstay of the computer-aided design industry (and an outgrowth of military R&D), scanning was first used on [live-action] actors in 1986 when ILM digitised the principals of *Star Trek IV: The Voyage Home* [directed by Leonard Nemoy] for a short time-travel scene in which their heads dissolve.[74]

A related technique is 'motion capture', a form of 'real time animation', which uses sensors to record the movement of an object; it might be said to represent the evolution of rotoscoping and, as a technique, is really closer to live-action than animation.[75] Media writer Rex Weiner explains that:

... motion capture is a computer-driven animation system that allows a director to rehearse and direct the movements of a three-dimensional cartoon character. Systems can use puppeteers manipulating models and hand controls, as well as actors connected by sensors, to achieve realistic human motion for animated characters.[76]

Motion capture was created for use by the military in the 1970s and has been employed in feature film production for many years, although only recently has it become 'cost-effective, time-efficient and reliable enough to fill the needs of television producers', according to business reporter Marla Matzer.[77] A number of American production companies have begun using motion capture for the production of television series (mostly aimed at children), some of which made their debut in Fall 1997.[78] These include the 'Wheel 2000' game show, which features a Vanna White-type character called Cyber Lucy (created by Modern Cartoons), on CBS; 'Bruno the Kid', which features a virtual Bruce Willis (created by SimGraphics), on Fox; and 'Secrets of the Cryptkeeper's Haunted House' (also by Simgraphics), on CBS. Other companies, such as Real Entertainment and Medialab (a division of France's Canal Plus) and a handful of other studios across the world are contributing to the expansion of the technique throughout television and home video.

Today, most production companies rely on motion capture hardware produced by such American manufacturers as Polehemus Inc. and Ascension Technology. It comes in both wireless and wired (or 'tethered) versions (costing $65,000 and $35,000, respectively, for Ascension hardware in 1997). The Cyber Lucy character in 'Wheel 2000' is created by an actress who wears a dozen motion-tracking magnets and nylon harnesses, in addition to a half-pound device worn on the head to track facial movements.[79] The products typically are run in conjuction with Silicon Graphics computers, although there is a movement toward a PC (personal computer) platform.

While the computer offers advantages to production personnel, the extent to which motion capture or any computer technique is more time and cost efficient than manual methods remains open to question and varies with each situation. For example, ILM President Jim Morris explains that a lot of motion capture was used for lip synching in *Toy Story* but adds, if any editing of the motion capture was needed, it turned out to be 'almost as easy to animate the movement from scratch'.[80] Facial capture also was used in another film released that year, the animated feature *Casper* (1995). According to Paula Parisi, director Brad Silberling 'initially hoped facial capture could be used extensively to save time, but he changed his mind. In the end, says ILM's Dennis Muren, the digital-character supervisor on the project, "We could get a better performance out of an animator than an actor" '.[81]

Fig. 9.7 *Star★Trak suit, designed to assist computer-generated human movement animation by Polehemus Inc. Courtesy Polehumus Inc.*

Today, motion capture on television primarily is used to show a real-time host within a live-action context. As Matlin explains, 'it's much more expensive and difficult to do motion capture animation involving character interaction. Right now, characters' hands appear to slice through others' hands rather than touch them'.[82] Of course, technology continues to change rapidly, and new advances help to assure producers that both the cost and the aesthetics of motion capture will continue to become more attractive to the industry (see CP 32).

ILM had used a variation of motion capture in 1991, in creating imagery for *Terminator 2: Judgment Day*. In their book on the studio, Mark Cotta Vaz and Patricia Rose Duignan explain:

> Just as traditional cartoon cel animation often utilized rotoscopes of live photography for realism, so too does CG incorporate live-action references into the digital realm. To produce a realistic moving chrome figure, a black grid-painted Robert Patrick was filmed and the reference footage scanned in. The resulting digital skeleton was used as a guide in creating the T-1000 animation.[83]

Today, animators go through considerable effort in attempting to depict an illusion of realism in terms of both movement and appearance. For example, in *Toy Story*, the face of the film's most complex character, Woody, was operated by 212 motion controls (out of 723 used to operate his entire body).[84] Within the 'ReBoot' series, Mainframe Entertainment has created proprietary software called GRIN to allow animators to 'quickly and realistically synchronise the animated characters' facial expressions with dialogue'.[85] Mainframe Entertainment's Director of Communications, Mairi Welman, boasts that, in 1997, the characters in 'ReBoot' underwent a great deal of remodelling: '[T]here is far more of a 3D effect, and they're amazingly life-like (see CP 29). You'll see subtle details now, like eyelashes. People will still recognise all of the characters, but they've evolved, just as the animation software we're using has evolved.'[86]

Certainly, limitations are posed by the state of computer technology, but a creative and resourceful artist recognises the boundaries of what is possible and works within them – perhaps expanding those boundaries in the process of creation. Experienced artists realise that technology is a significant factor, but by no means the only one that affects the potential of a work.

Eric Darnell, who directed the short film *Gas Planet* (1992) at PDI, is among those who recognise that the state of computer technology is just one consideration among many. In an interview with Emru Townsend, Darnell said that he and art director Michael Collery acknowledged that *Gas Planet* was to be completed within certain limitations. Two of them were, predictably, time and money. Other considerations included the cabilities of the technology, as well as the requirements of the design, story, and art direction. In addition, Darnell stressed another important factor, one that is under the control of the artist: the creator's own knowledge – knowing just what the technology can and cannot do.[87] The most capable artists are those who are fully rounded in both computer techniques and traditional methods, and can estimate what is viable for the project as a whole, given all the limitations.

Having a balanced blend of experience with computers, traditional animation, and other arts can help to overcome some of the problems that John Lasseter sees in the creation of computer animation. He explains that 'the tools needed for creating successful character animation with a computer are not just software tools but an understanding of the fundamental principles of animation' that are associated with traditional animation techniques.[88]

However, he cautions:

> While studying traditional animation is still the best vehicle for learning the principles of animation, making the transition from hand-drawn animation to computer animation can be challenging. Probably the biggest difference is the fact that computer animation is truly 3D within the computer. The first run cycle I ever animated looked great from the side view, but when I looked at it from the front, the arms were going through the body and the knees were bending the wrong way.[89]

In his interview with Jo Jürgens, he explains that traditional dimensional animators (e.g. those who use puppets or clay) also have their share of problems with computer technology. While they are used to thinking of a 3D environment, they have to 'adjust to not working in a straight ahead format, but with key frames and the ability to tweak and refine the animation'.[90] Knowing only one form of animation limits the success of anyone working in the field today. Apparently, the best strategy is to get a grounding in traditional 2D and 3D techniques, as well as training in computer technologies.

Certainly, most studios seem to believe in this approach, since they tend to seek employees who have diverse backgrounds in art and production. In recruitment materials, it is common to find that applicants for computer-animation jobs need various types of training. For instance, in its brochure on 'Computer Generated Imagery Career Information', Walt Disney Feature Animation tells future CGI animators to expect to 'animate and model characters, 3D props, and effects using your traditional as well as your computer animation background'.[91] DreamWorks Animation seeks CGI character animators 'who can utilise 2D/3D digital tools to bring to life unique character design for feature films. Traditional animation experience – including overlap and follow through, squash and stretch, staging and composition, and primary and secondary action – is a plus'.[92] ILM advises: '[T]o

Fig. 9.8 *The Cyber Lucy character from 'Wheel 2000', created by Modern Cartoons, is given motion by a performer in full bodysuit equipped with sensors*

Modern Cartoons/Copyright © Columbia Tri-Star Television 1998

become a successful candidate in the 3D department it is necessary to have a good educational and/or professional blend of computer knowledge and artistic studies.'[93] Its company employment information describes two positions, animator and technical director, for which it is 'ideal' to have not only training on SGI computer systems and knowledge of high-end software programs such as Softimage, Wavefront, Alias, Prisms or TDI Explore, but also a Bachelor of Fine Arts in art and design, or a variety of art courses.[94]

As more and more students grow up in an environment where computers are a familiar device, and as computer research and development progresses even further, it is certain that the separation between artist and technologist will become even narrower. As it does, the aesthetics of computer animation will continue to evolve.

This chapter completes the 'fundamentals' section of the book. The next chapter will turn to the first of several more general studies, in this case focusing on institutional regulators, such as Broadcast Standards and Practices departments within American television networks and governmental agencies.

Notes

1. Luc Hatlestad, 'Smoke and Mirrors: Industrial Light & Magic President Jim Morris Unveils the Secrets of the Illusion Business', *Red Herring* 38 (Jan. 1997): n.p. Published on-line at http://www.herring.com/mag/issue38/smoke.html
2. Tim McGovern, quoted in Anthony Perkins, 'Digital Wizards of Hollywood's Future', *Red Herring* 7 (Dec. 1993): n.p. Published on-line at http://www.herring.com/mag/issue07/future.html
3. Bill Hilf, 'Don't Believe Your Eyes: Is It Real or Is It Animation?', *Animation World Magazine* 2, 5 (Aug. 1977).
4. For more on the distinctions between 2D and 3D software, see Ross Harley (ed.), *New Media Technologies* (Sydney: Australian Film, Television and Radio School, 1993).
5. The claims of software manufacturers range considerably. Steve Wright of Atomix explains that his software is 'approximately five times more productive than manual ink and paint' while Shelley Miles of USAnimation contends that 'a manual painter can paint 20 to 30 cels a day and these digital systems can paint up to 500 cels a day'. Steve Wright and Shelley Miles, quoted in Debra Kaufman, 'Sketchy Budgets', *Hollywood Reporter* (26 June 1996): S3-S4.
6. Steven Chadwick referenced in Carl DiOrio, 'Cambridge's Ani Draws on Computer and Crayon', *Hollywood Reporter* (6 August 1996): 3+, 74.
7. Bill Hilf, 'Developing a Digital Aesthetic', *Animation Journal* 5, 1 (Fall 1996): 4–31, 8.
8. Id.
9. Id.
10. Wendy Aylsworth, quoted in Ann Fisher, 'Tips for Setting Up Digital Studios', *Animation Magazine* (June 1997): 31–35, 33.
11. Carl Rosendahl, in Perkins, op. cit.
12. Carl Rosendahl, quoted in Alex Gove, 'Toy Story: PDI has Remained a Top Digital Studio by Reinventing Itself Three Times. Now for Number Four ...', *Red Herring* 28 (Feb. 1996): n.p. Published on-line at http://www.herring.com/mag/issue28/toy.html
13. Rosendahl, quoted in Perkins, op. cit.
14. Id.
15. Paula Parisi, 'The New Hollywood', *Wired* 3, 12 (Dec. 1995): n.p. Published on-line at http://www.wired.com/wired/3.12
16. Ellen Wolff, 'Building Bodies Three Ways', *Daily Variety* (28 June 1996): 82+, 100.
17. Ibid., 100.

18. Tim Sarnoff, quoted in Ellen Wolff, 'WB Digital Says Reuse It Or Lose It', *Daily Variety* (22 March 1996): A14. For more information on digital backlots, see also Celia Duncan, 'Mighty Mouse', *Screen International* (22 March 1996): 14+.

19. Tim Guggenheim, quoted in Ellen Wolff, 'Welcome to Digital Backlot', *Daily Variety* (22 March 1996): A14+, A14.

20. Id.

21. Valliere Richard Auzenne, *The Visualisation Quest* (Cranbury, NJ: Associated University Presses, 1994), 26.

22. Ibid., 38.

23. Turner Whitted, quoted in Auzenne, op. cit., 67.

24. Auzenne, op. cit., 70.

25. Robi Roncarelli, in Giannalberto Bendazzi, *Cartoons: One Hundred Years of Cinema Animation* (Bloomington: Indiana UP, 1994), 441.

26. Lawrence French, 'Pixar – Writing the Book on CGI and Computer Animation', *Cinefantastique* (Nov. 1995): 23–25, 23, quoted in Hilf, 'Developing a Digital Aesthetic', op. cit., 16.

27. Auzenne, op. cit., 62.

28. Valliere Richard Auzenne, *The Visualisation Quest* (Cranbury, NJ: Associated University Presses, 1994), 62.

29. Robin Baker, 'Computer Technology and Special Effects in Contemporary Cinema', in Philip Hayward and Tana Wollen (eds), *Future Visions: New Technologies of the Screen* (London: BFI, 1993), n.p.

30. Bill Hilf, 'Developing a Digital Aesthetic', *Animation Journal* 5, 1 (Fall 1996): 14.

31. John Lasseter, interview with Jo Jürgens, San Francisco (April/May 1996).

32. Lasseter, interview with Jürgens; Bendazzi, *Cartoons*, op. cit., 441.

33. Auzenne, op. cit., 77.

34. Loren Carpenter, who worked on the fractals for *The Adventures of Andre & Wally B.*, explains that it was mostly Lasseter who 'was responsible for the story and the characters'. Loren Carpenter quoted in Auzenne, op. cit., 78.

35. Using the best resources available, *The Adventures of Andre and Wally B.*, running just short of two minutes in length, required sixteen computers (including the most powerful at that time, the Cray XMP–2 and XMP–4), and still took months to compute. Mark Cotta Vaz and Patricia Rose Duignan, *Industrial Light & Magic* (New York: Ballantine, 1996), 193.

36. Auzenne reports that 'in 1985, discussions and negotiations had already begun for the computer graphics group to split from Lucasfilm. There was a concern that Lucasfilm had branched out into too many areas and needed to focus once again on filmmaking. The last film the computer graphics group worked on as part of Lucasfilm was a Spielberg umbrella production called *Young Sherlock Holmes*' (directed by Barry Levinson, 1985). Ed Catmull, referenced in Auzenne, op. cit., 77.

37. John Lasseter, interview with Jürgens, San Francisco (April/May 1996).

38. Id.

39. Animatics are made by filming storyboard-type images in a way that approximates the timing and action of the final production. Craig Good, 'Filmmaking First, Computers Second: The Making of *Tin Toy*', *Animation Magazine* (Fall 1988): 30–32, 31.

40. For information on the company, focusing on the techniques used in *The Mask*, in particular, see Debra Kaufman, 'UnMasked: Industrial Light & Magic Animators' Use of Softimage', *Animation Magazine* (July/August 1994): 24–25.

41. Rosendahl, quoted in Alex Gove, 'Toy Story: PDI has Remained a Top Digital Studio by Reinventing Itself Three Times. Now for Number Four ...', *Red Herring* 28 (Feb. 1996): n.p. Published on-line at http://www.herring.com/mag/issue28/toy.html

42. For more information, see Debra Kaufman, 'Pacific Data Images: The Once & Future of CGI', *Animation Magazine* (July/Aug. 1994): 22–23+; Michelle Quinn, 'Beyond the Valley of the Morphs', published on-line at http://www.wired.com/wired/1.1/features/morphs.html
    In a document related to *Homer3*, PDI explains that production on the segment took approximately four months, with a core team consisting of a director, a producer, a technical director, three character-technical directors, three lighting specialists, eight character anima-

tors and nine effects animators. Elements in the landscapes allude to classic CGI images from such sources as *TRON* and the computer game, 'Myst'. Also, *TRON* is the subject of one of the episode's gags. When Homer asks if anyone in the room has seen the film, one by one they all answer 'no'. The segment appears in the 1995 *Treehouse of Horror VI* Halloween special of 'The Simpsons'. More information is published on-line at http://www.pdi.com/PDPage/how/homer3.html

43. Hilf, 'Developing a Digital Aesthetic', op. cit., 20.

44. Drew Takahashi, quoted in Perkins, 'Digital Wizards of Hollywood's Future', *Red Herring* 7 (Dec. 1993): n.p. Published on-line at http://www.herring.com/mag/issue07/future.html

45. Charlie Gibson, quoted in Perkins, op. cit.

46. Paula Parisi, 'Tools of the Trade: Computer Keyboards are Replacing the Traditional Paint and Brush', *The Hollywood Reporter* (26 January 1993): S24+, S24.

47. For information on Fantôme Animation and its series, see Harvey Deneroff, 'Fantôme: The First 10 Years', *Animation World Network* (April 1996); 'Fantôme', on-line at http://www.awn.com/fantome

48. Originally, 'Reboot' was produced by Mainframe Joint Venture, which was composed of several companies and a group of creators known as 'the hub'. In July 1996, Mainframe Entertainment was established as an independent firm. For more information on the 'Reboot' series, see Emru Townsend, 'Turn On and Plug In: The Alphanumeric World of 'Reboot', *fps* (Autumn 1995), 12–14.

49. 'Fantôme', on-line at http://www.awn.com/fantome

50. Rogier van Bakel, 'Features: Reboot', *Wired* 5, 3 (March 1997), n.p. Published on-line at http://www.wired.com/wired/5.03

51. Ian Pearson, quoted in Janet L. Hetherington, 'As Mainframe's Technology Reaches Adolescence, There's a Reboot Renaissance', *Animation Magazine* (Sept. 1997): 14–16+, 72.

52. Hetherington, op. cit., 14.

53. See Hetherington, op. cit., 16.

54. Tony Apodaca, quoted in Emru Townsend, 'Tony Apodaca & Flip Phillips: An Informal Chat with Two of Pixar's Old Hands', *fps* (Autumn 1995): 18–22, 22.

55. Ellen Wolff, 'Firms Plan CGI Pix for Infinity and Beyond', *Daily Variety* (24 March 1997): 8+, 8.

56. Harvey Deneroff, 'Fantôme: The First 10 Years', *Animation World Magazine* (April 1996).

57. Steven Levy and Katie Hafner, 'Pixar's Magic Kingdom', *Newsweek* (17 March 1997): 72–75.

58. Wolff, 'Firms Plan CGI Pix for Infinity and Beyond', op. cit., 14.

59. Hilf, 'Developing a Digital Aesthetic', op. cit., 9.

60. Debra Kaufman, 'Computer as Paintbrush', *Hollywood Reporter* (21 Jan. 1992): S36–S40, S38.

61. Paula Parisi, 'The New Hollywood', *Wired* 3, 12 (Dec. 1995): n.p. Published on-line at http://www.wired.com/wired/3.12

62. Michael Salinders, 'Revolutionary Animation Cleans Up During Holidays', *UCLA Bruin* (11 January 1996): 26.

63. John Lasseter, quoted in Celia Duncan, 'Quick on the Draw', *Screen International* (22 March 1996): 18+.

64. Beverly J. Jones, 'Computer Graphics: Effects of Origins', *Leonardo* (Special SIGGRAPH issue, 1990): 21–30, 26.

65. Parisi, 'The New Hollywood', op. cit.

66. Joe Johnston, quoted in Parisi, 'The New Hollywood', op. cit.

67. Paul Wells, 'Don't Talk to Me About Princess Leia: Integral Imaging and the Future of Animation', *Art & Design* 53 (1997): 90–92, 91.

68. Valerie Hall, synopsis of Bergeron P. (1985), 'Controlling Facial Expressions and Body Movements in the Computer-Generated Animated Short, *Tony de Peltrie*', tutorial, SIGGRAPH 1985. Published on-line at http://mambo.ucsc.edu/psl/bergeron.html

69. Id.

70. Id.

71. Valerie Hall identifies the 'three stages to be worked through' in the animation process as 'specifying the key positions, interpolating between the key positions, and fitting the 3D model on each interpolated skeleton. This fitting includes putting the clothes on Tony and making wrinkles in the clothes when the body moves'. Hall, op. cit.

72. Jones, op. cit., 27.

73. Craig Good, 'Filmmaking First, Computers Second: The Making of *Tin Toy*', *Animation Magazine* (Fall 1988): 31.

74. Parisi, 'The New Hollywood', op. cit.

75. Jamie Dixon, digital effects supervisor at Pacific Data Images, explains that 'having 3D motion data offers the animators the flexibility to fine-tune certain motions' because they can move the camera anywhere they want to. She adds, 'if we had rotoscoped a live scene we would have needed to set up all those different camera angles beforehand'. Jamie Dixon, quoted in Ellen Wolff, 'Cinemagicians: FX', *Daily Variety* (25 April 1995): 21+, 24.

76. Rex Weiner, 'Moved by Technology', *Daily Variety* (23 March 1995): n.p.

77. Marla Matzer, 'Animation's New 'Toon Advances Mean "Motion Capture" is about to Make a Splash', *Los Angeles Times* (8 Sept. 1997): n.p. (business section).

78. Id.

79. Id.

80. Jim Morris, quoted in Ellen Wolff, 'Cinemagicians: FX', op. cit., 24.

81. Dennis Muren, quoted in Parisi, 'The New Hollywood', op. cit.

82. Matzer, op. cit.

83. Mark Cotta Vaz and Patricia Rose Duignan, *Industrial Light & Magic* (New York: Ballantine, 1996), 204. The idea of filming an individual who is wearing a grid of some sort relates to the early motion studies of Jean Marey and others. Marey had some of his subjects wear a marked suit that would clearly indicate patterns of motion in the finished photograph.

84. Celia Duncan, 'Quick on the Draw', *Screen International* (22 March 1996): 18.

85. Janet Hetherington, 'As Mainframe's Technology Reaches Adolescence, There's a Reboot Renaissance', *Animation Magazine* (September 1997): 14.

86. Mairi Welman, quoted in Hetherington, op. cit.

87. Emru Townsend, 'Eric Darnell & Michael Collery: The Creators of *Gas Planet* on Art, Computers, and the Frankenstein Complex', *fps* (Autumn 1995): 24–27.

88. John Lasseter, 'Viewpoint', *Animation Magazine* (March/April 1994): 44–45, 44.

89. Ibid., 44.

90. Lasseter, interview with Jürgens, op. cit.

91. Walt Disney Feature Animation, 'Computer Generated Imagery', employment brochure (ca. 1997).

92. DreamWorks, 'DreamWorks Animation', employment brochure (1996).

93. Industrial Light & Magic, 'General Information' from the Human Resources Department (June 1996).

94. Id.

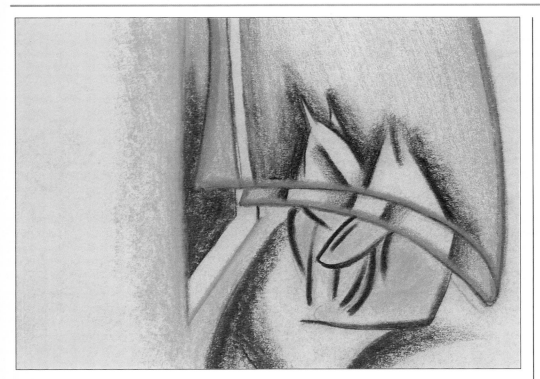

COLOUR PLATE 1
Furies *(1978)*
Sara Petty
Courtesy the artist/
© Sara Petty

COLOUR PLATE 2
The Man Who
Planted Trees *(1987)*
Frédéric Back
Courtesy CBC

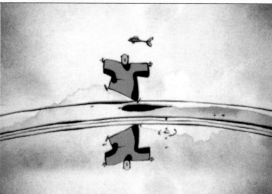

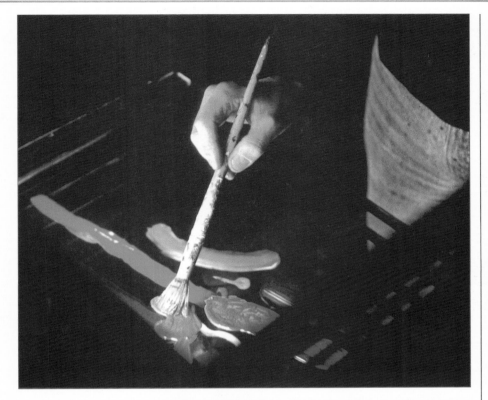

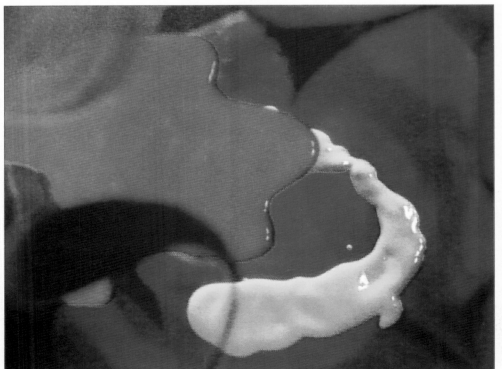

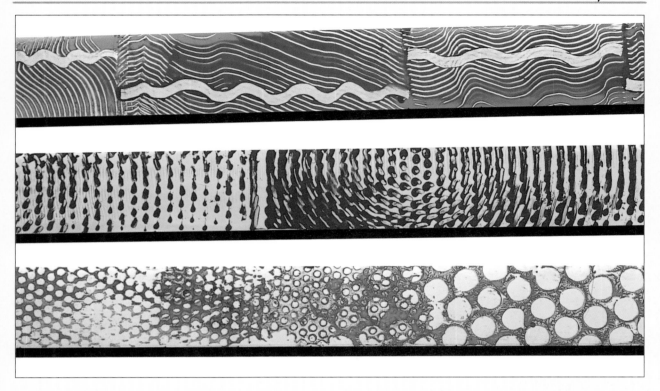

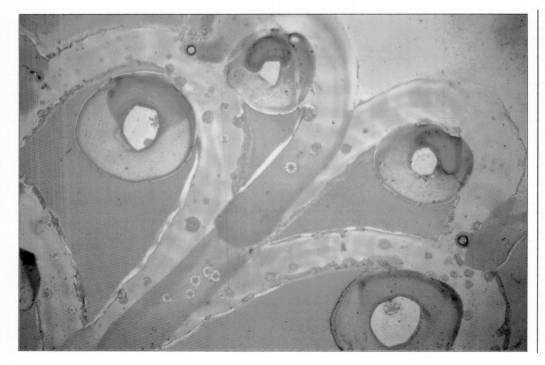

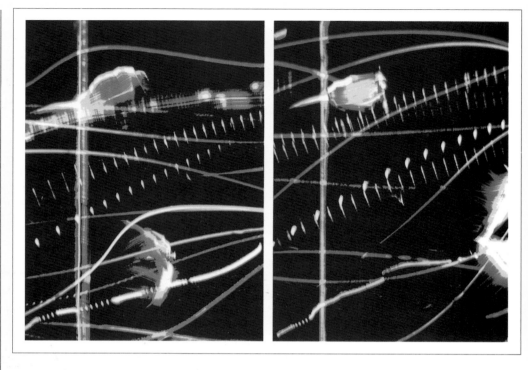

COLOUR PLATE 13
Moonlight *(1997)*
Bärbel Neubauer
Courtesy the artist

COLOUR PLATE 14
The Boy Alchemist
(1984), a collage box
by Larry Jordan
Courtesy the artist

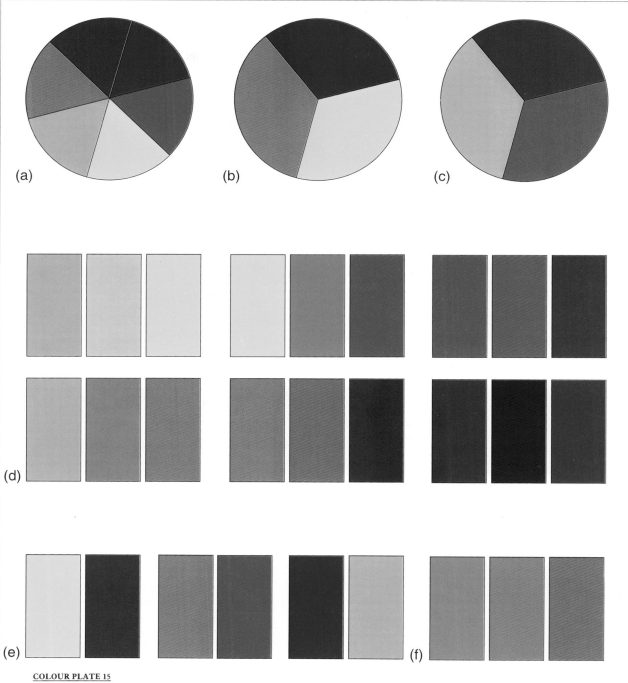

COLOUR PLATE 15

(a) *Colour wheel*
(b) *Primary colours: red, blue, yellow*
(c) *Secondary colours: orange, violet, green*
(d) *Analogous colour schemes*
(e) *Complementary colour schemes*
(f) *Example of a monochromatic colour scheme*

COLOUR PLATE 16
Frame from World
(1970) Jordan Belson
Collection of the artist/
© Jordan Belson

COLOUR PLATE 17
Fireflies I (1995)
Trnka Studio
Courtesy Trnka Studio

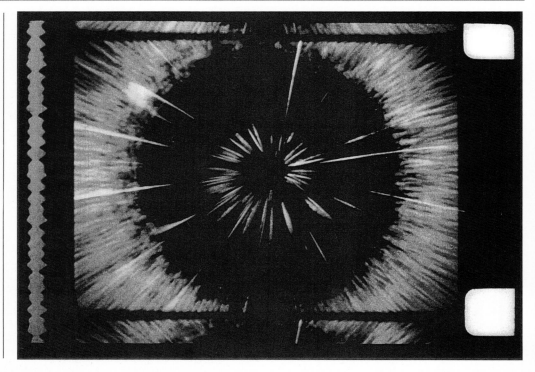

COLOUR PLATES
18 and 19
Gerald McBoing
Boing *(1951), directed
by Robert 'Bobe'
Cannon. UPA
included minimalist
backgrounds and fields
of colour to establish
mood. This marked the
studio as different from
Disney, which used
elaborate, subtle back-
grounds to create a
more realistic diegesis*
Courtesy Jules Engel

COLOUR PLATE 20
When the Stars
Came Dreaming
*(1997), directed by
Jean Poulot*
© *Will Vinton
Studios, Inc.*

COLOUR PLATE 21
Meet the Raisins,
*produced by the Will
Vinton Studios (1988)*
© *Will Vinton
Studios, Inc.*

COLOUR PLATE 22
*Gumby and Pokey
from 'The Gumby
Show' (1956–1957),
produced by Art Clokey*
Courtesy Art Clokey

COLOUR PLATE 23
The Hand *(1965)*
Jiří Trnka
© *Trnka Studio*

COLOUR PLATE 24
Toy Story (1995),
*directed by John
Lasseter for Walt
Disney Pictures*
© *Disney Enterprises, Inc.*

COLOUR PLATE 25
Gas Planet (1992),
*directed by Eric
Darnell and
Michael Collery*
© *Pacific Data Images*

COLOUR PLATE 26
Sleepy Guy *(1995)*
Raman Hui
© *Pacific Data Images*

COLOUR PLATE 27
The Cat and the
Two Sparrows,
*from 'Les fables
géométriques',
Fantôme Animation*
© *Fantôme*

COLOUR PLATE 28
Insektors *(1995)*
Fantôme Animation
© Fantôme

COLOUR PLATE 29
AndrAIa, a popular
Game Sprite from the
'ReBoot' series, Season
III (1998)

ReBoot is a registered
trademark of Mainframe
Entertainment, Inc.
ReBoot™ and ReBoot™
characters © 1998
Mainframe Entertainment,
Inc. All rights reserved.

COLOUR PLATE 32
*'Hippoposterous', a
new property being
developed by Modern
Cartoons, using
its real-time
animation system
© 1998 Modern
Cartoons, Inc.*

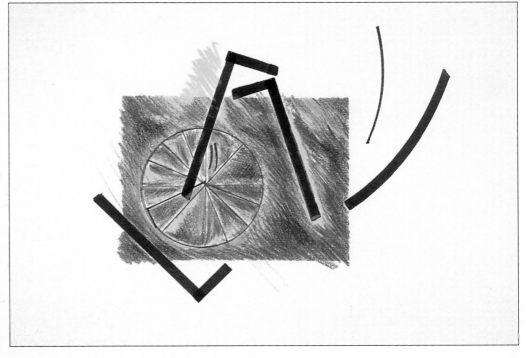

COLOUR PLATE 33
Meadow *(1995)*
Jules Engel
Courtesy the artist

Part 2

STUDIES
IN ANIMATION
AESTHETICS

10

Institutional regulators

TASTE AND CONTROL

Richard A. Blum and Richard D. Lindhem have identified two core concerns related to the censorship of American television: taste and control.[1] Taste affects the regulation of the content of programs to reflect some designated standard of morality. Control concerns access – the issue of who is able to view any given material. They note that much of television censorship:

> ... centers on the impact of programming on children ... the underlying assumption by most of those concerned about children being exposed to potentially harmful material is that the individuals watching television are unable to make intelligent choices and are incapable of monitoring and controlling the viewing selection of other family members. The only acceptable solution, therefore, seems to be to eliminate those programs or program elements that might be deemed undesirable or offensive.[2]

This chapter examines issues related to taste and control, particularly relating to child audiences and the way in which content is developed with their interests in mind. It focuses most of its attention on the American television industry, although some references are made to theatrical filmmaking and the television industry worldwide.

Aside from a given broadcast station, there are many 'key players' who affect what is shown on the air, including advertisers, who might make national deals or purchase air time from local broadcasters; syndicators, who distribute programming that is not produced for release by a specific network or is a re-run; networks, which provide popular programs at relatively low cost to local broadcasters; government regulators; and local community members, who provide feedback to station managers.[3]

Local community members influence broadcasters through phone calls or letters, as well as the decision to watch a given program. Sometimes, a number of people become united on an issue and express their opinions in unison; they may be known as special interest groups. Representing a particular point of view, special interest groups make it their duty to lobby legislators and pressure broadcasters into reacting to their demands. Some groups, such as Action for Children's Television (ACT) in particular, have exerted a great deal of influence on the American television industry. ACT was formed in 1968 and led by Peggy Charren to help raise the consciousness of the networks in regard to children's programming.[4] Blum and Lindhem identify four areas with which ACT and other special interest groups typically are concerned: the portrayal of minorities, violence, suitability for children, and wholesomeness.[5]

Susan Tyler Eastman and her associates note that it was the pressure of the special-interest group ACT upon the Federal Communications Commission (FCC), along with the success of 'Sesame Street' (1968–present), which airs on the Public Broadcasting System (PBS), that initially caused the networks to become more interested in children's shows.[6] They write:

> ... by the mid-1970s, all three commercial networks [ABC, CBS, and NBC] had named a vice-president in charge of children's programs. Before that, children's programming had been the last thing on the priority list for the daytime vice-presidents, whose attention was largely on the more competitive talk shows, soap operas and game shows.[7]

The campaigns by ACT and others for the improvement of children's entertainment were not by any means the first of their kind. In fact, youth entertainment had been the subject of public scrutiny throughout the 1900s. Richard deCordova explains, for example, that 'during the 1920s and early 1930s the cinema's address to children was contested ground and a matter of frenzied concern. Reformers denounced the movies' influence on children and mounted well-organised efforts across the country to regulate and control this aspect of children's leisure'.[8] One result of this increased concern was the formation of various censoring organisations, including the Production Code Administration, which already has been discussed in this book.

Some years later, debates arose concerning comic books. In the late 1940s and early 1950s, the E.C. Comics company, originally founded by M.C. Gaines to publish stories from the Bible and Western history, took a turn to the sordid after the business was inherited by the founder's son, William Gaines. Under the younger Gaines, the company experienced sensational success with comics sometimes involving significant, politically charged world events such as the Korean War and the Holocaust, but generally characterised by themes of horror and crime.[9] The rise of E.C. Comics and other comic books dealing with topics some thought to be in bad taste led to the publication of Frederic Wertham's infamous book, *The Seduction of the Innocent*, in 1954.[10] Wertham alleged that comic books were destroying the morality of American youth. The same year it was published, the United States Senate Judiciary Committee held hearings on the relationship between comic books and juvenile delinquency.[11] As a result of these and other actions, the Comic Book Code Authority was established in the United States as an industry censorship body; its 'Comic Book Code' lasts to this day, although it is less influential now than it was in the past.

The influence of ACT and other special interest groups upon animation aesthetics should not be dismissed lightly. However, because there are a number of special interest groups with diverse agendas, it would be a lengthy undertaking to provide much information on them all. Instead, this chapter will focus on the institutions that are influenced by these groups, including Network Broadcast Standards and Practices departments and government regulators.

Broadcast standards and practices

Within each American broadcasting network, a department generally called Broadcast Standards and Practices is endowed with the responsibility of internally monitoring the content of the materials the network airs.[12] The origins of these departments are found within the Television Code of Standards developed in 1952 by the National Association of Broadcasters (NAB), the oldest and largest broadcast trade association in the United States.[13] Cable television networks (Nickelodeon, MTV, the Cartoon Network, etc.) also have Standards and Practices departments, although they are not covered by the same code of standards as the broadcasters that use public airwaves (ABC, Fox, etc.).[14]

The function of Standards and Practices is, in part, to circumvent pressure from outside parties, whether special interest groups or government regulators. The primary areas of concern for Broadcast Standards and Practices are the depictions of violence and sexual content, although the issues of replication (i.e. can actions shown on the program be repeated by a viewer?), offensive language, and suitability for family viewing also come into play.[15]

Typically, Broadcast Standards and Practices review any production while it is in the script stage and indicates required changes. Once scripts have received final approval from Standards and Practices and other institutional offices, nothing about the story is to be changed in any significant way. When network television is broadcast over public airwaves, it is subject to greater regulation than theatrical films or cable television productions; governmental regulators have the right to control content because broadcast (as opposed to cable) television, like most radio, is transmitted over signals that are owned by the public, rather than any one individual or company.[16]

Eastman and her associates explain that:

> ... the broadcast standards and practices department, a behind-the-scenes group, exercises total authority over all network programming. Cynically and often angrily called the 'censors', this department at each network has absolute approval rights over every program ... It often finds itself walking a thin line between offending viewers or advertisers and destroying imaginative programming that may pull in high ratings.[17]

While the depiction of nudity (e.g. no full frontal nudity of men or women, or breasts of women) is a well-delineated area, some concerns such as violence or language are less clear in their parameters. Blum and Lindhem contend that 'the central issue between creators and censors concerns the standards that are used in decision making. The guidelines often seem arbitrary, leading to frustration among the creative people and hostility on the part of network standards executives', who answer only to the top executives in the studio.

A much-publicised case concerning Canadian John Kricfalusi and 'The Ren & Stimpy Show' series, which he created, serves as a good example. In early 1991 the series became a major hit and helped to launch the success of original animation on the Nickelodeon Television Network. Much of the appeal of the show was the outrageousness and sometimes the raunchiness of the two characters and their activities – never before had there been such a 'kid's show' broadcast on American television.

However, in 1992, Kricfalusi, who had sold his rights to the characters, was fired from the series. Linda Simensky, who was a Producer at the Network at the time, contended that their policy was to let creators operate with relative autonomy, 'to work out their own artistic visions', and that Kricfalusi was able to develop his story ideas without much interference. In his case, she argued, 'schedule and budget were the problems. There were things that standards didn't like, but Vanessa [Coffey, his Producer,] got them through'.[18] However, Mark Langer notes that some problems seemed to have developed because of continued requests for changes in the stories.[19] He writes that:

> Nickelodeon story editors continually requested script and other modifications, which were resisted by Kricfalusi. Revisions to *Stimpy's Big Day* included the deletion of a character sniffing kitty litter ... The original ending of this episode was to show Stimpy presenting himself for a smacking. Nickelodeon story editors deemed this to be 'Too masochistic for the younger viewers' ... Standards and Practices at Nickelodeon withheld network approval from such items as the episode titles *Ren and Stimpy Bugger Christmas* and *Stimpy's First Fart* ... Nickelodeon began to receive finished episodes that had to be censored in part. Eventually, two episodes featuring a new character named George Liquor were deemed unsuitable for broadcast altogether. *Man's Best Friend* featured Ren clubbing George Liquor with an oar in a black-and-white slow motion parody of *Raging Bull* (1980).[20]

Other problems arose when an episode showed the Pope clinging to the buttocks of a character called Powdered Toast Man, who was depicted using the American Bill of Rights and Constitution for kindling. Langer writes:

> ... when viewers complained to the FCC, Nickelodeon dropped the episode from replay on future air-dates. These shows presented real problems for the cable network. Each show represented an investment of approximately $400,000. Nickelodeon could not pump money into a program that did not conform to corporate perceptions regarding the needs of the 55 percent of its audience that was under 18.[21]

Although it is difficult to say just how much influence Standards and Practices had in the troubles of John Kricfalusi, in a general sense, the department assumes great importance in the production of American made-for-television series. Numerous anecdotes have been told about the censorship of items such as nudity, alcohol, and weapons in animated shows. Gabor Csupo, whose company originally animated 'The Simpsons' series, provides an example of a seemingly innocuous visual that was targeted by the censors. In one episode:

> ... the family is walking through an art gallery and one artist drew a statue of a naked woman – in the background, in silhouette. We didn't even realise it. I mean, when you walk into a museum, that is everywhere. Well, the executives at Fox banned it. They said: 'What are you trying to do? Sneak in pornography? Redo it!'[22]

The creators of the computer-generated television series 'ReBoot' (animated by the Canadian production house Mainframe Entertainment) ran across problems in dealing with the ABC network, which distributed the series for two seasons beginning in 1994. *Wired* reporter Rogier van Bakel explained that 'ABC's disapproval focused mainly on sexiness and interpersonal violence'.[23] As an example of the latter, Gavin Blair said the network would not allow 'jeopardy' to occur, 'meaning we couldn't end an act with Bob falling off a cliff and him yelling "Aaaaahh" as we cut to a commercial

– because that's jeopardy, and we'd upset the kiddies'.[24] The network also objected to the design of the leading female character, insisting:

> ... that Dot's shapely figure be toned down. Never a particularly large-breasted character to begin with and never one to expose much cleavage, Dot's chest had to be completely desexed. 'So she acquired this longish horizontal lump on the front of her torso', muses Blair. 'Her breasts sort of come out at the side and then go straight across the front without a hint that there are two of them.'[25]

Karl Cohen notes other areas where standards of taste are open to question. For example, he says that 'the word "asshole" isn't acceptable, but it is okay to call a person an "ass" on TV. MTV lets Beavis and Butt-Head say "ass wipe" and "ass munch" on the air as alternative expressions'.[26] In addition, the depiction of nudity is also an area that is becoming open to interpretation. Cohen notes that:

> ... nudity is beginning to be included in animated shows like 'Beavis and Butt-Head' and 'The Simpsons'. The most common image is an exposed male behind. [J.J.] Sedelmaier [whose company animated 'Beavis and ButtHead' episodes] said he couldn't show a bare butt if the pants were down to the character's ankles, but it was OK to expose the butt if the pants were only pulled down to the bottom of the character's behind.[27]

Eric Radomski, who was a Producer and Director for Warner Bros.' 'Batman: The Series', points out some relatively arbitrary restrictions that were applied to his work. He recalls:

> On 'Batman' they were very careful, and rightly so, not to show handguns, because kids can access a handgun in their parents' drawer. But we could have machine guns and shoot them at will. What kid has a machine gun in their closet? That's stupid, yet that was the deal.[28]

Guidelines set by Standards and Practices departments can limit the potential of foreign-produced animation broadcast on American television stations. A previous chapter discussed the difficulty that program lengths can create for the sale of animated productions internationally; for example, a show with a true 30-minute running time produced in the United Kingdom cannot easily play on American television, which requires shows of approximately 22 minutes to allow for the addition of commercials. But content, too, can create problems for global distribution. What is deemed acceptable for broadcasting in one country might not be welcomed in another. An examination of how a series of Japanese shows was adapted for use on American television helps to demonstrate the types of cultural differences that can exist.

During the 1960s, made-for-television animation had become very popular in Japan, leading to great growth in the industry. Among the most popular genres developed were toy-based fantasies featuring giant robots; by the mid 1980s, there were over 40 different giant-robot *anime* series in Japan.[29]

In the late 1970s, some of the earlier-produced animated series were imported to America, where they were subtitled and shown on Japanese community television channels. However, the programs were not very successful. According to Fred Ladd, one of the pioneering distributors of Japanese animation in the United States, there was a lot of 'pressure to reduce the amount of violence on TV' during the 1970s and, as a result, releases from that period were highly sanitised and did poorly.[30] It was not until the mid-1980s that Japanese animation became a significant force on American television. One of the most popular series released at that time was

'Robotech', which began in March 1985 (after a pilot was released in 1984) and remained in syndication for about a year.

The American incarnation of 'Robotech' is composed of three series that were broadcast individually in Japan: 'Super-Dimensional Fortress: Macross', which was a commercial success in Japan; and the less-popular series, 'Super Dimensional Cavalry: Southern Cross' and 'Genesis Climber: Mospeada'. Actually, there is only one way in which the series originally were related: they shared a similar visual design because all three were produced by Tatsunoko, a large studio located in Tokyo.

The rights to these and a number of other series had been purchased by an international distributor, Harmony Gold, which intended to distribute them in various markets, after dubbing the episodes into French, Italian and Spanish.[31] However, to enter the American market was problematic, since it remained difficult to air international work in the early 1980s. Complicating matters further was the fact that too few of each series had been produced to put them into syndication on American television (today, a minimum of approximately 52 episodes – about one per week – is needed for syndication).

During the 1980s, Carl Macek owned a comic art store in Orange, California, near Chapman University, where he had attended graduate school.[32] He learned that Harmony Gold owned the various series and that it was interested in adapting them for American television when individuals from the company came to his store seeking 'Macross' artwork to use for promotional purposes. To solve the problem of having too few episodes for syndication, Macek suggested that he might be able to combine the different series into one – which is why, eventually, three different series were used to make the 84 episodes known collectively as 'Robotech'.[33]

After completing a pilot episode of 'Robotech' in 1984, Macek was given the go-ahead to continue work. The series was adapted over a period of about six months, from late 1984 through the middle of 1985, which included the selection of materials, the re-editing of the episodes to remove abrupt butt splices, and the scripting and recording of dialogue, sound effects and music. On the average, five shows were mixed per week. It seems likely that the relatively fast production schedule enhanced Macek's ability to make the 'Robotech' series into a cohesive production, despite the differences among the source materials, because he probably could easily retain the total concept of the work in his mind over the entire period in which he worked.

In modifying the episodes, Macek stresses that his intention was to 'adapt' rather than 'translate' the series. He says he considered the cultural significance of the product in relation to its new audience, as well as the original language of the production, but he was interested in 'the soul of the work' rather than what each character said literally.

To be sure, significant changes were made to both the visual and aural components of the series. Macek believes that his prior study of live-action cinema influenced his choices in editing the series for what he envisioned would be a teenage and young adult audience. He claims that most of the decisions to modify the content of the episodes were based on his own aesthetic preferences, although some other forces contributed to the decision-making process. One of them was the National Broadcasting Corporation's (NBC's) Broadcast Standards and Practices regulations, which he said amounted to one primary mandate. Predictably, it was related to violence: there could be no blood coming from body parts.[34] In his analysis of the series, Anthony Beal points out a number of changes related to the depiction of death that likely were due to this regulation.[35] As an example, one might consider a scene in Episode 7, when an alien shoots down one of his own men. Beal writes:

> In the Japanese version, when the alien pod hits the ground, the door falls open and the alien inside is bloody and burned. In the American version, the pod hits the ground and then the image cuts to the next shot. Another example is in episode 10, when the battle fortress is attacked and the radar tower is destroyed. In the Japanese version, we see a shot of three men in a hallway that explodes and their bodies can be seen incinerating. In the American version, the explosion happens and, before the men start incinerating, it cuts to the next shot.

Beal comes to the conclusion that, ironically, the Japanese versions deal with 'sexual innuendoes and language more than the American version but the American version emphasises the violence ...'. The reason violence seems to receive more emphasis in the dubbed episodes, despite the fact that extremely violent actions were removed, is perhaps that 'balancing' content also was largely cut from the adapted work. As Beal's examination suggests, Macek's development of thematic consistency in the work entailed the removal of sexual and softer material. The three series were linked together as an action adventure, so relatively violent activities dominate the adapted storyline.

In his book, *Dreamland Japan: Writings on Modern Manga*, Frederik L. Schodt discusses the existence of both erotic and violent imagery in Japanese art. He argues that Japanese print comics 'are the direct descendants of popular art for the masses in the late Edo period (1600–1867), art in which exaggerated sexuality and stylised violence – scenes of samurai disemboweling themselves and blood spatters – were a standard feature'.[36] In terms of sexual content, particularly, standards in Japanese popular art have become fairly lenient; in recent years, erotic comics and animation have become widely available to adults as well as young people. However, American standards for the depiction of nudity in print or on television – especially in any medium targeted at children – are much more conservative.

In adapting the 'Robotech' series, Macek says he employed his own criteria to 'avoid pandering by overt sexuality'. Beal notes that nudity was cut from the series (e.g. in Episode 3, when a female character is taking a shower) and that a number of subtly sexual scenes were modified as well. For example, in Episode 1, the male characters watch a young woman walk away, but in the American version a close shot of her rear end is removed.

'Robotech's Episode 63 (Episode 3 of the 'Mospeada' series) includes a scene wherein a woman reveals her true identity as a man by disrobing in front of a group of embarrassed spectators. In the original version, a slow tilt reveals the sensual curves of the 'woman's' body, whereas the American version shows only the final seconds of the shot, a close up of her face as she winks. Another shot in the scene, revealing a curvaceous semi-profile of her body from behind, is left out of the adaptation altogether.

This brief examination only begins to reveal the process by which the 'Robotech' series was adapted for use on American television. It suggests some of the ways in which a production can be adapted to fulfill the aesthetic criteria of another culture – in this case, changes reflect the requirements of Standards and Practices, the personal aesthetics of Macek, and the industry's syndication needs, among other things.

Governmental regulation of content

Government regulators also are interested in the 'taste' and 'control' of animated programs. For example, in recent years, the United States has been considering the implementation of 'V-Chip' technology that will help parents to identify the amount of violence in a television program and control the family's access to it. The American government also has been in the position of requiring that broadcasters add certain kinds of programming and specifying when that programming should be run.

As Ladd suggests, a number of changes in children's programming occurred during the 1970s. Due in part to pressure from ACT, in the middle of that decade the NAB began issuing new guidelines as to the amount of advertising allowable on children's programming. By 1976, the air time had been decreased from sixteen minutes of commercials per hour to as low as nine-and-a-half minutes on the weekends and ten minutes per hour during the week (at first, ACT had argued to completely do away with advertising during children's programming). The NAB also declared that hosts of children's programs should not be allowed to present commercial messages and that vitamin commercials aimed at young viewers should be eliminated.[37]

Eastman and her associates explain that, in the early 1970s, networks were asked to portray constructive role models in storylines, communicate respect for the feelings of others, and provide youngsters with positive messages. The networks responded to this call for 'pro-social' content by seeking the assistance of experts from outside the television industry. For instance, CBS recruited a panel of educators and psychologists. One of the first programs it developed was the highly successful animated half-hour show, 'Fat Albert and the Cosby Kids' (1972–1979; under the title 'The New Fat Albert Show', 1979–1984), animated by Filmation and starring Bill Cosby. ABC worked with a group from Bankstreet College, which had been acclaimed for its experimental teaching programs. Bankstreet advisors reviewed scripts and, together with the network's Program Department and Broadcast Standards and Practices Department, issued guidelines on sex roles, role models, and age appropriateness for all scripts (these guidelines were similar to ones advocated by the other two networks, the Columbia Broadcasting System (CBS) and NBC). In 1972, the America Broadcasting Corporation (ABC) began an educational program called 'Schoolhouse Rock', a series of 3½-minute episodes that ran each hour during weekend children's programming, teaching multiplication tables.[38]

However, these gains were short-lived because, after deregulation of the television industry occurred during the 1980s, the mandates of the mid-1970s were virtually forgotten. Citing a number of studies, Patricia Aufderheide and Kathryn Montgomery explain that:

> ... over the years, citizen activism and government oversight have helped to temper the forces of the marketplace. In the 70s, responding to Federal Communications Commission (FCC) petitions by Action for Children's Television and other citizen groups, the networks launched a number of television programs designed to educate and inform children ... After the FCC deregulated the TV industry in the early 80s, these programs disappeared from the schedules. In fact, as the children's television business boomed, the amount of educational and informational programming plummeted.[39]

Deregulation of the industry occurred after Mark Fowler was appointed head of the organisation by President Ronald Reagan in 1981. Fowler viewed television and its programming purely as a business and, at the end of 1983, the FCC lifted policy guidelines of the 1970s concerning children's programming.[40] Partly as a result of his attitude, from 1979 to 1983, the average time that commercial stations allotted to children's programming dropped from 11.3 to 4.4 hours per week.[41]

Perhaps the most significant change in children's programming regulation occurred in 1984, when the FCC removed its ban on program-length commercials, or television series that are centred entirely upon toys and merchandise available in stores. Aufderheide and Montgomery explain that 'toy manufacturers immediately flooded the marketplace with TV series designed as merchandising vehicles for their toys ... Sales of licensed products more than doubled, to $64.6 billion, between 1983–1989, with the motor being television'.[42] They add that, 'by 1987, toy manufacturers financed 80 percent of children's programming, most of it animation. Licensing continues to drive children's programming today [ca. 1994], with product-related shows accounting for 90 percent of new production'.[43] During this same period, the spending power of children also rose dramatically, causing business analysts to view children as one of the 'hottest marketing trends of the 90s'.[44]

As one might expect, social activists did not take these developments quietly. During the late 1980s, the American Congress considered several bills intended to regulate the industry more closely, but none of them became law. However, in 1990, the Children's Television Act was passed. As Diane Aden Hays describes it, the Act contains three basic features:

> It places time restrictions on advertising during children's programming, re-
> quires broadcasters to make an effort to air programming that benefits children,
> and informs broadcasters that, at license renewal time, compliance with these
> factors will be considered as part of their duty to program in the public interest.[45]

One portion of the Act, the limitation of advertising during children's programming to ten-and-a-half minutes per hour on weekends and twelve minutes per hour on weekdays, is relatively clear. However, the majority of the wording in the Act is vague, which invited networks to take its mandates lightly. Aufderheide and Montgomery contend that 'after the Children's Television Act took effect in October, 1991, it initially had little impact on practices in the broadcasting industry'.[46] They argue that the Act was not implemented effectively because 'the FCC loosely defined educational and informational programming and made no stipulations on when programming must run or how much programming was necessary to meet the mandate'.[47] However, broadcasters disregarded even the more clearly defined area of advertising limits; the authors note a study by ACT that found 'stations airing as much as fourteen minutes per hour of advertising during children's programs'.[48]

After President Bill Clinton won the presidential election in 1992, he began to encourage more regulation throughout the government and the country as a whole.[49] Children's programming began to change in 1993, when the FCC delayed the renewal of licenses to several stations whose compliance with the Act was in question. After Congressional meetings that year, 'the broadcast networks began announcing new series scheduled for the upcoming Fall which were designed to comply with the law'.[50] Among the animated series to be made at that time were 'Where on Earth is Carmen Sandiego?', produced by DIC Enterprises,[51] and 'Cro', produced by Children's Television Workshop (CTW), the producers of 'Sesame Street'. Increasingly, the television industry employed such terms as 'FCC friendly', 'compliance show', and 'qualifier' to suggest that certain series would meet the FCC criteria.

Still, there was resistance to meeting the guidelines that were set down by the Children's Television Act. Media analysts have shown that very low production and promotion budgets were given to 'FCC friendly' shows (in comparison with other children's programming), which commonly were placed in early morning time slots when children would be asleep. An informal analysis of the top five television markets conducted by Aufderheide and Montgomery indicated that '44% of all "compliance shows" aired at 6:30 a.m. or earlier; of those 25% were on at either 5:00 or 5:30 a.m.'[52] They found that another common practice was to put these shows in pre-emptible time slots, when sports or other programming might take its place, or to schedule them irregularly, so that it would be difficult for viewers to know when they would appear. The authors conclude that 'the failure of most educational and informational programming demonstrates the weak commitment of broadcasters to such programming. The prevailing belief that "kids won't watch educational programs" has become a self-fulfilling prophecy'.[53]

The same opinion was expressed in an Annenberg Public Policy Center study of June 1996. It states that the 'broadcaster's beliefs about what attracts the largest audience may create a self-fulfilling prophecy. High quality programs for the desirable 6–11 year old audience are typically buried in the schedule (very early in the morning or weekend afternoons)'.[54] The study adds:

> ... there is a good deal of high quality programming generally available. Unfortunately, many of the high quality programs are aired on basic or premium cable television. Since approximately $1/3$ of children ages 2–11 do not have access to cable television (A.C. Nielsen), millions of parents and children have to rely on broadcast television for their educational programming needs.[55]

In August 1996, the Commission adopted new rules that were fully implemented on 1 September 1997, 'to strengthen its enforcement of the Children's Television Act of 1990'.[56] In order to clarify its mandates and to help broadcasters comply with them, the FCC implemented new measures and defined the terms of its legislation. Its public information initiative requires commercial stations to submit standardised reports on children's programming that will be placed in their public files on a quarterly basis. It also requires stations to 'identify core programming at the time it is aired and in information provided to publishers of television program guides'.[57]

The term 'core educational programming' also was defined to mean 'regularly scheduled, weekly programming of at least 30 minutes, aired between 7:00 a.m. and 10:00 p.m., that has serving the educational and information needs of children as a significant purpose'.[58] The new FCC rules also specify that 'at least three hours per week of regularly scheduled, weekly shows that are 30 minutes or longer' and otherwise meet the definition of core programming had to be shown.[59]

A study conducted in 1997 showed that broadcasters were attempting to comply with the FCC's new guidelines even before the compliance date of 1 September.[60] However, some broadcasters continued to feel that the exact definition of 'educational' programming had yet to be determined, and that the true guidelines would be discovered through a process of trial and error.

Because 'the local broadcaster is ultimately responsible for airing programs that meet the FCC criteria', programmers must be able to identify shows that in fact meet the requirements.[61] An Annenberg Public Policy Center study found that local broadcasters tended to mention four ways by which these shows were identified: trusting the syndicator to say if a program is 'pre-approved'; looking for a 'seal of approval' from the National Education Association, or some children's group; trusting the networks; or using their own judgement after reading a description of the program and perhaps watching an episode.[62]

Nancy Steingard, Executive Vice President of Universal Cartoon Studios, points to the series 'Doug', created by Jim Jinkins (owner of the Jumbo animation studio), as an example of a show that meets the criteria set forth by the regulators.[63] She explains that the series takes as its 'curriculum base' (i.e. the level of its educational content) children aged 8 or 9 to 12. It deals with the things that children of that age struggle with: situational ethics, the dynamics of friendships and group identity. A Nickelodeon press release describes the protagonist, Doug Funny, as 'an impressionable kid who feels painfully "average" ', although he is depicted as 'a reassuring, surprise hero. Despite all of his visions of failure, as well as those of grandeur, Doug often ultimately succeeds in life's typical situations in some wonderfully unexpected way'.[64] The series has been noted for clearly articulating its lessons through specific statements, by recasting its lessons in multiple ways throughout the episodes, and for tightly weaving its lessons through the episodes rather than tacking them onto the ends.[65]

Steingard contends that the FCC has supported the idea that 'pro-social content, or emotional experience, is as valid as a science or geography lesson' when it comes to educational or informational content. An Annenberg study confirms this opinion, stating that:

> ... educational and informational programming is simply defined as that which 'furthers the positive development of children 16 years of age and under in any respect, including the child's intellectual/cognitive or social/emotional needs'. Thus, 'prosocial' as well as traditional 'academic' programs will 'count' as long as they have education as a 'significant purpose'.[66]

To assist parents with the selection of appropriate materials, a television-ratings system was developed in 1997. The ratings are: TV-Y (all children), TV-G (all audiences), TV-Y7 (directed to older children), TV-PG (parental guidance suggested), TV-14 (parents strongly cautioned), and TV-M (mature audiences only). The code 'E/I' is applied to programs that are education or informational in nature. However, an Annenberg study suggests that, after implementation of the system, parents largely remained uncertain as to the meaning of specific indicators. For example, only 2.4 per cent of the parents surveyed knew what E/I stood for. The study also found that only 34.7 per cent were 'using the new rating system to guide their children's behavior'.[67]

The extent to which regulation of television occurs in different countries varies greatly, as do the areas of concern. In some countries, the content of artistic expression is strictly controlled. But, even in countries where there has been more freedom of expression, it is common to find regulators attempting to minimise violence throughout television programming and trying to improve the content of shows for children. Such is the case in New Zealand, where the Broadcasting Standards Authority (BSA) was set up by the Broadcasting Act of 1989 to establish and maintain 'acceptable standards of broadcasting' on all of the country's radio and television stations.[68] The BSA oversees code requirements in relation to:

> ... the protection of children; the portrayal of violence; fair and accurate programmes and procedures for correcting factual errors and redressing unfairness; safeguards against the portrayal of persons in programmes in a manner that encourages denigration of, or discrimination against, sections of the community on account of sex, race, age, disability, or occupational status or as a consequence of legitimate expression of religious, cultural or political beliefs; restrictions on the promotion of liquor; and presentation of appropriate warnings in respect of

programmes, including programmes that have been classified as suitable only for particular audiences.[69]

Canada is one of a number of countries that has incorporated the development of indigenous culture into its broadcasting requirements. A 'Factsheet' on the Canadian Radio-television and Telecommunications Commission explains that:

> Section 3 of the Broadcasting Act requires among other things that the Canadian broadcasting system encourage the development of Canadian expression. Public, private and community broadcasters must contribute to the creation and presentation of Canadian programming. They should also make maximum use, and in no case less than predominant use, of Canadian creative and other resources.'[70]

This agency, which was established after the Canadian Radio-television and Telecommunications Commission Act was proclaimed in 1976, has been involved with revamping Canadian broadcasting policy throughout the 1990s. One of the specific guidelines that has been established is the definition of quotas that explain the necessary amounts of 'Canadian content' that are to be broadcast on television. Specific guidelines read:

> The requirements for television are based on the amount of time devoted to Canadian programs. As set out in the TV Regulations, private television licensees generally must achieve a yearly Canadian content level of at least 60% overall, measured over the broadcast day, and 50% between 6 p.m. and midnight. As the national broadcaster, the CBC [Canadian Broadcasting Corporation] must ensure that at least 60% of its program schedule consists of Canadian productions.

To qualify as Canadian content, a program is evaluated using criteria based on the producer and key creative personnel used, the amounts paid to Canadians for services provided to make the program and on post production, as well as amounts spent in Canada on lab processing. Broadcasters may claim a 150 per cent time credit for Canadian dramas which have a full Canadian complement in all key creative roles, and which meet certain scheduling criteria.[71]

In France, national quotas also are in effect; they require that at least 40 per cent of the broadcast programs be of French origin, with additional requirements for shows falling within the more general category of 'European content'.[72] Undoubtedly, the efforts of Canada, France and other countries to encourage indigenous production are intended to help counteract the cultural domination of other market-share-aggressive countries – including (or one might say, primarily) the United States.

Two factors that have helped the Americans to retain a strong world position in the animation industry is the pervasiveness of licensing and the extensive use of merchandising techniques. In addition, audience-testing techniques are used to help assure the marketability of their products. These increasingly important considerations in the development of animated productions will be discussed in the following chapter.

Notes

1.   Richard A. Blum and Richard D. Lindhem, *Primetime: Network Television Programming* (Boston: Focal, 1987), 175.
2.   Ibid., 176.

3. This general list was taken from the Annenberg Public Policy Center, 'Children's Educational Television Regulations and the Local Broadcaster: Impact and Implementation', a study conducted by Amy B. Jordan and John L. Sullivan (9 June 1997).

4. For more on the subject, see 'Peggy Charren and 'Action for Children's Television', *Animation Magazine* (Fall 1989): 41–42.

5. Blum and Lindhem, op. cit., 179.

6. For more on the history of the Children's Television Workshop, as well as its present activities and general philosophies, see Gregory J. Gettas, 'Children's Television Workshop', *Drawing Insight: Communicating Development Through Animation* (Penang: Southbound, 1996), 78–81.

7. Susan Tyler Eastman, Sydney W. Head, and Lewis Klein, *Broadcast/Cable Programming: Strategies and Practices* (Belmont, CA: Wadsworth. 1985), 156.

8. Richard deCordova, 'The Mickey in Macy's Window: Childhood, Consumerism, and Disney Animation', in Eric Smoodin (ed.), *Disney Discourse: Producing the Magic Kingdom* (New York: Routledge, 1994), 203–213, 211.

9. For more on the rise of E.C. Comics, see Kirk Varnedoe and Adam Gopnik, *High & Low: Modern Art and Popular Culture* (New York: The Museum of Modern Art, 1990).

10. Frederic Wertham, *The Seduction of the Innocent* (New York: Rinehart, 1954).

11. United States Senate Judiciary Committee, 'Juvenile Delinquency (Comic Books): Hearings Before the Subcommittee to Investigate Juvenile Delinquency of the Committee on the Judiciary – United States Senate, 83rd Congress, Second Session, April 21, 22, and June 4, 1954' (Washington, DC: US Government Printing Office, 1954).

12. At CBS, the department is called Program Practices.

13. Sabrie Napier (NAB Library Assistant/Information Specialist), correspondence with the author (23 Sept. 1997).

14. Karl Cohen, 'Inside the Censor's Mind', *Animato!* 32 (Spring 1995): 32–34.

15. Blum and Lindhem, op. cit., 177. One imagines that the issue of replication was behind a decision to prevent the *Paint Thinner Rules* episode of 'Beavis and Butt-Head' from being broadcast in the future. As its title suggests, the episode depicts the characters inhaling paint thinner. Jim Fanning and Russ Miller, 'Huh, Huh, Huh ... Cool: The First Season Beavis and Butt-Head Episode Guide', *Animato!* 28 (Spring 1994): 46–49+.

16. Another reason for the tight control over changes to made-for-television series undoubtedly is economic. Television episodes generally have much smaller budgets and a shorter production schedule than theatrical features, so there is little room for improvisation. In contrast, story modifications might occur almost until the completion of a theatrical feature. Of course, it is preferable that few story changes occur after a feature film has progressed through layout, but there is nothing like the authority of Broadcast Standards and Practices to prevent continued modification of theatrical features.

17. Eastman, et al., op.cit., 142.

18. Linda Simensky, interview with the author, New York City (29 Jan. 1993).

19. Mark Langer, 'Animatophilia, Cultural Production and Corporate Interests: The Case of 'Ren & Stimpy', *Film History* 5, 2 (June 1993): 125–141, 136. The essay also appears in *A Reader in Animation Studies*, Jayne Pilling (ed.) (London: John Libbey, 1997): 143–161.

20. Later, the George Liquor episodes were broadcast on television.

21. Langer, op. cit., 137.

22. Gabor Csupo, quoted in an interview with Paula Parisi and Randall Thierney, 'Idol Chatter', *The Hollywood Reporter* (14 Jan. 1997): 29–38, 36.

23. After ABC stopped distributing 'ReBoot' it continued to be distributed to American stations independently. Rogier van Bakel, 'Features: ReBoot', *Wired* 5, 3 (March 1997), n.p. Published on-line at http://www.wired.com/wired/5.03

24. Gavin Blair, quoted in Bakel, ibid.

25. Id.

26. Karl Cohen, op. cit., 32.

27. Ibid., 33.

28. Eric Romonski, quoted in an interview with Paula Parisi and Randall Thierney, 'Idol Chatter', *The Hollywood Reporter* (14 Jan. 1997): 29–38, 36–38.

29. Fred Patten, 'A Capsule History of Anime', *Animation World Magazine* (Aug. 1996).

30. Harvey Deneroff, 'Fred Ladd: An Interview', *Animation World Magazine* (Aug. 1996).

31. Fred Patten, telephone interview with the author (19 Sept. 1996).

32. Carl Macek, interview with the author, Santa Monica (12 Sept. 1996). All subsequent references to Macek will be from this interview, unless otherwise specified.

33. Only one episode, number 37, is not based on an original episode from a series.

34. The other influence came from 'Robotech's' original producer, a French man named C.G. Revelle, who was concerned about material that might be offensive for foreign markets.

35. Anthony Beal, 'Japanese Animation and American Censorship', unpublished essay (6 May 1996). Beal and the author presented a paper on this topic at the Society for Animation Studies conference in Madison, Wisconsin, in October 1996. However, references to Beal pertain to his initial essay.

    Beal's analysis is based on viewing of the 'Perfect' video collection released by Streamline Pictures. Each video in the series includes two items: (1) the original Japanese version of an episode (actually two episodes) with subtitles, and (2) the edited and dubbed version of the episode as it was released for the American television. This chapter avoids discussion of changes in dialog that occurred because neither Beal nor myself is fluent in Japanese and, therefore, we could only rely on subtitles for an understanding of the dialogue in the Japanese version. Obviously, the English subtitles can be significantly different than what is heard in the spoken Japanese words. In any case, changes to the visual elements are enough to demonstrate the principles being discussed in this chapter.

36. Frederik L. Schodt, *Dreamland Japan: Writings on Modern Manga* (Berkeley: Stone Bridge, 1996), 50.

37. Eastman, et al., op. cit., 156; Cy Schneider, *Children's Television: The Art, the Business, and How It Works* (Chicago: NTC Business Books, 1987), 176.

38. Eastman, et al., op. cit., 157.

39. Patricia Aufderheide and Kathryn C. Montgomery, 'The Impact of the Children's Television Act on the Broadcast Market', published on the Internet (ca. 1994) at http://tap.epn.org/cme/ctact.html

    The authors cite B. Watkins, 'Improving Educational and Informational Television for Children When the Marketplace Falls', *Law & Policy Review* 5, 2 (1987), 365–367, and others.

40. Tom Engelhardt, 'The Shortcake Strategy', *Watching Television* (New York: Pantheon, 1986): 68–110, 76.

41. Ibid., 75–76.

42. Aufderheide and Montgomery, op. cit. The authors cite S. Cohen, 'Kidvideo Games', *Washington Post* (7 April 1991): 38, and others.

43. Aufderheide and Montgomery, op. cit. The authors cite S. Kline, *Out of the Garden: Toys and Children's Culture in the Age of TV Marketing* (New York, Verso, 1993), 139.

44. Aufderheide and Montgomery, op. cit. The authors cite D. Oldenburg, 'Children's Business: America's $90 billion-plus youth market', *Washington Post* (6 July 1993).

45. Diane Aden Hayes, 'The Children's Hour Revisited: The Children's Television Act of 1990' (ca. 1994), n.p. Published on the Internet (ca. 1994) at http://www.law.indiana.edu/fclj/v46/no2/hayes.html

46. Aufderheide and Montgomery, op. cit.

47. Aufderheide and Montgomery, op. cit. The authors cite the United States Federal Communications Commission, 'Report and Order: In the Matter of Policies and Rules Concerning Children's Television Programming' (1991), FCC Record 6: 2111–2127; and others.

48. H.R. Rep. No. 385, supra note 19, at 7–8, 1990 U.S.C.C.A.N. at 1611–1612 (discussing National Association of Broadcasters' Children's Television Commercialisation Survey and a report by Action for Children's Television), cited in Hayes, op. cit.

49. Hayes, op. cit.

50. Aufderheide and Montgomery, op. cit. For thoughts on the CTA as of 1993, see Judith Reboy, 'The Children's Television Act: Friend or Foe of Television Animation?' *Animato!* 26 (Summer 1993): 54–55+.

51.   For more on the 'Where in the World is Carmen Sandiego?' series, see Morrie Gelman, 'Lady in Red', *Animation Magazine* (Feb. 95): 26–31.

53.   Aufderheide and Montgomery, op. cit.

54.   Annenberg Public Policy Center, 'The State of Children's Television Report: An Examination of Quantity, Quality, and Industry Beliefs', a study conducted by Amy B. Jordan (17 June 1997), 37.

55.   Id.

56.   United States Federal Communications Commission, 'FCC Adopts New Children's TV Rules', (MM Docket 93–48), News Report No. DC 96–81 Action in Docket Case (8 Aug. 1996), n.p. Published on the Internet at http://www.epn.org/library/FCC6026.txt

57.   Ibid.

58.   Ibid.

59.   An FCC news release described a contingency plan, saying that a broadcaster also has the option to show 'a package of different types of educational and information programming that, while containing somewhat less than three hours per week of core programming, demonstrates a level of commitment to educating and informing children that is at least equivalent to airing three hours per week of core programming'. This 'package' might include specials, public service announcements, short-form programs and regularly scheduled non-weekly programs. United States Federal Communications Commission, op. cit.

60.   However, the study found that the broadcaster's attitudes were rather negative. It explains: '[T]he prevailing belief among broadcasters, particularly affiliates of the larger networks, is that children's educational programs do poorly in the ratings, no matter where they come from or when they are aired ... Coinciding with the belief that educational shows are destined to be poorly rated is the conviction that the public does not care. Over and over broadcasters said that the three-hour rule was the brainchild of the advocates and the public, by and large, would neither notice the change in programming nor care to watch the programs.' Annenberg Public Policy Center, 'Children's Educational Television Regulations and the Local Broadcaster', op. cit., 25.

61.   Annenberg Public Policy Center, ibid., 19.

62.   Ibid., 16–18.

63.   Nancy Steingard, 'FCC Panel', World Animation Celebration (29 June 1997). Unless otherwise noted, all further comments by Steingard were made at this event. Jinkins's past experience includes production design for the Children's Television Workshop's series, 'Square One TV', among other credits.

64.   Anonymous, 'Nickelodeon Gives the Average Kid an Animated Hero When It Debuts the New Series "Doug" ', Nickelodeon press release (12 March 1991).

65.   Annenberg Public Policy Center, 'The 1997 State of Children's Television Report: Programming for Children Over Broadcast and Cable', a study conducted by Amy B. Jordan and Emory H. Woodward (9 June 1997), 25.

66.   Ibid., 21.

67.   Annenberg Public Policy Center, 'Television in the Home: The 1997 Survey of Parents and Children', analysis by Jeffrey D. Stanger (9 June 1997).

68.   Broadcasting Standards Authority, 'Overview of the Broadcasting Standards Authority' (December 1995), n.p. Published on the Internet at http://www.liinz.org.nz/liinz/other/bsa/overview.html

69.   Broadcasting Standards Authority, 'Codes of Broadcasting Practice' (Nov. 1995), n.p. Published on the Internet at http://www.liinz.org.nz/liinz/other/bsa/codes

70.   Canadian Radio-television and Telecommunications Commission, 'Factsheet' (11 February 1996), n.p. Published on the Internet at http://www.crtc.gc.ca/eng/info_sht/g11e.html

71.   Id.

72.   Dominic Schreiber, 'International Broadcaster's Animation Buying Survey', *Animation Magazine* (October 1997): 10–11, 11.

11

Animation audiences

PREDICTING PROFITABILITY

*T*he previous chapter detailed some of the regulatory practices from outside the industry that affect the aesthetics of animation. In the United States, regulation by the Federal Communications Commission (FCC) and Congress clearly are types of external controls, and even broadcasters' internal Standards and Practices departments reflect the influence of outside parties that exert pressure on animation producers. This chapter will examine a number of internal factors that affect the content of animated productions – in particular, those related to profitability. Producers want to create work that will appeal to specific audiences (to attract advertisers) and do well in terms of licensing and ancillary markets. The stress on profitability is due in part to the highly competitive nature and soaring production costs of the entertainment industry today. It also reflects the potential for financial gain that is evident in the world of animation. This chapter will discuss the strategies of American animation companies in terms of merchandising and market research, and some of the ways in which producers in other countries have been strengthening their positions in the global marketplace.

Merchandising strategies

The May 1997 issue of *KidScreen*, a publication that focuses on the merchandising of entertainment products to children, contains the following 'newsbrief':

> Warner Bros. Consumer Products and Hospital Marketing Inc. (HMI) have teamed up for a licensing campaign that presents parents of newborns with a Baby Looney Tunes gift set. The package consists of a newborn baby shirt

Fig. 11.1 *Line drawings of the characters from the 'Meena' series, produced by UNICEF*

© *UNICEF*

featuring the Baby Looney Tunes characters and an imprint of the HMI slogan 'Life Begins', followed by the appropriate hospital's name. A matching birth certificate, featuring the characters and signed by the hospital administrator and nurse manager, is also presented. 'This unique agreement introduces children at birth to our lovable characters and strengthens our brand to parents and a new generation of children', says Karen Weiss, vice president of apparel licensing for Warner Bros. Consumer Products, in a release.[1]

Upon hearing of this strategy, one has to wonder why no one has developed an ultrasound treatment featuring the images of cartoon characters, so that children could be introduced to them even prior to birth!

Although one may greet Warner Bros. program with cynicism, the truth is that licensing (selling the right to use a company's brand name and copyrighted characters to sell products) and merchandising are part of the foundation of the American commercial animation industry.[2] It is becoming evident that no one who produces animation on a large scale can afford to ignore marketing these days – even not-for-profit organisations recognise the importance of a careful promotional plan. For example, the non-profit organisation UNICEF (United Nations Children's Fund) has published a strategy of 'Merchandising Program Management' that was presented at its 1996 Summit in Orlando, Florida. Among the advice given: 'capitalise on external trends or events', 'fulfill an experience of need', 'create or fulfill a demand', and 'focus on existing business drivers' (i.e. successful characters, products or trends).[3]

Indeed, animation producers across the world are beginning to develop aggressive marketing strategies in order to secure their positions in a global market, to achieve greater visibility and reap the financial rewards that come with popularity. It is increasingly frequent to hear of licensing workshops such as the one held at an Italian festival, 'Cartoons on the Bay'. Its object:

> ... was to discuss how characters of a European animated series can be commercialized, and to what extent a licensing and merchandising market can be established in Europe. Participants learned how to improve the presentation of European animated characters in order to compete with American and Japanese projects.[4]

The Japanese animation industry is one of the biggest in the world, and has been for many years. This achievement is in large measure due to well-developed merchandising programs; the success of animated productions is assured through close ties with the country's massive comic book (*manga*) industry. Frederik L. Schodt has cited a claim that 'in an average week in May 1981 there were over a hundred animated programs showing on Japanese television. More than half ... were based on comic stories'.[5] Schodt explains that after a comic book has been successfully serialised as a comic book (within Japan's huge manga industry), typically it is sold as a paperback series, then developed as an animated television series and then, if the success continues, made into an animated feature for theatrical release. He explains: '[A]nimation stimulates further sales of magazines, reprints of comic paperbacks, and massive merchandising. And often the entire cycle is repeated for a sequel.'[6]

Fig. 11.2 *Characters from the 'Meena' series* © *UNICEF*

In the United States, the true potential of merchandising was realised in the late 1970s. In his book, *Children's Television*, Cy Schneider writes: 'In 1977 the licensing industry took a giant leap forward and has been growing by enormous jumps ever since. One factor, more than any other, suddenly changed things – the success of the motion picture *Star Wars*.'[7] The three films of the 'Star Wars Trilogy' have earned billions of dollars in licensed product sales and generated a great deal of interest in licensing. According to Schneider, prior to *Star Wars*'s release, in 1976, licensed toys accounted for 20 per cent of all toy sales. By 1977, the number had climbed to 33 per cent, and by the mid-1980s, almost 80 per cent of toy sales were of licensed products.[8]

Along the way, many successful licensed products for children have been produced. For example, Strawberry Shortcake, introduced in 1980, was developed jointly by the Toy Group at General Mills and American Greetings Corporation; beginning in 1981, with *Strawberry Shortcake in Big Apple City*, the concept was developed into a number of half-hour animated television specials. The Smurfs, which began in 1957 as a strip by Belgian cartoonist Pierre 'Peyo' Culliford, was adapted as a concept by an American licensing firm; in 1981, the characters made their debut in both toy form and within a successful Saturday morning series animated by Hanna-Barbera in association with Sepp International (1981–1990) on the National Broadcasting Corporation (NBC). The series 'He-Man and the Masters of the Universe' (1985), animated by Filmation, was developed around a series of plastic toy figures made by Mattel and sold into syndication; it was followed by a 'girl's series', 'She-Ra: Princess of Power' (1985).[9] 'My Little Pony' was another successful toy series aimed at young girls; it was developed into a number of animated productions by Sunbow and Marvel, including two television specials (1984, 1985), two series (1986–1987, 1992), and a movie (1986).[10] According to Tom Engelhardt in his article 'The Shortcake Strategy', there was approximately a 300 per cent increase in licensed-character cartoons from

1984 to 1985, when the number of them on network television jumped from 14 to approximately 40.[11]

Without a doubt, the motivation for increased production of licensed-character series was economic. In respect to 'He-Man', Engelhardt points out that Mattel had sold '35 million of the action figures alone in 1984; 95,628 a day; 66.4 each minute'.[12] During its first year, the Transformers toy line made $100 million, promoted in part by its television series. Clearly, regulatory attitudes had changed a great deal since the late 1970s, when a series featuring the Hot Wheels toy cars was not allowed to air on ABC because it was perceived as being a commercial. By the mid 1980s, children's television and advertising were becoming inseparable.

Writing at around that time, Schneider explained that 'new children's characters are no longer originated by television or movies. Instead they are originated by toy companies as products, then turned into television series'.[13] Schneider finds fault with people who disparage the toy-based series as though they are inherently wrong. He contends that there is no injustice in developing a show around a toy, and poses the old 'chicken and egg' question – which came first? – to prove his point. He says that few people would complain about a toy coming out after a show has been successful, so why should they be upset about a show coming out after a toy has been successful?[14]

Although it might have taken the successful *Star Wars* for companies to realise the true potential of licensing, certainly the benefits of merchandising have been known for some time. The first licensed children's product in the United States was the Teddy Bear, a toy named after President Theodore (Teddy) Roosevelt, which was introduced by the Ideal Toy Company in 1913. Proceeds from the toy were used to fund the country's national parks.

In the realm of animation, merchandising also has a fairly long history. One of the first and probably the most accomplished producers of animation to maximise ancillary sales is, without a doubt, The Walt Disney Company. In his article, 'The Mickey in Macy's Window: Childhood, Consumerism, and Disney Animation', Richard deCordova maps out the company's early strategies for engaging a youth audience. DeCordova begins by 'distinguishing between two different registers of consumption that tied the child to the cinema: first the child was a consumer of films, someone who paid a certain amount to see a show. Second, the child was a consumer of products displayed through the films'.[15] He explains that 'today, something like a sacred connection exists between Mickey Mouse and idealized childhood. However, as the occasional early references to Mickey's vulgarity attests, that connection was by no means natural or unproblematic. It was the result of a particular historical work';[16] an ongoing, well-designed strategy to market Disney as wholesome youth entertainment.

Disney's first licensing agent was a man named Herman 'Kay' Kamen, who signed his first contract in 1932. That year, there were 21 licensees of Mickey Mouse merchandise in the United States alone, and the character became commonplace in toy stores across the country.[17] Mickey Mouse dolls and merchandise also appeared in theatres, as promotional giveaway products. Under the terms of his contract, Kamen received 40 per cent of the profits and Disney received the remaining 60 per cent. Kayman represented Disney until his death in 1949, at which time the studio created Walt Disney Character Merchandising.

Shortly thereafter, Disney launched two of its most ambitious merchandising feats, the 'Disneyland' television show (beginning in 1954) and the theme park (opening 17 July 1955). Christopher Anderson writes:

> ... in uniting the TV program and the amusement park under a single name, Disney made one of the most influential commercial decisions in postwar American culture. Expanding upon the lucrative character merchandising market that the studio had joined in the early 1930s, Disney now planned to create an all-encompassing consumer environment that he described as 'total merchandising'.[18]

Throughout the years, Disney has perfected the merchandising of its products, which has helped the company retain its dominance in the world market. In a *Los Angeles Times* article entitled 'Can Anyone Dethrone Disney?', John Horn writes: 'Disney has practically copyrighted the book both on how to make – and, equally important, to launch – an animated movie ... There's no limit to Disney's merchandising efforts.'[19] He provides an example of one of the company's biggest successes and some of the benefits of its marketing: 'Counting its domestic international home video and merchandise profits, *Toy Story* has spun off $400 million in profits ... The goods simultaneously reinforce namebrand identification and create a thirst for more *Toy Story* experiences.'[20]

Horn accounts for the box-office failure of the Warner Bros. feature *Cats Don't Dance* (1996) by citing a lack of merchandising efforts. He explains that the film garnered largely positive reviews but:

> ... the film's collapse had little to do with what was on the screen ... There was no Danny the Cat Happy Meal at McDonald's. Soft and fluffy *Cats Don't Dance* toys were not spilling from Toys R Us shelves ... In other words, producer Turner Pictures and distributor Warner Bros. thought *Cat's Don't Dance* was a movie and did not pursue tie-in deals. But successful animated movies are not movies. They are motors, and they don't go anywhere without the fuel of merchandising and the wheels of event marketing.[21]

Indeed, it is virtually impossible for an industrial animation producer to succeed without an extremely well-thought-out marketing plan – whether he or she is financing theatrical features or television series. As a *Hollywood Reporter* article on animation licensing points out, 'with quality [made-for-television] animation costing upward of $350,000 a half hour, few shows, if any, can turn a profit on their programming fees alone, and every producer hopes for the brass ring of merchandising bucks'.[22] Feature-length animation requires a much larger financial investment.

It also could be suggested that the most important thing that *Cat's Don't Dance* lacks is the actual Disney name, which seems to be the only real guarantee of success today. Horn cites an example showing the strength of brand loyalty that Disney has developed:

> Far from Los Angeles, Warner Bros. held two test screenings of *Thumbelina*, showing clips from its animated movie to gauge audience interest. The first time around, audience reaction was flat. For the next test, according to people familiar with the experiment, Warners stripped off its company logo – and slapped Disney's name on the exact same *Thumbelina* footage. The test scores soared. (Warner Bros. declined to comment.)[23]

The importance of brand name development has not been lost on international animation producers, who increasingly are becoming sensitive to the importance of a strong merchandising program. At a 'Cartoon Licensing' panel at the 1997 Marché International du Film d'Animation (MIFA – International Animated Film Market), Rainer Tschierschwitz, Head of TV Sales and Acquisitions for the German EM-Entertainment, spoke of his company's efforts at establishing a cartoon character named Tabaluga, a little fire-breathing dragon.[24] The inspiration for the series came from the music of Peter Maffay, who in 1983 composed an album for his fans' children that sold 2.5 million copies (accompanied by a book illustrated by Helme Heine); a second and third album were released in 1986 and 1993. In 1994, a stage show, *Tabaluga and Lilli*, developed in conjunction with a line of high-profile licensed products, became the most successful musical of its type in Germany. Finally, a co-production deal for 26 half-hours was signed by Tabaluga GmbH, the German public broadcaster ZDF-Enterprises, Yoram Gross Film Studios of Australia, and EM-Entertainment (the first three being co-producers, while the fourth is the merchandising company). The animated series made its debut in October 1997, but planning for the launch began as early as 1990, when deals with such major corporations as Lufthansa airlines and Coca Cola began to be arranged.[25]

Some of EM-Entertainment's strategies include the development of a 'Tabaluga Club',

Fig. 11.3 *Tabaluga, a little fire-breathing dragon, is the central character of a highly successful 26 half-hour series, a co-production of Yoram Gross, Tabaluga GmbH©, ZDF Enterprises and EM-Entertainment*
A Yoram Gross Film Production/© TABALUGA GmbH

which functions in a manner similar to a 'Mickey Mouse' club. The televised club airs 'Tabaluga' and other animated shorts and offers fans the opportunity to join for updates and information. In addition, a large promotional event has been planned annually, to increase consumer awareness. These events are promoted in tandem by each of the product's licensees. Tschierschwitz contends that one advantage of the Tabaluga character is its appeal to both children and adults. He says that 'parents in the range of thirty to fifty years of age buy the records, so they are also targeted'.

On the same MIFA panel, Liz Keynes from Aardman Animations in England outlined a somewhat different strategy in her company's promotion of the 'Wallace and Gromit' films and other productions.[26] She explained that, 'from the outset of production, marketing is a big consideration'. To promote its products, Aardman has representatives in fifteen territories of Europe and seven agents in other parts of the world. Aardman's productions are not specific to children; in fact, virtually all its merchandise is marketed towards an older consumer, to the company's advantage. Keynes explains: '[T]he adult market is not as crowded as the younger market. It has been said that Wallace and Gromit really has opened up the range of merchandising opportunities for adults.'

She notes that, in part, Aardman differentiates its productions by positioning them as films, as opposed to television work. In England, Aardman cannot do a theatrical release before showing its films on the British Broadcasting Corporation (BBC), which is its co-producer. However, Keynes says that elsewhere – in Australia or Germany, for example – big theatrical debuts are planned, so that Aardman productions will be reviewed as film releases.

For many years, merchandising and aggressive promotion largely remained a secondary consideration in many countries. Today, in somewhat of a turn-around, European producers are confronting the American market with more strength than ever before. A *Hollywood Reporter* article of April 1997 notes the trend that 'European toon houses are opening offices in the United States, a market that has traditionally been unkind to imports', and that production of animation in Europe has boomed from only 60 hours produced in 1987 to 750 hours in 1996.[27] Part of the growth of European animation is due to the support of an organisation called CARTOON, which is the animation platform for the European Union's MEDIA Program.[28] CARTOON is intended to boost film and television production in that region of the world. It offers training to European animators and financial assistance for pre-production. It also facilitates studio groupings intended to limit subcontracting with Asian countries to overcome 'competition from the American and Japanese giants'.[29]

A growing trend in animation production is toward international co-productions, which balance the financial and creative responsibilities among more than one company. For example, the American company DIC Entertainment and Scottish Television are co-producing the 'Sherlock Holmes in the 22nd Century' series; the Canadian Nelvana studio and France's Medialab are combining efforts on the series 'Stickin' Around'; and the American Children's Television Network is co-producing 'Zhima Je' (a Chinese version of 'Sesame Street') with Shanghai Television in China, considered to be one of the greatest up-and-coming markets for licensing opportunities.[30] *The Hollywood Reporter* notes:

> With more than 325 million children, China holds the greatest potential for licensors. But finding a property that crosses cultural boundaries and then getting on the shelves in such an insular marketplace will be no mean feat. 'Whoever

cracks the code to China will make an absolute fortune', says Pat Wyatt, president of Fox's licensing arm.[31]

Certainly, the success of American productions cannot be attributed only to business practices. Oliver Ellis, programming manager for the British animation distributor ITEL, explains that 'Europe has always been very good at gentle, narrative storytelling for preschool audiences. But when you're looking at animation for the 8- to 12-year olds, which is a little faster paced, Hollywood is still unchallenged'.[32] Hamilton explains that American series are so popular because 'the writing is good, fast, exciting – made by good script teams'. However, he also confirms that, in the final analysis, the success of the programs is guaranteed by effective sales strategies: '[I]t is clear that the commercial possibilities have been considered from the outset. Why will the public buy products based on that character? Very few British or European producers think that way.'

Hamilton recommends that producers strategise more effectively in order to make their series successful in today's competitive marketplace. He advises, 'the easiest way to kill a property is to launch it too soon. It takes eighteen months to two years to select products and negotiate with licensees' before they can be brought to market. He contends that 'licensing doesn't build awareness but only continues what is developed elsewhere', so a well-thought-out campaign is vital. This belief is echoed by David Kirschner, producer of Warner Bros.' ill-fated *Cats Don't Dance*: 'Launching these films takes a year and a half of planning.'[33]

According to Cy Schneider, some of the components of a successful merchandising promotion are an appeal to children, media exposure, an aggressive licensing agent, and good timing.[34] Hamilton stresses the importance of the last of these factors, timing, due to the seasonality of toy sales. He notes that 70 to 80 per cent of toy sales occur during the last three to four months of the year, and that merchandisers must get these products to toy fairs held the previous January.

However, merely getting the products to the toy fair is only half the battle because, in Wyatt's words, 'retailers hold the ultimate access to the consumer'.[35] As a result, merchandisers must think about gaining the support of major toy sellers from the very start. Tschierschwitz estimates that, in Germany, ten retailers control approximately 95 per cent of the market. The situation is not so different in the United States, where about four retailers control the majority of the toy market. Jonathon Davies writes:

> ... as demand for toy department shelf space has soared in the 1990s, retail executives have grown more savvy about the business. They are now much more likely to put conditions, including exclusivity, on a license, and they expect to see long-range commitment to the characters in the form of multi-million-dollar fast-food promotions and other support.[36]

Market research

With all this emphasis on censorship and marketing, one has to wonder if the actual audience has any say in what it sees. The answer is, certainly. As the stakes in animation production become higher and higher, every financial source wants some kind of guarantee that its investment will be a winner and not a financial disaster. One means by which such predictions are made is through audience testing, or focus groups. Although far from being an exact science, market research has become an integral part of business since World War II, so that in the United States it is now rare to find a made-for-television series or theatrical feature that has not in some way been tested before significant financial investments are made.

A potential animation project for television can be audience tested at a number of stages. In 'concept testing', the audience is asked whether or not it likes a given idea. Frequently, producers will conduct a 'pilot test', which means that an initial episode, or 'pilot', of a property is fully completed and then shown to a test audience to hear what it thinks. One of the companies most involved with this kind of testing is ASI Market Research. This company runs a theatre where viewers watch programs and commercials, indicating positive and negative reactions with the aid of a control on each seat, and then fill out questionnaires about their experiences. In some cases, 'program testing' is conducted when a series is under way but not experiencing success; audience research might suggest a way to alter a show's content in order to save it from failure.[37]

The way in which animation testing occurs has changed since the animation business took off during the early 1990s. In their 1985 book, Susan Tyler Eastman and her associates wrote that 'pilot programs are almost never commissioned for cartoons because of the long production time and high costs. Therefore, the decision to pick up a cartoon series costing nearly $3 million for 13 episodes is based solely on artwork and scripts'.[38] However, practices are now much different. Today, pilot testing of animated series is a relatively common strategy in the production of made-for-television animation in the United States, although exact practices differ from company to company.

When she was a producer at Nickelodeon, Linda Simensky was among those responsible for reviewing pitches for the development animated series. She approximates that, for every one hundred relatively formal pitches she received from would-be creators, only one would be commissioned as a pilot. After these pilots were created, they would be shown to focus groups in several cities across the United States. Roughly half the pilots eventually made it to the air, typically entailing the production of thirteen episodes in a series. Geraldine Laybourne has described the kind of market research conducted by Nickelodeon, which included 250 focus groups annually across the United States, as well as individual studies of children and even Internet contacts on a more informal basis. She explained that the use of the 'information highway' allowed them to 'talk to some 150 kids on an almost daily basis everyday after school'.[39]

A different strategy has been introduced by Hanna-Barbera, which in 1993 began a storyboard competition held in conjunction with the Cartoon Network. The idea came from Fred Seibert, who moved to Hanna-Barbera from MTV in 1992. His intention in starting the 'What a Cartoon' program was to 'give animators the creative freedom that had been missing since the industry's Golden Era to make new cartoons'.[40]

The company requested that entrants send in a conceptual storyboard for an animated short that could be produced and broadcast on television. In 1994, 30 storyboards were chosen for a final competition, based on the criteria of originality of concept, character development, and humour. The contest form states that the ten winners were required to 'negotiate in good faith solely with Hanna-Barbera regarding the acquisition of audiovisual and ancillary rights in and to the storyboard'.[41]

The point of the negotiation was to develop the concept into a short subject which could be braodcast as a 'World Premier Toon' on the Cartoon Network and also entered into film festival competitions. These exhibition opportunities provided a means for evaluating the marketability of the animated shorts. Rita Street reports that the Cartoon Network broadcasts 'became a convenient testing ground to see if any 'What a Cartoon' projects had the legs to expand into full-blown cartoon series'.[42] Through the use of focus groups, including a toll free number and Cartoon Network's America Online bulletin board, the company measured the popularity of their work. The series to develop out of this competition include 'Dexter's Laboratory', created by Genndy Tartak; 'Cow and Chicken', created by David Feiss; and 'Johnny Bravo', created by Van Partible.[43]

There are a number of ways that the television industry measures the success of its programming. Commonly, the term 'ratings' and 'shares' will be used to describe the level of viewership any program receives. Specifically, ratings reflect the percentage of viewers based on the total number of television homes in the United States. Shares refer to the percentage of viewers based on the number of homes using a television at the time. Ratings are used to set advertising rates, while shares are used to make programming decisions, because they show how well a program does against its competition.[44]

In the United States, most of the statistics regarding ratings and shares on television are produced by Nielsen Media Research. Drawing upon a random sample of individuals, Nielsen receives its information in a variety of ways.[45] For its national ratings estimates, it records data from more than 4000 households. The company installs metering equipment on television sets, video cassette recorders (VCRs), cable boxes, and satellite dishes in each residence. This equipment is linked to a 'black box' that forwards data to Nielsen's central computers. In order to identify what is being watched, Nielsen developed and patented a system called AMOL, or Automated Monitoring of Line-ups. With this system, almost every program that is broadcast is coded with an identification number that appears as a series of lines and dots at the top edge of its picture.

Another method used by the company to gather national statistics is the Nielsen People Meter, a small box that is placed near each television set. This box contains buttons that are assigned to each household member, with extras for guests, and can be operated by remote control. Viewers push their buttons when they begin watching a program. This test helps determine the types of people who are watching each show, which is of prime concern to advertisers.

Over 200 local markets are measured by Nielsen Media Research through the use of 'TV diaries'. These diaries record who is watching, what they are watching, and the channel on which they are watching it; this information is recorded in quarter-hour segments. Measurements are taken during a one-week period in February, May, July and November (commonly referred to as 'sweeps weeks', when broadcasters are particularly competitive in their programming, in order to receive higher ratings). Sometimes, Nielsen conducts 'Telephone Coincidentals' studies by calling thousands of randomly selected phone numbers, in order to test the general validity of results obtained by its other sampling methods.

Some programmers rely on TvQs (television quotients), another type of test that measures the popularity of a program and a viewer's familiarity with it, as a means for predicting its potential for success. Sometimes a 'vulnerability study' will be conducted, to evaluate the competitive strength of a given show. In this case, audiences are asked: 'If these two shows were on at the same time, which would you watch?'[46]

Any form of audience testing is imperfect, due to such factors as limited sample sizes, a lack of exact representation, or failure to measure all types of viewing situations (typically, hotels, college dorms, and other non-traditional living sites are not measured). However, Eastman and associates contend that:

> ... in practice, these limitations are rarely considered. This result is not one of ignorance or carelessness so much as of the pressure to do daily business using some yardstick ... The 'numbers' for any single market usually show a consistent pattern that makes sense in general to those who know local history.[47]

In other words, the measurements might not reflect actual viewing habits but, when considered along with past numbers, one can tell if a given rating is relatively strong or weak.

Ultimately, the strongest determinant of what kind of animation gets produced might be the preconceived ideas of those individuals who control the finances. Worldwide, animation has been stereotyped as a technique best suited for children. Certainly, this has been the case in many countries where the media has been largely State (i.e. government) supported and controlled. Giannalberto Bendazzi writes that, in Eastern European countries such as Czechoslovakia, Yugoslavia and Poland, the State became the sole producer, promoter and distributor, and:

> ... supported only certain kinds of animation, resisting market forces and using cinema for educational purposes. For the first 15 years following World War II, animation in Eastern Europe shared similar characteristics with 1930s Soviet animation: mainly created for children, oriented towards moral and civic teaching, and resistant to stylistic changes.[48]

England is among those countries where perceptions about animation audiences have been changing. Funding by Channel 4 and the BBC has permitted the development of numerous animated shorts that have widespread appeal, such as the 'Wallace and Gromit' films. It also has enabled the production of animation aimed at a specific portion of an older audience. For example, Joanna Quinn's *Body Beautiful* (1990) is set in a Welsh working-class community and addresses many issues of interest to women, in particular.

An adult audience was targeted with the production of the animated series 'Crapston Villas' (created by Sarah Ann Kennedy, beg. 1996) and 'Pond Life' (created by Candy Guard, beg. 1996).[49] In 1998, another breakthrough occurred with the completion of 'Bob and Margaret', a series that caused at least one writer to ask: 'Is it the UK's answer to the "Simpsons"?'[50] The initial thirteen half-hour episodes of the series, which was created by Alison Snowden and David Fine, were financed by Channel 4 (25 per cent) and the Canadian production company Nelvana (75 per cent).[51]

In the United States, ideas have been changing over the years. In the 1970s, Ralph Bakshi stunned viewers by creating the first X-rated animated feature, *Fritz the Cat* (1972), which was followed by a number of other long format films aimed at older audiences. In recent years, the success of such television series as 'The Simpsons' (beg. 1989) and 'The Ren & Stimpy Show' (beg. 1991), as well as the travelling programs of 'Sick and Twisted' short films (produced by the San Diego company, Spike and Mike) showing in American theatres, has helped to convince financial backers that animation can indeed appeal to a wide range of viewers. Over the last few years, the appearance of such shows as 'King of the Hill' (beg. 1997), 'Spawn' (beg. 1997), and 'Ralph Bakshi's Spicy City' (beg. 1997) has provided an indication that beliefs are indeed changing.

This chapter has examined a number of audience-related forces that affect the content of animated films and television programs. The next chapter will continue to focus on content to some extent, but will take a slightly different angle. Today, more than ever, people have become sensitised to the types of images that are presented on the screen – not just in terms of violence or sexual content – but also the portrayal of cultural diversity. The next chapter will overview the subject of representation, in terms of race and ethnicity as well as gender, including some additional industrial and social factors that have influenced the creation of animated images.

Notes

1. Anonymous, 'Newsbrief: Life Begins with Looney Tunes', *KidScreen* (May 1997): 16. Of course, many companies take advantage of the birth of a child as a merchandising opportunity. At the hospital, new parents typically are given a variety of samples from companies that make products for infants (diapers, food, and so forth). The 'Looney Tunes' strategy is different in that it is merchandising a character, rather than a tangible product, and that 'Looney Tunes' products are not infant-specific.

2. It seems that promoters cannot do enough to top one another in their give-aways. In September 1997, the Fox Television Network gave away a life-sized replica of the Simpsons' home in a promotion held in conjunction with Pepsi-Cola Co., the home builders Kaufman and Broad, and a variety of other housing-related companies. The house was built in Henderson, Nevada, near Las Vegas. According to an advertisement, the 'architects designed the home to include the same vivid colours. The exterior is a combination of "solar yellow" and "power orange". The kitchen has "radiant lilac" cabinets and a "lemon-twist yellow" sink ... High arches have been provided to accommodate Marge's hair and Homer's hips'. Anonymous, 'Morning Report', *Los Angeles Times* (11 July 1997): F2; Anonymous (advertising supplement), 'Builder Creates Cartoon Home as Top Contest Prize', *Los Angeles Times* (10 Aug. 1997): CC2; see also the nearly full-page ad on CC4. A fairly detailed account of the series' merchandising strategies and sales, once very strong but having 'dwindled in the U.S. to a trickle', are provided in Marla Matzer, ' "Simpsons" Sales: Halving a Cow', *Los Angeles Times* (25 Sept. 1997): D1+.

3. Glenda Banales, 'Merchandising Programme Management: It All Begins with a Strategy', *Drawing Insight: Communicating Development Through Animation* (Penang: Southbound, 1996), 55–58.

4. Florian Haffa, 'Cartoons on the Bay Creates Licensing Workshop', *KidScreen* (May 1997): 18.

5. Toshio Naiki, quoted in Frederik L. Schodt, *Manga! Manga! The World of Japanese Comics* (New York: Kodansha, 1986), 146.

6. Id.

7. Cy Schneider, *Children's Television: The Art, the Business, and How It Works*, foreword by Fred Silverman (Lincolnwood, IL: NTC Business Books, 1987), 114.

8. Ibid., 115.

9. Tom Engelhardt, 'The Shortcake Strategy', *Watching Television* (New York: Pantheon, 1986): 68–110, 76.

10. For information on 'My Little Pony' and other series, see Ellen Seiter, *Sold Separately: Parents & Children in Consumer Culture* (New Brunswick, NJ: Rutgers UP, 1995).

11. Engelhardt, op. cit., 78.

12. Ibid., 77.

13. Schneider, op. cit., 111.

14. Ibid., 113.

15. Richard deCordova, 'The Mickey in Macy's Window: Childhood, Consumerism, and Disney Animation', in Eric Smoodin (ed.), *Disney Discourse: Producing the Magic Kingdom* (New York: Routledge, 1994): 203–213, 204.

16. deCordova, ibid., 211.

17. Ibid., 205.

18. Christopher Anderson, *Hollywood TV: The Studio System in the Fifties* (Austin: University of Texas Press, 1994), 134.

19. John Horn, 'Can Anyone Dethrone Disney?', *Los Angeles Times Calendar* (1 June 1997): 4+, 82.

20. Ibid., 83.

21. Ibid., 82.

22. Jonathon Davies, 'Shelf Life', *The Hollywood Reporter* (14 Jan. 1997): 15–16+, 16.

23. Horn, op. cit., 4.

24. Rainer Tschierschwitz, 'Cartoon Licensing' panel, MIFA (30 May 1997). Unless otherwise noted, all further comments by Tschierschwitz were made at this event.

25. EM-Entertainment, 'Tabaluga Press Kit' (ca. 1996).

26. Liz Keynes, 'Cartoon Licensing' panel, MIFA (30 May 1997). Unless otherwise noted, all further comments by Keynes in regard to Aardman were made at this event.

27. Nick Vivarelli, 'Eurotoons!' *Hollywood Reporter* (1 April 1997): S1–S7. For more information on the buying patterns of television companies across the world, consult Dominic Schreiber, 'International Broadcaster's Animation Buying Survey', *Animation Magazine* (Oct. 1997): 10–11.

28. Iain Harvey writes, 'there has been a growing recognition within Europe that animation and the art of animation is very much a part of the European heritage. A key body that has helped this fact to be realised is the European Association of Animated Film, better known as CARTOON. This body was created under the original MEDIA program, a pan-European initiative set up in 1989 to try [to] add financial and marketing weight to the highly divided audiovisual media industries scattered around Europe ... CARTOON isolated the key points in trying to develop a substantial European animation industry: development, transnational cooperation and training, but it also highlighted the talent working within Europe'. Iain Harvey, 'Europe: A Storyboard Success', *Animation World Network* (April 1996). For other essays on MEDIA and European production, see John Hill, Martin McLoone and Paul Hainsworth (eds), *Border Crossing: Film in Ireland, Britain and Europe* (Ulster: Institute of Irish Studies in association with the University of Ulster and the British Film Institute, 1994).

29. European Association of Animation Film (Cartoon), 'Cartoon supports animation film all over Europe', brochure (ca. 1995).

30. Information on these and other international co-productions is found in 'Mipcom Special Report: Co-production Diary', *KidScreen* (Oct. 1996): 30–48.

31. Pat Wyatt, quoted in Davies, 'Shelf Life', op. cit., 16.

32. Oliver Ellis, quoted in Vivarelli, 'Eurotoons!' *Hollywood Reporter* (1 April 1997).

33. David Kirschner, quoted in Horn, 'Can Anyone Dethrone Disney?', *Los Angeles Times Calendar* (1 June 1997): 5, 82.

34. Cy Schneider, op. cit., 116–117.

35. Wyatt, quoted in Davies, 'Shelf Life', *The Hollywood Reporter* (14 Jan. 1997): 16.

36. Davies, ibid., 16.

37. Susan Tyler Eastman, Sydney W. Head, and Lewis Klein, *Broadcast/Cable Programming: Strategies and Practices* (Belmont, CA: Wadsworth, 1985), 41

38. Ibid., 159.

39. Geraldine Laybourne, 'Kids Deserve to be Heard', *Drawing Insight: Communicating Development through Animation* (Penang: Southbound, 1996), 74–77.

40. Rita Street, 'H-B is Showing its Initiative, Literally', *Daily Variety* (22 March 1996): A18+, A18. See also Ferdinand Lewis, 'The Great Cartoon Experiment', *Animation Magazine* (July 1995): 28–29+; and G. Michael Dobbs, 'The Return of Creator-Driven Cartoons', *Animato!* 29 (Summer 1994): 28–29+.

41. Anonymous, 'Announcing the 2nd Annual Hanna-Barbera/Cartoon Network Storyboard Contest', entry form (ca. June 1994).

42. Street, op. cit., A20.

43. Roberta G. Wax, 'World Cartoon Headquarters', *Animation Magazine* (March 1997): n.p.

44. Eastman, op. cit., 50.

45. A.C. Nielsen, 'What TV Ratings Really Mean', company brochure (1995). This information remained accurate in 1997, when the author received the brochure.

46. Richard A. Blum and Richard D. Lindhem, *Primetime: Network Television Programming* (Boston: Focal Press, 1987), 7.

47. Eastman, op. cit., 76.

48. Giannalberto Bendazzi, *Cartoons: One Hundred Years of Cinema Animation* (Bloomington: Indiana UP, 1994), 151.

49. For more on Kennedy's and Guard's series, and the women at Channel 4 who accepted them for development, see Jill McGreal, 'Out of the Animation Ghetto: Clare Kitson and Her Muffia' (Animation World Network). On-line at http://www.awn.com/mag/issue1.2/articles1.2/mcgreal1.2.html

50. Ed Waller, 'Animated Anxiety', *Televisual* (Jan. 1988): 33+.

51. Snowden Fine, as the animators are known, are a British and Canadian wife and husband team. They won an Academy Award, among other honours, for their short *Bob's Birthday* (1995). In Fine's words, that 'made the pitch for a 13 × 30-minute series "Bob and Margaret" [based on the short] a whole lot easier'. David Fine, quoted in Waller, ibid., 33.

12

Issues of representation

RESOLVING CULTURAL DIFFERENCE

When we discuss representation in motion pictures, in many cases we draw our attention to what we see on the screen. However, what is not seen should be an equally large concern. What is missing from films and television shows often can say as much about social attitudes and business practices as what is actually depicted. This chapter will overview the representation and the lack of representation of certain kinds of images in animation. To some extent, it also will discuss issues of representation as they pertain to the workplace – to the places where those images are created.

Throughout the twentieth century, but with increased emphasis since World War II, issues of racial, ethnic and gender representation have been of concern in day-to-day life and in the images presented by all kinds of media. People have grown sensitive to the use of stereotypes that have dominated entertainment and, in an effort to bring equality in society, have demanded that films and television shows adopt a more even-handed way of dealing with cultural difference.

Whether one is discussing racist imagery, sexism, or any other form of seemingly derogatory representations, the origins of stereotypes and the reasons for their perpetuation are many. In terms of film and television, one finds that certain depictions are deeply ingrained in traditions of popular humour. David Crafton is among those who has discussed the practices of racial and ethnic jokes in vaudeville, which had great influence upon many aspects of the development of early film practices.[1] In his analysis of 'Racism and Resistance: Black Stereotypes in Animation', Karl Cohen observes that 'racial stereotypes in cartoons date back to the silent era;

by the early sound era, unflattering caricatures of almost every nationality had appeared in animated cartoons'.[2]

Cohen's work demonstrates that public resistance to stereotyping seemed to influence production practices, with the effect that racist imagery was greatly diminished by the end of the 1950s. He notes that Walter Lantz produced his last cartoon with racist imagery in 1943 (however, in 1948, the National Association for the Advancement of Colored People or NAACP requested that the 1941 film *Scrub Me Momma with a Boogie Beat* be withdrawn from re-release). At Warner Bros., racist images began to disappear by the end of the 1940s; Cohen identifies the 1949 film *Which is Witch* as the last 'Bugs Bunny' short to contain racist imagery, although Chuck Jones's 'Inki' films ran from 1939 to 1950. At MGM, the 'Bosko' series was ended in 1934, while Mammy Two Shoes, another of MGM's characters, co-starred in seventeen 'Tom and Jerry' shorts between 1940 and 1952. Cohen notes that Paramount, which had distributed the work of the Fleischer and Famous Studios, as well as George Pal, continued to distribute racist imagery until about 1958.

Although resistance by individuals and groups such as the NAACP seems to have had a positive affect on the animation industry, that conclusion is open to question. Unfortunately, while racist imagery did diminish, positive images did not increase. Indeed, the net result of public pressure upon the industry seems to have been greater reluctance to depict cultural diversity at all. As Cohen notes, black characters in animation were relatively rare until the 1970s, when series like 'The Harlem Globe-trotters' (1970–1973; rebroadcast as 'Go Go Globetrotters', 1978), 'The Jackson Five' (1971–1973), 'Fat Albert and the Cosby Kids' (1972–1979; under the title 'The New Fat Albert Show', 1979–1984) and 'I Am the Greatest: The Adventures of Muhammad Ali' (1977–1978) appeared.[3]

To demonstrate one evasive technique, Cohen gives the example of the 'Tom and Jerry' series, which was re-released for television in the mid-1960s. He explains that the black Mammy Two-Shoes character from the original series, who is shown only from the legs down (in one instance from the neck down), actually was re-animated, her skin being painted a lighter shade. In addition, she was given a new voice, an Irish brogue by June Foray, to replace the original voice track by Lillian Randolph.[4]

In recent years, there has been more of an attempt to depict diversity and inter-racial harmony. Apparently, the strategy used in the animated series 'Doug' is to neutralise colour issues by using unnatural skin tones (e.g. his friend Skeeter is blue) to depict characters that can represent any ethnic or racial background. However, it is significant to note that a creamy skinned (i.e. 'white') character, Doug, remains the star.

The influential (primarily live-action) children's series 'Sesame Street' shows diversity but in general does not address skin-colour differences among the characters. In his book on *Television and America's Children*, Edward L. Palmer discusses the series' effectiveness in presenting, 'without any explicit comment [about acceptance] ... blacks and whites, on the street, engaged in the simple events of everyday living'.[5] Incidentally, 'Sesame Street' has employed a similar strategy in encouraging other types of acceptance as well. For example, it also includes within its 'everyday society' people of varying physical and mental abilities; according to Palmer, these 'unre-markable' interactions encourage 'the non-disabled members of the audience to give up stereotypes and relate to the disabled in accepting, sensitive, and supportive ways'.[6]

Certainly, the issues concerning the representation of cultural diversity are many and varied. Sometimes, depictions reflect specific agendas, perhaps commercial (to sell a product) or political (to sell a belief). In the anti-Semitic film *Van den vos*

Reynaerde (About Reynard the Fox), a 'cunning, money-grabbing' rhinoceros named Judocus is depicted as a Jewish character. The film was produced in Holland in 1941, under the jurisdiction of the German Nazi government, and clearly shows the political agenda of that regime.[7] Other times, the ways in which characters are depicted reflects the 'naturalised' relationships within society (i.e. depictions that many people take for granted as being realistic) or relate to conventions established within a given practice. For example, in 'The Flintstones' (1960–1966; rebroadcast 1967–1970), like many animated family sitcoms, fathers go to work and mothers stay home, while boy and girl children also fulfill the roles (e.g. active–passive) traditionally assigned to them.

In any case, one must again return to the issue of cultural context when attempting to evaluate the content of any animated work. When beginning an analysis of representation, some of the questions a researcher should ask include:

1. Who made the product?

2. For whom was the product made, in what year and historical context?

3. What mediating forces came between the creator and the audience?

4. What is the nature of spectatorship, in general? That is, how do people derive pleasure from what they watch and to what extent does viewing affect behaviour?

5. In which ways is the researcher qualified to speak for the group whose representation he or she examines, and how can he or she make assumptions about that group's interests, abilities, and needs?

6. Whose standards are being employed in the analysis?

While all these questions could be discussed at length, the last one especially warrants extra attention at this point. Recognition of one's own values, or the values being employed in writing the study, is imperative. For example, to generalise that violence in films and television is harmful to all viewers, or children in particular, might be more of an assumption than a fact. To argue that certain depictions of ethnic groups in films made decades ago are inherently bad and should be banned also reflects a given set of values. To contend that stereotypes produced today are acceptable as just one of many means of expression is also a value statement and subject to debate. All values are subjective; naturally, the researcher's task is to recognise his or her own point of view and understand how it affects his or her perceptions of a given situation. Sometimes, values are supported by previously conducted research; in that case, writers should support their points by citing studies in the field.

Just as complex are questions concerning exhibition and creation. If a stereotypical work made in the past is considered offensive by many people, or even just a few, should it be publicly displayed? Should it be banned from theatres or television broadcasts, and not even distributed on video cassettes? Today, should artists be discouraged from creating these kinds of images in their work? One must decide whether the freedom to show and create images that might be unpopular outweighs a responsibility to represent characters in a more 'socially responsible' manner, assuming that one can really define that term.

It is all too easy to dismiss stereotypes simply as 'bad things' that should not be tolerated by an enlightened society. However, such an attitude teaches us very little: it seems more fruitful to confront issues that might make us feel uncomfortable, in order to learn more about the reasons why they have been created and why we feel as we do. Although the subject of representation is virtually limitless, this chapter will focus only on areas relating to representations of women and women's issues.

GENDER AND THE ANIMATION INDUSTRY

In a letter entitled 'Wanted: Girl Heroes', published in 1993, in the commentary section of the *Los Angeles Times* newspaper, a young girl named Alexandra Early expresses anger over the fact that 'there aren't enough girl superheroes on TV'.[8] She closes by noting: 'I hope the people who make these shows know that girls like me are watching. We want fairness.' What Early has witnessed is actually part of a long-standing tradition in the field of animation; as Sharon Couzin has remarked, with few exceptions, 'historically the woman had no voice at all'.[9]

Fortunately, the voice of women in animation has become stronger during the past several years, not only in the realm of independent animation but commercially as well. Although many women are still struggling to be recognised for their abilities, many already have attained positions of relative power. Increasingly, studios and networks are making an effort to hire and promote females as creators and producers (as well as in various other capacities) in order to rectify an imbalance created in the past by institutionalised policies of sexual discrimination – in part because women have made it to the top of the labour hierarchy and are now looking out for the future of other women.

The importance of this goal was made clear at the first meeting of a professional organisation entitled 'Women in Animation', which occurred at the home of *Animation Magazine* publisher Rita Street on 29 October 1993. Street explains that:

> ... just as [live-action] film has a 'Women in Film' organisation and theatre has a 'Women in Theater' organisation, the time has come to develop a similar organisation in our industry. We need opportunities to network, to guard the future of our growing industry and to address important issues. In the years to come, this group could prove to be a powerful influence.[10]

Historically, the creative side of American animation production has been characterised by rigid gender-based hierarchies that have been characteristic of the media industry as a whole.[11] Early Disney recruitment material illustrates the institutionalised divisions as it assures potential (male) applicants that they will be occupied with creative work, while a large staff of women attend to the routine jobs of inking and painting animation cels.[12] When women did begin to advance within the Disney organisation, evidently there was dissent among the employees; in a 1941 speech delivered to striking animation staff, Walt Disney tried to diffuse an 'ugly rumor' that 'we are trying to develop girls for animation to replace higher-priced men'.[13]

Of course, worldwide, some women did achieve some measure of success as animators and directors. In his article on 'Splendid Artists: Central and East European Women Animators', Marcin Gisycki mentions the work of puppeteer Hermina Tyrolova, who gained renown after World War II; Franciszka Themerson, who made several short films with her husband Stefan between 1930 and 1945; and a list of women he says 'never imprinted [their] presence in the deeper memory of foreign specialists' because of, at least in part, 'the male-oriented promotional policies of Film Polski, the state run film agency' in Poland.[14] Also noteworthy is the success of German silhouette animator Lotte Reiniger, whose best-known work is the feature-length *Die Abenteuer des Prinzen Achmed* (The Adventures of Prince Achmed, 1926).[15]

Many other women made a name for themselves working in conjunction with a male partner, as Themerson did. American Claire Parker collaborated with her Russian-born husband, Alexander Alexeieff. Evelyn Lambart worked on several productions with Norman McLaren at the National Film Board of Canada. However, in most cases, women partners tended to be greatly overshadowed by the men they worked with. Gizycki refers to a number of Polish artists (without mentioning any names), writing that 'there were always women behind the men, writing scripts for their husband-directors, helping them as art directors, and working as an army of anonymous aides'.[16] An exception occurred in the case of American Mary Ellen Bute, who achieved success creating abstract animation with her husband/producer Ted Nemeth. Today, she remains the primary name associated with her works, such as *Rhythm in Light* (1933), *Tarantella* (1939), and *Spook Sport* (1940, with animation by Norman McLaren).

In any case, it was not until relatively recently that women have seen significant advances in hiring practices within the realm of industrial production, in part due to changes in training opportunities. During the 1970s, particularly, women became more active as college film programs developed (and animation courses were established within them) and the enrollment of women in colleges grew as a whole.

Before then, only a small number of women had managed to make a name for themselves within the animation industry. For example, Lillian Friedman and La Verne Harding were animators at the New York Fleischer studio and the Hollywood Walter Lantz studio, respectively. At the Disney studio, Mary Blair and Sylvia

Fig. 12.1 *Norman McLaren and Evelyn Lambart working together on* Begone Dull Care *(1949)*
Courtesy NFB

Holland, both inspirational artists, were among the highly respected – if few – females employed in so-called 'creative' positions.[17]

Even earlier, one woman played a very significant role in relation to the Disney studio: Margaret J. Winkler. The most successful American distributor of animation during the silent era, she agreed to promote the studio's 'Alice Comedies' along with the popular 'Felix the Cat' and 'Out of the Inkwell' films she represented. A newspaper article from the early 1920s makes her novelty clear. Subtitled 'Only Woman Distributor Handles Short Subjects', the article begins: 'Gentlemen, one of the few remaining fields in which you have not had to face feminine competition is now being invaded. It is the business of distributing motion pictures.' The article adds: 'Few of the motion picture men who have done business with M.J. Winkler Productions know that M.J. is Margaret Winkler, and that she is young and nice looking.'[18] It is significant to note that, after Winkler got married to Charles Mintz in 1923, her husband took over the business and she soon retired.[19]

Winkler's strategy of using initials is not particularly unusual. To try to overcome the possibility of sexual discrimination, women in a related field, the comic book industry, in some cases also have adopted working names or monikers that are masculine-sounding or at least gender neutral.[20] Among the best known of these artists is Dale Merrick, who was born with the name of Dalia. According to Trina Robbins, Merrick has explained that she:

> ... changed her name to the more sexually ambiguous Dale because editors would reject her strips and then put the make on her. The way she finally sold 'Brenda [Starr Reporter]', she says in all her interviews, was to become Dale and mail the strips in.[21]

Unlike Winkler and some cartoonists, females who wished to pursue a career in animation were not able to work anonymously; they had to be physically present at the studio each day and could not operate through the postal service. However, it is interesting to note that, as Tom Klein reveals, the first woman animator in Hollywood, La Verne Harding (who briefly worked as a cartoonist), also used a masculine-sounding name upon occasion. Klein notes that Harding 'was often referred to as "Verne", in name and sometimes in print'.[22]

It was more often the case that women settled into the roles of inking and painting, colour keying, or background painting, which were the primary positions open to them. Within these vital roles, some established themselves as artists in their own right. One example of a woman who became well respected in these areas was Phyllis Craig, who spent many years working for the Disney, Hanna-Barbera, Marvel, and Film Roman studios.[23] Another is Helen Nerbovig, who had an important role at Disney as the individual in charge of the Courvoisier animation art program, through the studio's Cel Setup Department.[24] Libby Simon has written about some of the other ' "unsung heroes" of the animation process' in her 'History of the Ink and Paint Studio' articles.[25] She notes that, during the 1940s and 1950s, a number of ink and paint companies were born which were:

> ... mostly run and owned by women. These businesses, in many instances, started in their own homes. As they found their homes being taken over by cels drying and paint staining their kitchen sinks, these companies moved to other locations.[26]

In her articles, she overviews her own contributions to the field in addition to the work of Betty Brennan, Mary Cain, Auril Thompson, Celine Mills, Betty Brooks,

Fig. 12.2 *'Cynical Susie',*
created by Becky Sharp
and La Verne Harding,
the first woman animator
in Hollywood
Courtesy Tim Klein

Cindy Wallin, Judi Cassell, Millie Simon (her mother) and Bill Hanna's two sisters, Marion O'Callahan and Connie Crawley, most of whom began their careers at large Hollywood animation companies before starting their own ink and paint studios.

In 1964, an Occupational Guide published by the State of California explained that 'the one-time prejudice against women animation artists has all but vanished' but noted that women still 'predominate in inking and duplicating work, which requires infinite patience'.[27] However, a 1990 summary of the Los Angeles-area Motion Picture Screen Cartoonists Union Local 839 statistics revealed that there had not been much change to the imbalance: while total membership was 34 per cent female, women made up only sixteen per cent of the top of the employment hierarchy. On the other hand, they made up 68 per cent of the 'technical workers' – such as inkers and painters – in the union's membership.[28] In 1997, Union spokesperson Jeff Massie said he was surprised to find there had been relatively little change in the percentage of women members overall, despite the rapid growth of the animation industry during the intervening years.[29]

Although the number of women in union jobs might not be increasing at an impressive rate, at the management level there seems to have been a positive change. By 1997, a number of women occupied executive positions in the United States, particularly in relation to the children's television industry; for example, Betty Cohen as President of the Cartoon Network Worldwide and TNT International; Lucy Johnson as Senior Vice President of Daytime-Children's Programming and Special Projects for CBS; Geraldine Laybourne as President of Disney/ABC Cable Networks; Margaret Loesch as Chair(wo)man and Chief Executive Officer of Fox Kid's Network, Worldwide; Jean MacCurdy as President of Warner Bros. Television Animation; and Anne Sweeney as President of The Disney Channel and Vice President of Disney/ABC Cable Networks.

Some women are managing to 'work their way up' the hierarchy as directors and animators in the commercial realm. For example, Jun Falkenstein, who was hired as an animation director at Hanna-Barbera just two years after her graduation from film school, writes: 'I have never felt held back in any way because of my gender. In fact it has worked to my advantage at Hanna-Barbera because they were looking to specifically hire more female producers/directors.'[30]

Another woman, who had become the first female animation director at a major Hollywood studio, had quite a different experience. She explains that her promotion was met by surprise:

> ... many of my co-workers hit me with 'Wow! A *woman* director!' or 'Gee! The first female director at [the studio]!' Those kind of comments left me nonplussed. I realised that I kind of take myself for granted ... As someone said during the Academy Awards a while ago (the industry was celebrating 'The Year of the Woman'), the real time for celebrating will be when women in the industry are so common as to be hardly worth noting. I certainly agree![31]

Now that a number of women have managed to secure positions of power within the industry, there is a greater sense of group identity developing among females in all aspects of the field. The formation of 'Women in Animation' brings increasing awareness and solidarity and removes any doubt about the 'ambition' of women within the field to be accepted on equal terms with their male colleagues.

Representations of femininity in animation

One area of concern for today's animation producers is the way in which women and girls are represented in their productions. Repeatedly, one hears the so-called 'fact' that men and boys will not watch female-oriented programming – that is, productions with females in central roles and centring on issues related to the experience of being a girl or woman – but that girls and women will watch programming that deals with males. As a result, it is reasoned, animation about females cannot be a commercial success and that it is safer to show stories about males. A study conducted by the Annenberg Public Policy Center in June 1996 states that 'boy-oriented, violence-laden programs dominate the more favorable parts of the schedule to such a degree that it is unusual to find programs that are girl-oriented or even gender neutral', adding, 'industry experts argue that advertisers want the largest possible audience, and programmers and producers believe the way to obtain it is to program ... for 6–11 year old boys'.[32]

In speaking about her experience as President and Chief Executive Officer at Nickelodeon, Geraldine Laybourne comments on this situation, writing:

> In many countries girls are treated not even as second-class citizens, but as property. At Nickelodeon we have a strong commitment to demonstrate to girls that we listen to what they have to say. We learned early on that when programmers talked about kids and kids' issues, they usually meant boys. For years, the conventional wisdom was that kids, boys and girls alike, would respond positively to programming designed exclusively for boys. The broadcast industry seemed to feel that girls would watch anything, but that boys would not watch programs that had girls at the center of the action. Over the years, we at Nickelodeon have

Fig. 12.3 *From the series 'Pond Life' (beg. 1996) by Candy Guard Courtesy Pond Life Productions*

gone out of our way to challenge these myths. The response from our viewers has consistently proven us right.

The success of programs like *Clarissa Knows All*, *The Secret World of Alex Mack* and *Eureeka's Castle* have demonstrated that girls have been starving to see female characters portrayed and female issues explored in children's programming. It showed that boys – and they don't even mind admitting it – find these shows interesting as well.[33]

However, the shows that Laybourne uses as examples are all live-action series. In the United States, it has less often been the case that animated series are designed with women as the central focus; however, recent efforts include 'Daria', a spin-off of the 'Beavis and Butt-Head' series created by Mike Judge, and 'Where on Earth is Carmen Sandiego?', a series created by the American company DIC, based on a successful educational software line.[34] In 1997, other new female-centred shows appeared on American television, including 'Pepper Ann' on ABC and 'The Legend of Calamity Jane' on the Warner Bros. network.

In other countries, efforts also have been made to create female characters in central positions. One example is a British series, 'Pond Life', created by Candy Guard for Channel 4 and SC4. The Canadian animation company Cinar has found success with 'Little Lulu', which was developed from the comic strip by Marjorie Henderson Buell. One of the most popular series featuring a female lead is 'Pretty Soldier Sailor Moon', which comes out of the Japanese studio Toei. It became the number one show in Japan and proved to be a great success in other countries as well, such as France, Spain and Hong Kong. Later, DIC secured television and merchandising rights to the series within the United States and all other English-speaking countries, so that it could be adapted for use in these areas.[35] Also notable is UNICEF's development of the female Meena character to address prejudices against girls in many countries throughout the world.

Linda Simensky, who worked at Nickelodeon as a Producer before moving to The Cartoon Network, found it difficult to generate series about women because the creators she worked with predominantly were male. She explains that, in her experience, male animation creators and directors usually do not design female characters who have substance and provide strong, positive role models; most of the men pitched her concepts that had male characters in central roles, with women included only as objects of affection or as common stereotypes. The artists whose series concepts and sense of humour appealed to the Nickelodeon producers have generally been unwilling or unable to create strong central female characters. When asked by Simensky why a long list of series concepts did not contain even one that focused on a female, the representative of an award-winning English animation studio replied: '[W]e don't do women. They're not funny.'

One can find this kind of attitude deeply rooted in culture. For example, in discussing the vaudeville era, June Sochen explains that physical humour (such as slapstick) and femininity were considered incompatible because:

> ... showing personal weakness, an essential trait of humor, was considered funny when big, burly men did it, but women? After all, members of the 'fairer sex' were known to be physically weak; that was their nature. What was funny about that?[36]

Although Nickelodeon has been able to develop some female characters in their series, such as Patti Mayonnaise in 'Doug',[37] more common was the type of experience Simensky had with the creators of the series 'Rocko's Modern Life', all of whom were male. She explains: '[W]e asked them if they could stop drawing the women so "top-heavy" and they said they couldn't – because it was *easier* to draw them the traditional way!' At the time, Simensky said:

> I feel as though I'm constantly faced with the issue of 'is it funny' versus the 'is it politically conscious' (meaning gender stuff) while working on 'Rocko'. They are a bunch of talented guys who seem to have formed a boys' club. We push them to be funny, but a lot of their women are stereotypical.[38]

One way that producers have tried avoid problems associated with gender is to use animal characters. Although they are often clearly gendered through a combination of names, voices and narrative conventions (such as passive and active roles), animals at least provide the possibility of a more neutral sexual identity. They also can solve problems about representing race. When the Nickelodeon producers requested story ideas for the 1992 season, they noted their preference for animal characters because, according to Simensky, they offer better licensing opportunities and can do 'crazy things' (such as fall off a roof or get hit on the head) more easily than human characters. Despite their original preference, very few of the acceptable pitches contained animals. Two of the three pitches that Nickelodeon eventually developed into series involve human characters (e.g. 'Rugrats' and 'Doug') and even 'Ren & Stimpy' originally was pitched as a series built around humans.[39]

Simensky, like many women today, is sensitised to the fact that – as Walker explains – for many years:

> ... humor did not play a large part in feminism. Indeed, the anger and grim determination that characterised the early women's movement, like the civil

rights movement that instigated it, led to renewed accusations that women – especially 'women's libbers' – had no sense of humor.[40]

Simensky says she was self-conscious about the fact that the male artists tried to 'shock' her and the other female producers with offensive material but felt she would look like 'a prude' if she rejected every single thing that seemed out of line. To avoid such a problem, she sometimes let the material slip through to Standards and Practices, which then became the 'bad guys' (although, in that case, they were the 'bad women') who deemed things too offensive. It seems clear that, despite her experience and confidence as a producer, Simensky remained acutely aware of her position as a woman working within a system that remains male dominated.

Although it is unlikely that differences between producers and their creative teams will ever diminish, it does seem that the relationship between males and females within the animation industry is improving at all levels and that women are finding more opportunities to work side by side with men. There are also positive signs in terms of the representation of women as animated characters.

Developing an alternative form of expression

In regard to the success of women in the animation industry, one question that has arisen is whether or not, for social or biological reasons, women actually tend to express themselves differently than do men, or if any perceived difference between the sexes is imaginary. Jun Falkenstein believes that her aesthetic sensibilities contributed to her success in the field, explaining:

> ... there are very few women like me. This may explain why there are very few women directors in animation – not that I'm saying that I represent the ultimate female director in any way. What I mean is, and I hate to say it, I have more of a 'masculine' approach to thoughts and ideas than most women I know ... I remember an incident [in college] when a visiting Russian animator came to look at our work on the wall; he told me that I drew like a man. He meant it as a great compliment.[41]

In her book on women and animation, Jayne Pilling maintains there is 'no overriding thesis about the specificity of women's animation', although she suggests that:

> ... men and women are socialised as children in different ways, with the result that women tend to be more able to explore and share personal experience ... Animator Susan Young has commented interestingly in relation to this, [saying] that the socialisation of boys encourages hierarchical play and a tendency to act out as a possible explanation why men tend to dominate character animation.[42]

Animators Faith Hubley and Mary Beams both contend that women's experience – or at least 'feminine' nature – tends to be more cyclical than that of men (or masculinity), which they describe as more linear.[43] In the opinion of these two artists, the difference can manifest itself in an artist's style and choice of content.

Many of these two women's works have been concerned with such issues as the family, the environment and global unity. For example, that kind of focus is apparent in Beams's *Whale Songs* (1980), based on the experience of a whale-watching expedition. Similar concerns are evident in virtually every film by Hubley, from *Second Chance: Sea* (1976), which urges 'international responsibility in preserving our oceans', and

Upside Down (1991), which illuminates 'our foolish misconceptions and delusions about our participation in the Earth's complex and delicate ecosystem'.[44] For Beams, Hubley and many other animators, cyclical and thematic structures provide the most appropriate means for expressing personal world views, as well as the 'content' of their films. A quick survey of a number of women's films helps to illustrate this point.

For example, Hubley is an artist who has avoided linearity in her work, generally opting for what she describes as a cyclical structure, a formal pattern she derives from her experience of life. She explains:

> It's how I breathe. It is something I feel so naturally. I feel it especially in music. You state a theme, and you repeat it in many different ways ... The cyclical approach is very healing, very reassuring ... life without cycles is unthinkable to me.[45]

Hubley's aesthetics have been influenced by many art forms, including jazz music.[46] A recently released series of her films (completed in partnership with her husband) is entitled 'Art and Jazz in Animation: The Films of John and Faith Hubley', and includes soundtracks featuring Quincy Jones, Ella Fitzgerald, Dizzy Gillespie and Benny Carter. In her films, one also can see that she has been greatly influenced by children's artwork as well as tribal art, including petroglyphs, pictographs and goddess sculpture. [47]

Another artist, American Karen Aqua, has employed elements of non-modern culture in films that are 'non-narrative, often playing with metamorphosis, lyrical curvolinear, personal journeys'. Interesting in this respect is Aqua's *Shrine to Ritualized Time* (1989), which features tribal motifs and ritualised movement, and *Kakania* (1989) (see CP 6), in which 'the urban strife of overcrowding, conflict, crime and poverty is transformed into cooperative living and rejuvenation. Nine figures multiply to fifteen, change into dancing symbols, don animal masks for ritual dances, link arms and begin to move into harmony'.[48]

American animator Sara Petty employs a thematic structure in her film *Furies* (1977), using metamorphosis to shift between the images of two cats and fluid abstract forms to provide a sense of ambiance rather than a record of physical actions – the film says less about the actual events of a cat fight (to which it alludes) than the energy that sort of occurrence entails. William Moritz explains that 'pure non-objective and non-linear representation coexist in Sara Petty's films. Her *Furies* ... clearly shows how the daily life and consciousness of two cats blends from sharply-observed moments of realism into "abstractions" ' of geometric forms.[49] Jayne Pilling writes that '*Furies* has been described as both a study in movement and composition and a projection in imagination of the mysterious consciousness that is other than human'.[50] Both commentators hint at a mystical quality in the film that creates visual appeal.

Another female artist, Aleksandra Korejwo of Poland, also employs a thematic structure in films like *Carmen Habanera* (1995), which explores the relationship between music and movement. Korejwo, who studied painting, music and poetry before beginning to animate, creates the images in her films with salt. In an essay entitled, 'My Small World', she explains how she employs an everyday item to create images of great beauty:

> Everybody knows salt. It is a common material. But for me, it is more than just salt. In this material, I discovered my new way for Art, my new way for animation. There were many years of research and hard work. People often ask me, 'How

can you do such difficult animation so fast? It is impossible'. But I have been working for this moment all my life.[51]

In Korejwo's explanation, one can begin to see what Jayne Pilling means when she says that 'animation as a form offers such potential to explore women's issues in a way that simply isn't possible in live-action filmmaking. At the most basic level is the production process itself'.[52] This statement reflects Pilling's belief that the ability to work independently, without dependence on a large crew, allows one to explore his or her personal visions to a greater extent. Certainly, Korejwo's use of salt fits perfectly into Mary Beams's perspective when she writes: 'What characterizes the feminine side of the creative process? It is the tendency to work with what is at hand.'[53]

The question of what constitutes a 'feminine sensibility' – which is perhaps the quality that ties these and other works together – is an important consideration when one begins to examine the representation of women, or women's experience, in animation. One can argue that the media is dominated by images representing the priorities of a white male culture, but how does one go about depicting an alternative? How does one define 'women's experience'? And, even if it were possible to come up with a definition, could it encompass the realities of women across the world? Of course, the answer to the latter question is 'no': the experience of being a woman differs from country to country, class to class, skin colour to skin colour, person to person. So, then, we return to the first question: How does one go about creating an alternative?

In her study of British female animators, Sandra Law has examined some of the strategies employed in works that represent aspects of women's experience. She reaches the conclusion that, despite the aesthetic differences among the animation she studies, the works all:

> ... explore, through their use of imagery, the existence of the female form as something that is malleable and whose femaleness can be enhanced or reduced. They illustrate that femininity, as it is traditionally represented, is something that can be put on and taken off at will.

She adds that the women in each of the animators' works 'are depicted as duplicitous in their own enslavement by the mirror or by society's expectations of what femaleness represents'.[54]

One of the artists whose work Law studies is Joanna Quinn, who began her career as an illustrator and graphic designer. Eventually, Quinn moved to Cardiff, Wales, where she continues to work today. Quinn's environment is reflected in her 1990 film *Body Beautiful*, which is set in Wales, involving a group of labourers who are employed in a factory.

The film features one of Quinn's recurring characters, Beryl, whose representation is far from the feminine 'ideal'. Simply put, she is middle aged and fat. At first, she is also insecure and unwilling to stand up for herself. As Law explains, 'at certain moments throughout the film, Beryl actually effaces herself by giving up the right to speak on her own behalf', allowing herself to be verbally abused by her pompous co-worker, Vince.[55] A good deal of metamorphosis is employed within the film, and both characters at times are depicted as a variety of animals: Vince as a rodent and braying donkey, for example, and Beryl as a whale and a pig.

According to Law, the power of *Body Beautiful* comes in shifting the point of view from the domineering male to the initially disempowered female. As she explains:

In *Body Beautiful,* Quinn provides us with a glimpse of the possibilities animated films offer in terms of the representation of female images and the experience of being female. Though Beryl's malleability is a feature that is initially under the control of other individuals, it eventually comes to be something that she personally directs – and therein lies the difference between her character's appeal and that of Vince. Beryl's ability to change is under her own, internal control and the metamorphoses she experiences reflect her potential to be whatever she chooses. The act of personal deconstruction and eventual reconstruction of her own form becomes an affirmative sequence ...[56]

Candy Guard employs quite a different strategy in her work, not only visually but also in terms of content. In comparing Guard's style with that of Quinn's, Law says it is 'unadorned and direct. In an interview, she describes her technique as "very simple, very economical" '.[57] However, in other ways the two animators share common techniques. For example, as Law suggests:

Guard's female characters are not idealised in either physical or behavioral terms. They discuss their concerns, which vary from the everyday ... to the profound ... The significance of these concerns, which are also found in Quinn's work, resides in how they affect women's experience and behavior.[58]

It is often the case that Guard's characters worry about things that affect their appearances, including weight and clothing. For example, these two topics provide the focus of an exactingly familiar slice of life vignette *What About Me?* (1990), in which two women exchange comments about each other that grow increasingly barbed. In a previous film, *Wishful Thinking* (1988), Guard had developed these same concerns in a longer format. *Wishful Thinking* focuses on two female pals whose illusions of popularity and social possibilities at a party are crushed when they find

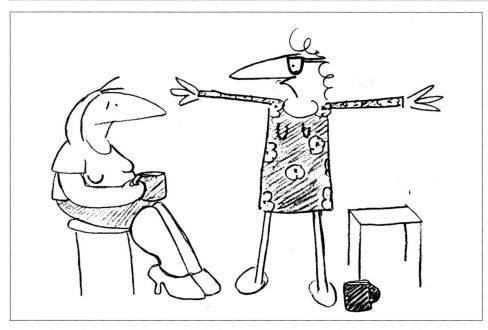

Fig. 12.5 What About Me?, *created by Candy Guard (1990)*
Courtesy the artist

themselves alone in the hostess's kitchen, eating the party food but speaking to none of the other guests, all of whom are completely self-absorbed.

Law notes that Guard's work is located in:

> ... very definite geographic, temporal and class locations. Through the act of putting on different clothing, or playing different parts in domestic scenarios, Guard's characters delve into the experience of being female in a particular location, at a particular point in time.[59]

Fig. 12.6 Wishful Thinking, *created by Candy Guard (1988)*
Courtesy the artist

However, elements of the acts performed by the characters have resonance on a larger scale, for a larger audience of female – if not male – viewers. Law interprets the ritual of changing clothes in this work (and in other films by Guard) as 'an act of self-re-creation; it represents the potential for a change in style of life, identity, or relationships that [the characters] seem to desire'.[60] This common performance can be recognised by many women throughout the world.

Quinn and Guard offer two distinct interpretations of feminine experience. Law concludes that, 'in Quinn's films, Beryl rejects societal dictates of what it is to be female, instead choosing a form that is comfortable for her' while 'Guard's characters are trapped into a masquerade of the feminine'.[61] She further elaborates:

> Guard's work exposes to us, in embarrassing detail, the true nature of our own folly ... The less-than-skin-deep transformations that are undergone by Guard's characters are cosmetic and ultimately transient, whereas Beryl's transformation in *Body Beautiful* has lasting significance. The eventual defeat of Guard's characters is located in their unwillingness to discard the stereotypes to which they will never be able to measure up.[62]

Despite their differences, the aesthetics of the animation created by Quinn and Guard have more in common with each other than they do with the animation made by the four artists mentioned previously: Hubley, Aqua, Petty and Korejwo. Quinn and Guard employ narratives, using dialogue to move forward their linear structures. They also use humour to a great extent and a drawing style that is relatively representational, rather than abstract. The other four animators have created works that tend to be non-linear (either cyclical or thematic); lacking in narrative; less humorous than intellectual; and symbolic, archetypal or dreamlike in their use of imagery. It is likely that these differences have resulted not only from the tastes and experiences of each artist, but also from the fact that Quinn's and Guard's works were broadcast on television, which suggests that a somewhat more commercial strategy was welcomed. In contrast, the other four artists' works were produced as independent projects.[63]

In any case, the point of using such widely different examples is to underscore the fact that there is no such thing as a unified body of 'women's films' or any best way of representing femininity and issues pertaining to women. It will be interesting to see how the further integration of women into the field of commercial animation, both at the levels of management and creative personnel, will affect the form and content of work being produced in the future.

In order to understand better the new forms of expressions as they arise, we will have to continue to redefine our strategies of investigation, taking into account the priorities and concerns of their creators. The next chapter explores this notion in a different context, focusing on a relatively marginalised form within animation production, whether industrial or independent: abstract animation. In general, abstract animation has proven to be one of the most challenging types to introduce to new viewers because it differs so greatly from the narrative-based, representational animated productions that are familiar to most of people. The final chapter of the book provides information on the aesthetics of abstract animation, in an effort to increase our appreciation of this type of work and provide additional analytical tools for the study of it.

Notes

1. Donald Crafton, *Before Mickey: The Animated Film 1898–1928* (Chicago: Chicago UP, 1993), 55.

2. Karl Cohen, 'Racism and Resistance: Black Stereotypes in Animation', *Animation Journal* 4, 2 (Spring 1996): 43–68, 43.

3. Ibid., 63.

4. Ibid., 49.

5. Edward L. Palmer, *Television and America's Children* (New York: Oxford UP, 1988), 95.

6. Ibid., 95.

7. This film is discussed in an adapted article, Egbert Barten and Gerard Groeneveld, 'Reynard the Fox and the Jew Animal', *Animation World Network* 1, 7 (Oct. 1996). The original English-language article is '*Van den vos Reynaerde* (1943): How a Medieval Fable became a Dutch Anti-Semitic Animation Film', *Historical Journal of Film, Radio and Television* 14, 2 (1994): n.p.

8. Alexandra Early, 'Wanted: Girl Heroes', *Los Angeles Times* (Orange County Edition) (9 Nov. 1993): B1.

9. Sharon Couzin, 'The Woman's Voice in Contemporary American Animation: An Analysis of Suzan Pitt's *Asparagus* and Joanna Priestley's *All My Relations*', in Jayne Pilling (ed.), *Women & Animation: A Compendium* (London: British Film Institute, 1992), 71–75.

10. Rita Street, letter to the author (17 Nov. 1993). WIA is the not the first organisation of its type. In 1982, a group called WANDA, or Women's Animation Network Directory Alliance, was formed in an effort to 'assemble an inexpensively printed directory of women in animation, both students and professionals, who are willing to share the benefits of their expertise, as well as provide job-search information'. The 'committee' list includes Kathy Barrows, Carole Beers, Marija Dail, Ruth Kissane and Rosemary O'Connor. Like WIA, WANDA was created by women from the Los Angeles area. Anonymous, WANDA questionnaire form (Fall 1982), send to the author by Prescott Wright.

11. Art historian Linda Nochlin has suggested that women have not created 'great art' because 'they have been excluded from the societal institutions that make artistic greatness possible'. In her view, the attitudinal and legal barriers that have oppressed women as artists include 'domestic expectations placed on women that precluded professional art careers; the practice of denying women access to art academies (or when admitting them, forbidding the essential study of the nude model); and the prevailing notion that females were not capable of possessing the genius that separates the artist from the rest of humanity'. Elizabeth Chew, 'Introduction – Women Artists', in *National Museum of American Art Online: Tour the Galleries*, America On Line computer service (14 Sept. 1993). She refers to Linda Nochlin, 'Why Have There Been No Great Women Artists?' *Art News* 69 (Jan. 1971): 22–39+.

12. This booklet might be available at the Walt Disney archive. It was published during the late 1930s, when Disney was increasing the size of his staff in order to prepare for the production of *Snow White* (1937), the studio's first animated feature. It is mentioned in an article, 'Mickey Mouse Makers: Those From Ranks Given Trial As Artists, Then Up-Grade; 100 Yearly Enter Portals', *Daily Variety* (24 Nov. 1935): 146. The article says that 'age or nationality is no barrier to artists', while explaining that 'principal artists in demand by Disney studio are men, but women too find a spot on the staff, as inkers and painters'.

13. The reason for training them, he explained, was not because they earned less money but because he wanted to increase employees' versatility, to protect himself in face of the impending war (when men would be called to fight) and because 'the girl artists have the right to expect the same chances for advancement as men, and I honestly believe that they may eventually contribute something to this business that men never would or could. In the present group that are training for in-betweens there are definite prospects, and a good example is to mention the work of Ethel Kulsar and Sylvia Holland on *The Nutcracker Suite*, and little Rhetta Scott, of whom you will hear more when you see *Bambi*'. Walt Disney, 'Speech to Strikers' (10–11 Feb. 1941), 16–17, located at the Disney archives.

14. Marcin Gizycki, 'Splendid Artists: Central and East European Women Animators', *Animation World Magazine* 1, 2 (May 1996).

15. For more on Lotte Reiniger, see William Moritz, 'Some Critical Perspectives on Lotte Reiniger', *Animation Journal* 5, 1 (Fall 1996): 40–51.

16. Gizycki, op. cit.

17. For information on these artists, see Robin Allan, 'Mary Blair: An Indelible Imprint', *Animation Magazine* (July 1995): 58–61; Robin Allan, 'Sylvia Holland: Disney Artist', *Animation Journal* 2, 2 (Spring 1994): 32–41; John Canemaker, *Before the Animaton Begins: The Art and Lives of Disney Inspirational Sketch Artists* (New York: Hyperion, 1996).

18. Anonymous, 'Right off the Reel: To the Ladies!' source unknown (ca. 1923). This clipping is located in Winkler's scrapbook. A microfiche copy can be found in the M.J. Winkler file at the Museum of Modern Art Film Study Center.

19. They married in November 1923 and by 1925, when her first child was born, she had made the decision to retire. Ron Magliozzi, 'Notes for a History of Winkler Productions, Inc.', unpublished essay (10 Dec. 1990).

20. The name changes occurred especially if they wished to work on strips that were dramatic action-adventures. Trina Robbins suggests that 'a male pseudonym did seem to be required for action strips.' Some women who used nicknames include Cecelia Paddock Munson, who worked as Pad or Paddock Munson; Caroline 'C.M.' Sexton; Ramona 'Pat' Patenaude; Mabel 'Odin' Burvich; June 'Tarpe' Mills; Marjorie 'Neysa' McMein. Trina Robins, *A Century of Women Cartoonists* (Northampton, MA: Kitchen Sink, 1993), 70.

21. Robbins, ibid., 58–59.

22. Klein also notes that Nellie Chouinard, the founder of the Chouinard Art Institute (which became California Institute of the Arts), 'professionally went by the name "Nelbert" Chouinard, which she invented'. Harding attended Chouinard before being hired by Walter Lantz. Atom Klein, 'La Verne Harding: Hollywood's First Woman Animator', *Animation Journal* 2, 2 (Spring 1994): 54–67, 63. Klein has returned to using the name Tom, rather than Atom.

23. Maureen Furniss, 'Animation and Color Key: The Career of Phyllis Craig', *Animation Journal* 5, 1 (Fall 1996): 58–70.

24. Ron Barbagallo, 'Cel Art Pioneer: Discovering Helen', *Animation Magazine* (Aug. 1997): 37–39.

25. Libby Simon, 'History of the Ink and Paint Studio', *Work in Progress* (WIA Newsletter) 1, 6 (Spring 1997): 1+; 'History of the Ink and Paint Studio: Part II', *Work in Progress* (WIA Newsletter) 2, 2 (Summer/Fall 1997): 5.

26. Simon, 'History of the Ink and Paint Studio', ibid., 5.

27. 'Artist – Animation', *Occupational Guide* published by the State of California, Department of Employment (Aug. 1964).

28. Figures compiled by Jeff Massie, Assistant to the Business Representative, Motion Picture Screen Cartoonists, Local 839 IATSE (1990).

29. Jeff Massie, telephone interview with the author (23 June 1997).

30. Jun Falkenstein, letter to the author (21 Nov. 1993).

31. Anonymous, e-mail to the author (27 Oct. 1993).

32. Annenberg Public Policy Center, 'The State of Children's Television Report: An Examination of Quantity, Quality, and Industry Beliefs', a study conducted by Amy B. Jordan (17 June 1997), 37. The statement also says that the largest possible audience comes from programming for entertainment rather than for educational purposes.

33. Geraldine Laybourne, 'Kids Deserve to be Heard', *Drawing Insight: Communicating Development through Animation* (Penang: Southbound, 1996), 74–77, 76. The article contains typographical errors, so it incorrectly lists two of the series as *Alice* and *Mack and Eureka's Castle*. The correct titles are used in the quote as I have printed it.

34. Morrie Gelman, 'Lady in Red', *Animation Magazine* (Feb. 1995): 26–31.

35. Morrie Gelman, 'Sailor Moon', *Animation Magazine* (Feb. 1995): 42.

36. June Sochen, 'Slapsticks, Screwballs, and Bawds: The Long Road to the Performing Talents of Lucy and Bette', *Women's Comic Visions* (Detroit: Wayne State UP, 1991), n.p.

37. Simensky feels that Patti Mayonnaise provides a good role model because she is relatively independent (and certainly more assertive than the series' male star) but that the series'

creators almost 'go out of their way to make her too good' – it seems like she has to be perfect, because she is the only well-developed female character around.

38. Simensky, interview with the author. For more on the subject, see Maureen Furniss, 'What's So Funny About Cheese? and Other Dilemmas: The Nickelodeon Television Network and Its (Female) Animation Producers', *Animation Journal* 2, 2 (Spring 1994): 4–22; G. Michael Dobbs, 'Women in Animation', *Animato!* 31 (Winter 1995): 32–34.

39. The choice to use humans was, it seems, a purely evasive one. Kricfalusi explains that, before he pitched to Nickelodeon, he had tried to sell 'Ren & Stimpy' to other networks but 'there was no way in the world they would buy my stuff undiluted'. As a result, he says, 'I hid the Ren and Stimpy characters, surrounding them by a bunch of kids in a show called 'Your Gang''. And I made up a bogus pitch about it being socially conscious'. When Kricfalusi pitched the idea to Nickelodeon producer Vanessa Coffey, evidently she did not like the concept but was interested in the Ren and Stimpy characters. John Kricfalusi, quoted in Daniel Cerone, 'Nickelodeon Betting on Cartoons', *Los Angeles Times* (8 Aug. 1991): F1+.

40. Nancy Walker, 'Toward Solidarity: Women's Humor and Group Identity', *Women's Comic Visions* (Detroit: Wayne State UP, 1991), 57–81, 73.

41. Falkenstein, letter to the author (21 Nov. 1993).

42. Jayne Pilling (ed.), *Women & Animation: A Compendium* (London: British Film Institute, 1992), 6.

43. See Joanna Priestley, 'Creating a Healing Mythology: The Art of Faith Hubley', *Animation Journal* 2, 2 (Spring 1994): 23–31; Mary Beams, 'Subverting Time: A Woman's Perspective', *Animation Journal* 2, 2 (Spring 1994): 42–53; 'Artist – Animation', Occupational Guide, op. cit.

44. 'Films by Faith Hubley', Pyramid Film & Video brochure (ca. 1989), with an added description of films from 1990 and 1991.

45. Priestley, op. cit., 28.

46. Hubley is also trained in acting, music, writing and film editing.

47. Priestley, op. cit., 26.

48. Jayne Pilling (ed.), 'Karen Aqua', *Women & Animation: A Compendium* (London: British Film Institute, 1992), 117.

49. William Moritz, 'Some Observations on Non-objective and Non-linear Film', in John Canemaker (ed.), *Storytelling in Animation: The Art of the Animated Image* (Los Angeles: American Film Institute, 1988), 27.

50. Pilling, *Women & Animation*, 134.

51. Aleksandra Korejwo, 'My Small World', *Animation World Network* 1, 2 (May 1996).

52. Pilling, op. cit., xx.

53. Beams, op. cit., 43.

54. Sandra Law, 'Putting Themselves in the Pictures: Images of Women in the Work of Selected Female Animators in the UK', *Animation Journal* 4, 1 (Fall 1995): 21–55, 47.

55. Ibid., 27.

56. Ibid., 29.

57. Law quotes Candy Guard, 'Candy Guard: An Interview with Linda Pariser', in Jayne Pilling (ed.), *Women & Animation: A Compendium* (London: British Film Institute, 1992), 88.

58. Law, 'Putting Themselves in the Pictures', op. cit., 32.

59. Ibid., 32.

60. Ibid., 34.

61. Ibid., 47.

62. Ibid., 38.

63. This is not to say that the artists and their techniques are not compatible with more commercial production. For example, Sara Petty was employed by the Disney studio and Aleksandra Korejwo has created commercials.

13

Considering form in abstract animation

STRUCTURAL MODELS

*I*n the Academy-award winning animated short, *The Critic* (directed by Ernest Pintoff, 1963), the voice of an elderly, somewhat confused spectator is heard over the visuals of an abstract film. With every new form that appears, the man (voiced by Mel Brooks) is sure he has finally figured out what the images *really* mean.

Fifty years previously, Wassily Kandinsky had lamented that:

> ... the spectator is too ready to look for a meaning in a picture – i.e. some outward connection between its various parts. Our materialistic age has produced a type of spectator or 'connoisseur', who is not content to put himself opposite a picture and let it say its own message. Instead of allowing the inner value of the picture to work, he worries himself in looking for 'closeness to nature' or 'temperament', or 'handling', or 'tonality', or 'perspective' or what not. His eye does not probe the outer expression to arrive at inner meaning.[1]

The problem Kandinsky described so early in the century in relation to painting has been even more apparent in the situation of the film medium, the conventions of which became solidified in the decades after he made his observation. It is really no wonder that Pintoff's critic is so confused, since overwhelmingly dominant conventions of the Hollywood classical film have prepared him only for representational images and narrative forms, which typically have little to probe beyond surface meaning.[2]

This chapter will provide information that will assist viewers in watching and analysing abstract animation. It begins by discussing some ways in which specific viewing practices can assist in an appreciation of the work, and concludes with attention to some visual and aural concerns that are useful in a study of abstract animation.

Watching abstract animation

As Kandinsky suggested, many people find that an appreciation of abstraction requires a re-alignment of one's process of interpretation. Rather than following the story or assessing the rendering of representational figures, a viewer of abstract work typically must assume a much more intuitive and contemplative approach to the material.

In abstract animation, there are no characters with which to identify, there is no diegesis to transport the viewer to a different time and place and, when the animation is over, the viewer does not have a complete 'understanding' of its meaning as he or she would with a closed narrative structure. Clearly, abstract animation does not offer the viewer many of the pleasures found in watching a classically structured film. That is not to say that abstract animation does not offer pleasure. It does, but as an 'open text', which leads beyond the film itself, as opposed to a 'closed text' which provides tangible information within the film and, at the end, a clear resolution of the film's plot. It seems that abstract motion pictures are often 'about' the need to expand our ability to see, experience, and comprehend things in day-to-day life. For that reason, they challenge the viewer to participate in the process of creating meaning.

In a best-case scenario, abstract animation would be viewed a number of times during a single screening session, as well as across a period of time during different screening sessions. Unlike the classical Hollywood film, abstract images generally are not easily grasped upon the first viewing – nor are they meant to be. This kind of work relies heavily on personal interaction (or the 'process' of viewing) and an individual should participate in several screenings just to create a frame of reference within which to develop feelings about the work. The development of this framework can be facilitated by exhibiting abstract animation in the company of other works of an abstract nature, including painting and music. Among these arts, abstract animation is not an anomaly, as it might seem to be when viewed among more conventional motion pictures. Other forms of art can provide models for the discussion of aesthetics concerning abstract animation.

In contrast to industrially produced live-action productions, abstract animation defies the naturalised logic of a forward-moving cause-and-effect narrative. Rather, they tend to be developed around an aesthetic of thematic stasis or cycles. For instance, much of Jordan Belson's work is structured this way. A good example is found in *Momentum* (1968), the title of which ironically suggests forward movement. The film itself begins with a solarised image of a rocket launch – another hint of linear development. However, the body of the film contains nothing in the way of an unravelling narrative, but only a series of hazy gaseous orbs and other relatively vague images.

To the spectator unaccustomed to viewing Belson's films, it might appear that they have no point other than to illustrate the theme of 'the cosmos' or 'the environment' in very loose terms. In that respect, the films are structured thematically, rather than linearly. Belson explains that, actually, '*Momentum* is a kind of revelation regarding the sun as a source of life. The end shows the paradoxical reality in which the subatomic phenomena and the cosmologically vast are identical'.[3] Clearly, there is no attempt made to develop a storyline to any extent; rather, the film seems to exist as an effort to alter peoples' general perceptions about the world as a whole.

Some theorists and practitioners have speculated that one's ability to create and appreciate cinematic images, abstract or otherwise, is tied into the functioning of different areas of the brain. The classical model of film, with its linear narrative structure of uni-directional cause-and-effect relationships, is one that seems to draw largely on abilities controlled by the left hemisphere of the brain. Logical thinking is required to connect plot actions together into a meaningful 'syntagmatic' stream of events, quite like we do in other situations where we engage in verbal activities of a narrative nature (e.g. constructing or comprehending sentences). In contrast, abstract animation demands much more of the right hemisphere, since it requires the viewer to think intuitively and to process sensory data in a 'paradigmatic' mode.[4]

All people are capable of switching between ways of conceptualising, and to varying degrees rely on functions controlled by both the left and right hemispheres of the brain. It has been theorised that the two parts work in tandem throughout the day and night, although the left side of the brain dominates during waking hours while the right side is most active during periods of sleep and dreaming.

Barbara Lex suggests that, while hemispheric dominance (generally, left-brain dominance) might be culturally determined, 'specific acts involve complimentary shifts between the functions of the two hemisphere'.[5] For example, she has argued that, in meditational practice, the effect of using mantras is to 'evoke and place preeminence in right hemisphere functions' by inhibiting or holding-constant left-brain functions.[6] She believes that this occurs because the mantram is verbal in nature; while the left hemisphere of the brain (which tends to dominate during waking periods) is fixated on the re-occurring sound, the right hemisphere of the brain is less likely to be inhibited. As a result, right-hemispheric behaviours and sensations, such as a sense of euphoria and timelessness, are more likely to occur. This same kind of experience occurs during other activities, such as the drinking of alcohol or the use of hallucinogenic drugs, when left-hemispheric functions are also somewhat incapacitated, thereby encouraging right-hemispheric perception.

Since the process of watching films in many ways replicates the experience of sleeping and dreaming, it is arguable that the pleasure of film viewing also hinges to some extent on the assertion of right-hemispheric activity. In his book, *Film and the Dream Screen: A Sleep and a Forgetting*, Robert Eberwein writes:

> Many people have noticed that watching a film is like having a dream. Narrative elements sometimes seem to be outside spatial and temporal laws. The viewing conditions in the theater (such as the darkened room and the relative sense of isolation) are reminiscent of our solitary existence as dreamers alone in the night. The overpowering images on the screen sometimes frighten us and make us feel the same kind of paralysis we feel in nightmares. In addition, films seem 'real' in the way dreams do; in fact, their ability to make us believe we are a part of the action is for many one of film's most important achievements as a form of art.[7]

When watching a live-action film, it is likely that the left hemisphere becomes 'tied up' by recognisable actions and a complex narrative structure, which require the processing of verbal material as well as logic. With the left hemisphere engaged in thought, the right hemisphere is left with relatively little inhibition; narrative conventions minimise chaos and so the individual feels at ease, especially as a sense of dreaminess is encouraged by the environmental factors that Eberwein describes.

It is likely that a similar situation occurs when an individual views abstract animation. However, with the abstract work, the viewer has nothing tangible with which to occupy 'the logical part' of his or her mind. If asked to interpret an experience that is highly reliant on right-hemispheric capabilities, the inexperienced viewer might feel anxiety because his or her 'normal' left-hemispheric cognitive faculties are left untethered.

Shamus Culhane is among those who have suggested that the onset of behaviours controlled by the right hemisphere can cause a person to feel anxiety. He contended that people have an aversion to thinking with right side of the brain, the part that is 'strictly intuitive, willing to forego reason and logic', because they do not like the loss of 'control' that comes with intuitive thinking.[8] However, once an individual realigns his or her expectations and learns to be comfortable with the less-structured experience, the process of viewing abstract work generally becomes increasingly pleasurable.

One must realise that a change in perceptual modes may be at the heart of what the abstract artist strives for, with the work functioning as a means of altering not only the viewer's outlook but also the creator's own level of understanding. For example, *Momentum* seems to illustrate Belson's desire for homeostasis and a deeper understanding of the self and the nature of life.

Norman McLaren, too, seemed to use at least some of his artwork to gain a sense of mastery within a world generally characterised by chaos. In comparing photographed animation with cameraless animation, he explains:

> ... with the standard animation technique, one breathes life into a static world; with hand-drawn technique, one slows down, to observable speed, the world of frantic mobility. (When beginners draw footage by hand and the result is projected at normal speed, the image-flow is so fast that it gives the impression of looking at thought, if thought were visible.)

In the words of Wolf Koenig, 'the lesson that McLaren teaches (and which is so hard to remember in the confusion of this world) is that chaos can be made into order only by applying the rules of art'.[10] In fact, McLaren found a number of ways to confront chaos in his life. He also practiced 'Tai-chi-ish' exercises[11] and was prescribed to take Xanax in an effort to control the factors which caused him to suffer from severe depression.[12]

Despite the difficulty of maintaining order in life and understanding its many mysteries, a number of abstract animators – like Belson and McLaren – have participated in activities and studied techniques that might help them do so. Many found creative inspiration by encouraging the dominance of right-hemispheric brain functions through the use of 'automatic techniques' that were thought to minimise intervention between the subconscious and the expressive act; the use of hallucinogenic drugs to encourage intuitive thought processes; and meditational practices. Upon examination, one can see that these and other activities generally were interrelated, as varied means for achieving inner peace as well as knowledge. The next section of this book will examine how one of these activities, meditational practice, has influenced the aesthetics of some abstract animation.

Mandalas

While it is true that many abstract films were made as formal investigations – for example, the work of Mary Ellen Bute and John Whitney tend to fall into that category – a significant number of them were created as part of a quest for expanded consciousness and spiritual fulfillment. To varying degrees, artists such as Norman McLaren, Oskar Fischinger, Len Lye, Harry Smith, Jordan Belson and James Whitney saw abstract art as a means of understanding themselves and the world around them. Their work in abstract animation paralleled other activities in their lives, such as meditation.

The overlapping of artistic practice and the quest for enlightenment is evidenced, in some cases, by the appearance of images that can be described as 'mandalas' within these artists works. A 'mandala' (Sanskrit for 'round' or 'circle') is a symmetrical image, usually circular but sometimes square, lotus-shaped or of another geometrical form, that is an important component of Hindu and Buddhist religious practices. In that context, mandalas have symbolic meaning – generally representing the cosmos, deities, knowledge, magic and other powerful forces – and often are used to assist concentration and meditation.

By fixing the eyes on a solid object such as a mandala, an image becomes stabilised on the retina and will soon disappear. In place of images of the 'real world', the meditating practitioner instead may 'see' colours and forms that result from a physiological reaction to the lack of sensory stimuli. One of the primary goals of meditational practice is to achieve a deeper understanding of oneself and the meaning of life. The attainment of this goal, enlightenment (also known as 'samadhi'), is sometimes symbolised by a brightly shining white light.

The use of mandalas in film, especially in relation to the work of James Whitney and Jordan Belson, has been widely recognised in histories of the avant-garde.[13] However, it is important to stress that the filmed mandala operates very differently from a traditional meditational device because, in the film medium, the images move, whereas the traditional mandala is static. When viewing a meditational film, an individual does not experience visual deprivation and the resultant stabilised retinal image because the mandala is constantly in motion. Nonetheless, he or she can become entranced by the light in combination with the rhythmic, hypnotic imagery projected on the screen. The moving mandala works in time, more like music, to induce a trance-like state.

William Moritz has noted the influence of meditational imagery on the work of Oskar Fischinger, who studied Tibetan Buddhism. He explains that the film, *Radio Dynamics* (1942), was 'designed specifically as a meditative vehicle' and many of his other works are highly spiritual in nature.[14] Fischinger's wife, Elfriede, explains that Oskar was greatly influenced by:

> ... Tibetan Buddhism. He believed in it strongly and he did meditate. [Our] house sold itself only because of the very big bathroom. That was his retreat. He would lock the room up and disappear for two or three hours and you would never know what was going on. We only sometimes heard his breathing exercises – that we knew. Whatever else was his meditation.[15]

In his meditations, Fischinger displayed the kind of ease that Barbara Lex finds characteristic of a person who has been entranced many times.[16] According to Elfriede, her husband 'could sit in the living room with lots of children, people, me, everyone milling around – and he was gone. You could say "Oskar!" and it was like a blank wall. He couldn't hear you'.[17]

Despite their differences from a static mandala, many of the abstract films made by Oskar Fischinger, James Whitney and Jordan Belson are intended to be viewed in much the same manner. According to Moritz, these artists' abstract animations are often:

> ... meant to be looked at with a centered gaze, where you are actually looking at the center of the screen ... They are designed for that concentration, which is different from a lot of ordinary cinema, where the eye is meant to wander around and pick out details and have its own discourse with the film.[18]

Belson's distributor, Pyramid Films, released a guide to the artist's work, explaining that, 'to derive the most from this film style, viewers should be encouraged to allow themselves to become fully attentive, receptive. Surrender to the experience ...'[19]

In *Lapis* (1966), James Whitney employs several visual strategies to encourage the viewer to fix his or her vision on, or become entranced by, his images. For example, near the beginning of the film, shortly after the title appears, images grow smaller and seem to recede into the frame, pulling the spectator's vision in with them. This design technique is used at other points in the film, along with a widening of a black circle within a circle (i.e. the center of the mandala), which also tends to pull in the viewer's focus (the viewer feels as if he or she is being drawn into the figure). The use of light and colour fields also affects the viewing experience, as images in *Lapis* transform fluidly from dark to light, or strobe effects send out a shocking pulse of white light (perhaps an attempt to replicate or at least symbolise the white light said to characterise the transcendent state of enlightenment). In these instances, brightness creates a natural attraction to the eye and opens up the pupil, increasing one's ability to absorb sensory information. Although the means of entrainment differ between a static mandala and a moving one (such as *Lapis*), both potentially lead to an entranced state and the stimulation of similar physiological reactions.

Although they are not mandala films, one can see a similar aesthetic operating in McLaren's 'Lines' films – *Lines Vertical* (1960) and *Lines Horizontal* (1962) – and *Mosaic* (1965), which are made from the same images combined in different ways (as explained in Chapter 3). Similar to *Lapis*, the progression of 'action' (i.e. the movement of images on the screen) in the 'Lines' films follows 'the structure of much Hindu classical music, with its very slow, thin opening, its very gradual uninterrupted build-up in complexity, rhythm and richness to a final stunning climax'.[20] In *Lines Vertical* and *Lines Horizontal*, as a single line gradually multiplies, and the resulting groups of lines deflect off the edge of the frame with increasing rapidity, one will find a sort of optical illusion beginning to occur. As in *Lapis*, the eye is drawn into the film by the visuals. As images change from flat to dimensional, seeming to roll into the deepened screen space, the viewer's gaze tends to follow them; if one becomes engaged by the optical illusion, the result is relaxing and mildly entrancing.

The optical effects in *Mosaic* are less attractive in a sense, since the film is composed of bright pinpoints of light that flicker on and off, rather than gently rolling lines. McLaren created the film in part as an experiment with stroboscopic imagery, which interested him very much, presumably because of the hallucinatory optical effects produced by strobing lights.[21] The pacing and pattern of the flickers follows the model of the two 'Lines' films.

Some people have suggested that the mandala image, whether static or in motion, does more than just induce the meditative state. They contend that the mandala form itself originally derives from meditational or dream imagery and that it is based on archetypal forms retained somewhere in the minds of all people. William C. Wees explains that 'despite the mandala's specific significance within particular cultural and religious practices, its visual origins are universal: they are to be found in hallucinations anyone might experience'.[22] C.G. Jung devoted a great deal of attention to the mandala, which he theorised 'originated in dreams and visions' and could function as a 'concealed pole round which everything ultimately revolves' within a person's psyche.[23]

In addition to its symbolic functions, then, it seems that the mandala form might work in two ways: one, by providing a fixed form that can activate entrainment; and two, by providing a form recognisable to the subconscious that will help to structure the experience of meditation. Marlene Dobkin de Rios has made a similar suggestion regarding the function of music in the hallucinogenic trance. She claims that a rhythmic beat can induce a trance state and, further, that the music can then operate 'as a "jungle gym", providing a series of pathways and banisters throughout which the [ritual participant] negotiates his way'.[24] In this respect, the filmed mandala might in fact provide a stronger aid to entrancement than does a static mandala, especially when optical strategies are used to increase the attractiveness of images, as Whitney did in *Lapis*. In any case, in its temporal element, the meditational film seems to share with music a potential for structuring the experience of entrancement. The remainder of this book will further explore the relationship between music and abstract animation.

MUSICAL INFLUENCES ON CONTENT AND FORM

In 1968, Norman McLaren suggested:

> If a person's a static artist and a musician, the chances that he or she will be an animator are much higher, because he's interested in motion – the whole flux and flow of what's happening. Music is organised in terms of small phrases, bigger phrases, sentences, whole movements and so on. To my mind, animation is the same kind of thing.[25]

Nowhere is McLaren's point better supported than in a statement by Mary Ellen Bute, regarding her start as an abstract animator in the 1930s. She writes that, while working with musicologist-mathematician-painter Joseph Schillinger:

> I learned to compose paintings using form, line and color, as counterparts to compositions in sound, but I felt keenly the limitations inherent in the plastic and graphic mediums and [became] determined to find a medium in which movement would be the primary design factor. Motion picture sound film seemed to be the answer and I began to make films, most of them abstract in content.[26]

Perhaps there is an actual connection, since almost 30 years previously, in 1940, McLaren had animated Bute's film, *Spook Sport*.[27]

It is unquestionable that many abstract animators have been greatly inspired by music, which, like painting, has provided models in terms of content as well as form. For example, the improvised 'automatic' compositions of bop music served as the basis for the 1950s' 'Beat' aesthetic that had great impact on the filmmaking of such independent animators as Harry Smith and Jordan Belson.[28]

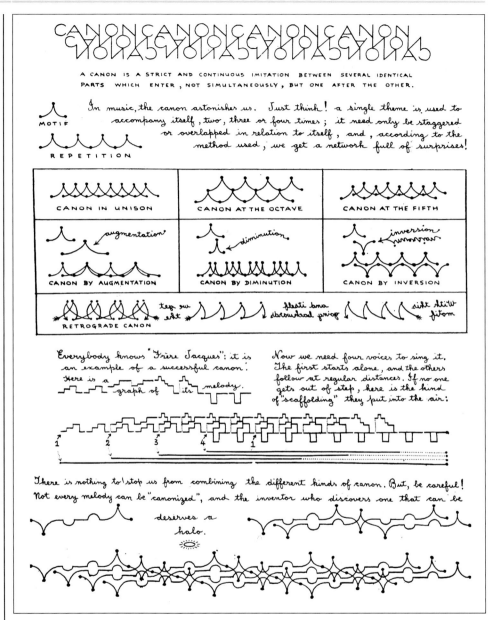

For John Whitney, the processes of composing visual and aural images were insepa-rable. He explained: '[Y]ou would not ask if a musical composition is driven by a piano or by a violin – I think of [the aural and the visual] as two voices, so at one moment a sound pattern inspires a graphics pattern and at the next moment it's vice versa.'[29]

Norman McLaren often structured his films with music in mind, even when the soundtrack was chosen or created after the animation was complete; he created movements that occurred in rhythmic beats, so it was relatively easy to compose a score to complement the visuals and post-synchronise a soundtrack. Donald McWilliams says that the 'planning of movements in terms of musical rhythms' was a 'normal activity for Norman'.[29] For example, in McLaren's notes on *Neighbors* (1952), the artist discusses his use of a 'tempo-control factor ... to tie in [the visuals] with steady musical beats and phrases of the as yet un-made sound track'.[30]

Abstract painter and animator Jules Engel also sees his animated works as being compatible with music (although, like McLaren, he does not create his images to be direct visualisations of sounds) (see CP 33). Engel writes that 'conductors, composers and musicians have all spoken to me about my work. They describe the composition, timing and direction they sense from my films as musical. They are moved by the rhythm and by the "complete, fulfilling process" '.[32] But Engel's definition of sound ranges far beyond music. He writes:

> ... sound is natural. When visiting a museum, there is not a musical score playing in the background as we gaze at the painting. But sound is always present: someone's footsteps, a throat being cleared, or whispers of viewers sharing thoughts. So as it is in my films, 'sound score' is often far more appropriate, since a formal music composition is not always necessary to provide enhancement, nor is it always the basis of stimulus.[33]

Wassily Kandinsky, whose artworks and theories have inspired many abstract animators, had a great interest in music. He contended:

> ... a painter who finds no satisfaction in mere representation, however artistic, in his longing to express his inner life, cannot but envy the ease with which music, the most non-material of the arts today, achieves this end. He naturally seeks to apply the methods of music to his own art. And from this results that modern desire for rhythm in painting, for mathematical, abstract construction, for repeated notes of colour, for setting colour in motion.[34]

Arnold Schoenberg and atonal music

Among the musicians Kandinsky praises most is Arnold Schoenberg, whose 'music leads us into a realm where musical experience is a matter not of the ear but of the soul alone ...'[35] Schoenberg, whose influence as a composer has been immeasurable, also was a painter. For example, his paintings *Rotes Blick* and *Christ, Vision* were shown in a 1911 exhibition of the *Blaue Reiter* group (of which Kandinsky was also a member) and he sketched and painted set designs for such operas as *Die Glückliche Hand*.[36] Like Kandinsky, Schoenberg was motivated to a great extent in his artwork by spiritual and philosophical inquiry.[37] And, also like Kandinsky, Schoenberg's artworks and theories made a significant impact upon abstract animation, particularly in the work of James and John Whitney.

A resident of Los Angeles for a number of years (teaching at the University of Southern California and the University of California at Los Angeles), Schoenberg met with and influenced both of the Whitneys. John Whitney, whose 'theoretical considerations have ... centered around the analogies between film structure and music or language', counted Schoenberg among his most important influences.[38] For John Whitney, the composer's theories of twelve-tone music provided a rational structural model by which to pursue his primary goal, 'the idea ... of finally achieving a fluid visualisation of the qualities, of the architecture, of music'.[39] About the early part of his career, John Whitney writes:

> I became obsessed and charmed with such thoughts about the art of music –
> rhythm and harmony – and why just twelve tones were infinitely applicable. I
> began to explore ideas of creating structures of visual pattern. I commenced a
> search for the simplest building block, an alphabet, with which to construct an
> art of vision to match the art of music ... Arnold Schoenberg's principles of
> twelve-tone composition, while bearing only the most superficial similarities to
> my optical design problems, still influenced my film projects ...[40]

While the spiritual elements of Schoenberg's work have been noted by Kandinsky
and many others, Whitney feels they were not significant to his own investigations,
explaining:

> I felt no need to justify. If you look at the spread of western music, there are
> composers like Bach, for example, who achieved very profound emotional
> associations with religious experience but also much of their work is simply
> elegantly formal and very simple. It doesn't need to have any amplification, any
> relations other than what it is. It is entirely self-reflective. I felt no need to go
> beyond that. I was looking for formal patterns and dynamics, fluidity.[41]

John Whitney found models for the investigation of visual aesthetic issues in music
and musical concepts. But others went beyond visual experimentation for art's sake,
finding that music provided guidelines for an equally engaging spiritual quest.

After completing the *Five Film Exercises* with his brother during 1943 and 1944, James
Whitney said he:

> ... went through a period of intense research trying to reduce movement-form to
> a modular system which I could use as a visual graphic matrix. It was somewhat
> patterned after the twelve-tone serial compositions principles of Arnold Schoen-
> berg. My thinking at that time was very much influenced by music ...[42]

But for James Whitney, music often was employed as a model for both aesthetic *and*
spiritual investigations. The same is true of Oskar Fischinger, Jordan Belson, Len
Lye and Harry Smith.

Pythagoras

The relationship between music and spirituality was explored by Pythagoras, a
philosopher who lived during the fifth century BC (a century before Plato), and about
whom a mixture of fact and legend has accrued. For most people, the name recalls
high school mathematics courses, in which one is required to memorise the Pythagorean Theorem, stating that the square of the hypotenuse of a right-angled triangle
equals the sum of the squares of its other two sides (a formula that was, in fact, known
well before Pythagoras's time).[43] What is less discussed is Pythagoras's motivation
for his mathematical formulations, which was the concern 'to find the essence of
matter, the single force or center from which all life and matter spring'.[44] However,
it was in this respect that the theorist's thinking affected the work of such abstract
animators as Oskar Fischinger and Jordan Belson.[45]

It is difficult to summarise briefly the tenets of any mystical belief system, including
the Pythagorean system of numbers. Essentially, it was believed that 'all developments
in the universe can be derived with the tetrad 1, 2, 3, 4. These numbers were thought
to contain the secrets of all life and matter as well as divine truth'.[46] Each of the
numbers was associated with a different geometric form – respectively, the point, the

straight line, the triangle and the pyramid – and each takes on its own significance in various contexts. For example, the number four represents the four basic elements (air, water, earth and fire) as well as the four disciplines 'thought to be essential for the mastery of true knowledge ... the quadrivium: arithmetic, music, geometry, and astronomy'.[47]

Taken altogether, the numbers 1:2:3:4 include all the ratios necessary to achieve what was considered harmonic perfection in musical terms; that is, they provide the proportions for the intervals of the octave, the fifth and the fourth. With the ratio 1:2, one takes a taught string of a given length and divides it in half (1/2) to achieve an octave of the sound produced by the original length. The ratio 2:3, or two-thirds of the string, produces a fifth and the ratio 3:4, or three-fourths, produces a fourth.

Walker explains that 'music, for the Pythagoreans, was the science that dealt with relationships between whole numbers expressed as ratios, or proportions. It was regarded by them as the physical manifestation of the perfectness of ideal numerical relationships'.[48] Out of this perfection grew a model of natural order, or 'armonia', a concept that has been elucidated by James Vincent Kavanaugh:

> Pythagoras designated the concept of order which he had discovered by the term 'armonia' or harmony. *Armonia* originally meant simply the order of any well-organised structure of parts fitted together in due proportion. The discovery of the mathematical basis for the order of the universe in the harmony of earthly music led Pythagoras and his followers to extend the concept to all aspects of existence. Harmony was assumed to govern the operation of the simplest natural law as well as the ordered motion of the planets in their orbits. It determined the harmonious integration of body and soul and of the intellect and the emotions in the human sphere and, as a consequence, it structured the ethical relationships within society. Harmony shaped the ordered exposition of art, science, and philosophy. At the highest level, universal harmony functioned as the objective form of that pervasive cosmic soul which bound the universe into spiritual unity.[49]

Although he was evidently not drawn to the spiritual elements of Pythagoras's theories, John Whitney was nonetheless immensely influenced by the philosopher's conception of harmony. In his book, *Digital Harmony*, John Whitney writes:

> ... the foundation of my work rests first upon laws of harmony, then in turn, upon proof that the harmony is matched, part for part, in the world of visual design ... This hypothesis assumes the existence of a new foundation for a new art. It assumes a broader context in which Pythagorean laws of harmony operate.[50]

He notes that 'Pythagorean influences' and a 'casual connection between Islamic ideas of cosmos, music, geometry and architecture' significantly influenced the creation of his film, *Arabesque* (1975).[51] However, for many other artists, Pythagorean laws have provided a model for the exploration of spiritual, as well as aesthetic, issues.

At one point, a 'Pythagorean table' was developed to illustrate the theoretical relationships that the philosopher had described. As Joscelyn Godwin explains, the table became 'an incomparable aid to speculative music, as a means toward symbolic explanation and possible illumination concerning cosmic and metaphysical realities. The table is an image of the Universe. If extended to mathematical infinity it would contain every rational fraction and integer'.[52]

Although Pythagorean cosmology lost most of its influence in Western thought and creativity with the advancement of modern sciences and philosophies, it has continued to resurface periodically. For example, it has been noted in the work of composer

Claude Debussy, whose influence upon the field of music has been 'incalculable'.[53] As Kavanaugh has shown, Pythagoreanism also has proven to be a significant force upon American artists, including the Transcendentalist writers Henry David Thoreau and Nathaniel Hawthorne, as well as Charles Ives, who is thought by many to be America's greatest composer. Incidentally, the two authors' direct influence upon Ives is revealed in such compositions as the 'Second Pianoforte Sonata', subtitled 'Concord, Mass., 1840–1860', which contains movements devoted to the characterisations of both Thoreau and Hawthorne (Thoreau also had a direct influence on the work of John Cage, most obviously in the score for the 1976 composition, *Renga*, which uses Thoreau's drawings rather than traditional musical notation).[54]

Vibration and the music of the spheres

Like many abstract artists, Ives had a fascination with mystical concepts, including the idea that vibration is the basis of the life force, a notion shared by many writers and abstract artists. Among them was Kandinsky, who, like Len Lye, was influenced in this matter by his study of theosophy, the doctrine of which is based upon 'ancient wisdoms' found in all religions.[55]

In the years surrounding Kandinsky's writing of *Concerning the Spiritual in Art*, the Theosophical Society – founded in New York in 1875 – was having a great influence on the cultural scene.[56] Sixten Ringbom explains that, according to theosophical aesthetics, the work of art is 'in its own way a thought-form, shaped by the artist's thought vibrations and itself transmitting these vibrations to the beholder'.[57] Taking a similar position in *Concerning the Spiritual in Art*, Kandinsky discusses vibration specifically in relation to colour. After noting the physical effects of colour, he explains that '... to a more sensitive soul the effect of colours is deeper and intensely moving. And so we come to the second main result of looking at colours: *their psychic effect*. They produce a corresponding spiritual vibration ...'[58]

In the drawings and paintings of Kandinsky, Piet Mondrian, Frantisek Kupka and others it is possible to see the soft edges of figures that represent spiritual vibrations, which complement the more subtle vibrations apparently given off by colours used in the artwork itself. Because motion pictures include an element of time, it is much easier to get a sense of actual vibration (in terms of physical movement). This is especially true in relation to cameraless (direct-on-film) animation.

One of the most notable features of direct-on-film figures is their great kinetic energy, which occurs because it is difficult to register images exactly and, therefore, light falls differently on every frame; as a result, the vibration of images is practically unavoidable. Although in his *Lines* films McLaren produced an extremely disciplined exercise in direct-on-film animation, he explains that 'if you want a very slow image in hand-drawn film, it is tedious and difficult, because you have to register the image so precisely with such a minute difference that it becomes almost impossible'.[59]

Len Lye discovered that his artworks – direct-on-film animation and otherwise – as well as his sense of motion were 'tied in a lot with vibration'.[60] In that aspect of his work Lye found the potential for more than mere decoration or entertainment. For Lye, the vibration of images contains a spiritual component. He writes that:

> ... consciousness of movement may be purely receptive, as a passive sensing of
> the vibration-pattern: so that we might speak of a sense of movement just as we
> speak of a sense of telepathy, meaning a receptive intuition of other people's

thoughts, or a theosophist sense, meaning a receptive intuition of things unknown ... Or we might say, speaking in terms of light, colour, sound, atoms, that nothing physical exists in a static state.[61]

Another direct-on-film animator who seemed particularly attuned to internal movement, or bodily rhythms, is Harry Smith. Smith explained that his films, especially those drawn on film, are 'organised in specific patterns derived from the interlocking beats of the respiration, the heart and the EEG Alpha component ...'[62]

Composer Charles Ives also incorporated his interest in vibration into his work. His 'Universe Symphony', for example, seems to have been 'planned to have a number of pianos in the performance that would serve the purpose of rendering the vibrations of natural phenomena audible through sympathetic vibration of the piano strings'.[63] The title, 'Universe Symphony', alludes to another Pythagorean conception that has significantly affected the aesthetics of Belson and other abstract animators: the 'Music of the Spheres'.

Walker explains:

> ... the music of the spheres is the sound of the planets expressed in the proportions of 1:2:3:4, or, musically speaking, the intervals of the octave, fifth and fourth. Pythagoras argued that they sound continually, thus preventing humans from hearing them, and that only if they were to stop, which they never do, could the heavenly music be discerned.[64]

Godwin notes that the notion of 'cosmic harmonies' has been developed in various cultures. He explains that 'although hearing the planetary music is usually reserved for those in supernatural states, there is a widespread and recurrent tradition that the Sun, at least, makes sounds which are audible on Earth'.[65] He also points out:

> ... the writings of the Jewish Kabbalah contain a vision of a harmonious universe in which 'not only the angels sing: the stars, the spheres, the merkavah [Chariot-Throne] and the beasts, the trees in the Garden of Eden and their perfumes, indeed the whole universe sings before God'.[66]

The influence of the 'Music of the Spheres' theory upon Belson is clear; to begin with, he gave the same name to a film he made in 1977. A promotional brochure for Belson's *Music of the Spheres* references a quote from Pythagoras: 'There is geometry in the humming of the strings. There is music in the spacing of the spheres.'[67] But also evident in this brochure is a certain cautiousness in approaching the commercial market with such an esoteric notion. One of the possible 'study questions', provided in the publicity material is 'Do you think there is actually music in outer space, or is it just a metaphor?', suggesting that the idea is not to be taken too seriously. The brochure also includes an 'outline and brief description [of the film] for those who may wish to identify the images as they develop', creating a mini-narrative for viewers who feel uncomfortable with the unconventional subject matter and structure found in the film. Seeking a broad commercial market, Belson's distributor wisely recognises that most viewers are, as Kandinsky once lamented, very eager to 'look for meaning in a picture',[68] particularly meaning that conforms to the rational nature of mainstream Western thought.

This chapter already has suggested that, given the possibility of learning to switch between right- and left-hemispheric modes, it seems likely that a viewer could make the transition between modes of cognition without much difficulty, particularly after being exposed to numerous abstract films and other experiences that are of a similar nature (e.g. meditational practice). The question remains, however, whether or not individuals in our society would desire to do so, since to some extent our ways of thinking are associated with a perceived position of power. To abandon the uni-directional model of cause-and-effect relations that binds together not only our firmly entrenched ideals of the cinematic form but also our entire social structure is to position oneself on the borders and, in so doing, to (apparently) disempower oneself.

However, it can be argued that expanding one's ways of thinking can *never* be disempowering. On that note, this book will close. It is hoped that *Art in Motion: Animation Aesthetics* leaves the reader with an increased understanding of abstract animation as well as a greater appreciation for the breadth of aesthetic possibilities within animation production as a whole.

Notes

1. Wassily Kandinsky, *Concerning the Spiritual in Art*, ed. and trans. M.T.H. Sadler (1914. New York: Dover, 1977), 49.
2. Although Faith Hubley's works are not wholly abstract, her intentions seem to overlap with those of many abstract artists. She writes: 'My films do not provide solutions, but they do make people stop and feel.' Faith Hubley, in Joanna Priestley, 'Creating a Healing Mythology', *Animation Journal* 2, 2 (Spring 1994): 23–31, 28. William C. Wees makes a similar observation about the work of Stan Brakhage. He writes: '[H]ere is an indication of the social role Brakhage's films can play. If viewers recognise equivalents of their own seeing in Brakhage's films, they may become increasingly open to ways of seeing that do not conform to the social conventions respected by the "tutored eye" and that are not incessantly reinforced by conventional techniques of image making.' William C. Wees, *Light Moving in Time: Studies in the Visual Aesthetics of Avant-garde Film* (Berkeley: University of California Press, 1992), 80.
3. Jordan Belson, '*Momentum*', publicity material from Pyramid Films, Santa Monica, California.
4. For additional information on nondiscursive thinking and abstract art, see Alwynn Mackie, *Art/Talk: Theory and Practice in Abstract Expressionism* (New York: Columbia University Press, 1989).
5. Barbara Lex, 'The Neurobiology of Ritual Trance', in Eugene G. d'Aquili et al. (eds), *The Spectrum of Ritual: A Biogenetic Structural Analysis* (New York: Columbia UP, 1979), 117–151, 125, 129.
6. Ibid., 126.
7. Robert Eberwein, *Film and the Dream Screen: A Sleep and a Forgetting* (Princeton: Princeton University Press, 1984).
8. Shamus Culhane, *Animation: From Script to Screen* (New York: St. Martin's, 1988), 30.
9. Cecile Starr, 'Norman McLaren', in Robert Russett and Cecile Starr (eds), *Experimental Animation* (1976. New York: Da Capo, 1988): 117–128, 122.
10. Wolf Koenig, quoted in Starr, 'Norman McLaren', ibid., 116. Although it is extremely difficult to control the pace of images rendered directly on film, McLaren proved himself capable of doing so. Technically, this most amazing feat was accomplished not only once, but three times, in the 'Lines films' (including *Mosaic*). In the production notes for *Lines Vertical*, McLaren describes the difficulty of etching the straight lines on long lengths of black leader. Sometimes, the brittleness of the film's emulsion made it 'almost impossible to get a clean line out of it. No matter how carefully the knife was handled, the line came out ragged and weak with patches in it. There were quite a number of these places in the film, they were kept because it was almost impossible to duplicate the "shot" '. McLaren describes the *Lines* films as 'a disciplined exercise' which reflects that he is 'obsessed with unity'. Norman McLaren, 'Technical Notes on *Lines Vertical* (1960)', in *Technical Notes on McLaren Films (1934–1983)*, unpublished manuscript available from the National Film Board of Canada.
    It probably was McLaren's obsession with unity that compelled him to write (sometimes very detailed) technical notes after completing each of his films at the National Film Board

of Canada. Every work was 'finished off' with the notes. Norman McLaren, quoted in Donald McWilliams (ed.), *Norman McLaren on the Creative Process* (Montreal: National Film Board of Canada, 1991), 20. McLaren, in a letter to Philip Stapp, estimates that 70 per cent of his notes were completed 'just after finishing each film'. McLaren, letter to Philip Stapp (28 Jan. 1984), 'Norman McLaren' file, Museum of Modern Art Film Library.

11. Ibid. McLaren was interested in Eastern cultures, having spent time in both India and China. However, Donald McWilliams writes that 'although he had read much about Eastern religion (and Allan Watts), and had witnessed the East at first-hand in India and China, Norman never really shook off the 'Kirk'. Norman was a remarkably down-to-earth man in many ways, despite being a dreamer'. Donald McWilliams, letter to the author (24 March 1994).

12. Colin Low, quoted in Starr, op. cit., 117. Also see the film (or video), *Creative Process: Norman McLaren*. It would seem that, throughout his life, McLaren struggled with opposing forces. Known publicly as gentle man who would 'never speak harshly of another filmmaker, artist, or technician' and who was characterised by 'patience and kindness', privately he seemed to harbour a great deal of 'pain and suffering'. Lesser known are the pieces of McLaren's art that reveal the artist's dark side (indications of which can be found in what McLaren deemed the favourite of his publicly released films, *Neighbors*, and in the unfinished film, *Head Test*), and personal letters reflect his concern about revealing his homosexuality to the public.

13. For example, P. Adams Sitney calls *Lapis*, by James Whitney, 'the most elaborate example of a mandala in cinema'. Of Belson, Sitney says that, 'simply stated, the early films, up until and including *Allures* [1961], are objects of meditation. The subsequent works, his nine major films, describe the meditative quest through a radical interiorisation of mandalic objects and cosmological imagery'. P. Adams Sitney (1974), *Visionary Film: The American Avant-Garde 1943–1978* (Oxford: Oxford University Press, 1979), 263.

14. Bill Moritz, interview with the author (25 Jan. 1992).

15. Elfriede Fischinger, interview with the author (25 Jan. 1992).

16. Barbara Lex explains that 'cortical and subcortical centers controlling autonomic responses appear to become conditioned to react to emotional stimuli, and once learning has occurred, autonomic fluctuations are no longer essential to emotional experience. This may explain the onset of trance in response to only a single cue ... as well as the observation that novices seem to be less able to control their behavior than experienced trancers'. Lex, op. cit., 134.

17. It might be that Fischinger became similarly entranced while painting, which became his primary medium beginning in the late 1940s. Although he had made films during the night to avoid daytime interruptions, he could conduct his painting during the day, 'with all the children around him and it didn't bother him one bit'. Elfriede Fischinger, interview with the author (25 Jan. 1992).

18. William Moritz, interview with the author (25 Jan. 1992).

19. 'General Guide to the Films of Jordan Belson', Pyramid Films, n.d.

20. McLaren, in Donald McWilliams's personal McLaren papers. In the same correspondence, McLaren explains that *Synchrony* was also structured according to the aesthetic. In addition, 'even non-abstract films like *Neighbors*, *Canon* (the last sequence) and *Pas De Deux* were also shaped to some extent by this concept'.

21. In 'An Anecdote', McLaren recounts his use of the strobe attack machine at the Film Board. He explains: 'When you look at [its light] ... you get the most fabulous brilliant colours and patterns, which would change. The purity of the colours is fabulous. It was a time that mescaline first was being written about a lot and this flicker thing was mentioned in relation to mescaline in articles I read. I used to borrow this thing for months on end, have it in my room and at lunch time I would go and have visions. It was sheer pleasure.' Norman McLaren, quoted in Donald McWilliams (ed.), *Norman McLaren on the Creative Process* (Montreal: National Film Board of Canada, 1991), 42.

Perhaps to counteract the slightly alienating effect of the strobing lights, the film begins and ends with the figure of a live man walking on screen. The flickers in the body of the film then take on the appearance of magic, at first thrown into the air by the man and later recaptured in his hand.

22.   William C. Wees, *Light Moving in Time: Studies in the Visual Aesthetics of Avant-garde Film* (Berkeley: University of California Press, 1992), 6, 129.

23.   For example, see 'The Symbolism of Mandalas', in C.G. Jung, *Psychology and Alchemy*, trans. R.F.C. Hull, from *The Collected Works of C.G. Jung*, Vol. 12, Bollingen Series XX, in Herbert Read et al. (eds) (New York: Pantheon, 1953): 91–213, 92, 212.

24.   Marlene Dobkin de Rios, *The Wilderness of the Mind: Sacred Plants in Cross-cultural Perspective*, Sage Research Papers in the Social Sciences, No. 90-039 (Beverly Hills, CA: Sage 1976), 67.

25.   McLaren himself studied a year of piano and three years of violin (including musical theory) as a child. As a teenager his interests narrowed to jazz, popular and folk music, but he became 'excited about classical music' after his teens. Norman McLaren, quoted in McWilliams, *Norman McLaren on the Creative Process*, op. cit., 29.

26.   Mary Ellen Bute, 'Abstronics', *Films in Review* (June–July 1954), reprinted in Cecile Starr (1976), 'Pioneers of Abstract Animation in America – Mary Ellen Bute', in Robert Russett and Cecile Starr (eds), *Experimental Animation: Origins of a New Art* (Da Capo, 1988): 104–105.

27.   David James writes that James Whitney and Jordan Belson built upon the tradition of abstract art established by Bute and others, although they added references to 'interior or transcendental realities'. David James, *Allegories of Cinema: American Film in the Sixties* (Princeton: Princeton University Press, 1989), 128.

28.   Jordan Belson, letter to the author (21 March 1994).

29.   John Whitney, interview with the author (1 March 1992).

30.   Donald McWilliams, letter to the author (16 April 1994).

31.   Norman McLaren, 'Some Notes on Stop-Motion Live-Actor Techniques as used in the visuals of *Neighbors* (1952) and *Two Bagatelles* (1952)', unpublished film notes available from the National Film Board of Canada.

32.   Jules Engel, 'Experimental Animation ... Art in Motion', *ASIFA-Canada* 21, 3 (Dec. 1993): 26–27, 27.

33.   Ibid., 27.

34.   Wassily Kandinsky (1914), *Concerning the Spiritual in Art*, ed. and trans. M.T.H. Sadler (New York: Dover, 1977), 19.

35.   Ibid., 17.

36.   Most of Schoenberg's paintings are in the private collection of his heirs, but a large number are compiled in two editions of a book entitled *Arnold Schönberg: Paintings and Drawings*. The German/English edition was published by Belmont Music, Los Angeles, in 1991. A more complete Spanish/Catalan edition was published by Fundaci – 'la Caixa', Barcelona, in 1992. See also, Pamela C. White (1983), *Schoenberg and the God-Idea: The Opera Moses und Aron* (Ann Arbor, MI: UMI Research, 1985), 63. See also Edward Lockspeiser, *Music and Painting: A Study in Comparative Ideas from Turner to Schoenberg* (NY: Harper & Row, 1973).

37.   White, *Schoenberg and the God-Idea*, ibid., 1, 64. It seems safe to say that Kandinsky and Schoenberg were mutually admiring of each other's work. Schoenberg says that it was 'with great joy that I read Kandinsky's *On the Spiritual in Art*, in which the road for painting is pointed out and the hope is aroused that those who ask about the text, about the subject-matter, will soon ask no more'. Arnold Schoenberg, *Style and Idea* (New York: Philosophical Library, 1950), n.p.

38.   Malcolm Le Grice, *Abstract Film and Beyond* (Cambridge, MA: MIT, 1977), 80. John Whitney acknowledged being influenced by Schoenberg, as well as Claude Debussy, a composer who, Kandinsky notes, is also 'deeply concerned with spiritual harmony'. John Whitney, interview with the author (1 March 1992). William Moritz also discusses the influence of Schoenberg on Whitney's work in Moritz, 'Non-Objective Film: The Second Generation', *Film as Film: Formal Experiment in Film 1910–1975* (London: Hayward Gallery, 1979), 59–71. See also Kandinsky, op. cit., 16.

39.   John Whitney, interview with the author (1 March 1992).

40.   John Whitney, *Digital Harmony: On the Complementarity of Music and Visual Art* (Peterborough, NH: McGraw-Hill, 1980), 25.

41.   John Whitney, interview with the author (1 March 1992).

42. James Whitney, 'Towards Being Choicelessly Aware: Conversations with James Whitney', unpublished interview with T. Teramaye (1974).

43. Walker notes that the formula 'was also known to the ancient Sumerians more than 1,500 years before Pythagoras lived'. Robert Walker, *Musical Beliefs: Psychoacoustic, Mythical, and Educational Perspectives* (New York: Teachers College, 1990), 63. For more on Pythagoras's theories of numbers, see Walker, ibid., 63–68.

44. Ibid., 63.

45. Although Mary Ellen Bute evidently was not as spiritually inclined as Fischinger and Belson, her animations are also closely tied in with numerical systems, having been greatly influenced by her association with Joseph Schillinger. William Moritz contends that she was much like John Whitney in that she saw music as providing a logical system for creating visual art. William Moritz, phone conversation with the author (27 April 1994).

46. Walker, op. cit., 64.

47. Ibid., 64–65.

48. Ibid., 65.

49. James Vincent Kavanaugh, *Music and American Transcendentalism: A Study of Transcendental Pythagoreanism in the Works of Henry David Thoreau, Nathaniel Hawthorne, and Charles Ives* (Yale University, Ph.D. dissertation, 1978), 6–7.

50. Whitney, *Digital Harmony*, op. cit., 5.

51. Ibid., 113. For more information on the specific design of the film, see a chapter in the book, '*Arabesque* – An Analysis', 97–113.

52. Joscelyn Godwin, *Harmonies of Heaven and Earth: The Spiritual Dimensions of Music from Antiquity to the Avant-Garde* (Rochester, NY: Inner Traditions, 1987), 190–191.

53. Roger Reynolds, *Mind Models: New Forms of Musical Experience* (New York: Praeger, 1975), 90–92; see also Edward Lockspeiser, *Music and Painting: A Study in Comparative Ideas from Turner to Schoenberg* (New York: Harper & Row, 1973), 35–46. In 1992, John Whitney mentioned Debussy as an influence in describing the aesthetics of his production, *Moondrum*, then a work in progress. John Whitney, interview with the author (1 March 1992).

54. *Renga* was commissioned by Seiji Ozawa and the Boston Symphony Orchestra for a major bicentennial work. The score utilises 361 of Thoreau's drawings. Anon., 'Biological Chronology based on similar surveys by Ellsworth Snyder and particularly Anne d'Harnoncourt', in Peter Gena and Jonathon Brent (eds), *A John Cage Reader in Celebration of his 70th Birthday*, (New York: CF Peters, 1982), 184–93, 191.

55. For more information and a list of works by such authors as Claude Bragdon and Charles W. Leadbeater, see Maurice Tuchman, 'Hidden Meanings in Abstract Art', *The Spiritual in Art: Abstract Painting 1890–1985*, catalogue for an exhibition organised by Maurice Tuchman with the assistance of Judi Freeman in collaboration with Carel Blotkamp (New York: Abbeville, 1985), 17–61, 26. Also see Sixten Ringbom, 'Transcending the Visible: The Generation of the Abstract Pioneers', *The Spiritual in Art: Abstract Painting 1890–1985* (New York: Abbeville, 1986), 131–153, 137.

56. Robert Ellwood, *Eastern Spirituality in America* (New York: Paulist, 1987), 19, 35.

57. Ringbom, ibid., 137.

58. Kandinsky, op. cit., 24.

59. McLaren, quoted in Donald McWilliams (ed.), *Norman McLaren on the Creative Process* (Montreal: National Film Board of Canada, 1991), 9.

60. Len Lye, quoted in Wystan Curnow and Roger Horrocks (eds), *Figures of Motion: Len Lye – Selected Writings* (Auckland: Auckland University Press, 1984), xx.

61. Len Lye and Laura Riding, 'Film-Making', *Epilogue* 1 (1935), reprinted in Wystan Curnow and Roger Horrocks (eds), *Figures of Motion: Len Lye – Selected Writings* (Auckland: Auckland UP, 1984), 39–42, 41.

62. Harry Smith, *Film-Maker's Cooperative Catalogue* 3 (New York: Anthology, 1965): 57–58, reprinted in P. Adams Sitney (1974), *Visionary Film: The American Avant-Garde 1943–1978* (Oxford: Oxford University Press, 1979), 232. Smith explains that his 'handpainted' films are 'basically derived from the heartbeat and the respiration which are, roughly, the heart beats 72 times a … minute, and you expire 13 times a minute. You see, those are important Cabalistic

numbers – 13 is half of 26 – so I had taken those two basic rhythms, the rhythm of the heartbeat which is about 72 and the rhythm of the breathing which is about 13, and I had then interlocked them in certain ways'. Mary Hill, 'Harry Smith Interviewed: January 5th and January 15th, 1972, New York', *Film Culture* 76 (June 1992): 1–7, 5.

63. Kavanaugh, op. cit., 208. For a discussion of 'Universe Symphony', see ibid., 204–217.

64. Walker, op. cit., 66.

65. Godwin, op. cit., 60.

66. Amnon Shiloah, 'The Symbolism of Music in the Kabbalistic Tradition', *World of Music* 22 (1978): 56–69, 4, cited in Godwin, ibid., 64–65.

67. 'Music of the Spheres' promotional material (Pyramid Films, n.d).

68. Kandinsky, op. cit., 49.

Index